# THEORIZING FOLKLORE FROM
# THE MARGINS

ACTIVIST ENCOUNTERS IN FOLKLORE AND ETHNOMUSICOLOGY
*David A. McDonald, editor*

# THEORIZING FOLKLORE FROM THE MARGINS

## CRITICAL AND ETHICAL APPROACHES

EDITED BY
SOLIMAR OTERO
AND
MINTZI AUANDA MARTÍNEZ-RIVERA

INDIANA UNIVERSITY PRESS

*This book is a publication of*

Indiana University Press
Office of Scholarly Publishing
Herman B Wells Library 350
1320 East 10th Street
Bloomington, Indiana 47405 USA

iupress.org

*Manufactured in the United States of America*

Cataloging information is available from the Library of Congress.

ISBN 978-0-253-05606-1 (hardback)
ISBN 978-0-253-05607-8 (paperback)
ISBN 978-0-253-05608-5 (ebook)

First printing 2021

*This volume is dedicated to
our intellectual and family ancestors,
who opened, cleared, and created the roads
on which we now walk.*

# CONTENTS

# ACKNOWLEDGMENTS

Community is central to what we do and who we are as scholars, activists, and individuals. This work is the result of a multiplicity and diversity of communities that supported us through *Theorizing Folklore from the Margins*'s different stages of conceptualization, creation, and production.

To some degree, *Theorizing Folklore from the Margins* would not have come to fruition without John Nieto-Phillips's invitation, in 2017, to edit a special volume of Latinx folklore for *Chiricú Journal*. The seeds for this project were planted while we worked with the *Chiricú Journal* community, as we were able to think of different paths for folklore studies and play with ideas that found a home in this volume.

At Indiana University Press, we would first like to thank Janice Frisch, who believed in this project since the beginning and brought us into the press. We are also thankful to our editor Jennika Baines and the whole team at Indiana University Press for their hard work and willingness to collaborate with us to complete our vision. We also want to thank the two anonymous reviewers for their detailed comments and suggestions, as they made this volume stronger.

We would also like to thank our authors, as *Theorizing Folklore from the Margins* would not be possible without their contributions. We are grateful that they trusted us to curate their stories, ideas, and creations with care, respect, and love.

Many individuals communicated vital suggestions to us as we vetted the work at the American Folklore Society annual conferences. Norma Cantú, Olivia Cadaval, and Guillermo de los Reyes gave particularly insightful interpretations of this collaborative project at different stages of its development at the meetings. We also appreciate the support of the Cultural Diversity Committee; the Chicana/o section; and the Folklore Latino, Latinoamericano, and Caribeño section in providing venues for related discussions aimed to include scholars of color in AFS leadership and projects.

We are grateful for the artwork of Juana Alicia that graces the cover of this book. Her righteous spirit and vision of new and ancient worlds illustrate what we hope to evoke in this collection.

On a personal note, Mintzi wishes to acknowledge the support, encouragement, and love that she received from her family and friends during this process. She is especially thankful to Solimar Otero for her guidance, mentorship, friendship, wisdom, and generosity. It was a joy to work on this project with Solimar, and Mintzi looks forward to future collaborations and adventures.

Solimar would like to thank her husband, Eric Mayer-García, and her family in Cuba, Puerto Rico, and the United States for their love and guidance. She is especially grateful to Arturo Lindsay and Ana-Maurine Lara for sharing their art, words, and wisdom. She is indebted to her coeditor, Mintzi Martínez-Rivera, for being a light and an inspiration. A real *comadre* in birthing projects, Mintzi keeps it real and fills her with hope for the future generations of scholars to come.

To all that supported and encouraged this project, ¡mil gracias!

# PART I

Critical Paths

# Introduction

## How Does Folklore Find Its Voice in the Twenty-First Century?
## An Offering/Invitation from the Margins

SOLIMAR OTERO AND
MINTZI AUANDA MARTÍNEZ-RIVERA

The genesis of this book began with a collaborative project with *Chiricú Journal* in January 2017. John Nieto-Phillips, general editor of *Chiricú*, invited us to coedit a special volume on Latinx folklore. The 2016 presidential elections had just passed, and hate crimes and violence against ethnic, racial, sexual, religious, national, and differently-abled-body minorities were rising quickly. Hence, we decided to focus on how *poder y cultura* work together to create, model, and express a different society, a society more equal and just. The terms *poder y cultura* loosely translate to "power and culture," and the valence of their pairing in Latinx and Latin American contexts signifies a relational process. That is, poder y cultura work through each other in helping create individual and communal reinventions of the self, tradition, and belonging. We were especially interested in how practices of poder y cultura inform vernacular cultural expressions in ways that serve to empower minority communities across contexts, cultures, and borders and that can also challenge the status quo. Contributions focused on issues of migration, violence (both intellectual and physical), spirituality, digital humanities, and other topics. We also aimed to challenge the ways in which academic knowledge is presented (mainly the format of "academic" writing) by incorporating pieces that mixed academic and creative writing in the academic/article section. The special volume was published in December 2017, and by February 2018, *Chiricú Journal* was recognized by Project Muse as journal of the month, in large part because of the reception of our special volume. The work done for *Chiricú Journal* inspired the ethics, methods, and outcomes of this volume. We wanted to further examine the elusive yet visceral nature of the conception and experience of poder y cultura by centralizing the epistemologies of the communities typically the subject of folklore studies. In many ways, the seeds for this project were planted much earlier.

## MINTZI'S MEMORIES

I remember my first meeting with the American Folklore Society (AFS), when I met Solimar. I was starting my second year of graduate school, and while I had an amazing supporting community, in my department I was one of the few Latinas and women of color. I remember feeling intellectually isolated.

During my undergraduate career at the University of Puerto Rico, I had been exposed to European (mainly French) and Latin American postmodernism. I had been trained to question the status quo and to analyze how people, through cultural vernacular practices, create, imagine, and challenge hegemonic structures. Recognizing the privilege that a higher education means, as students at the University of Puerto Rico, living and growing up in a colony, we were also taught that what we research matters and can have a real impact in the world. Therefore, whatever we studied and researched had to have a positive impact in the communities that we inhabit.

Excited to join the Folklore and Ethnomusicology Department at Indiana University Bloomington, I arrived in Bloomington thirsty for knowledge and eager to learn. But that first year, with very few exceptions, the scholarship that I read and engaged with did not speak to me, my reality, or the reality of the communities where I do fieldwork. However, in one course, in my second semester, I was briefly exposed to Indian postcolonial and subaltern studies, such as those of Gayatri Chakravorty Spivak and Dipesh Chakrabarty, and I clung to those scholars as if they were lifeboats. From there I discovered Latin American postcolonial and subaltern studies (including those by Walter Mignolo, John Beverly, and Florencia Mallon). I was so happy that I had found scholars that spoke to me. But as I read and engaged with those ideas, I had trouble incorporating them into my coursework. I was ignored by both faculty and classmates every time I tried to mention that scholarship in class discussions, and in some cases, professors even penalized me for citing Latin American scholars in my work.

So, I arrived at the AFS meeting looking for a community that spoke my intellectual language, that shared my experience of being the "only one, or one of the few," and that felt a core and intrinsic responsibility, love, and engagement with the communities that open their homes to us as researchers and folklorists. That is when I met Solimar and other members of the Latinx, Latin American, and Caribbean community. This amazing community welcomed, embraced, mentored, and adopted me. The conversations that we had and still have are, contrary to what some may believe, full of love and joy for what we do and aim to accomplish with our work. We do not shy from difficult conversations regarding our work or our positionality (both within academia and within our communities), nor are we afraid to push each other to help make our work stronger. As a community, we also recognize the legacy of our intellectual ancestors, other folklorists of color that have paved the way for us. And while our work is not considered mainstream, and we remain in the margins of the discipline, we have benefited from the transdisciplinary exchange of ideas that germinate only in the most unexpected places. This is what I found at my first AFS meeting many years ago.

This book is for the young Mintzi who needed it when she began graduate school. This is the book that she would have loved to read then.

## SOLI'S SAINTS

I am sitting in my godmother Tomasa's living room in front of her saints and *orichas*, listening to the noisy Havana afternoon traffic. Shouts of "¡*Tamalero!*" and "¡*Oye ven acá!*" are sprinkled between blaring horns, clanking engines, and whooshing truck beds bouncing metallically off the potholes found on the *calzada*. My job is to help clean the altars and dust around the tureens that house my aunt's divinities. Music is added to the layers of sound and accompanies my work, as my cousin, Devist, begins to blare Ozuna, a Puerto Rican trap artist, from his room. The orichas seem to like the music, and I feel newly inspired as I reposition the huge *racimo de plátanos indios*, bunch of red plantains, in front of both Changó and Santa Bárbara, who share a place of honor at the center of the house's altars (see fig. I.1). As I am saluting and speaking to my aunt's orichas, I feel a sense of kinship and recognition.

These entities touch my life in both ephemeral and tangible ways that feel familial. The orichas' presence reminds me of the story told to me earlier this morning by my great uncle, Tío Enrique, about the last meal my deceased mother, Maria Julia, ever had in Cuba, in that very living room about fifty years ago. Like that revelation, touching and cleaning the santos provides keys to mysteries and connections that bind me to my family and culture. There are endless details to be discovered, memories to capture, and future work to be done in rituals that commemorate ancient knowledge with new understanding and purpose.

There are likewise a multitude of similar moments that span a day of living and "doing fieldwork" with my family and interlocutors in Cuba. Some of them are untranslatable, some of them are indescribable, and some of them are secret. How do they relate to my own understanding of folklore, a field and subject of study that I have devoted over twenty-five years of my life to? How do the sensations, stories, and ritual experiences of my time in Cuba connect to the papers, books, and lessons I create in the United States? What do my connections and dislocations have in common with other people I know, similarly engaged in religiosity and scholarship and art? Like the young, wonderful Mintzi, I am still waiting for some of the answers that will help me navigate these questions.

Fig. I.1 Santa Barbara and Changó Altar, Havana, Cuba, 2019. Photo by Solimar Otero.

## HISTORICAL INTERVENTIONS

*Theorizing Folklore from the Margins* is an invitation from the margins, points of contact and disconnection that make up the emerging landscape of folklorists who study and belong to communities that engage in everyday forms of culture in order to thrive, resist, and enact ways of being in an often hostile world. The virulent legacies of white supremacy, patriarchy, and homophobia that persist in our society make studying transnational expressive cultures such as Cuban Santería a particularly important and daunting task. The colonial plantation system that set up the racial and religious inequalities found in the Caribbean, Latin America, and the southern United States left institutional patterns of silencing and co-opting the histories and communities responsible for creating the texture of tradition and resistance that makes each of these places unique. What does the study of folklore look like if we assume a different starting point, one located in the center of the rhizomatic and dense location of cultural contact, conflict, and borrowing rather than "discovery"? What if we embrace the notions of mystery, confusion, and apprenticeship in working with communities in shared projects? This would take a shift in authority and change the way that we write, work, and build relationships. The work in this volume invites interaction with people, ideas, and creative expression in dynamic frameworks that question and reposition the power of representation, analysis, and interpretation. As a way to demonstrate this reformulation of perspectives, the chapters in this book are geographically and culturally diverse and embedded; they are written with a transnational intersectionality in mind.

We seek to do more than critique the institutional structures and scholarly practices that marginalize and yet also romanticize the cultures and persons often studied under folklore. We invite readers to consider reconceptualizing the very notions of history, power, and culture from the locations of their vernacular creation, invoking Édouard Glissant's provocative phrasing: "We demand the right to opacity" (1990, 189–190).[1] In other words, we suggest embracing the complexity of marginalized cultures that resist the universalizing tendency, the knowability of the other, that Western philosophy and academic discourses impose on non-Western subjects. Glissant roots his philosophical critique of colonialism in the diversity of Caribbean cultures and folklore. Our approach mirrors his in suggesting that everyday forms of multiplicity and specificity are essential tools for generating anticolonial creative and academic work. We are not alone in suggesting that practices like "listening in detail"[2] can be the first step to doing critical and ethical work in the study of folklore.

The study of folklore has historically focused on showcasing the daily life of regular people, such as artisans and storytellers, as well as analyzing vernacular expressive cultural practices. One of the main concerns of the field since its inception in the nineteenth century has been the issue of authentic representation in the expression of discernable cultures. We would like to turn away from this search for authenticity and the verifiability of the vernacular as a means to justify the study of folklore. Rather, this volume asks folklorists to consider how effective they have been in theorizing with collaborators and from the location of expressive culture in understanding their mutual roles and exchanges. At play here is recognizing the necessity for reflexivity on the part of the researchers with regard to the ways their presence and work affect the communities they engage with. Conversely, we also are curious as to what the communities that we study, and at times are a part of, reveal about vernacular strategies of belonging, survival, and reinvention in times of trouble.

This anthology builds on and also departs from existing scholarship on folkloristics. During the late twentieth and early twenty-first centuries, the field adopted several critical turns that certain anthologies exemplify. Collections like *Towards New Perspectives in Folklore*, edited by Américo Paredes and Richard Bauman (1972), and *Women's Folklore, Women's Culture*, by Rosan Jordan and Susan Kalcik (1985), set the stage for real considerations of performance traditions and women's culture, respectively. A more recent collection is Domino Renee Perez and Rachel González-Martin's (2018) *Race and Cultural Practice in Popular Culture*, which invites cultural critics to think about the interconnection between popular culture and folklore and this connection's relationship with the intersectionality of race, class, gender, sexuality, and citizenship. This collection opens similar paths to our own by introducing new approaches to the study of popular culture grounded firmly on communities' receptive creativity and meta-analysis.

*Theorizing Folklore from the Margins* also engages in the study of marginalized beliefs and groups. Volumes that deal with belief and subaltern studies, such as *Out of the Ordinary*, by Barbara Walker (1995), and *The Stigmatized Vernacular*, edited by Diane Goldstein (2016), reflect the kinds of original insight and discussion for folklore studies that we seek to build on. One especially influential collection for us in building this anthology is *Chicana Traditions*, edited by Norma Cantú and Olga Nájera-Ramírez (2002). Our book likewise uses a racially critical lens with which to investigate key questions concerning power, representation, and epistemology from the perspective of groups that have transnational and translocal roots. The chapters offered here also move in the spirit of Jacqui Alexander's (2005) *Pedagogies of Crossing* by simultaneously archiving and creating paths that resist empire and invoke hope for the multiple communities and cultures we engage with.

## CRITICAL PATHS

The central concerns that inform this volume's call for the critical are intimately tied to social activism. To be clear, the essays in this book do not relegate the practice of social activism solely to the realm of discernable civil organizations or political movements. Instead, we invite readers to consider how the creators of folk culture deploy their expressions to specific social and personal ends that make spaces for liberation. Here, liberation is defined in multiple ways and refers to a range of registers and experiences that are cocreated, including those of race, gender, sexuality, ethnicity, religion, (dis)ability, and national identity. Thus, we urge folkloristics to consider the long-overdue intersections between the study of folklore and such approaches as postcolonial studies, critical race studies, ethnic studies, gender and sexuality studies, disability studies, and continuing forays into performance studies and cultural studies. Working with communities on the ground forces us to challenge and expand our understanding of vernacular expressive cultural practices, as well as the theoretical approaches used by folklorists.

Our colleagues in the public sector understand the need for collaboration with community partners and artists, and their contributions to how we all experience folklore as a civil society have been underrepresented in academic discussions of folklore studies (Baron and Spitzer 2007). Recent works such as Steve Zeitlin's (2016) *The Poetry of Everyday Life* and Joseph Sciorra's (2015) *Built with Faith* bring forth this valuable community perspective. Folklorists working for federal, state, city, and private entities juggle a multitude of expectations while trying to stay true to their folk constituents. We mention this component of folklore work because it illustrates a kind of sustained interaction with communities that embodies the tension and negotiation we want to embrace. Their work is situated within an understanding that their publics are also generators of culture and art and have a vested interest in their representation.

This volume likewise presents necessary interventions and directions needed to critically engage in the study of folklore in the twenty-first century. The experience of living in hostile conditions in the contemporary political era is at the heart of the creation of vernacular culture for communities under attack culturally, socially, politically, and economically. The authors in this book touch on issues that most folklorists tend to avoid: racism, sexism, ableism, ethnocentrism, homophobia, elitism, violence, and regionalism.[3] Some of the work presented in this book complicates what is considered scholarly or academic knowledge production in their form and content. This is because we believe that form informs content and that the texture of a text produces certain affects and responses that matter (Dundes 1980, 20–32; Bakhtin 1981).

Studying one's own community and culture is precarious yet productive work. As Kirin Narayan (1993) and Ruth Behar (1996) have explored in their reflexive approaches to ethnography, the act of positioning the self, in and out of multiple contexts of belonging, questions the limits of knowability. More importantly, their work rightly critiques the project of creating a disconnected narrative of culture that erases the very means and perspectives that produce it. This elision obscures the power dynamics at play between researchers and their "subjects," dynamics that often include institutional and economic advantages that the former holds over the latter. Some of the authors in this volume choose to address these issues of positionality in their scholarship through autoethnography. Autoethnography as a methodology includes the self as subject and primary guide to the study of culture and society. It spans multiple disciplines and approaches, including anthropology, performance studies, and sexuality studies.[4]

Stacy Holman Jones and Anne M. Harris (2019), in *Queering Autoethnography*, include radical social engagement, natural ecologies, and nonhumanist approaches in their reconceptualization of autoethnography. They assert that autoethnography can "lead humankind to begin attending to and emphasizing with the non- and more-than-human" (5). Queering here does the work of embracing nonnormative and fluid subjects as a starting point for inquiry. The autoethnography found in this volume demonstrates this adoption of a multiplicity of interactions that necessarily include race, gender, and sexuality. Philosophical, spiritual, and cultural approaches that embrace queer, nonhuman, and divine forms of intervention and agency in society require a recalibration of the purposes of ethnography and autoethnography along the lines of collaboration and advocacy. For example, the autoethnographic perspectives from which Rachel González-Martin, Mintzi Auanda Martínez-Rivera, Rhonda R. Dass, and Phyllis M. May-Machunda write their chapters situate the importance of visibility to viability in the continued development of scholars of color in the field of folklore studies. In doing so, these perspectives include voices, information, and positions that do not fit neatly into the accepted paradigms, discourses, and taxonomies of ethnography and autoethnography. This is why this volume's creative pieces by Mabel Cuesta and Itzel Guadalupe Garcia open up generative spaces where the aesthetics of autoethnography are challenged by different kinds of witnessing, telling, and documentation. The aim is to highlight how folklorists' methods and outcomes need to be tethered to the larger world-building visions of the communities they belong to and work with.

The chapters that follow produce innovative theoretical, topical, and methodological pairings that move folklore studies to the center of contemporary debates confronting the humanities and social sciences. The authors grapple directly with the issues of the relevance of scholarship to everyday people's lives, well-being, and art. Approaches and areas of study put into conversation with folkloristics in this book include critical race theory, transnational feminism, disability studies, Indigenous studies, LGBTQI studies, African and African American studies, Native American studies, and Latinx studies. The quotidian epistemologies and pedagogies of the communities explored in this volume illustrate how folklore studies has the potential and responsibility to bridge the gap between theory and practice in ways that make an impact.

## ETHICAL PATHS

Moving beyond and among different ways of understanding, grappling with, and addressing ethics, each chapter in this volume approaches ideas of ethics differently as our contributors propose alternative ways in which to ethically engage in research, what stories can be told, and ways in which to tell those stories. Moreover, we encouraged our contributors to reflect on the ways in which they interact with their interlocutors, research participants, and research communities. In a similar way to our approach to critical paths, we understand ethics and our ethical paths as connected to social activism and rooted in anti-oppressive praxis. As discussed further down and throughout the volume, the ethical paths that we are proposing in this volume do not stem from Eurocentric perspectives or philosophies as their starting point. These paths, however, do not discard or ignore European scholarship (such as Marxism or Deleuzian philosophy) but seek to create reciprocal dialogues among different epistemological frameworks that inform and enrich our understanding of the multiplicity of expressions of the human experience. Furthermore, such a dialogical approach allows for ethical collaborations that are anti-oppressive, decolonial, and rooted in practices that stem from an honest and disinterested love (Sandoval 2000; hooks 2018).

Folklore, as a colonial discipline that, at its inception, focused on studying the "national other" (contrary to anthropology, for example, which specialized in the "foreign other"), claims an interest in studying everyday life and giving voice to those that do not have one. However, as folklorists and scholars in other disciplines have argued, "to give voice to the other" is a colonial, hegemonic act that can also disguise itself as racial ventriloquism (Spivak 1988; Glaser 2016). Moving away from the inherent problems with this approach, folklorists, especially folklorists that work in the public sector, have developed practices that are imbued with sincere collaborative intention and that have a reciprocal transformative effect in all those who participate in the project (a model proposed by Xóchitl Chávez in this volume). An example of this practice was discussed during the first panel of the 2018 American Folklore Society Annual Meeting, "Silent Partners: Allyship, Collaboration and Research Practice in American Folklore," which focused on allyship as a form of "building ethical, mutually beneficial, collaborative relationships with individuals and groups" (AFS 2018). More than anything, the members of the panel highlighted that to be an ally is a work in progress, constantly checking our privilege and positionality as well as engaging in anti-oppressive practices. They mentioned that it was not about giving voice to others but about collaboratively imagining spaces where everybody could talk and create together.

As a precursor to situating the kind of strategies we are suggesting in performing folklore studies as a method for negotiating power and representation, we are especially engaging with Chela Sandoval's (2000) *Methodology of the Oppressed*. In her revolutionary text, Sandoval proposes a model for the decolonization of academia, knowledge production, and, more generally, neoliberal globalization. By analyzing canonical works by scholars from multiple disciplines (such as Frantz Fanon, Gloria Anzaldúa, Audre Lorde, Michel Foucault, and Jacques Derrida) that have challenged hegemonic political-economic-social-cultural constructions of the world order, she proposes a methodology of emancipation or liberation. This methodology comprises five skills or elements (semiotics, deconstruction, meta-ideologizing, democratics, and differential movement) that, when combined, contribute to the decolonization of twenty-first century globalization. More importantly, the guiding force, or what unites all the different skills or elements, is love, which, in this framework, is a tool for social transformation.

Connecting Sandoval's work with Leslie Brown and Susan Strega's (2005) seminal edited volume *Research as Resistance: Critical, Indigenous and Anti-oppressive Approaches*, which positions social justice as an integral component of research practices and products, *Theorizing Folklore from the Margins* seeks not only to create a space for marginalized scholars and ideas but also to transform academia from the ground up by using emancipatory and anti-oppressive approaches. Anti-oppressive approaches must be developed from a sense of commitment to, respect for, and personal engagement with the communities where we collaborate in research. In this regard, anti-oppressive researchers do not study particular communities but study with communities.

For scholars conducting anti-oppressive research in their own communities of origin, like the majority of the contributors of this volume, a sense of responsibility and love (as espoused by Brown and Strega [2005], Sandoval [2000], and hooks [2018]) will influence their decisions on what their research is about and how they will conduct it. But doing research in our communities of origin is not without its challenges—it's not as easy as some may naively think (Richards-Greeves 2013). As scholars and members of our communities, we are constantly in a liminal space of not belonging, which is a dance that we have to do as insiders and outsiders while doing fieldwork. And this sense of not belonging also translates into academia, because as "native scholars" our work is considered "easier," not "really research." However, these challenges also provide rich opportunities to forge new academic and intellectual paths. Autoethnography, for example, and as previously discussed here, is one of those tools that allow us to be firmly reflexive about the process of negotiating, always revising how we are doing the work with our communities.

As part of the ethical, collaborative, and critically grounded work that we are encouraging, during the creation of this volume we also recommended that our collaborators think about the ethics and politics of citations, of who we are citing and why. Unfortunately, people of color, and especially women of color, are cited less frequently than their white and male counterparts in academia (Mott and Cockayne 2017; Ray 2018). With few exceptions, the work of people of color remains in the periphery and is heavily marginalized in most fields. Some scholars believe that citing "well-intentioned white-liberal scholars" is enough, but it is not (Dupree and Fiske 2019; Kauffman 2018). The work of scholars of color should be part of the canon, not a curious interest or an elective, as their work is necessarily innovative, reflexive, and tied to community concerns. It is the work that our field deeply needs to be relevant at this social and cultural conjuncture.

In this volume, therefore, we approach and engage with the topic of ethics from myriad angles: from the way that research and knowledge are conceptualized, performed, and shared, to who is included in the conversation. Together with critical theoretical approaches and borrowing from Sandoval's framework, this project of critical and ethical folkloristics, born at the margins of the discipline, is an act of revolutionary and transformative love.

## STRUCTURE OF THE BOOK

Moving among, and with, Mexican, Wolof, Native American, Cuban, Puerto Rican, Haitian, Martinican, Andean, North American, African Diaspora, and LGBTQI folk cultures and communities, the collaborators of this volume employ a range of discursive strategies in order to illustrate alternative intellectual paths. The volume is divided into four sections: "Critical Paths," "Framing the Narrative," "Visualizing the Present," and "Placing Community." Each section engages with ideas of critical and ethical folkloristics and invite us to rethink folklore studies from multiple perspectives, from the concrete to the abstract. And while we have divided and organized the contributions in this book based on overarching themes, chapters overlap and cross into other sections. For example, we encouraged our contributors to directly provide alternative or new theoretical and methodological paths in the first section, *Critical Paths*, and we suggested that chapters in other sections offer alternative models for interpreting folklore. We also invited our contributors to play with their contributions in format, topic, and approach. Many of these experimental chapters contain components of autoethnography, as discussed previously. We find that as these researchers move away from a type of scholarship that is meant to be impersonal, objective, and detached, they lean into a scholarship that is rooted in deep experiential and personal epistemologies. Moreover, the authors in this volume grapple with the honesty of their intellectual journeys and reveal their processes of trying to make sense of their experiences and data. As a result, the contributions found in this collection come from a profound sense of personal responsibility toward the communities where we do our work.

The first section, "Critical Paths," aims to (re)frame our understanding of folklore studies by providing alternative readings of our disciplinary history and theoretical paths. Rachel González-Martin's "White Traditioning and Bruja Epistemologies: Rebuilding the House of USAmerican Folklore Studies" invites us to rebuild folklore studies by centering theoretical frameworks that have been marginalized by mainstream scholarship. Proposing a bruja epistemology, González-Martin means to "spur the intersectional futurity of critical folkloristics in and of the United States." By centering marginal and diverse authorial voices, González-Martin argues that we may learn that those voices create "spaces for knowledge that may actually offer a renewed magical stability" and help move folklore studies away from its colonial legacy.

Similar to González-Martin's contribution, Juan Eduardo Wolf's chapter, "Un Tumbe Ch'ixi: Incorporating Afro-Descendant Ideas into an Andean Anticolonial Methodology," explores folklore studies' colonial past, specifically folklore's quest to find that which is premodern. In order to forge a new path for folklore studies, Wolf builds and expands Silvia Rivera Cusicanqui's anticolonial frameworks, specifically her *ch'ixi* methodology, in order to incorporate Afro-descendant epistemologies into a form of cultural critique. By analyzing dance and music cultural practices, specifically the *tumba de rueda carnaval*, Wolf argues that by "considering multiple perspectives to describe these rueda performances . . . [we can] . . . sketch out alternatives to politics rooted in Western modernity, alternatives that can influence the way we practice folkloristics."

In the last chapter of this section, "Disrupting the Archive," Miriam Melton-Villanueva and Sheila Bock explore the history of silencing women of color in the archive. By highlighting the *historias* of Lily and Doña Anita, Melton-Villanueva and Bock share the tale of how two women of color helped create the only archival collection that focuses on the Ures region of Sonora, Mexico, yet are invisible inside the archive. By using Gloria Anzaldúa's concept of *desconocimiento*, incorporating the rhizomatic framing of Deleuze and Guattari, and interviewing both Lily and Doña Anita, the authors provide a liberating discussion of how occluded labor in the archive can be excavated and recontextualized.

"Framing the Narrative" contains chapters that grapple with representation with regard to the stories that make up the building of community, history, place, and power. This section investigates expressions of connectivity and division through poetry, talk, ritual, and film in Afrolatinx, Native American, African, Caribbean, and Mexican American contexts. The authors focus on how memory, futurity, and the imagination fuel the ways that communities make story and kin. The pieces also stay firmly grounded in the specificity of the cultural, political, and historical contexts that emerge from these narratives. Here, then, framing is an important modality that necessarily includes voices from the margins. The first selection, Solimar Otero's chapter, "Afrolatinx Folklore and Representation: Interstices and Antiauthenticity," questions the parameters and problematic of authenticity and replaces it with the LGBTQI aesthetic and practice of "realness." She investigates how Afrolatinx spirituality and sexuality must coexist in narratives of liberation and healing. Using examples of poetry, visual art, and ethnographic interviews, Otero situates a retelling of colonial history that is rooted in antiracist and feminist imaginative practices.

Rhonda R. Dass also explores the importance of kinship in decolonializing the academic discipline of folklore in the next chapter, "Behaving like Relatives: Or, We Don't Sit Around and Talk Politics with Strangers." Dass's piece evaluates the role that representations of native voices and folklore have played in the field and in her own work. Thinking through community, she situates her own struggle to reconcile her academic training with her native cultural heritage. An important framing in the chapter is the discussion on native strategies for dealing with outsiders and researchers whose claim to the community is tenuous. Ultimately, we learn the valuable lesson that "behaving like a relative" requires a situatedness in a community that includes ecologies, places, and people in ways that challenge narrow notions of kinship and our place in the world.

In a similar look toward community ethics and aesthetics, Cheikh Tidiane Lo's chapter, "Political Protest, Ideology, and Social Criticism in Wolof Folk Poetry," moves folklore away from the traditional arguments made about the "value" of oral literature in Africa. Instead, Lo presents a thoroughly contextualized analysis of Wolof poetry performed by fishermen and rural workers. He sees the songs as expressing a call for activism in fighting the everyday struggles against exploitation and poverty. More specifically, he visualizes the poems as providing a glimpse into the "ontological preoccupations" of the communities who express this form of resistance.

Katherine Borland's "*Sugar Cane Alley*: Teaching the Concept of 'Group' from a Critical Folkloristics Perspective" likewise investigates the parameters of resistance through representation. Borland seeks to rethink the important concept of "group" through a pedagogical lens that takes into account the interstices between folklore studies, critical race theory, and Caribbean postcolonial theory. She looks at *Sugar Cane Alley* as a cinematic representation of a transnational, polylingual, and Black Caribbean social imaginary. In doing so, Borland examines how filmic folklore can and cannot hash out the complexity of group association in regard to anticolonial consciousness. Her analysis of group representation instructs us on the importance of understanding specificity historically and geographically.

Itzel Garcia's chapter, "movimiento armado / armed movement," finishes this section on narrative. Her creative piece explores the many fissures and also the connective tissue that make up the southern US border with Mexico. The fierceness, beauty, and pain with which Garcia relates her life full of comings, goings, and magic exemplifies the texturing of story that dry academic accounts of recorded tales leave out. Yet Garcia's writing also gives us a vivid phenomenological rendering of Anzaldúa's *nepantla*,[5] a location of death and rebirth for so many Chicanxs and Mexican Americans. As with the other chapters in this section, the location of culture and place continuously shifts, and the resulting challenges are painful yet productive.

The book's next section, "Visualizing the Present," investigates what it means to think through the visualization of belonging and breaking away. We include innovative pieces, such as collages and creative work in Spanish, that challenge how academics think through visual and linguistic representation. The overall result is a revisualization of expectations surrounding the work folklorists can do and how. We begin "Visualizing the Present" with author Mabel Cuesta's piece, "Ni lacras, ni lesbianas normalizadas: Trauma, matrimonio, conectividad y representación audiovisual para la comunidad lesbiana en Cuba." The chapter explores writing the self, culture, and sexuality in Cuba. It concerns trauma, firsthand accounts of repression, and liberation through everyday interactions of the LGBTQI community in Cuba. We want to honor the comparative and international nature of the field of folklore by presenting this piece in its original language, Spanish. Furthermore, Cuesta's exploration of sexuality and place in its intended linguistic register creates an opportunity for audiences to engage with feelings of both inclusion and exclusion as a reflexive exercise that promotes an awareness of one's situatedness and adaptability as a reader.

Similarly, Gloria M. Colom Braña's innovative piece, "'¿Batata? ¡Batata!': Examining Puerto Rican Visual Folk Expression in Times of Adversity," underscores the importance of form in exploring issues of trauma, recovery, and resilience. Colom's unconventional exploration of visual folk expressions by multisited Puerto Rican communities challenges us to see in different ways. The chapter reflects the fragmentation and conglomeration of responses to political, economic, and natural crises on the island through a combination of physical and digital means. The work presents an innovative pedagogy of "reading" the visual with a digital sensibility that mimics virtual experiences and expressions.

The following chapter likewise asks us to look more carefully. Martin A. Tsang's "Forming Strands and Ties in the Knotted Atlantic: Methodologies of Color and Practice of Beadwork in Lucumí Religion" takes us into the world of transatlantic beading. A master bead artist, priest, and anthropologist, Tsang's exploration of the process of beading in Lucumí[6] traditions offers a shift from looking at sacred objects as museum items. His discussion of the colors, numbers, and procedures involved in beading for ritual and memory illustrates how beaded objects in Afro-Cuban religion offer physical and metaphysical chains to multiple pasts and locations. Rather than codifying these objects, Tsang asks readers, viewers, and wearers to consider the trajectories these beautiful art pieces offer for making community connections.

The Haitian tradition of Vodou also gives us a visual scape with which to track memory through divinity. Alexander Fernández's chapter, "Of Blithe Spirits: Narratives of Rebellion, Violence, and Cosmic Memory in Haitian Vodou," centers on the historical and ritual import of *veves*, or metaphysical designs of the gods. Literally drawn on the ground for invocation, veves carry the weight of a past of rebellion, liberation, and struggle. Fernández's extensive fieldwork and knowledge as an ethnographer-priest of Afro-Diasporic religions richly inform his discussion of the relationship of violence to spirit possession and postcolonial embodied memory. His piece provides an apt closing for this section of *Theorizing Folklore from the Margins* on how certain lived histories perpetually make themselves known in the body and in art.

The last section of the volume, "Placing Community," explores different ways in which communities are created, performed, and marginalized and, more importantly, how each community frames its own stories. In the first chapter of this section, "'No One Would Believe Us': An Autoethnography of Conducting Fieldwork in a Conflict Zone," Mintzi Auanda Martínez-Rivera places herself inside her community, and the community where she does fieldwork, in order to explore the impacts of living and conducting research in a conflict zone. Using the poetry of Abegunde Maria Hamilton as a framing device, Martínez-Rivera's autoethnography challenges folklorists to think of the ways in which we can humanize the fieldwork experience and protect researchers, especially those of us that are more vulnerable when we are out in the field.

In her chapter, "La Sierra Juárez en Riverside": The Inaugural Oaxacan Philharmonic Bands Audition on a University Campus," Xóchitl Chávez presents a "methodological approach of sincere collaborative intention that is based on a framework of ethics and commitment to the Oaxacan migrant community on how knowledge is produced and represented." Taking the opportunity to organize a music event on her university campus, Chávez worked on a reciprocal collaborative project with communal leaders both in California and in Oaxaca,

Mexico, in order to transform a university space into a community-wide traditional music space. Through documenting the different stages of the preparation of this event, Chávez was able to witness the "reciprocal transformative effect" that sincere collaborative intentions can have.

In order to explore the invisibilization and exoticization of queer masculinities, Cory Thorne's "Hidden Thoughts and Exposed Bodies: Art, Everyday Life, and Queering Cuban Masculinities" challenges our understanding of how everyday life is defined. He puts into conversation the experiences of everyday life of his research participants, who are engaged in MSM sex work or underground economies in Cuba, with Global North epistemologies of what the authentic quotidian should look like. By engaging with the work of two Cuban artists, Thorne concludes that "art helps us escape these confines in a way that ethnography merely strives for, forcing us to consider a diversity of ways of seeing regardless of our own personal identities." That is, his visual foray into masculinity and desire resituates the conversation about the everyday in Cuba in a manner that is intimately translocal.

Criticizing folklore studies' obsession with the perfect traditional practitioner, in "Complexifying Identity through Disability: Critical Folkloristic Perspectives on Being a Parent and Experiencing Illness and Disability through My Child," Phyllis M. May-Machunda brings attention to a community that is mostly invisibilized and ignored in folkloristics: people with disabilities, chronic illness, or trauma. May-Machunda shares her family's experience of taking care of her differently abled daughter by framing it as a never-ending rite of passage where the family is constantly negotiating between liminality and reincorporation. Moreover, May-Machunda proposes different research avenues for folklore studies that can help us move beyond the limited understanding of community, vernacular traditional practices, and what is "worthy" of folklore research.

## CONCLUSION: CRITICAL JOURNEYING TOWARD FUTURE WORK

The volume that follows this introduction asks readers to expand the ways in which they think the study of folklore can operate on the ground and in academia. We are inviting alternate conceptions of context and meaning from what we have called the "margins" of the field. To be sure, the margins contain trained folklorists who are also members of cultures and communities that have too often been static objects of study. Opening up authority, we believe, means breaking with norms and canons in regard to form, representation, and the supposedly objective perspective of scientific observation. Rather, we encourage innovative and provocative avenues for rethinking engagement with folklore and the communities that create the culture and work we study. This means that claiming a clear positionality and a reflexive apparatus is necessary for doing folklore critically and ethically in the twenty-first century.

For many of the collaborators of this book, their contributions are personal, deeply rooted in their experience both as scholars and as members of their communities. As editors and contributors to this volume, it is a challenge as well as a joy to engage in difficult topics and to push each other outside of our comfort zones. For all of us, this volume is an opportunity to share stories that otherwise may not be told, to experiment with format and content, and to (re)create, (re)think, and (re)model our discipline. More questions linger and are or will be born out of this collaboration. What other paths may be opened for interdisciplinary work? What are other models and ways of creating collaborative and ethical communal work? What are the strategies that communities are creating to survive and thrive despite legacies of white supremacy, homophobia, misogyny, xenophobia, ableism, and other injustices and forms of discrimination? More than anything, we hope that this volume is the first of many where we can explore different ways in which we can create partnerships with communities that have traditionally been subjects of study, or even ignored. *Theorizing Folklore from the Margins* proposes, invites, and offers alternative paths that can enrich and strengthen folklore studies in ways that are relevant and necessary for the twenty-first century.

## NOTES

1. "Nous réclamons le droit à l'opacité" (Glissant 1981, 11).

2. Here, we are borrowing the phrasing of Cuban music and performance scholar Alexandra Vazquez, who understands details "as events that instantly reveal and honor what can't be said" (2013, 21).

3. Notable exceptions here are Patricia's Turner's (1993) work on African American rumor and Kay Turner and Pauline Greenhill's (2012) work on LGBTQI readings of fairy tales.

4. See, for example, Ramón Rivera-Servera's (2012, 137–143) autoethnographic exploration of race, sexuality, and place.

5. For more on nepantla, see Anzaldúa ([1987] 1999).

6. *Lucumí* is a term used to describe Afro-Cuban religious practices that include ritual, narrative, and artwork.

## BIBLIOGRAPHY

Alexander, Jacqui M. 2005. *Pedagogies of Crossing*. Durham, NC: Duke University Press.

American Folklore Society (AFS). 2018. *No Illusions, No Exclusions: 2018 Annual Meeting Program and Abstracts*. Bloomington, IN: American Folklore Society.

https://cdn.ymaws.com/www.afsnet.org/resource/resmgr/am18/AM18_program
_book,_online.pdf.

Anzaldúa, Gloria. (1987) 1999. *Borderlands / La Frontera*. San Francisco: Aunt Lute
Books.

Bakhtin, Mikhail. 1981. *The Dialogic Imagination*. Austin: University of Texas Press.

Baron, Robert, and Nick Spitzer, eds. 2007. *Public Folklore*. Jackson: University Press
of Mississippi.

Behar, Ruth. 1996. *The Vulnerable Observer: Anthropology That Breaks Your Heart*.
Boston: Beacon.

Brown, Leslie, and Susan Strega, eds. 2005. *Research as Resistance: Critical, Indigenous
and Anti-oppressive Approaches*. Toronto: Canadian Scholars' Press/Women's Press.

Cantú, Norma, and Olga Nájera-Ramírez, eds. 2002. *Chicana Traditions*.
Champaign: University of Illinois Press.

Dundes, Alan. 1980. *Interpreting Folklore*. Bloomington: Indiana University Press.

Dupree, Cidney H., and Fiske, Susan T. 2019. "Self-Presentation in Interracial
Settings: The Competence Downshift by White Liberals." *Journal of Personality
and Social Psychology* 117 (3): 579–604.

Glaser, Jennifer. 2016. *Borrowed Voices: Writing and Racial Ventriloquism in the Jewish
American Imagination*. New Brunswick, NJ: Rutgers University Press.

Glissant, Édouard. 1981. *Le discours antillais*. Ann Arbor: University of Michigan
Press.

———. 1990. *Poetics of Relation*. Translated by Betsy Wing. Ann Arbor: University of
Michigan Press.

Goldstein, Diane, ed. 2016. *The Stigmatized Vernacular*. Bloomington: Indiana
University Press.

hooks, bell. 2018. *All About Love: New Visions*. New York: William Morrow.

Jones, Stacy Holman, and Anne M. Harris. 2019. *Queering Autoethnography*. New
York: Routledge.

Jordan, Rosan A., and Susan Kalcik. 1985. *Women's Folklore, Women's Culture*.
Philadelphia: University of Pennsylvania Press, Publications of the American
Folklore Society.

Kauffman, Eric. 2018. "White Privilege Is Real, but Well-Meaning White Liberals
Are Helping to Perpetuate It." *Quillet*, October 27, 2018. https://quillette.com/2018
/10/27/white-privilege-is-real-but-well-meaning-white-liberals-are-helping-to
-perpetuate-it/.

Mott, Carrie, and Daniel Cockayne. 2017. "Citation Matters: Mobilizing the Politics
of Citation toward a Practice of 'Conscientious Engagement.'" *Gender, Place and
Culture* 24 (7): 954–973.

Narayan, Kirin. 1993. "How 'Native' Is a Native Anthropologist?" *American
Anthropologist* 95 (3): 671–686.

Paredes, Américo, and Richard Bauman, eds. 1972. *Towards New Perspectives in Folklore*.
Austin: University of Texas Press, Publications of the American Folklore Society.

Perez, Domino Renee, and Rachel González-Martin, eds. 2018. *Race and Cultural Practice in Popular Culture*. New Jersey: Rutgers University Press.

Ray, Victor. 2018. "The Racial Politics of Citation." *Inside Higher Ed*, April 27, 2018. https://www.insidehighered.com/advice/2018/04/27/racial-exclusions-scholarly-citations-opinion.

Richards-Greeves, Gillian. 2013. "Going Home: The Native Ethnographer's Baggage and the Crisis of Representation." *Anthropology News* 54:11–12, 15–16.

Rivera-Servera, Ramón H. 2012. *Performing Queer Latinidad: Dance, Sexuality, Politics*. Ann Arbor: University of Michigan Press.

Sandoval, Chela. 2000. *Methodology of the Oppressed*. Minneapolis: University of Minnesota Press.

Sciorra, Joseph. 2015. *Built with Faith*. Knoxville: University of Tennessee Press.

Spivak, Gayatri Chakravorty. 1988. "Can the Subaltern Speak?" In *Colonial Discourse and Post-colonial Theory*, edited by Patrick Williams and Laura Chrisman, 66–111. New York: Columbia University Press.

Turner, Kay, and Pauline Greenhill, eds. 2012. *Transgressive Tales*. Detroit: Wayne State University Press.

Turner, Patricia. 1993. *I Heard It through the Grapevine*. Berkeley: University of California Press.

Vazquez, Alexandra T. 2013. *Listening in Detail*. Durham, NC: Duke University Press.

Walker, Barbara. 1995. *Out of the Ordinary*. Logan: Utah State University Press.

Zeitlin, Steve. 2016. *The Poetry of Everyday Life*. Ithaca, NY: Cornell University Press.

SOLIMAR OTERO is Professor of Folklore at Indiana University in the Department of Folklore and Ethnomusicology. She is author of *Archives of Conjure: Stories of the Dead in Afrolatinx Cultures* (Columbia University Press, 2020) and *Afro-Cuban Diasporas in the Atlantic World* (University of Rochester Press, 2010). She is also coeditor with Toyin Falola of *Yemoja: Gender, Sexuality, and Creativity in the Latina/o and Afro-Atlantic Diasporas* (SUNY Press, 2013).

MINTZI AUANDA MARTÍNEZ-RIVERA is Assistant Professor of Anthropology in the Department of Sociology and Anthropology at Providence College. Since 2005, she has conducted research on the P'urhépecha culture of Michoacán, México, spending most of her time in the community of Santo Santiago de Angahuan. She has published articles on the Indigenous rock movement in Mexico, Indigenous popular culture, and the use of food as decorations. She is currently working on her first monograph, *Getting Married in Angahuan: Creating Culture, Performing Community*.

ONE

# White Traditioning and Bruja Epistemologies

## Rebuilding the House of USAmerican Folklore Studies

RACHEL V. GONZÁLEZ-MARTIN

### DISLOCATION

Tradition is a racialized concept that is imbued with an abstract aura as well as practical power. In response to generations of disciplinary tradition, I offer Irene Lara's (2005) concept of bruja positionality as a means to spur the intersectional futurity of critical folkloristics in and of the United States. This position is rooted in a deeply held cultural respect for magic as a transformative system for the disbursement of power in communities of believers and as a discursive disruption in the imperialist logics of Western rationality. Centering magic and magical thinking as logics for interpreting community practice creates a space to center non-Western sensibilities in the production of knowledge, sensibilities that have been previously weaponized against communities degraded as primitives and others. In this case, the bruja's magic articulates an alterity that challenges ideals "against which the ideals of modern social order have been articulated" (Styers 2004, 17). She inspires an epistemological lens that centers the marginal feminine and devalued spiritual and intuitive self in Western contexts while also representing the feared power of feminine sexuality: "Though we aim to transform our selves and our worlds, the reality is that we are part of a society still largely organized around racist and sexist binary ways of knowing. As we carve transformative spaces in a profession built on a rigid foundation of reason that invalidates and binarizes with spiritual intuitive knowledges, we are still judged by that value system" (Lara 2005, 28). Additionally, I use *Chicana Traditions: Continuity and Change* (Cantú and Nájera-Ramírez 2002) to revisit the work of queer, Chicanx, female voices as transformative sources of discursive innovation, urging USAmerican folklore studies toward the spiritual, the intuitive, and the magical.

## BUILDING A NEW HOUSE

In her famous *Sister Outsider*, Black feminist philosopher and activist Audre Lorde invokes the following warning: "For the master's tools will never dismantle the master's house. They may allow us to temporarily beat him at his own game, but they will never enable us to bring about genuine change" (1984, 78). In this essay, delivered at "The Personal and the Political Panel" at the Second Sex Conference held at New York University in the fall of 1979, Lorde shares her perspective, one rooted in challenging the enduring power of White heteromasculinity. In doing so, she illustrates why engaging bruja epistemologies may be a necessary step toward carving out new disciplinary ideologies in USAmerican folklore studies that have the potential to endure the upheaval of contested transitions. The conference took place seven years after the original publishing of *Toward New Perspectives in Folklore*, edited by Américo Paredes and Richard Bauman (1972). That volume set out not only to challenge the segmented view of North and South American perspectives in the fields of "American" folklore but also to address, among other formative frameworks, "the tension between the collective force of tradition and individual experience," "the situational context of expressive practice," and "the negotiations of difference" (Paredes and Bauman [1972] 2000, x). Lorde's impassioned talk, more akin to lyrical poetry, addresses the arrogance of erasure, in particular that by White feminist scholars who failed to see how race, age, class, and sexuality are critical factors of difference that link the personal and the political in feminist theoretical inquiry and that cannot be subsumed under an umbrella of common gender identification, lest it be distorted and trivialized (Lorde 1984, 66–71). Lorde's most potent synthesis of the White feminist blind spot in progressive feminist theorizing emerges when she asks how such theories—those that fail to engage critical differences—persist as they ignore the very people who make these scholars' labor possible.[1]

## THE *WHITE* IN WHITE TRADITIONING

A disciplinary identity has been cultivated by the field of academic folklore in the contemporary United States.[2] Tradition and variation are the twins at the core of folklore and have become prominent characteristics of folklore's disciplinary identity; they are the patterns through which discursive formations come to be categorized as the professional field of USAmerican folklore (Toelken 1996). Traditions of the field come to implicate the assumed active bearers and constituent audiences. Within highly variable intellectual genealogies, I consider what connects these paths to the present moment. I use the term *USAmerican folklore studies* to describe the purview of "American" folklore studies in order to decenter Whiteness from its intellectual core.[3] I do this with three practical and ideological intentions in mind. First, as my work straddles anthropological folklore and Latinx studies, the term *American* unduly prioritizes the culture of Anglo-descent communities, those who represent historically dominant demographics and specific settler-colonialist agendas in the Western Hemisphere. Second, the shift helps avoid confusion, as diasporic Latinx communities claim multinational subjectivities that span Latin America and the Caribbean, where people also identify as Americans.[4] The continued oversimplified use of the term "American" also implies that the study of discrete US Latinx communities is irrelevant to students of dominant populations, who are allowed to hide behind assumptions of generic pluralism, never made to account for their methodological and theoretical limitations. Third, *USAmerican folklore* clarifies distinctions between Latin American scholars and hemispheric scholars working from the United States who also research cultural practices across the Americas. To continue to use the term *American folklore* without reference to both its limitations as a term and its political bent is to ignore the theoretical and methodological impacts of views from the Global South and from scholars of Latinx and Latin American descent who identify as living in diaspora, migration, exile, and other states of racialized alienation. Accounting for such perspectives potentially sets us on a path toward intersectional inclusivity, one that could account for gaps in gender, racialized institutional power structures, and history in theoretical critique (Paredes and Bauman 2000, xi).

The term *White* in the context of the title of this chapter is not meant to target ethnically White professionals in the field or ethnically White communities. Instead, I mean to point to the racialized power dynamics that have impacted and continue to impact folklore's disciplinary identity in the United States. Open discussions of a politics of Whiteness can construct inclusive boundaries around racialization, where the high stakes of racial inequity implicate us all. Critical Whiteness studies is a growing field of critical race inquiry that, at its most basic, invites White- and Euro-American-identifying scholars and professionals to be as responsible for discourses about race and social racialization as those who are easily identified as ethnic and racialized minorities. Incorporating this line of thought reflects an attention to structurally competent scholarship as a service to communities, students, and peers. It also facilitates new contexts from which to theorize the cultivation and maintenance of White ethnic identity in USAmerican culture as a racialized identity. *American* is a deracialized social descriptor akin to *mainstream* or *normal*; it has a silent racial subtext but can still be argued to be inclusive in mixed company. The use of such terms manifests an invisible center. If race is an ideological construct shared across populations in the United States, then the responsibility for addressing racial inequality and abuse of race-blind privilege becomes a shared burden and a shared goal in the production of transformative theoretical discourse. Yet unrealized, the responsibility to address concerns of racial inequality in the field falls to scholars of color, who host difficult conversations about the impact of race in their research and who, in their professional contexts, are characterized as scholars of less value and, indeed, as hostile to their thematic field of study.

Claiming Whiteness is recognition of power, regardless of ethno-racial identification. It is a mutable state of being that informs the socially active relations of power at the conception of the professional field of folklore and the inception of the American Folklore Society. Using *North American* to designate the scope of the early journal and society elides the racialized divide between those producing discourse and those whose lives were reduced to discourse (Newell 1888).[5] Whiteness is a way to "construct boundaries in order to exclude certain groups" (Dowling 2015, 239). Avoiding race as a social factor is a tactical strategy that implicitly prioritizes a demographic majority, normalizing their primacy and subsuming challenges to this racialized hierarchy. In USAmerican folkloristics, Whiteness indicates the position of the scholar-professional, at times collector, whereas non-Whiteness is ascribed to the subjects. At this twenty-first-century moment, as a growing body of minoritarian professionals enter leadership roles in the field and academic appointments in tenure-track jobs, our disciplinary identity is up for review. To this end, our scholarly community must reconsider the role that Whiteness as a position of social dominance plays in the future of the field by acknowledging where this scholarly community began.

Studying folklore in the United States was a settler-colonial enterprise predicated on the racialization of a Native American other. Patrick Wolfe posits that the heart of settler-colonial practice is a "logic of elimination" (2006, 387). Using a biological comparison to a bacterial form, Lorenzo Veracini (2014, 622) asserts that this logic of elimination works through an ethos of domination and reproduction. Its efficiency is accomplished through an ability to reproduce through bacterial mats on dead cells. Settler-colonialism functions by replacing Indigenous populations with invasive settler societies that, over time, develop a distinctive identity and sovereignty. This brand of colonialism normalizes continuous settler occupation, exploiting lands and resources to which Indigenous people have genealogical ties and fomenting the dispossession of Indigenous resources, including cultural resources. In *American Folklore Scholarship*, Rosemary Lévy Zumwalt writes, "In the nineteenth century when folklore was established as a subject worthy of investigation, the orientation of American scholars to the study of folklore was greatly influenced by the presence of the American Indian" (1988, 5). This premise was called into question, as the European scholars interpreted the peasant classes as occupying a different social evolutionary position from that of Native Americans: as "savages or primitives," they were the subject not of folklorists but of ethnologists (5). Collection practices of the late nineteenth century and early twentieth century then become less romantic salvage expeditions and more strategic exploitation, from which riches came in the form of thematically organized folklore collections.[6] The settler-colonial origins and the functional early methods of the field form the basis of USAmerican folklore studies, and it must be acknowledged that this persists in oblique ways. While the origins of the field are rooted in a racist social discourse, this is only one of the complexities of doing folkloristics in the United States in the present day.

## BUILDING, CREATING, CONJURING

Academic discourse is magical. It has the capacity to affect material reality with the use of symbols arranged in a ritual space, the blank white template. As Sabina Magliocco asserts, ethnographic writing is a conscious act of construction (2004, 17). While scholars would prefer to situate academic discourse as the reporting of reality, a narrative of neutral scientific methodologies, ethnography in particular is closer to alchemy. It is in the combination of volatility and (at times) elusive thoughts and experiences that communities are constituted through discourse. This is power; it is world making through ink reorganized by those people previously fragmented by language and history (Glave 2003, 615). Moreover, the capacity for hegemonic social influences is higher, as those whose words are the most efficacious as performative utterances are those with the greatest social capital in academia.[7] Social capital is directly related to the legibility of one's intellectual genealogy and is limited by race, class, and gender distinctions. The foundation of the House of Folklore is built from similar materials to that of early twentieth-century anthropology: a desire to order the world using a European colonial mindset. Those whose intellectual artistry and labor built the field delineated where power resided and how to use that power to impose a certain classificatory order on a social world that, without that power, was inaccessible to them.

In the introduction to *Folklore and Folklife: An Introduction*, Richard M. Dorson (1972), eminent folklorist of the mid-twentieth century and first chair of the Folklore Institute at Indiana University, writes that it is only in the mid-1960s that the character of folklore study in the United States firmly shifts away from its antiquarian roots to become a formidable academic field. In his words, in the 1960s, "the American Folklore Society underwent a considerable transformation from a loose and floundering organization dependent on amateurs or academics studying folklore as a secondary interest" to a professional society gaining a foothold in American universities (5). However, if we think of USAmerican folkloristics as the critical study rooted in the folkloric cultural practices of those living in the continental United States, then it seems strange that in his statements, Dorson does not acknowledge the work of educated, intellectual scholars that preceded this professionalizing turn. One such example is the fieldwork and literary contributions of Jovita González Mireles (e.g., 2006), who examined the folklore of the Texas-Mexican borderlands and was formally trained at the University of Texas. Her work in Starr County in the late 1920s was not simply a logging of experiences with an exotic other but an assessment of the relationships of social power that affected Mexicans living in the borderlands. Similarly, in his book *Américo Paredes: Culture and Critique*, José E. Limón (2012) has taken a critical stance toward the intellectual genealogies of folklorists who have overlooked the contributions of Américo Paredes, whose work predated the recognized critical turns in the field, relegating him to the intellectual margins, a specialist in the border whose work can speak only for others of the same ethno-racial community—in many ways, allowing Paredes, as well as González Mireles, to enter House of Folklore only through the back door. Here, access to the familiar of one's own backyard is positioned in stark contrast to those whose racialized social positions allow them only shadow access to the cultural capital of other professional academics.

Moreover, such ordering established a disciplinary premise of othering that continues into the present day. This othering was initially conceived of as a way of preserving the culture of Native peoples who were seen as victims of social and cultural devastation, even before such devastation was certain. In many ways, such a perspective only contributed to and supported the continued slaughter and disenfranchisement of Native communities, whose narratives and rituals, rendered artifice in print, were stripped of their power within community contexts.[8] While the documentation of this process begins in the field in the late nineteenth and early twentieth centuries, such a framework continues, albeit more subtly, as the rotted floorboards of the House of Folklore begin to buckle under the weight of redressive discourses that question disciplinary origins while also acknowledging the future that is yet to be built. One way that we can begin to shape the new structure of folklore is to question the theoretical premises and methodological language that scaffold a system that is rooted in racialization but unwilling to engage with contemporary politics of race in the United States. Moreover, those scholars, particularly those of color who have made it their careers to engage with race politics, remain minimized beyond their capacity to collect interesting materials from communities that might be otherwise inaccessible to White, cis, heterosexual academics. This is most potently seen in the work of scholars examining borderland spaces at the seams of cultural collisions.

The other entryways, those visible from the street and to the public, are defined by a relationship to European origins and male scholars. I make no claim that folklore was at all different from other intellectual academic pursuits at the time, and yet, in 2021, if we cannot question the ground from which we grow, we are in danger of laying fallow. Dorson (1972) lists the tools of the folklorist, those that would separate "him" from the anthropologist proper or the historian. His first claim regards the practice of fieldwork. He asserts, "*Fieldwork* enables [the folklorist] to penetrate into alien cultures—at his back door, not necessarily in remote lands" (6; emphasis in original). First, to consider the cultures present in US territory as "alien" with respect to those academic collectors is implicitly a racist discourse. Within the formal discourse of the United States Citizen and Immigration Services, the term *alien*, specifically *nonqualified alien*, refers to those people residing in the geographic United States but who have no standing as legal citizens or as US nationals. This term has been in use since the early English and British nationality law, and in the United States proper, it dates back to the Alien and Sedition Acts of 1798. That being said, *alien* had the same significance in Dorson's day as it does today. It is a term of hierarchical categorization of rightful belonging in the United States. In this way, as exemplified by Dorson's use of *alien* and the acknowledgement that "alien cultures" are "at your back door," folklore has been built and reaffirmed in the mid-twentieth century as a field that, through its mere attention, renders people alien in their own homes.

This ideological premise is dangerous as it opens the door to subhumanizing practices that impose symmetrical value on living, breathing individuals and static collections in print. It is further reinforced in the elite resources at the present day (Dorson 1972) made useful by and to US-based scholars. Dorson goes on to explain that alongside archival sources and bibliographic tools, US scholars can and should use indexes he calls "ingenious classificatory systems" (1972, 6). These include Stith Thompson's (1955) expansive *Motif-Index of Folk Literature*, the Aarne-Thompson type-index of folktales, Archer Taylor's (1931) arrangement of English riddles, and Francis James Child's (1965) canon of English and Scottish popular ballads. Each of these tools is based on the study of Western European "peasant" communities. Thompson, Taylor, and Child were all White USAmerican men with intellectual pedigrees leading back to Harvard University. Antti A. Aarne was Finnish and is credited with establishing the historic-geographic model in folklore studies to analyze the diffusion of oral literature, also known as the Finnish method. Thompson (1953) used this model to examine "The Star Husband Tale," said to be "confined to North American Indian tribes" (Dorson 1972, 10). Thompson was criticized for his reliance on descriptive details rather than an analysis of circulation and change, an approach that reflects a lack of interest in engaging critically or deeply in the experiences of Native North American communities. However, his work continues to be canonical in the field.

Just as Dorson was publishing this work that became a definitive source for training folkloristics, particularly at Indiana University, US culture was going through key historical moments that make the frame of this work seem painfully weak as methods that actually "explore the relationships of folklore to culture," as Dorson asserts (1972, 7). As Dorson's work is was received, the US Supreme Court ruled on *Roe v. Wade*, legalizing abortion across the United States; President Richard Nixon pulled out of offensive actions in North Vietnam; the American Indian Movement stood against federal authorities at the Pine Ridge reservation in Wounded Knee, South Dakota; the American Psychiatric Association removed homosexuality from the DSM-II; and Bruce Lee died. The litany of texts praised by Dorson in this seminal publication of the mid-twentieth century centralizes analytic tools that are honed for European-origin communities and yet are used specifically to address cultural practice in the United States. Such a framework asks the communities of the Americas to fit into a model of European cultural exchange, setting them up to fail and justify their marginalization in wider disciplinary history. At the same time, this arrangement ignores the heterogeneity of "European" experiences. How could these tools, which implicitly devalue the cultures of the Americas and were formulated in different cultural, racial, and colonial contexts, hope to speak to the experiences of US communities of color, LGBTQI communities, women, the poor, and the undereducated, among others? One productive response to this historic premise is recognition of epistemologies of the *Américas*, rather than those rooted in Western hegemony and European idealism.

## MAGICAL THINKING

If we collectively pivot away from Eurocentric epistemologies that implicitly invalidate analyses that privilege the perspectives of communities who do not identify with European histories of conquest, we acknowledge the power wielded by scholars producing academic discourse to conjure the communities they study through the act of entextualization. The act of conjuring or evoking the image of a community when decontextualized from its social, political, and geographic center through the imposition of Eurocentric theoretical models is itself another form of intellectual and rhetorical colonization, a settler-colonial ethos in action. Redressing cultural annihilation through race-resistant scholarship requires decentering European-origin discourse by incorporating intersectional epistemologies not as descriptive novelties but as models of ethical future-making.[9] The remainder of this work is concerned with a presentist frame in the vein of Jack Halberstam's (1998, 54) notion of "perverse presentism." Perverse presentism works as a corrective methodology that rejects determinative historiography in sexuality studies where logics of intimacy from the present are imposed on social actors of the past. Halberstam acknowledges historical expressions as independent of interpretive frames of the present that limit the potential for variability and complexity of past forms. While we cannot travel through time and change the politics of the past, we can hope to institute correctives in the present. One way we can do this is by acknowledging magical thinking as an alternate system of knowing, a system that acknowledges "magic as a form of science, a means of acquiring knowledge and exercising control" (Shweder 1977, 637), and by acknowledging at the same time the manner in which entextualizing forms of folklore works to constitute community imaginaries.

The power of the written word cannot be overstated. Whether one is debating Shakespearean monologues as the pinnacle of Western creativity or making unadvisable comments about one's boss on Twitter, words have power, and those who wield words, those who speak and are heard, manage said power. Entextualization, as framed by Bauman and Briggs (1990), is a manner of framing or the "reconstitution and traditionalizing" of discourse, "whether quoted, repeated or embedded" (Muana 1998, 44). It follows that entextualization, particularly of discursive forms drawn from fieldwork, is the start of a larger process implicating the role of decontextualization and recontextualization in the larger circulation of a cultural text. The creation of movable parts allows for texts to be taken out of their context and placed into theoretical and social frames from which they were not intended to be considered. While we can use this process as an analytic framework for the study of intertextual relationships, we still need to articulate the political stakes of this process: the othering of everyday affective behaviors and speech. When such frames pass between academics and community members, especially those who study the Americas through the lens of hemispheric connectivity, the result is not ethical scholarship; it is alienation. Scholars can build illustrious careers on alienation. The question then becomes, How do we conjure connection through our work, rather than alienation? One answer is that we acknowledge our rhetorics as part of a system of magical thinking that academics call "theoretical discourse," and we incorporate the magic we find in the field into our discourse as a method of community-based intellectualizing.

The way to break the path of intellectual chain migration is to stop cold and pivot. The epistemological pivot away from following and replicating the work of previous generations does not require a wholesale rejection of the disciplinary past; it requires only the promise to help create a new, radically improved disciplinary identity through a modified focus and critical repurposing of the established methods of inquiry. Fieldwork, collection, interpretive models, and historical geography can all be approached in a way that actively takes on the issues of contemporary US society—namely, experiences of race, class, and power. While previous generations have approached the study of USAmerican folklore as the practice of imposing order onto the people and practices who call the

United States home by means of voyeuristic collecting practices, fetishization of poverty and the poor, and a tendency to romanticize cultural differences, critical folkloristic practice in the twenty-first century will valorize the practice of disordering.

In this context, the concept of disordering emerges from critical practices in Chicana feminist theorizing, particularly the work of Laura E. Pérez (1999). Strategic disorder destabilizes discourses of the past by challenging old perspectives with new authors, methodologies, and theoretical framing. The ensuing chaos draws attention to the facade of orderly texts and identities to suit intellectual rather than humanistic purposes, with a note that the normalized order is about making non-Western others legible to Western audiences. Drawing on hooks (1994), Lara notes that such Western ideologies create cracks in a profession built on rigid foundations of a Western, male, heteronormative logic that "invalidates and binarizes" itself with alternative, intuitive ways of knowing (2005, 28). With such a logic, I offer to the folklore canon the notion of bruja positionality as a way of engaging with Latinx folklore and as an example of reconciling group logics with transformative academics (28). Bruja positionality as an epistemological revisioning emerges from scholars and activists committed to socially transformative work that is invested in social justice. In Chicana feminist philosophies, the image of the bruja or witch is an ambivalent character. She builds solidarity with "the dark, india, puta, queer, outcast and 'maligned' other" (28). This foregrounding of the feminine as a way to fragment male-centric discourses of the past has been part of USAmerican folkloristics since the early twentieth century and yet has failed to gain status as canon. One such work, now close to twenty years old, is the volume *Chicana Traditions: Continuity and Change*, edited by two senior figures in USAmerican folklore study, Norma E. Cantú and Olga Nájera-Ramírez (2002).

*Chicana Traditions* is a work of feminist folklore that engages in an ethos of bruja positionality. The volume aims to address the absence of visible discourse in and of Chicana studies in the field of USAmerican folklore by centering Native scholars writing about their own experiences and communities. This perspective pushes back on the race-blind history of academic folklore. Cantú and Nájera-Ramírez cite how as a viable subject of inquiry, folklore is a subjective construction of authors, noting Danish literary folklorist Bengt Holbek's assertion that "our views of folk traditions are formed probably to a much higher degree than we think by prejudices, experiences, and interests that are characteristic of the class we come from. If the social position of this class changes or if the recruitment of folklorists changes, then the tacit assumptions in our work change and, along with them, our theories and working hypotheses" (1981, 140). A crucial aspect of this statement is this notion of tacit bias. Tacit bias is no longer acceptable. To move forward, folklorists must directly unearth such biases and decide whether we can live with their continued impact on our collective work. While *Chicana Traditions* facilitates the potential for many more metadiscursive folklore projects, I examine four chapters to illustrate how this volume has already conjured a version of bruja positionality—a quotidian manifestation of the interstitial space occupied by minoritarian communities (Muñoz 2009) that embraces ambiguities in research production—and offers a lens through which we can reassess the wider project of USAmerican folklore in the twenty-first century. I examine aspects of research practice and production that exemplify my understanding of bruja positionality as it can be adapted to the realm of USAmerican folkloristics using chapters by Domino R. Perez, Yolanda Broyles-Gonzalez, Cándida F. Jáquez, and Deborah R. Vargas.

FRESH LUMBER

Domino R. Perez is the foremost expert on the legend of La Llorona, the Weeping Woman, in the Americas. Her 2008 book *There Was a Woman: La Llorona from Folklore to Popular Culture* reflects a new canon of interdisciplinary texts that straddle the intellectual worlds of folklore, English, popular culture studies, and Chicana studies. Her work emerges as part of a new tool kit that scholars of folklore may draw from to begin constructing the new House of Folklore.

In part 1, "Enduring Traditions," Perez's "Caminando con La Llorona: Traditional and Contemporary Narratives" lays out a detailed account of the cultural products emerging from the circulation of this legend of a "sexualized mestiza" among Mexican American and Latinx storytellers and audiences (2002, 101). Her work documents the shifts in the legend text and its functionality as products of a shifting multicultural Chicanx population in the United States. While Perez documents an exhaustive survey of versions, she begins with self-knowledge. She places herself into the narrative at the beginning of the text and at the end. She begins with a version of the legend that she herself has heard told. To those looking for methodological nuance, this creates an implicit equity between herself as author and her coethnic community while never taking up an uncritical "us" position. What is also unique about Perez's explication is the self-conscious desire to narrate from within a specific community context, which is followed later in greater depth in her book-length work (2008). This position is a localizing premise, but it also creates spaces to understand the legend as the product of many authors in many contexts, authors who are laboring within a complex representational process. When I discussed the chapter with the author, she explained that the chapter does not sync with later developments in her stance on the metanarrations of the legend, in particular the dichotomy between what is categorically traditional and what is labeled contemporary. She abides by living scholarship, which, like the legend itself, is in flux and subject to the contours of context. As the story evolves, so does the scholarship. And as community members become scholars, the legend is regarded with potentially new generational insights, as well as conflicts.

In part 2, "Practicing Traditions," Broyles-Gonzalez's chapter, "Indianizing Catholicism: Chicana/India/Mexicana Indigenous Spiritual Practices in Our Image," examines spiritual practice as a tool of gendered and racialized survival. Unlike that of Perez, Broyles-Gonzalez's narrative form frames her piece as one of stream of conscious remembering, a practice in time travel where readers are brought into her memories of her *abuelita*, Polita. This narrative style in particular speaks to the latter half of the title, in which "Practices in Our Image" relate back to the desire to foreground the spiritual labor of Mexican women as the chief authorities in her text. While cultural outsiders might resist calling the chapter theoretically rich, the truth is that its discussion centers on bringing together gender, power, and temporality—drawing historical trauma into the light of the present and reassessing the efficacy of spiritual survival. In her work, Broyles-Gonzalez creates a sense of urgency. The incantation intimates a syncretic practice that does not serve as detritus of true Native identity—in this case, Yaqui identity—but instead shifts in practice serve as "*disimulo* (camouflage)," rhetorical protection (2002, 120). The lens of camouflage asserts that rather than succumbing to colonial powers, Native women in particular are agentive social actors, hiding in plain sight, living to tell their stories.

Moreover, her work pinpoints an issue that often goes overlooked in the study of folklore in the United States, that of the "matter of speculation" (120). While Broyles-Gonzalez's work speaks directly to Chicana-identifying communities, the issue of speculative histories becomes particularly valuable to a wider discussion of communities who identify as living in diaspora. These communities' identities are geographically and emotionally split across space and time, complicating their relationships to present practices and their antecedents. The speculative status comes with the chosen and forced migration of communities fleeing settler-colonial violence, as well as those who later would be identified as "economic migrants" fleeing ideological and physical violence of structurally embedded poverty. This realm of ambivalent occupation of places in time means that histories are blurred and practices are blended, and this is itself a defining state of being that requires critical attention to the systemic dehumanization of Native women across the Americas, rather than benevolent absolution for existing at all. While the link between Chicanx communities and rhetorics of indigeneity makes precarious connections to the social realties of contemporary

Native North American communities, Broyles-Gonzalez's work emphasizes lingering at the gaps of knowledge and allowing those who live to fill those gaps and rightfully change the future. This is the tension that folklorists need to address, futurity and change.

This unapologetic narrative of *mujerista* agency,[10] while not completely applicable to cross-cultural communities (though perhaps translating well to experiences of diverse communities of women), is also part of the narrative contribution of Jáquez in her piece, "Meeting La Cantante through Verse, Song and Performance." Jáquez, a professor of music, was formerly a faculty member at Indiana University, and I was fortunate enough to overlap with her in my first semester of graduate school. An ethnomusicologist by training, her work adds a transnational link drawing on nationalism and gendered symbology of Mexican mariachi performance in urban US centers. She herself is a trained musician and *cantante*, and her chapter locates themes of fragmentation and dualities in the performance of gender in mariachi performance and practice in the US. She takes a decidedly intersectional lens to relate the fragmentations and internal contradictions evinced in the mutually constitutive character of nationalism, tradition, race, ethnicity, and gender in mariachi practice (2002, 179). This layering of constitutive elements draws attention to the ethical necessity of a non-isolating model of cultural texts: rather than decontextualizing one element of mariachi performance—such as lyrical content—the concert of factors and the contextualization of the practice in quotidian reality offers genuine insight into its roles as a politicized cultural practice instead of simply as a skill, hobby, art form, or teaching tool. The most incisive point Jáquez draws is a rejection of the social value of coherence, or order, of neatly defined classificatory systems. She asserts that the inherent contradictions she outlines in terms of gender performance in contemporary urban mariachi practice "are not social puzzles in need of solutions; rather, they collectively define a performance plane that form a coherency in the act of a performative statement (despite the dualities) in daily practice" (179). Here, the author offers us two nuggets of wisdom that we can instrumentalize in the study of cultural practice. The first is the need to prioritize coherency from an internal perspective, with the acknowledgement that the antiquarian models of collection and categorization rooted in European models fall outside the cultural logics of USAmerican communities. Second, the phrase *performative statement* offers the artist agency in the production of self through practice rather than being a passive purveyor of tradition for the benefit of curious audiences or professional appreciators; it creates an identity for performance external to that of cultural fetish. Disorder in this case comes through a process of decentering assumed interpretations of universal legibility in favor of a locally defined in-group discourse.

Social location resides at the heart of Vargas's chapter, "Cruzando Frontejas: Remapping Selena's Tejano Music 'Crossover.'" Again, this chapter draws on a Chicanx studies lens to merge traditional practice with the study of popular culture. Vargas discusses the career of the late Tejana music sensation Selena Quintanilla, who died young before realizing the full impact of what was imagined to be her illustrious English-language crossover career. Using the cultural trope of "crossing," Vargas points to a more abstracted or ambient form of folklore tradition that begins with verbal artistry but morphs into a kind of folk belief that centers Tejana/o, Chicanx life at the interstices of US and Mexican life and culture. While Selena's artistry comes in the form of regional Tejano music, her persona was more than a musician; she was a cultural icon and, after her death, a folk saint. She allows us to dip into the idea of folklore as a cultural product, one that is marketable and profitable. This relation to a sense of a Latinx public allows us to broaden our understanding of how communities, particularly minority communities under the auspices of folklore, are contextualized with regard to their social positions in the United States. Vargas's use of the music industry crossover, which signaled Selena's growing audience in the United States, alludes to the ambiguity of interethnic identities, of bordered living, which Selena's life and career have come to symbolize in music and the cultural productions that have circulated since her death. The Latinx public is a concept of US Latinxs in the public sphere that is framed through explicit narratives of racialized economics, consumer citizenship, and demographic variability. This is not a regional ethnic enclave to be left to the area studies specialist but a shift in national discourses of social location in the United States. These realities inform the shifts in social location of new generations of Chicanx and Latinx communities, whose traditions are not the same as those of their grandparents and yet are dependent on the relations of technology and commerce in the Americas.

## FRAMING

If the above discussion is to resonate with the field of USAmerican folklore, then the House of Folklore will also need reframing. I would like to return to the idea of magical thinking for a moment and to have us collectively imagine an intellectual pivot, a pivot that reframes the authoritative discourse in the field by decentering White hegemonic discourse and instead anticipating folklore's mestizo futurity. In her narrative of life as a *curandera* (healer) and community activist in Nyssa, Oregon, Eva Castellanoz advocates for revised traditions. Working with Joanna Mulcahy, Eva shares her belief that tradition must serve the individual and social good; and while (in Eva's community) "Mexican culture provides the root, new growth may be stimulated by practices and beliefs germinated in new soil" (Mulcahy 2007, 454). This ideology is supported by a central notion of folklore as coming from a "usable past" (446). Usable artistry, not simply entertainment, becomes a different register for cultural practice that draws together belief systems in the logic of material goods. This frame of artistry as therapy, as labor, and as social production speaks to the value of tradition in minority communities, where folklore is a tool used within strategies of social survival. However, in contexts of migration, diaspora, and other forms of social dislocation, rooting becomes a constant process of revision and reimagination, one that cannot be static, as for many it is wholly speculative. Rooting therefore works as a form of conjuring stability.

The intellectual *brujería* of Perez, Broyles-Gonzalez, Jáquez, and Vargas, among other authors in the text, creates rhetorical stability by honoring disorder, ambivalence, and speculation, allowing in-group social logics to ground their folkloristic work in the realities of community life, of speaking wholeness into partial stories. Rooting therefore occurs at the level of the representational process rather than in place-space. Eva's words as a healer, a woman, a mother, and a Latina migrant rooted in her Oregon community signal a right to transformation, to a value in relevance over presumptions of authenticity. She asserts, "There are traditional things not good for a person. They have to die; [we] even kill them and keep what's good" (Mulcahy 2007, 454). The healer foretells the destruction of the house. We must keep what's good, discard the rotted wood, and replace the cracked concrete if we are ever to live in the house again. The efficacy of magical thinking and healing comes from complex cultural collisions, much of which are rooted in memory and necessary forgetting. What can we keep from the institutional memory, and what must be "killed" before we are able to imagine who we might become?

Tradition is a racialized tool. The academic concept of tradition is an organizational device that undervalues racialized communities in our contemporary Western, White supremacist society, where Whiteness is synonymous with "unmarked" and tradition is part of a validation of a community's capacity to historicize its existence in place and time. Tradition is a set of practices that hold both literal and symbolic values, values that are mobilized in different ways but also received socially and culturally in different ways depending on subjective positionality. This essay has been an experiment in centralizing a different authorial voice and, by doing so, interrogating intellectual genealogies and the colonial power that allowed their advancement. What can we learn from the margins? What can we learn from the voices of those who have been historically disenfranchised? We might find that we have a lot to learn from precariously situated theory and methodologies, which facilities spaces for knowledge that may actually offer a renewed magical stability.

NOTES

1.  In an intimate letter to author Mary Daly in response to her book *Gyn/Ecology* (1978), Lorde confronts Daly over her desire to examine all women's experiences of oppression as shared, rather than acknowledging the racialized divisions experienced by non-White women. Referencing Daly's discussions of goddess worship, Lorde notes that the author's work is wholly blind to non-European case studies, and yet she makes no claim to be narrowing her theories to only European-origin women. She asks Daly, "So I wondered, why doesn't Mary deal with Afrekete as an example? Why are her goddess images only white, western european, judeo-christian?" (1984, 67).

2.  White traditioning is not a totalizing discourse and has been challenged on many fronts for generations. Feminist scholars such as Norma E. Cantú, Olga Nájera-Ramirez, Olivia Cadaval, Shirley Moody-Turner, Kimberly Lau, and Phyllis May-Machunda have labored in critical ways that have made the process of White traditioning legible and therefore challengeable. Similarly, scholars working in the public sector have always had to find ethical ways of working with communities in order to be productive. Their work must be recognized as part of this disciplinary history, a revisioning process to refute old binaries in the face of critical integration. Some key intergenerational interlocutors include Maribel Alvarez (Southwest Folklife Alliance), Debora Kodish (founding director of the Philadelphia Folklore Project), Kay Turner (Brooklyn Arts Council), Selina Morales (director of the Philadelphia Folklore Project), and Sojin Kim (Smithsonian Center for Folklife and Cultural Heritage).

3.  The first rule of "the American Folk-Lore society" published in the first issue of the *Journal of American Folklore* elides diversity in the face of pluralism, noting, "The American Folk-Lore society has for its object the study of Folk-Lore in general, and in particular the collection and publication of the Folk-Lore of North America" (Newell 1888).

4.  In "The American Concept of Folklore," Alan Dundes (1966) was specifically aware of this distinction: "By 'American' I refer to North American and more specifically United States of America. The peoples of Latin America also refer to themselves as themselves 'Americans' and folklorists in Latin America have been extremely active in the last few decades, particularly with respect to formulating 'concepts' of folklore" (226).

5.  The first issue of the *Journal of American Folklore* cites collections from a variety of Native North American tribal communities: Briton's "Lenapé Conversations," Beauchamp's "Onondaga Tales," and Boas's "On Certain Songs and Dances of the Kwakiutl of British Columbia." Given their place at the inception of the field, it would be logical if these communities or a thriving body of pan-Indigenous scholars were an active and powerful intellectual force of the contemporary American Folklore Society. This is not the case.

6. One such example that accentuates folklore's direct connection to American anthropology is Kroeber (1925).

7. In *Women Writing Culture*, Ruth Behar and Deborah A. Gordon (1995) provide a feminist critique of the oral predicament of ethnographic writing, in particular sexual politics and the silencing of women's voices that are apparent in the seminal critique of ethnographic production, *Writing Culture* (Clifford and Marcus 1986).

8. Cutcha Risling Baldy (2018) offers a powerful premise of reclaiming community history and practice after the trauma of rhetorical and material colonization. Angela Cavender Wilson (2005), a member of the Dakota people, narrates resistance focused on reclaiming Indigenous epistemologies of health.

9. Karin Ingersol (2016) does a fascinating interpretation of this very premise in her ethnography of Indigenous Hawaiian ways of knowing founded on a sensorial, intellectual, and embodied literacy of the ocean.

10. For an expanded history on mujerista ideologies, see Ada Maria Isasi-Diaz et al. (1992).

## BIBLIOGRAPHY

Baldy, Cutcha Risling. 2018. *We Are Dancing for You: Native Feminisms and the Revitalization of Women's Coming-of-Age Ceremonies*. Seattle: University of Washington Press.

Bauman, Richard, and Charles L. Briggs. 1990. "Poetics and Performance as Critical Perspectives on Language and Social Life." *Annual Review of Anthropology* 19:59–88.

Behar, Ruth, and Deborah A. Gordon, eds. 1995. *Women Writing Culture*. Berkeley: University of California Press.

Broyles-Gonzalez, Yolanda. 2002. "Indianizing Catholicism: Chicana/India/ Mexicana Indigenous Spiritual Practices in Our Image." In Cantú and Nájera-Ramírez (2002), 117–132.

Bychowski, M. W., Howard Chiang, Jack Halberstam, Jacob Lau, Kathleen P. Long, Marcia Ochoa, C. Riley Snorton, Leah DeVun, and Zeb Tortorici. 2018. "'Trans*historicities': A Roundtable Discussion." *TSQ: Transgender Studies Quarterly* 5 (4): 658–685.

Campa, Arthur L. 1946. *Spanish Folk-Poetry in New Mexico*. Albuquerque: University of New Mexico Press.

Cantú, Norma E., and Olga Nájera-Ramírez, eds. 2002. *Chicana Traditions: Continuity and Change*. Urbana: University of Illinois Press.

Child, Francis James. 1965. *The English and Scottish Popular Ballads*. New York: Dover.

Clements, William M. 1988. *100 Years of American Folklore Studies: A Conceptual History*. American Folklore Society. https://scholarworks.iu.edu/dspace/handle /2022/9009.

Clifford, James, and George E. Marcus. 1986. *Writing Culture: The Poetics and Politics of Ethnography.* Berkeley: University of California Press.

Cox, Alice. 2017. "Settler Colonialism." In *Oxford Bibliographies.* July 26, 2017. http://www.oxfordbibliographies.com/abstract/document/obo-9780190221911/obo-9780190221911-0029.xml.

Daly, Mary. 1978. *Gyn/Ecology: The Metaethics of Radical Feminism.* Boston: Beacon Press.

Dorson, Richard M. 1972. *Folklore and Folklife: An Introduction.* Chicago: University of Chicago Press.

Dowling, Julie A. 2015. *Mexican Americans and the Question of Race.* Austin: University of Texas Press.

Dundes, Alan. 1966. "The American Concept of Folklore." *Journal of the Folklore Institute* 3 (3): 226–249.

Espinosa, Aurelio M. 1909. *Studies in New Mexican Spanish: Part I—Phonology.* Albuquerque: University of New Mexico Press.

Glave, Thomas. 2003. "Fire and Ink: Toward a Quest for Language, History, and a Moral Imagination." *Callaloo* 26 (3): 614–621.

González Mireles, Jovita 2006. *Life along the Border: A Landmark Tejana Thesis.* Elma Dill Russell Spencer Series in the West and Southwest 26. College Station: Texas A&M University Press.

Halberstam, Jack. 1998. *Female Masculinity.* Durham, NC: Duke University Press.

Holbek, Bengt. 1981. "Tacit Assumptions." *Folklore Forum* 14 (2): 121–140.

hooks, bell. 1994. *Teaching to Transgress: Education as the Practice of Freedom.* New York: Routledge.

Hurston, Zora Neale. 1990. *Mules and Men.* New York: Perennial Library.

Ingersol, Karin. 2016. *Waves of Knowing: A Seascape Epistemology.* Durham, NC: Duke University Press.

Isasi-Diaz, Ada Maria, Elena Olazagasti-Segovia, Sandra Mangual-Rodriguez, Maria Antonietta Berriozábal, Daisy L. Machado, Lourdes Arguelles, and Raven-Anne Rivero. 1992. "Roundtable Discussion: Mujeristas Who We Are and What We Are About." *Journal of Feminist Studies in Religion* 8 (1): 105–125.

Jáquez, Cándida F. 2002. "Meeting La Cantante through Verse, Song and Performance." In Cantú and Nájera-Ramírez (2002), 167–182.

Kaplan, Caren, and Norma Alarcon. 1999. *Between Woman and Nation: Nationalisms, Transnational Feminisms, and the State.* Durham, NC: Duke University Press.

Kroeber, Alfred L. 1925. "Handbook of the Indianas of California." *Bureau of American Ethnology Bulletin.* Washington, DC: Smithsonian.

Lara, Irene. 2005. "Bruja Positionalities: Toward a Chicana/Latina Spiritual Activism." *Chicana/Latina Studies* 4 (2): 10–45.

Limón, José E. 2012. *Américo Paredes: Culture and Critique.* Austin: University of Texas Press.

Lorde, Audre. 1984. *Sister Outsider: Essays and Speeches.* Crossing Press Feminist Series. Trumansburg, NY: Crossing Press.

Magliocco, Sabina. 2004. *Witching Culture: Folklore and Neo-paganism in America.* Contemporary Ethnography. Philadelphia: University of Pennsylvania Press.

Moraga, Cherríe, and Gloria Anzaldúa, eds. 2015. *This Bridge Called My Back: Writings by Radical Women of Color.* 4th ed. Albany: State University of New York Press.

Muana, Patrick Kagbeni. 1998. "Beyond Frontiers: A Review of Analytical Paradigms in Folklore Studies." *Journal of African Cultural Studies* 11 (1): 39–58.

Mulcahy, Joanne B. 2007. "Oregon Voices: 'Know Who You Are'; Regional Identity in the Teachings of Eva Castellanoz." *Oregon Historical Quarterly* 108 (3): 444–457.

———. 2010. "Magical Thinking: Magical Thinking." *Anthropology and Humanism* 35 (1): 38–46.

Muñoz, José Esteban. *Cruising Utopia: The Then and There of Queer Futurity.* New York: New York University Press, 2009.

National Conference of State Legislatures. 2018. "Common Immigration Terms." October 15, 2018. https://www.ncsl.org/research/immigration/common -immigration-terms.aspx.

Newell, W. W. 1888. "Rules of the American Folk-Lore Society." *Journal of American Folklore* 1 (1): n.p.

Paredes, Américo. 1958. *With His Pistol in His Hand: A Border Ballad and Its Hero.* Austin: University of Texas Press.

Paredes, Américo, and Richard Bauman. (1972) 2000. *Toward New Perspectives in Folklore.* Bloomington: Trickster.

Perez, Domino Renee. 2002. "Caminando con La Llorona: Traditional and Contemporary Narratives." In Cantú and Nájera-Ramírez (2002), 100–116.

———. 2008. *There Was a Woman: La Llorona from Folklore to Popular Culture.* Austin: University of Texas Press.

Pérez, Laura E. 1999. "El desorden, Nationalism, and Chicana/o Aesthetics." In *Between Women and Nation Transnational Feminisms and the State,* edited by Caren Kaplan, Norma Alarcón, and Minoo Moallem, 19–46. Durham, NC: Duke University Press.

Ruiz, Vicki L. 2006. "Nuestra América: Latino History as United States History." *Journal of American History* 93 (3): 655–672.

Shweder, Richard A. 1977. "Likeness and Likelihood in Everyday Thought: Magical Thinking in Judgments about Personality." *Current Anthropology* 18 (4): 637–658.

Styers, Randall. 2004. *Making Magic: Religion, Magic, and Science in the Modern World.* New York: Oxford University Press.

Taylor, Archer. 1931. *The Proverb.* Cambridge, MA: Harvard University Press.

Thompson, Stith. 1953. "The Star Husband Tale." *Studia Septentrionalia* 4:93–163.

———. 1955. *Motif-Index of Folk-Literature: A Classification of Narrative Elements in Folktales, Ballads, Myths, Fables, Mediaeval Romances, Exempla, Fabliaux, Jest-Books, and Local Legends.* Bloomington: Indiana University Press.

Toelken, Barre. 1996. *The Dynamics of Folklore*. Rev. and expanded ed. Logan: Utah State University Press.

Vargas, Deborah R. 2002. "Cruzando Frontejas: Remapping Selena's Tejano Music 'Crossover.'" In Cantú and Nájera-Ramírez (2002), 224–36.

Vargas, Deborah R., Lawrence La Fountain-Stokes, Lawrence M., and Nancy R. Mirabal. 2017. *Keywords for Latina/o Studies*. New York: New York University Press.

Veracini, Lorenzo. 2014. "Understanding Colonialism and Settler Colonialism as Distinct Formations." *Interventions* 16 (5): 615–633.

Wilson, Angela Cavender. 2005. "Reclaiming Indigenous Knowledge." In *War and Border Crossings: Ethics When Cultures Clash*, edited by Peter A. French and Jason A. Short, 255–264. New York: Rowan and Littlefield.

Wolfe, Patrick. 2006. "Settler Colonialism and the Elimination of the Native." *Journal of Genocide Research* 8 (4): 387–409.

Young, Frank W. 1970. "A Fifth Analysis of the Star Husband Tale." *Ethnology* 9 (4): 389–413.

Zumwalt, Rosemary Lévy. 1988. *American Folklore Scholarship: A Dialogue of Dissent*. Folkloristics. Bloomington: Indiana University Press.

RACHEL V. GONZÁLEZ-MARTIN is Folklorist and Associate Professor of Mexican American and Latina/o Studies at the University of Texas at Austin. Her award-winning book *Quinceañera Style: Social Belonging and Latinx Consumer Identities* (University of Texas Press, 2019) examines the politics of representation and materiality of inter-American quinceañera traditions informed by US Latinx consumer practice.

# TWO

# Un Tumbe Ch'ixi

## Incorporating Afro-Descendant Ideas into an Andean Anticolonial Methodology

### JUAN EDUARDO WOLF

During the weeklong carnival celebration in the highland town of Socoroma in northern Chile, participants follow a schedule of events that is different for each day. Most of these events are accompanied by at least one of three types of traditional musicians: *tarkeada, orquesta andina,* and the *cantor de pueblo.* The harsh sound of the consort of duct flutes known as tarkeada is designed to bring rain, and, in the past, it was associated with the town's older members.[1] The string band known as orquesta andina plays popular waynos and romantic songs with lyrics adapted to its local setting.[2] It inspires couple-dancing and was previously linked to Socoroma's younger residents. According to the acclaimed culture bearer Rodomiro Huanca Vásquez,[3] however, the oldest repertoire belongs to the cantor de pueblo, or town bard. With his guitar, occasionally accompanied by additional guitars, a violin, or an accordion, the cantor de pueblo plays *ruedas de carnaval* (carnival rounds), singing couplets in both Spanish and the Indigenous language of Aymara. The participating dancers respond by forming a large circle, surrounding the bard and any accompanying musicians.

Three ruedas, each having a different melody and dance practice, are part of the carnival repertoire. The *jach'a anata* (or Grand Play) occurs every day of that carnival, and for that rueda, the dancers create a circle by weaving their arms in front of one another while repeating the couplets the bard sings. The energy of the dance reaches a climax when the bard starts singing a melody only with syllables and the men begin stomping their feet on the ground, a *zapateo.* In contemporary practice, the cantor de pueblo immediately follows the jach'a anata with the *rueda*

The videos referenced in this chapter can be found at the following URL: https://purl.dlib .indiana.edu/iudl/media/z40k81r01s.

*del caderazo.* Now the dancers trace a circle around the cantor as couples, until the singer changes his guitar accompaniment from a continuous pulse to single accents on the chord changes. The dancers then map out the circle by grabbing a partner in each hand and follow the cantor's command to *hacerse pedazos,* or make pieces of one another. Each dancer tries to bump one or the other partner with their hips, and the circle stretches in multiple directions as the dancers avoid or knock into one another. Beyond this medley of ruedas performed throughout the week, the cantor de pueblo also leads a special rueda called the *tumay tuma.* It is only performed on Ash Wednesday, as a way of marking the horse race that happens on that day. On the last day of carnival, the cantor performs a fourth rueda, the *cuculi,* which technically belongs to the repertoire of the May Cross celebration. Its appearance is a way of inviting people to that feast (Huanca Vásquez 2016). To watch an example of a rueda danced while being sung by the cantor, see video 2.1.[4]

Socoromeños understand these expressions as traditional, a way of honoring the community's elders, but Huanca Vásquez observed that they had begun to fall into disuse by the late 1960s.[5] This period corresponds to the midcentury migration of many of the town's residents to the city of Arica in search of labor. At that key moment, a group in Arica known as Los Peregrinos del Norte began to collect information about regional traditions and to actively participate in Socoroma's ritual carnival space. Currently, many people interested in Chile's Andean folklore consider Socoroma to be "one of the towns that is most faithful to the traditions of its ancestors."[6] Chile's return to democracy in the early 1990s came with a law recognizing the existence of certain Indigenous groups, allowing individuals to openly identify as Indigenous, and offering these discriminated groups certain opportunities. Today, many Socoromeños generally recognize their Aymara roots, so that these carnival practices are considered Indigenous Aymara expressions.

Since the beginning of the twenty-first century, however, another revival has been underway in the region, this time focused on people of African descent, or Afro-descendants. As of 2018, the Chilean state had yet to pass a law recognizing such communities as participants in and contributors to Chilean society, similar to the one passed for Indigenous peoples. Part of the resistance to passing this law springs from the conscious omission of Afro-descendants in Chilean historiography after manumission and the subsequent dismissal of their influence in Chilean culture. To raise awareness of the Afro-descendant community in the Arica-Parinacota region, the emerging Afro-descendant activist groups collected oral histories and used them as source materials to stage public performances of music-dance. The most successful music-dance expression to emerge from these endeavors is the *tumbe carnaval.* Afro-descendant elders interviewed for the oral history project recalled that during carnival season in the Azapa Valley adjoining Arica, their parents danced in a circle to the sounds of drums, a donkey jawbone called a *quijada,* and other instruments. At a certain moment during the dance, participants would yell, "Tumba!" and women would try to knock over their male partners with their hips. Members of these activist organizations made creative decisions to produce an alternate form of this dance—the tumbe carnaval—suitable for parading through the streets of Arica. For an example of this street performance, see video 2.2.[7] Performing the tumbe carnaval has become an essential part of public events that assert Afro-descendant identity and one of the primary cultural signs associated with the region's Afro-descendant organizations.

In the eyes of international institutions, the Chilean state, and many individuals (including folklore scholars), the cultural categories of Afro-descendant and Indigenous peoples are separate. Indeed, the politics of culture depend on these distinctions, offering special funds to support performances and culture bearers of each strain to illustrate diversity and multiculturalism. I began my fieldwork in Arica to research Afro-descendant expressions in the region but eventually realized that distinguishing cultural elements between multiple communities who had shared and interacted for such a long time was a quixotic task. I was particularly struck by similarities between the rueda del caderazo as performed in Socoroma and the rueda de tumba carnaval that the Afro-descendant elders described. Since I supported the cause of the Chilean state officially recognizing its Afro-descendant communities, these similarities presented a challenge to illustrating the difference required by the racial politics of contemporary cosmopolitan societies.[8]

While recognizing the existence and importance of the Afro-descendant and Indigenous categories within this political setting, scholars of decoloniality or anticoloniality question whether these current policies can fundamentally change the status quo. These scholars have argued that such categories sprang from Western conceptions of modernity, enabling the colonial system that led us to the current global conditions in which many individuals face inequality and discrimination. What is needed, they argue, is to promote alternate ways of thinking to arrive at different foundations on which to build institutions. One of these alternate ways of thinking, rooted in Andean modes of thought, is what Silvia Rivera Cusicanqui calls *ch'ixi* methodology—*ch'ixi* being the Aymara word for *stained* or *motley.* In this essay, I use ch'ixi methodology to examine the similarities between Socoroma's ruedas de carnaval and the rueda de tumba carnaval that the Afro-descendant oral history project discovered. I first describe this methodology with a note on the relationship between folkloristics and coloniality studies. I then illustrate how ch'ixi ideas can help one approach elements of rueda de carnaval performance from an Indigenous perspective. While Rivera Cusicanqui tends to focus on the complementary binaries of Andean philosophy, I examine the challenges that the rueda de tumba carnaval offers, expanding the ch'ixi methodology to consider Afro-Andean cultural contributions. Considering multiple perspectives to describe these rueda performances helps sketch out alternatives to politics rooted in Western modernity, alternatives that can influence the way we practice folkloristics.

## POSTCOLONIALISM, FOLKLORISTICS, AND A DECOLONIAL APPROACH

Postcolonial scholars concentrate on revealing the persistence of coloniality, those structures of power in thoughts and institutions that remain even after the formal departure of a colonial presence. As Homi K. Bhabha (1994) has suggested, however, the *post* prefix brings with it more than just a reference to a past moment or simple opposition to an ideological way of thinking. It offers an "awareness that the epistemological 'limits' of those ethnocentric ideas are also the enunciative boundaries of a range of other dissonant, even dissident histories and voices" (6). The ethnocentric ideas that Bhabha refers to are those that contributed to the concept of modernity that emerged from Western European elites after the Columbian Encounter.[9] These ideas included (but were not limited to) understanding the mind and body as separate, interpreting progress in terms of urbanization and the exploitation of resources, and assuming the written to be more permanent and binding than the oral. Together with the newfound awareness of available resources in Abiayala, the concept of modernity fashioned in this way helped both produce and justify European colonization of the world.[10] Bhabha's statement reminds us that, beyond basic opposition to being exploited, the colonized also often had ideas that spoke past the precepts of modernity, ideologies that the colonizers would misinterpret or dismiss due to their fundamentally different epistemologies.

To a certain degree, folkloristics was born out of an interest to counter the experience of this modernity as manifested in urbanization and the Industrial Revolution. Richard Bauman and Charles Briggs (2003) have demonstrated how European intellectuals constructed an antimodernity based on a variety of characteristics that they imagined in opposition to these industrial evils. These oppositional characteristics would conglomerate into the concept of "the folk," and Regina Bendix (1997) deftly illustrated how folklore scholars used the constructed category of authenticity to judge which behaviors were truly of the folk. In many ways, the works of these cited authors resonate with the goals of postcolonial theorists in their desire to illustrate how modernity was constructed according to Western European ideals—ideals that continue to perpetuate existing power structures.

These studies also illustrated, however, how classic folklore research has been a product of the same mode of thinking. By opposing the principles of modernity, early folklorists often reinforced what those principles were. The folk were grounded in the body rather than the mind; they were rural and inefficient, valuing tradition over the full exploitation of the resources at hand. Over time, of course, folklore scholars have become more nuanced, problematizing the idea of a "pure folk" with representations of a blending of cultures and its spaces. The idea that folklore in urban environments went beyond rural survivals, for example, complicated the urban as a space for the modern and contributed to the application of the concept of community in these spaces (Dorson 1970; Kirshenblatt-Gimlett 1983). Then again, these same scholars might have struggled when they encountered the presence of commerce in folkloric expressions, as capitalism was supposed to be the engine for modernity. These mixtures—what some refer to as hybrids—complicated the neat binary categories of the modern versus the folkloric. Scholars such as Bhabha have considered the notion of hybridity as a particularly important phenomenon that contests these colonialist structures by being difficult to categorize. Hybrid expressions often support the values of the colonizers while simultaneously incorporating ideas associated with people the colonizers oppressed. Bhabha postulated that this juxtaposition creates a cognitive dissonance in the minds of colonial elites that calls into question the validity of colonial structures, creating an opening for a claim to power on the part of the colonially oppressed.

Hybridity (and its ideological family members such as creolization) comes with several caveats. First, it relies on a biological metaphor to describe the creative process, and theorists should be cautious in their application of this metaphor. The pseudoscientific use of biology to justify racialized forms helped prop up many colonial systems, and an awareness of how popular ideas of race functioned during colonialism is useful in analyzing the social interactions that created emerging cultural expressions. I caution, however, against examining "the birth" of creative forms solely on popular understandings of racial mixture; these understandings often revolve around simple binary biological-parentage structures that do not actually follow the rules of genetics and replicate a colonial mindset. A second issue with hybridity is the assumption that it confounds those in power. This perspective takes a primarily top-down approach (i.e., from the view of the colonizers) and thus rarely results in the promised dismantling of power. As ethnomusicologist Jonathan Ritter (2011) noted for the case of the Afro-Ecuadorian bomba, hybrid musical forms can be co-opted by the politically dominant group without necessarily advancing the agenda of activists seeking the political and economic advancement of marginalized peoples. Arguably, then, hybridity as a way of understanding cultural processes of exchange still functions from a perspective of modernity.

What decolonial scholars have called for instead is what Walter Mignolo (2011) terms "epistemological disobedience." Beyond recognizing the existence and mechanisms of colonialism, decolonial scholars express a desire to reimagine societies in terms other than the binaries of modern/folkloric or the westerniza-tion/nonwesternization.[11] Mignolo used the term *border thinking* to encourage scholars to explore the epistemologies of embodied thought found in the limits of coloniality, the spaces that Bhabha referenced earlier. For Mignolo, to do bor-der thinking means to value the perspectives of those peoples whose cultures were subjugated and give these perspectives equal weight as those found in mo-dernity, with the ultimate goal of advocating for those ideas that lead to more just and equitable societies. In *Borderland/La Frontera: The New Mestiza*, Gloria Anzaldúa (1987) identified the concepts grounded in Aztec-Mexica thought and the US-Mexico border experience that helped her arrive at a new "Borderlands" consciousness, inclusive of her positionality as both lesbian and Chicana. As an example of the diverse perspectives that needed to be valued, Anzaldúa's writing inspired Mignolo's border thinking concept.[12]

Like Mignolo and Catherine Walsh (2018), I recognize that taking this deco-lonial approach as a scholar and individual is an option; the individual must ask what it is they value and what the best response to these values is for the local situ-ation. To assume that a universal decolonial approach works for every situation would be simply to parallel the ways in which colonizers assumed modernity was universally applicable. While recent ethnographic approaches tend to shy away from overly ambitious claims of universality, abandoning universality implies that theorists accept that their work should lead to multivocality—or multiverses as Mignolo might frame it—based on multiple locations and multiple communi-ties. With these ideas in mind, I now sketch out some of the characteristics that define the town of Socoroma, the setting for the ruedas de carnaval of the cantor de pueblo. I also consider how those people who participate in this expression might identify and what kind of decolonial ideas might be useful given these contexts.

## SOCOROMA AND RIVERA CUSICANQUI'S CH'IXI APPROACH TO THE ANDES

Socoroma is nestled in what is often referred to in Chile as the *precordillera*—a "vertical environment" that lies between the coastal lowlands and the highland plains (Keller 1946, 174–191; Zimmerer 2011). At an altitude of thirty-two hundred meters above sea level, Socoroma's surroundings feature a variety of climates amid mountains and valleys that see a significant amount of rain during a certain portion of the year (usually December through March). The fruits of the lower valleys become more difficult to grow in this environment, and potatoes, oregano, and alfalfa are more common crops. Beginning in the late 1930s, Peruvian geographer Javier Pulgar Vidal (2014) criticized this oversimplified tripartite division of altitudes (coast, precordillera, and highlands), which he attributed to Spanish modes of characterizing geographic features. Following *Indigenista* perspectives and appealing to local folk categories of topography, Pulgar Vidal created an eightfold division of Peru's vertical environments, assigning them titles meant both to reflect Peru's Inca ancestry and to reference local ethnic groups. To support his naming system, Pulgar Vidal pointed to the appearance of these terms in folktales, song texts, and dances. He limited his system to Peru, but it easily extends to Chile's Arica-Parinacota region, in which Socoroma lies, since this region was part of Peru before the War of the Pacific. Socoroma's qualities place it in the category that Pulgar Vidal named "Quechua" (Choque and Pizarro 2013, 55). This Quechua categorization reflects one of the many ways in which Socoromeños can be associated with regional cultural practices as well as the multiple ways in which Socoromeños can identify.

Amid Chile's contemporary multicultural politics, the fact that Socoromeños have identified in multiple ways over time is often overlooked. Today, people associated with Socoroma are often characterized as Aymara, the most dominant of Chile's nine nationally recognized Indigenous groups in the Arica-Parinacota region. As with any of these groups, individuals who identify and are officially recognized as Aymara are eligible to receive some benefits from the Chilean government to offset the discrimination that Indigenous peoples have faced and continue to face. Anthropologist Carlos Choque Mariño (2009) points out, however, that this linguistically based category is a relatively new way of identifying, influenced by the Katarista political ideologies that were popular in Bolivia and that worked their way into Arica's politics during the 1980s via descendants of Bolivian immigrants. At the beginning of the twentieth century, in the wake of the War of the Pacific, the Chilean state had imposed assimilationist policies on Socoromeños in an attempt to absorb them into their imagined community. Chilean president Carlos Ibañez del Campo made Arica a "duty-free port" in 1959, and the newly available employment opportunities attracted many rural residents to migrate to Arica's urban space. Like other people from the interior, Socoromeño migrants to the city created an organization that united them via group participation in sporting and cultural events. These groups were collectively known as *hijos de pueblos* ("sons of the towns") organizations, and members of these different groups often unified under the common label of *andinos* (Andeans).

They would travel back to their respective towns to participate in their patron saint festival or carnival celebrations, as well as lobby for infrastructure projects such as roads or buildings that would benefit these towns. This hijos de pueblos movement continued until the arrival of Chile's military coup, when all such organizations were banned. This prohibition gave other individuals the opportunity to help redefine the ways that Socoromeños would identify, eventually leading to the contemporary category based on the language that many Socoromeños spoke at the beginning of the twentieth century. This history means that, when analyzing Socoromeño cultural expressions from a decolonial perspective, one can and should at least consider the multiverses of Quechua agricultural and environmental practice, Aymara linguistic ideas, and Andean ways of identifying.

Consequently, I have been particularly drawn to the work of Rivera Cusicanqui, whose ideas about cultural dynamics take a bottom-up perspective, rooted in multivalent Andean cultures. Frustrated by the elitist discourse of decoloniality that she has seen emerge in academia, she has preferred to understand her work as anticolonial, aimed at demolishing colonial prejudices, not just deconstructing them (2014). One of her primary methods of interpreting cultural interaction has been through the metaphor of tapestry, in which threads of many colors can be tensioned in both perpendicular and parallel ways. Each of these threads has an original color, but upon being woven together, they blend into different colors when seen at a distance. This recognition of a third, motley state while still being able to recognize the initial color foundations can be referred to in Aymara as *ch'ixi*. Indeed, *ch'ixi* is the word that Rivera Cusicanqui (2012) uses to refer to her own sociocultural situation, what historically has been referred to in Spanish as *mestizo*. The term *mestizo*, however, shares issues with the idea of hybridity and has been criticized for its homogenizing character. In contrast, the quality of *ch'ixi* can be made metaphorically even more complex in the sense that the initial threads themselves can be stained (ch'ixi) before or as they become part of the tapestry. Rivera Cusicanqui's ch'ixi philosophy envisions the "active recombination of opposed worlds and contradictory meaning" (2014), but rather than frame this recombination such that this opposition remains with the colonialist value structure intact (e.g., modernist capitalist versus backward Indian), Rivera Cusicanqui has tried to demonstrate that the ch'ixi recombination emerges from a consistent reworking of colonialist practices into a Native value structure.

An important tool in Rivera Cusicanqui's work is what she calls the "re-appropriation of bilingualism" (2012, 106), which entails treating those languages that coloniality has suppressed as equal tools to think with. She has taught herself Aymara, her mother's native language, and woven theoretical concepts both present in and interpreted through the language into her work. Many scholars have called attention to the apparent dualities that appear in

Andean language and philosophy—ideas such as *chacha-warmi* (man-woman) and *akaxpacha-araxpacha* (present time-space–above time-space). As Josef Estermann (1998) has explained, however, these dualities must be understood not as binary oppositions but rather as concepts that do not exist except in relationship with one another. The practice of *siku* or *lakita* performance may serve as an analogous, culturally rooted practice here. Each musician, having a limited number of notes on their portion of the instrument, must rely on their partner to provide the other notes necessary to create a complete melody. The melody does not exist without the participation of both the *arka-irka* sides of the instrument as performed by two complementary sets of musicians. This example illustrates the search for complementarity that is reflected in Andean language and thought.

Extending this idea, Rivera Cusicanqui has used the paired heteronyms prevalent in Andean languages to explore possible complementary relationships. These heteronyms are words that sound similar but have a different meaning due to a minor variation in phonemes. Exploring the relationships between pairs of certain heteronyms can offer an Andean hermeneutic for Andean expressions. In her work, Rivera Cusicanqui has used the heteronymic pairs of *khiyki-kirki* and *thaki-taki* to demonstrate how locals reworked Spanish colonial practices that were imposed on them into persistent Andean value structures to create ch'ixi understandings of contemporary situations. As a way of demonstrating Rivera Cusicanqui's technique and looking for a deeper understanding of Socoroma's expressive culture, I now apply her ideas to the rueda del caderazo and tumay-tuma of the cantor de pueblo.

### PAIRED HETERONYM ANALYSIS OF THE RUEDAS DE CADERAZO AND THE TUMAY TUMA

In analyzing a music-dance expression, one useful heteronym pair is *khiyki-kirki*, because the Aymara verb *kirkiña* refers to song or intoning a melody. The other part of the pair, *khiyki*, refers to complaint. While analyzing this heteronym pair, Rivera Cusicanqui points out that Andean song often expresses complaints in the catharsis of music-dance but that colonialist structures write these songs off as quaint folklore—useful for displays of multiculturalism but not to be taken seriously. Examples of two couplets from the rueda del caderazo suggest otherwise:

Couplet 1:
*Armense la rueda (ay agua y anatay) con formalidad (ay agua y anatay)*
Build a circle (Oh water and play) with formality (Oh water and play)
*que dira la gente (ay agua y anatay), somos para nada. (ay agua y anatay)*
what will the people say (Oh water and play), we are good-for-nothings.
   (Oh water and play)

Couplet 2:

*Alegres cantemos (ay agua y anatay), alegres bailemos, (ay agua y anatay)*
Happily, let us sing (Oh water and play), happily, let us dance,
   (Oh water and play)
*pa'l año que viene (ay agua y anatay) cuantos faltaremos (ay agua y anatay)*
next year, who knows (Oh water and play) how many (people) will we lack?
   (Oh water and play)

Each couplet contains what can easily be understood as an initial call to partic-ipate in entertainment, followed by complaints of the stark reality of Indigenous life that include discrimination by others and the reality of death or separation. The cantor de pueblo accompanies these lyrics on guitar, strumming a steady pulse with the classic Andean harmonic device of moving back and forth between an initial minor chord and its relative major. While the European tradition would hear this harmonic shift as one between sadness and happiness, such associa-tions are not always so in the Andes, where the combination of these harmonies with an upbeat tempo is often the staple of celebrations (Tucker 2013, 38–39). In fact, the Andean idea of complementarity suggests that European harmonic de-vices could have been co-opted and transformed to serve an Indigenous mindset, such that the alternating ambiguity of Andean harmony simply reflects how the character of each chord complements the other. Similarly, while the appearance of complaints in the space of celebration might seem contradictory, the call to participate is not just to enjoy oneself but to do so in a ritual that recognizes how celebrations exist in relationship with the difficulties of everyday life. Indeed, the acknowledgment of these difficulties within the rueda's lyrics and musical practice suggests that the celebration could not exist without them.

Another set of heteronym pairs that Rivera Cusicanqui has proposed comes from placing a Quechua word adjacent to an Aymara word: *taki-thaki. Taki* is the Quechua word for song, and *thaki* is the Aymara for path. The historical coexis-tence of the two languages in the same cultural space justifies their juxtaposition. *Thaki*, however, can have deeper connotations than just a simple trail. It can also imply the pathways between traditional locations of sacred power, linking not only spaces but also important practices that must take place at specified times in order for nature to reciprocate in abundance. Applying Rivera Cusicanqui's analysis of this heteronym pair to the case of these ruedas recognizes how many Socoromeños travel the path from the urban environment of Arica to spend time singing and dancing in Socoroma during carnival. They participate in the ritual offerings that bring fertility to the town, and, from the town, they receive the abil-ity to define and associate themselves more strongly with the "Andean." As Rivera Cusicanqui points out, many times these contemporary paths are consistent with past sacred and trade routes. Trade between the highlands and the coast certainly has been an ancient practice and would have also been consistent with Andean pilgrimages during the Inca Empire and beyond. To accommodate the many visitors that arrive in Socoroma for the celebration, travelers from Arica bring up supplies, thus requiring trade for this expression to occur. This ch'ixi interpretation of *taki-thaki* reinforces the idea that those who identify as Indigenous find in their current situation both continuity and compatibility with their past.

Following this ch'ixi hermeneutical practice, I propose supplementing Rivera Cusicanqui's heteronyms with another ch'ixi pair, following her concept of bilingualism: *tomar-tumaña*. Having never heard an explanation of the word *tumay* during my fieldwork, I had just assumed its use in the rueda tumay tuma to be an Aymarization of the Spanish verb *tomar*, which can alternately be translated as both "to drink" and "to take."[13] Both Spanish interpretations make sense in the rueda context. Since plenty of alcohol is offered and consumed during carnival, the expression can be understood as encouragement to drink or partake with the understanding that, before you do, you will pour libation to *pachamama*, Mother Earth. Woven together with this meaning, the phrase *tumai!* can also indicate "take this!" In the context of the rueda del caderazo, such a command could refer to the application of a rather strong hip bump. Anecdotes abound about dancers getting knocked to the ground from such blows. This action invokes other types of festive violence in the Andes, such as the *tinku* ceremony performed in Macha, Bolivia, in which the blood spilled from any injuries is understood as a particularly powerful offering to the pachamama (Stobart 2006, 134). Comments I overheard from participants talking about people who got hurt during the carnival testified to their awareness of this type of interpretation.

In exploring Manuel Mamani Mamani's Chilean Aymara dictionary (2002), however, I encountered an alternate strand, the word *tumaña*, meaning "to go from house to house" or "to encircle," both actions intimately associated with carnival practice. Throughout the week of carnival, a large group of dancers parades through the town accompanied by the tarkeada, visiting houses of different well-known members of the community. This practice points to one understanding of *tumaña*. Mamani Mamani's other definition of *tumaña* might relate to the counterclockwise circle that rueda dancers define when encompassing the cantor de pueblo and any other musicians. Ethnomusicologist Henry Stobart has documented a music-dance practice called *qhata* in the Bolivian state of Potosí that resonates very much with the performance of the jach'a anata. In the qhata, the encircling practice denotes the creation of an especially fertile space, with the dancers analogous to the walls of the highland corral that encircle llamas and alpacas (Stobart 2006, 229–231). While the Socoroma rueda practices may differ slightly, with the circle formed by alternating men and women who surround the male musicians, the interpretation of the creation of a fertile space resonates strongly with the other carnival practices designed to produce the final seasonal rainfalls in the hope of an abundant harvest season.

From these Andean Indigenous perspectives, the *tomar-tumay* duality suggests an ideology of reciprocity, "taking to give" and "encircling to produce." This way of thinking-being contrasts with the colonial modernist ideology of "taking to extract" and "encircling to limit" that decimated the resources of many Latin American regions and reduced Indigenous populations into reservations. The point here, however, is not victimization but rather the juxtaposition of these ideas as warp and weft to understand how Indigenous peoples use both threads in their daily lives and to suggest that local societies give them equal opportunity to impact their social practice.

## AN AFRO-DESCENDANT CONTRIBUTION TO ANDEAN CULTURE: TUMBA

As part of her ch'ixi, anticolonial thinking, Rivera Cusicanqui's paired-heteronym analysis is a tool that can call attention both to the details of contemporary cultural practices and to how those practices are laden with multiple, coexisting meanings. Like the Indigenous languages that the analysis used, these cultural meanings might otherwise remain unvoiced because they have been forgotten or suppressed as a result of coloniality. Unfortunately, the emphasis that this technique places on recognized Indigenous languages can exclude the understandings of those populations from which colonialism has severed their connection to a specific language or space. For Afro-descendants, this kind of exclusion can mimic that of multicultural policies common to many Latin American states. Anthropologist Shane Greene has pointed out that these policies require a "holy trinity" of multicultural "peoplehood": culture, language, and territory (2007, 345). As slaves, Afro-descendants often were separated from members of their language groups in an attempt to prevent rebellions, resulting in language loss. Under recent multicultural policies, only Afro-descendant groups that developed in isolated runaway slave communities have had much success in claiming "ancestral" territories. The result is that Afro-descendant communities often have had to depend heavily on displays of expressive culture, especially music-dance, to illustrate how their worldview and experience are different from the "mainstream" society of the Latin American state under whose jurisdiction they live.

Importantly, Rivera Cusicanqui recognizes Afro-descendants as belonging to the *pueblos originarios*, or First Nations, because they are "constitutive of the makeup of our continental being" (2014). This line of thinking resonates with Afro-descendant anthropologist and activist Jhon Antón Sánchez, who, influenced by French sociologist Roger Bastide, has noted that "the concept of

Afro-descendant refers to the distinct 'Black' or 'Afro-American' cultures that emerged from the descendants of Africans, who survived the slave trade or commerce that was present in the Atlantic from the sixteenth to the nineteenth centuries" (2013, 40).[14]

Antón Sánchez has emphasized that this understanding of the concept sets up slavery as the defining experience for recognizing Afro-descendants as a people. Obtaining status as a people is an important legal distinction. The United Nations and the International Labour Organization have both released statements on the rights of Indigenous and tribal peoples. In their general intention and interpretation of these documents, some Chilean Afro-descendant activists have argued that they should be recognized as tribal peoples.[15] Whether First Nations or tribal peoples, the Middle Passage experience cements the ch'ixi position of Afro-descendants in the Americas. Antón Sanchez argues that "in America, beyond understanding the African as someone who was exploited as a profit-making resource that developed Western capitalism, it is necessary to understand the African as a cultural being that accumulated Africa's rich experiences, demonstrating that a person despoiled of their culture and environment is capable of recreating and enriching their ideas to generate their foundational traditional values" (2003, 13). Despite being denigrated by the dominant hegemonies that they live in, Afro-descendant communities have developed a set of expressions that are grounded in African value structures. This assertion thus challenges Rivera Cusicanqui's anticolonial discourse to include this foundational voice.

By way of offering one specific answer to this challenge, I now return to the expression that elders from the Azapa Valley described to the participants in the oral history project early on in Chile's Afro-descendant movement. I will use the phrase *rueda de tumba carnaval* to distinguish this expression from the contemporary tumbe carnaval. Recall that, like Socoroma's rueda del caderazo, the rueda del tumba carnaval featured dancers moving around a circle and bumping their partners with their hips. The bumping action happened as someone yelled, "Tumba!" To see a staged reenactment of this rueda, see video 2.3.[16] As a result of these similarities, I adjust my previous use of Rivera Cusicanqui's heteronym analysis and make the pair a trio to explore Afro-descendant thought: *tomar-tumay-tumba*.

Beyond sharing choreographic features, both expressions appear to have similarity in a few *coplas*, the couplets that a leader sings and the group repeats. For example, in the rueda del caderazo, the cantor de pueblo sings,

> *Estos carnavales quien los inventaría, el que lo invento un borracho sería.*
> Who invented these carnivals, who did must have been a drunk.

One of the verses collected from the Afro-descendant elders is:

*Estos carnavales quien los inventaría, un negro borracho como yo sería.*
Who invented these carnivals, probably a Black drunk like me.

Such shared couplets might contain the khiyki (complaining) quality discussed earlier, but including the word *negro* more clearly marks the verse as a line that Afro-descendants might identify with. Furthermore, while not many couplets have been recorded for the rueda de tumba carnaval, those collected tend to offer a humorous tone:

*Marido, Marido, sácalo a mear, que animal tan feo, vuelvo guardar.*
Husband, husband, take him out to pee, what an ugly creature, put him away again.[17]

On the one hand, the ugliness registers as a complaint, but the context of reference being the husband of the person to whom the couplet is directed makes for a humorous insult. Several of the younger Afro-descendant activists I interviewed singled out the use of humor as an important characteristic of their culture. They would describe interactions between their organization's members during meetings as especially prone to laughter. They asserted that, because the majority of people present at these meetings were Afro-descendant, the members knew such behavior would not be misinterpreted negatively. John Miller Chernoff has generally commented that satire was the preferred comedic mode among the West Africans with whom he worked, as a way to encourage participation in and show concern for the community (1979, 163). The way Chernoff describes satire fits within Henry Louis Gates's broader ideas of signifyin(g), which refers to the multiple ways of performing that Africans and Afro-descendants use to undermine literal interpretations of phrases to imply others (2014). In the couplet above, a simple complaint about how an Afro-descendant man has been treated like an animal might be too straightforward; instead, the exaggerated act of taking an animal out to relieve itself and putting it back in some enclosure offers an over-the-top image that elicits laughter while commenting on the status of the Afro-descendant man in local society. That the wife is the one in charge could also be read as a critique of her position in that same society. Unfortunately, the couplets available for the rueda del tumba carnaval are not numerous enough to come to firm conclusions about the use of signifyin(g) in this space, but I feel that the anticolonial move here is to understand the possibility of an alternative, complementary rhetorical approach to the khyirki in the rueda de tumba carnaval expression.

This complementarity exemplifies the ways in which adding *tumba* can contribute to the *toma-tumay* pairing. The word *tumba* is found in seventeenth-century Spanish literature as an onomatopoeic phrase indicating a raucous party and came to be associated with several music-dance genres in the African diaspora. In the 1950s, Cuban intellectual Fernando Ortiz famously worked on a music-dance genre from eastern

Cuba known as the *tumba francesca* in which the word also refers to the drums them-selves. The conga drums are known as *tumbadoras* in Cuba, literally meaning those that tumba. Following this Spanish train of thought, this name might mean those that make a raucous sound. The Afro-descendant elders that spoke of the rueda del tumba carnaval all describe the presence of drums during the performance, some-thing that is absent in Socoroma's ruedas, which rely on guitar strumming to keep the beat. There has been some debate about what types of drums were used in the rueda de tumba carnaval. Pedro Cornejo Albarracín asserted that the drums were called bombo and tambora but that these resembled older hide-head versions of bass and snare drums rather than anything like the barrels used in performing contemporary tumbe carnaval (Báez Lazcano 2010, 110–111). The exact type of drum, however, is not as important as the presence of the drums, which suggests a value placed on the presence of drums, even if those drums arise from a colonial setting.

As mentioned earlier, the verb form *tumbar* in Spanish has come to mean to knock over. From an African-informed perspective, the key element of the choreography—the hip bump—has a different set of aesthetic values than the ones offered in the Socoroma caderazo. The sudden movement of attempting to knock over one's partner references what Robert Farris Thompson calls "cutting the dance." He encountered a number of West Africans who placed value on a sharp movement to end the choreographic phrase. When executed properly, this gesture has all the humor of a well-timed proverb (Thompson 1974, 20). This ori-entation toward the hip bump stands in complement to the caderazo of Socoro-ma's rueda, which, despite being ordered, allows some flexibility in its execution. It also connects to a number of expressions through the African Diaspora that share the value in the sharpness of the movement, even if the gesture is different.[18]

The anticolonial gesture here is not in the search for the origin of the word or the expression. The questioning of such origins and the emphasis solely on chronological, causal relationships have been part of the intellectual structures of modernity that created and sustained coloniality. The value here is in hearing, as Afro-descendant activists do, how the elders' tumba carnaval descriptions reso-nate with other African diasporic expressions—what scholars Jacqueline Nassy Brown (2005, 42) and Petra R. Rivera-Rideau (2015, 16) have termed "diasporic resources." From a performance standpoint, additional dance-music resources include the circle formation in dancing (the classic ring-shout paradigm) and call-and-response singing. This latter characteristic, call-response, was what Sam-uel Floyd Jr. ([1991] 1999, 146) chose to refer to as the "master musical trope," musi-cally paralleling Gates's idea of signifyin(g). For African Americans, Floyd wrote that the value of the ring lay as a sign of community and discipline, inviting par-ticipatory performance while reaffirming one's cultural memory, justified "by the strong African values of fertility and sexual prowess that fuel the erotic impulse"

(1995, 39). What is important here is how compatible these ring values are with those of the ring in Socoroma.[19] The juxtaposition of toma-tumay-tumba reveals not only the possibility of Afro-descendant values playing an important role in the development of these expressions but also the ch'ixi nature of those expressions.

## THE CH'IXI QUALITY OF THE ANTICOLONIAL GESTURE

In my interpretation of Rivera Cusicanqui's anticolonial thinking, directly tracing the origins of each expression is not as important as the resignification that each group has or could have given to a cultural expression to complement existing logics. This attitude springs from assuming the orientation that expressive culture exists in a ch'ixi state, and, in the Americas, this state results from the colonial enterprise that brought Afro-descendant, Asian, Indigenous, and European peoples into contact with one another under specific power relationships. Drawing from the weaving metaphor, the ch'ixi state is not the same as hybrid, mestizo, or creole, all of which are tied up in unpalatable biological logics. The ch'ixi perspective allows researchers to focus in and out on certain performance characteristics, admitting their complexity while recognizing that performers can emphasize or de-emphasize these facets as desired.

Assuming this ch'ixi perspective is important, because the task of people interested in anticolonialism (or as I prefer, dismantling coloniality) is imagining practices that amplify these multiple readings to equal volume levels to arrive at alternate, more equitable futures. In this regard, multiculturalism or pluriculturalism as practiced, with its demands of demonstrating cultural difference without acknowledging coloniality's ch'ixi nature, perpetuates colonialism—as does a decolonial practice that places value on only "pure" Indigenous language concepts. As an example, given that the Americas are ch'ixi societies, would not dismantling coloniality need to incorporate aspects of the social management principles of Afro-Indigenous groups into current cosmopolitan policing practices? Here is where I believe Rivera Cusicanqui's thinking challenges us as folklorists and beyond: to recognize and make space in our own lives for threads of the ch'ixi communities we work with and are a part of to be woven into the tapestry of personal and public practice.

### NOTES

1. For similar and perhaps related cases, see Stobart's (2006, 208–217) description of how different sound qualities are associated with rainfall in Bolivia.

2. The instruments in the orquesta andina include the violin, mandolin, guitar, charango, and quena flute. This ensemble shares similarities with *estudiantina*

practice in other parts of the Andes (Tucker 2013). Lyric modifications are usually limited to inserting the names of local towns.

3. Born in Socoroma and migrating to the city of Arica during his youth, Huanca Vásquez cofounded the folklore group Phusiri Marka over forty years ago. Arica's city council formally declared him an Illustrious Son of Arica in 2015.

4. https://purl.dlib.indiana.edu/iudl/media/425k324s5x.

5. Socoromeños are people who live in or identify as being from Socoroma.

6. "Hoy en día es considerado uno de los pueblos más fieles a las tradiciones de sus antepasados." From a DVD recording of "Socoroma, Tradición y Cultura en una noche de muestra," a performance in Arica's Municipal Theater, November 30, 2017.

7. https://purl.dlib.indiana.edu/iudl/media/t24w52mq4m.

8. The state government finally passed a law (Ley 21.151) recognizing the existence of Chile's Afro-descendants as a tribal people on April 16, 2019.

9. Here, I am following Enrique Dussel's (2011) argument that the resources provided by Europe's colonization, particularly of the Americas, enabled the concepts of modernity to flourish.

10. *Abiayala* is the Guna term for "land in full maturity" and is used by some Indigenous groups to refer to the land that later became known as the Americas after colonization.

11. The term *dewesternization* is borrowed from Mignolo and Walsh (2018). The use of *Western* here refers to the geographic roots of colonial ideologies. Non-Western countries have adopted Western ideologies, so *dewesternization* is used here the opposite of *westernization*.

12. See the preface to Mignolo (2012).

13. Other towns in the region have dances with similar names that support this etymology. In his 1998 documentary film *Carnaval de Chapiquiña*, for example, Mamani Mamani referred to a dance in the nearby Andean town of Chapiquiña as *"Toma y toma"* or simply *"El Membrillazo"* (The Quincing). In this dance, participants throw quince fruits at the thighs of their partner, often resulting in bruises. Such fruits grow only at lower altitudes.

14. All translations from the Spanish are mine.

15. The Chilean government published the decree (21.151) legally recognizing Afro-descendants *as a tribal people* as part of the Chilean nation on April 16, 2019.

16. https://purl.dlib.indiana.edu/iudl/media/x11x41q67m.

17. Several Afro-descendant community members cited these verses to me during my early fieldwork in 2006.

18. See Daniel (1995, 74–75) for a similar discussion of the *vacunao* in the Cuban rumba.

19. Carnival fertility in Socoroma is not limited to agriculture. Many people in the region recognize the phenomenon of "carnival babies," those born nine months after the celebration.

BIBLIOGRAPHY

Antón Sánchez, Jhon. 2003. "Diagnóstico de la problemática afroecuatoriana y propuestas de acciones prioritarias." CT BID ATN/SF-7759-EC. Quito: Organizaciones de la Sociedad Civil Afroecuatoriana.

———. 2013. "El conocimiento ancestral desde una perspectiva afrodescendiente." In *Amawta: Seminarios de investigación*, edited by Freddy Javier Álvarez González, Palmira Chavero Ramírez, and Martín Oller Alonso, 1:31–60. Quito: Editorial IAEN.

Anzaldúa, Gloria. 1987. *Borderland/La Frontera: The New Mestiza*. San Francisco: Spinsters/Aunt Lute.

Báez Lazcano, Cristian. 2010. *Lumbanga: Memorias orales de la cultura Afrochilena*. Arica, Chile: Herco Editores.

Bauman, Richard, and Charles Briggs. 2003. *Voice of Modernity: Language Ideologies and the Politics of Inequality*. Cambridge: Cambridge University Press.

Bendix, Regina. 1997. *In Search of Authenticity: The Formation of Folklore Studies*. Madison: University of Wisconsin Press.

Bhabha, Homi K. 1994. *The Location of Culture*. London: Routledge.

Brown, Jacqueline Nassy. 2005. *Dropping Anchor, Setting Sail: Geographies of Race in Black Liverpool*. Princeton, NJ: Princeton University Press.

Chernoff, John Miller. 1979. *African Rhythm and African Sensibility*. Chicago: University of Chicago Press.

Choque, Carlos, and Elías Pizarro. 2013. "Identidades, continuidades y rupturas en el culto al agua y a los cerros en Socoroma, una comunidad andina de los Altos de Arica." *Estudios atacameños* 45:55–74. https://dx.doi.org/10.4067/S0718-10432013000100005.

Choque Mariño, Carlos. 2009. "Divergencias y antagonismos del movimiento social indígena en la Región de Arica y Parinacota (1965–1985)." *Confluenze: Rivista di studi Iberoamericani* 1 (2): 267–289.

Daniel, Yvonne. 1995. *Rumba: Dance and Social Change in Contemporary Cuba*. Bloomington: Indiana University Press.

Dorson, Richard. 1970. "Is There a Folk in the City?" *Journal of American Folklore* 83 (328): 185–216.

Dussel, Enrique. 2011. *Politics of Liberation: A Critical Global History*. Translated by Thia Cooper. London: SCM.

Estermann, Josef. 1998. "APY TAYTAYKU: Theological Implications of Andean Thought." *Studies in World Christianity* 4 (1): 1–20.

Floyd, Samuel A., Jr. (1991) 1999. "Ring Shout! Literary Studies, Historical Studies, and Black Music Inquiry." In *Signifyin(g), Santicfyin', and Slam Dunking: A Reader in African American Expressive Culture*, edited by Gina Dagel Caponi, 135–156. Amherst: University of Massachusetts Press.

———. 1995. *The Power of Black Music*. Oxford: Oxford University Press.

Gates, Henry Louis, Jr. 2014. *The Signifying Monkey: A Theory of African American Literary Criticism*. 25th anniversary ed. Oxford: Oxford University Press.

Greene, Shane. 2007. "On Race, Roots/Routes, and Sovereignty in Latin America's Afro-Indigenous Multiculturalisms." *Journal for Latin American Anthropology* 11 (2): 294–328.

Huanca Vásquez, Rodomiro. 2016. *Armemos la rueda con formalidad . . . Carnaval de Socoroma*. Arica: Produccíon Imagen Publicidad Arica.

Keller, Carlos. 1946. *El departamento de Arica*. Santiago: Zig-zag.

Kirshenblatt-Gimlett, Barbara. 1983. "The Future of Folklore Studies: The Urban Frontier." *Folklore Forum* 16 (2): 175–234.

Mamani Mamani, Manuel. 2002. *Diccionario practico bilingüe: Aymara-Castellano Zona Norte de Chile (Suma Chuymamp Parlt'asiñani)*. Antofagasta, Chile: EMELNOR NORprint.

Mignolo, Walter D. 2011. "Geopolitics of Sensing and Knowing: On (De) Coloniality, Border Thinking, and Epistemic Disobedience." European Institute for Progressive Cultural Policies. September 2011. https://transversal.at/transversal /0112/mignolo/en.

———. 2012. *Local Histories/Global Designs: Coloniality, Subaltern Knowledges, and Border Thinking*. Princeton, NJ: Princeton University Press.

Mignolo, Walter D., and Catherine Walsh. 2018. *On Decoloniality: Concepts, Analytics, Praxis*. Durham, NC: Duke University Press.

Pulgar Vidal, Javier. 2014. "Las ocho regiones naturales del Perú." *Terra Brasilis (Nova Série)* 3 (October 16). https://doi.org/10.4000/terrabrasilis.1027.

Ritter, Jonathan. 2011. "Chocolate, Cocoa, and Honey: Race, Music, and the Politics of Hybridity in the Ecuadorian Black Pacific." *Popular Music and Society* 30 (5): 571–592.

Rivera Cusicanqui, Silvia. 2012. "*Ch'ixinakax utxiwa*: A Reflection on the Practices and Discourses of Decoloniality." *South Atlantic Quarterly* 111 (1): 95–109. Originally published as *Ch'ixinakax utxiwa: Una reflexión sobre prácticas y discursos descolonizadores*. 2010. Buenos Aires: Tinta Limón.

———. 2014. "The Potosí Principle: Another View of Totality." *E-misférica* 11 (1). http://hemisphericinstitute.org/hemi/en/emisferica-111-decolonial-gesture/e111 -essay-the-potosi-principle-another-view-of-totality.

Rivera-Rideau, Petra R. 2015. *Remixing Reggaeton: The Cultural Politics of Race in Puerto Rico*. Durham, NC: Duke University Press.

Stobart, Henry. 2006. *Music and the Poetics of Production in the Bolivian Andes*. Burlington, VT: Ashgate.

Thompson, Robert Farris. 1974. *African Art in Motion: Icon and Act in the Collection of Katherine Coryton White*. Los Angeles: University of California Press.

Tucker, Joshua. 2013. *Gentlemen Troubadores and Andean Pop Stars: Huayno Music, Media Work, and Ethnic Imaginaries in Urban Peru*. Chicago: University of Chicago Press.

Zimmerer, Karl S. 2011. "Vertical Environments." In *Mapping Latin America: A Cartographic Reader*, edited by Jordan Dym and Karl Offen, 263–268. Chicago: University of Chicago Press.

JUAN EDUARDO WOLF is Associate Professor of Ethnomusicology at the School of Music and Dance of the University of Oregon. He also serves as a core faculty and executive committee member in the university's Folklore and Public Culture Program. His first monograph is entitled *Styling Blackness in Chile: Music and Dance in the African Diaspora* (Indiana University Press, 2019).

# THREE

# Disrupting the Archive

MIRIAM MELTON-VILLANUEVA AND SHEILA BOCK

## CONSTRUCTION OF THE SONORAN COLLECTION:
## LIVING ARCHIVES OF DESCONOCIMIENTO

Witnessing Mariana Ortega's salient warning that "the intellectual production of U.S. women of color is . . . not getting appropriate attention" (2017, 506) spurred this essay. In the process of reencountering old fieldwork materials collected from Sonora, Mexico, by a white American man who was pursuing his PhD at UCLA in the 1970s, the historical silences (E. Pérez 1999, 5) became the centrifugal force that disrupted the hierarchies of authority structuring the genre of the tale collection. Contemporary interviews unraveled our understanding of how the original fieldwork was produced, leading us to the women's voices that challenged our methodological standards. What came forward were voices even more marginalized than those of the foundational Chicana scholars not being cited by decolonial literature: the local voices of Mexican women who continue to be crossed by a border that does not recognize their regional integrity in the United States. In other words, our struggle became how to integrate the very voices that Chicana scholars point us toward, in order to transform the archive itself.

How did two young Mexican mothers, friends who met at the Carson Street Elementary School PTA in California, help create the first significant tale collection from the Ures region of Sonora, Mexico? The roles of these women were not recorded—at least in any official capacity—when the materials were collected, processed, and initially analyzed in the past, though they were crucial to the construction of the archive of texts we find ourselves working with now. Doña Anita befriended her Mexican friend Lily the 1970s and later helped Lily's American folklorist husband collect stories from her northern Mexico birthplace

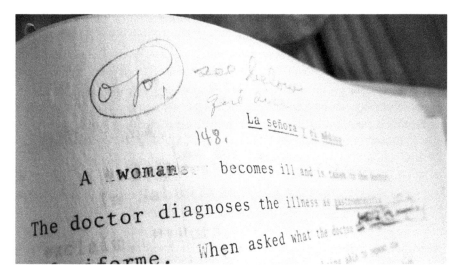

Fig. 3.1 Lily's notes to her deceased husband appear on the only surviving draft; his presence guides researchers as the archive continues to be accessed, engaged, and interpreted anew.

by offering entry to family and community in provincial Rayón. Through interviews conducted in the present, their generative encounter was reclaimed from the *desencuentro* (Ortega 2017, 506) of being excluded, a historical dislocation (L. Pérez 2007, 147) that creates new meanings.

Both friends survive; their presence decenters the original 1975–76 fieldwork data, a project that left the Mexican women unnamed, even though they helped create the corpus. That project, an archive of collected stories, remains significant in that it is the only known substantial corpus of folktales from the Ures region of Sonora, Mexico. But the collection was left unpublished since Lily's graduate-student husband died in 1989. Lily's authorial status was first recognized because of her significant labor—she was the one who edited, typed, and facilitated the fieldwork recording sessions.[1] Her handwriting is found in the margins of the only extant draft of the fieldwork transcriptions (see fig. 3.1). In a perfect irony, her marginalia themselves become the link to reclaiming her place beyond the "unseen, unthought . . . shadow in the background of the colonial imaginary" (E. Pérez 1999, 7). Lily's notes dialogue with her now deceased husband, creating a "living archive" that "is co-produced by the dead" as we interpret it today (Otero 2018, 4). Solimar Otero's concept of residual transcriptions helped open the archive's "tangled narratives" (2020, 189) and "reveal bonds of extended kinships where archives provide a living texture that is missed in traditional approaches to history and ethnography" (2018, 14).

That first step, looking through those drafts, served to foreground the voices of those originally relegated to background service or support positions of a UCLA doctoral dissertation project. Now that so much material exists almost exclusively in digital spaces, one wonders if and how that avenue of handwritten manuscripts will continue to be produced in the future. Nevertheless, returning to the data required "making space for the Chicana" (Ortega 2017, 508) on different levels. It is of note that the authors of this essay received pushback for their larger project, being told that it is well understood that women are silenced and that there is nothing new in that. It is time to own that much of US intellectual culture continues to tell scholars of women to get over it. Foregrounding the margins is no longer conceptually unintelligible, but it still remains to be practiced (Johnson 2010) to the point that women's work is understood to be "part of the story, but . . . is left off the 'main' page" (Hammad 2004, xi) of the colonial canon (E. Pérez 1999, 7). Even when consciously practiced, inclusion itself can be founded in "silence and erasure," in academic customs that continue to consider not only "man" normative but also the male voice authoritative, creating "practices of unknowing" that create scholarly genealogies absent of Chicana authors (Ortega 2017, 510). In this way, canonization has served to silence generative voices to leave us motherless and rootless, because only tall branches were recorded. Further, the unpublished Sonoran archive survived in a cardboard box in Lily's garage—created, housed, and maintained by Lily, not an institution, a fact that facilitated this study in that the authors of this essay gained access to Lily's voice, to first drafts, to marginalia, and to drafts of a conference paper that outlined her late husband's goals for the project. The irony of institutional *desconocimiento* (Anzaldúa 2015, 216n68), or invisibility of Lily, is that it promoted the *conocimiento* of her *historia*. Only by her preservation of the materials locally does her intimate knowledge of the interviewed people and places survive to create the narratives of its construction. For if Lily had donated the fieldwork—and its data had been held in an institutional setting—Lily's part in collecting, transcribing, translating, editing, and even typing every page in the archive could have remained obscured.

### DISRUPTING THE ARCHIVE: THE TROUBLE OF KNOWLEDGE

This section describes the unseen negotiations between these different kinds of knowing, and how our work disrupting the archive took us into a practice that made visible the relationship between local and institutional, knowing and desconocimiento. Working collaboratively exposed these edges against which disciplinary integrity splintered in sometimes uncomfortable ways. Because our research programs both focus on underrepresented voices, we didn't expect dissonance. The historian (Miriam, author of *Aztecs at Independence: Nahua Culture*

*Makers in Central Mexico 1799–1832*) felt complete studying the textual collection, so the folklorist (Sheila, author of numerous articles employing narrative and performance approaches to examine vernacular responses to stigma) had to strenuously advocate for new interviews, which the historian initially refused to accept as explanations of the past. Then the historian, trained as an ethnohistorical new philologian, found herself establishing a fortress around the original draft, but her mother and the coproducer of the original collection (Lily) considered it something to be amended. This tension lifted a mirror in which the historian witnessed her own outdated disciplinary directives that fetishize notions of authenticity. The folklorist, a white American woman, felt discomfort with interpreting the stories beyond their local performance contexts, while the historian, a Mexican migrant, pushed her to consider how the stories include expressions of broader colonial anxieties and descriptions of long-standing indigenous patterns that transcend one specific time and place. The folklorist found difficulty working with drafts without a theoretical construct when the historian chose textual arguments—signposting a productive tension that can exist when historicizing fieldwork. Folkloric training itself disrupted the study of this project's historical layer; the disciplinary impulse to record new interviews made the project stronger and allowed the project to grow beyond ethnohistorical approaches to indigenous colonial texts.

We could have ignored the disruptions, but it's in the trouble that new ways of knowing emerge. Inside the heart of this work, we found ourselves questioning what is considered scholarly and finding unanticipated dissonances that needed to be reconceived and repurposed in order to avoid recreating more silence. Simply put, finding women's voices in the past through contemporary evidence (interviews) in order to better understand the construction of the original fieldwork created complex methodological landscapes. Such challenges require researchers with every decision to return to their shared commitments to underrepresented points of view to find ways to procedurally recenter Chicana labor and historias as scholarly.

What conceptual steps can be taken to redefine *scholarly* and still retain disciplinary integrities within our "decolonial imaginary" (E. Pérez 1999), the cooperative space Emma Perez manifests for academia? Observing the anxieties of relationships between interviewers, knowledge sharers, time frames, and textual analysis led to a process of interrogation that was met with varying degrees of success. Adapting ethnohistorical methodology (Melton-Villanueva 2016, 155–156) from James Lockhart's "cycle of sources" (Lockhart 1991, 30, 60) suggested a preliminary practice with which to find often-concealed points of view during research planning and data analysis. The goal is not to eliminate "gaps that become visible as problems" in the interviewing process (Briggs 2007, 562) but to make conscious decisions in the data collection and curation based on the perennially imperfect parameters of a research design. To repurpose the local as scholarly and reimagine an archival canon, a simple positionality for a data set (and actors' influences on it) locates institutional and local as not neutral but opposing points in a continuum of archival production:

1. Evaluate difficulty of interpretation.
2. Evaluate accessibility.
3. Use steps 1 and 2 to position data as internal (local) or external (institutional).

The more institutional a voice one chooses to study, the less local a point of view can be represented in research outcomes, which made finding the point of view in our data an essential step. This binary oversimplifies but aids in making power visible, especially when distorted by well-meaning but caustic "regimes of knowledge"—the point here is to "look at our own practices so as to hold ourselves accountable" (Ortega 2017, 511, 512). For it is well understood that through our "decontextualization and recontextualization of others' discourse . . . we exercise power" (Bauman and Briggs 1990, 78). But the impact of quiet archival processes, of preparation, networking, collecting, and textual production, is often less understood in practice in terms of its influence on research agendas. In this case, it was Lily's local position to the project that made her unmarked labor desirable for this project—an internal point of view that was consciously made central to the research plan. However, her interviewers did not easily see that their methods were introducing an external point of view, associated with institutional status and disciplinary training. "In terms of negotiating the flow of the authority" (Otero 2015, 197), methods that tease out exactly why it is productive to recognize our complicities are useful in understanding the effects of institutional practices. We understand ourselves as participating in structures of oppression, so our job is to figure out how to intervene from the inside (Deleuze and Guattari 1987, 25, 87). But living and working in connection to each other, our multiplicities collide; our interstitial paths can occlude our centralized, hierarchical positionalities, however fleeting they might be, as we "ceaselessly jump from one register to another" (Deleuze and Guattari 1987, 75). In this sense, local data practices might be understood as invisibilized interbeing, while institutional data practices represent vertical, effortlessly visible arborescence. In our processes of conducting interviews, well-meaning institutional interventions were so assumed that they became hard to see. In this way, rhizomatic metaphors can illustrate an echo chamber of self-replication, fraught with unwanted traits. For, biologically speaking, plants that multiply via rhizomes are clones, echoing institutional replications. This does not negate the Deleuzian challenge to "write at n–1 dimensions" (Deleuze and Guattari 1987, 7), for we need thought practices that take us into horizontal dimensions in a way that outgrows the metaphor itself.

Categorizing the local voice as scholarly in research moved us toward using theoretical frameworks outside the canon in which we each were trained; manifestations of Chicana lived experience forced us to look at our dismemberment and rememberment in ways not easily adapted to or accepted by male hierarchical norms. Faced with Chicana critical theories, rhizomatic thought fulfills its potential in Gloria Anzaldúa's desconocimiento—or in relationship to the mycelial structures that both consume and connect all life (multispecies as well as mineral elements) while decomposing, feeding, watering, and healing. In turning over essential rocks, our academic foundations, we found ourselves analyzing marginal local data in a "temporal polyphony" (Tsing 2017, vii) that we didn't always like, especially when we were candid about our disciplinary edges, but it took us nearer to that center without beginning or ending (Deleuze and Guattari 1987, 25)—imperfectly closer to the "in-between spaces that can be found in many sites of symbolic and cultural production" (Otero 2015, 195).

Despite being committed to the unrepresented voice, we did not always enjoy step 1, evaluate difficulty of interpretation, because local horizontal data are often harder for researchers to interpret than standardized institutional data. Local interview transcripts, marginal or "residual transcripts" (Otero 2018, 5), and archival documents (as opposed to synthesized records or transcripts from more dominant cultures) often come in unfamiliar languages, contexts, and temporal dimensions and imply unseen interactions. Without Lily and doña Anita's ability to interpret the Sonoran Collection of folktales, their roles would have been impossible to determine. This project aimed to recover their labor, but it remained just as important to recognize how, if an institutional archive had managed and curated the presentation of the Sonoran Collection fieldwork, both their contributions would have been very difficult to ascertain. Had the archive been taken away from Lily's own curation, Chicana labor may never have become visible, because beyond her handwritten initials in the margins, Lily was never explicitly named. The crucial relationship-building that doña Anita facilitated before the first fieldwork trip would certainly not be recognized, for this key information emerged through informal conversations and more formal interviews with Lily. Lily and doña Anita's potential invisibility, had the archive migrated to an institutional setting, has far-reaching implications. Research often flows downstream, following the more easily interpreted information. This makes sense for myriad reasons, such as publication deadlines, but researchers often are not aware that in choosing to study the most easily interpreted data, one may overlook potentially complex authorship.

Choosing expediency and productivity can have unintended consequences for research, with implications of Anzaldúan unknowing as a form of violence. Regional language structures, especially Mexican Spanish, which developed within the grammatical structure of Nahuatl (Melton-Villanueva 2016, 45–63), require specialized translation skills, or their multiplicity is silenced. Our differences create barriers to interpretation. In other words, knowledge from underrepresented groups is often bypassed in Anzaldúan desconocimiento for institutional data that can be more readily analyzed. Instead of "falling prey to that which is easy" (E. Pérez 2003, 123), evaluating a topic for ease of interpretation allows researchers to at least make these choices consciously. As applied to the above proposed framework, institutional desconocimiento, in its structural "unwillingness to see, or of being forced not to look" (Anzaldúa 2009, 277), creates data sets that are categorically less complex—reference points in the data could have remained devoid of Mexican women's essential contributions. Can phones, cameras, or audio recorders detect the pot of beans on the stove that gathered everyone around the table? The least mentioned aspect of life is often the most taken for granted, not seen as needing an explanation and therefore not readily noticed or documented by common tools and procedures (Frink and Harry 2008). Following consideration of "the tape recorder" and "different media," as issues "central to the enterprise of ethnopoetics. . . . Texts both shape and are shaped by the situational contexts in which they are produced" (Bauman and Briggs 1990, 71, 76). Equipment and the archives they create reflect these challenges to interpretation.

In terms of step 2, evaluate accessibility, given that Lily's position is local to this project, one can contrast her Sonoran archive with institutional curation to weigh differences in accessibility. How does one even locate data kept in personal archives? If these archives are found, how can researchers extend access to others? As Charles Briggs notes, "Scholars have often seen circulation as a purely mechanical process, one that does not require ethnographic scrutiny" (2007, 565). Highlighting accessibility in the preliminary framework gives researchers a chance to see that our choices to use easily accessible subjects and records often lead to transposing local voices with those considered important by archivists. Less accessible data include the very materials not marked as valuable (or practical or economically feasible) in an institutional archive, such as "beads, stiches, herbs, cloth" or marginal notes of "living archives" (Otero 2018, 5). Facing the question of accessibility addresses the weight of "expert" gatekeeping in traditional archives. Noncentral ideas and objects, such as those pictured in figure 3.2, are often not recorded or maintained. Even if local records are made available, their "contaminated diversity" (to extend A. L. Tsing's [2017, 29] mycorrhizal metaphor as a new value) can still be difficult to access and interpret—hence the trouble institutions often have getting traffic to folk records.

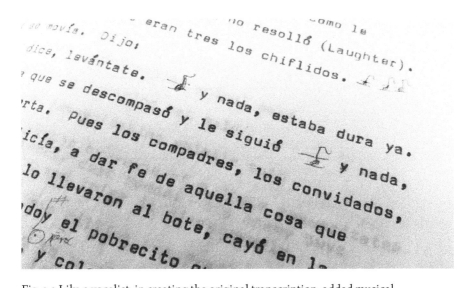

Fig. 3.2 Lily, a vocalist, in creating the original transcription, added musical notation to represent the exact notes and rhythm of a storyteller's whistles. Her expertise in musical notation captures the telling in a way that might not readily be understood by other listeners or researchers or grasped by archivists.

This "residual transcripts" (Otero 2018, 5) approach opens up nuanced understandings about the researchers (in both the past and present) and about the communities where the original fieldwork took place, and it identifies multiple meanings in the stories themselves. For if we follow the growing number of indigenous scholars into considering local concepts vital in their disciplines (Hoover 2017; Barker 2017; Bauer 2016; Kimmerer 2015), we are valuing less accessible, more difficult-to-analyze ideas that challenge established conceptual frameworks and that allow us to "move into the decolonial imaginary" (E. Pérez 2003, 123) of what we "haven't been taught to read yet" (Anzaldúa 2015, 110). In this study, the storytellers in both the past and the present are considered local intellectuals (McDonough 2014), *scholars of community literacy*. Thus, the lives of two friends, doña Anita and Lily, as they intersect in the construction of the Sonoran story archive, invert its creation story and, as detailed in the following section, continue to impart formal Mexican ethics and *conocimiento* today.

This preliminary research-design method explains the feedback loop outside of which Chicanas (defined broadly in this essay as indigenous-identified Latinas) in the United States find themselves, as scholars, as subjects, and as archivists. A methodological practice of access reinforces the need to commit to seeking out local data or at least owning up to making conscious choices to

| Anita 2018july audio codes | M's transcription | M's Translation of Dialog | M's Translation & interviewer notes 16 |
|---|---|---|---|
| 2009.164626 | tambien la historia de mi tata david nos contaba muchos cuentos bonitos que es donde yo aprendi una historia bonita de la sandia | | A's first use of word story, cuento, in a phrase surrounded with the word history |
| | | Also the history of my tata (grandfather) David would tell us, and there were many stories bonitos – that is where I learned a nice historia about the watermelon | |
| 2019.799365 | decia, te la voy a platicar. decia mi tata david: a ver mi hijitas! el que me adivina le voy a dar un cinco, un nickle | | |
| | | he said, and i'm going to tell it to you, my tata David would say: " let's see mijitas! [my daughters] To the one that guesses right will get a cinco, a nickle | |
| 2031.026213 | y decia, aver vamos a ver aquella, que nacio sin brazos, para hacer le el corazon, ls tenmos que hacer pedazos. Como la vieron?! | | [lilting cadence draws one in with drawl] |
| | | and he'd say " let's see the one that was born without | |

Fig. 3.3 Transcription and translation with embedded audio location codes (left column) of doña Anita's first recorded interview.

exclude underrepresented ideas in order to make a deadline. In this project, most of the original contributors no longer live. Doña Anita and Lily not only played key roles; their interviews were facilitated by accessibility to researchers, as opposed to community members still living in Ures and Rayón, Sonora.

The distance created with archival transcriptions can appear insurmountable, but specific practices offer solutions for digital records. A broader problem identified by querying the issue of access could be addressed with citation of digital audio files for folklore research. Simply put, even as digitization opens possibilities for making materials more accessible to a wider public, practical challenges remain in going back to double-check a quote in the audio file itself. If I cite a book, I give you a page number. But if I cite a transcription, it is much more challenging to find the original recording to analyze emotional affect or vernacular meaning, describe the audio context of background events, or (in the case of texts translated from local languages) question the translation of a word. And once an original recording session is accessed, how do you find the specific phrase you wanted to hear? Citation of digital recordings facilitates these types of data-dependent questions and addresses the needs of nondominant populations whose records may not be standardized, making them even more difficult to analyze and access.

The use of open-source software has the potential to address this need for accessible archival constructions. Transcriptions typed right into "labels" (we used Audacity) directly underneath a recording's graphical sound waves can generate instant reports that can be pasted and formatted in a word-processing program to become easily searchable (see fig. 3.3). This facilitated collaboration for this essay among people with varying skill sets. How did she say that? can be answered by following a numerical placement in the transcript, a citation that directs readers to the exact spot in an audio file. Such a citation convention would also obligate the reader to listen to the recording, extending the ethics of relationships that has shaped the archival collection throughout its process of becoming into the act of research itself.

Something as simple as a digital citation, particularly useful for accessing vernacular information, has the added potential to encourage community engagement. In this project, Sonoran Spanish carries complex intonation that conveys emphasis and meaning in itself. Thus, a free, open-source software can open the archive to nontraditional voices in a way that may also support museum studies. Curators struggle to keep oral recordings accessible and relevant. Making digital platforms accessible would facilitate audio's correlation to text and other cultural materials (audio online duplicated in physical space next to clothing collections?) in museum collections. This digital tool, when cross-referenced, could have far-ranging implications for archival management in terms of institutional relevance, making folk archives more easily interpreted and accessible.

Ultimately, these kinds of archival engagements facilitate access and dialogue. When community members and scholars alike engage with folk collections, evidence-centered research can be extended to local voices. Methodologically, revealing the complex authorship of archives not only allows unseen contributors to be named but also allows them to participate more fully in the production, maintenance, and analysis of archival data—even if they didn't write or have official status in the collection process. The idea that transnational women could de- and recontextualize a significant Sonoran tale collection is certainly not the narrative that Lily's graduate-student husband initially planned for as he embarked on his dissertation research in 1976. In this way, the authors considered themselves to be entering into an ongoing, dialogic collaboration that began decades ago when Lily and doña Anita first met at the PTA meeting to forge relationships and collect stories, a collaboration that now encompasses the voices and perspectives of women as creators and keepers of knowledge. By recovering Mexican women as contributors involved in the processes of preparation, networking, collecting, and textual production that led to the creation of the unpublished Sonoran tale collection, this project is creating new kinds of critical collaborations with far-ranging implications for archival management.

## CONOCIMIENTOS

In the disruption, a cardboard box became the archive, a mother's friend the scholar, and new conversations emerged. Opening the archive and laying bare the structural choices of research birthed conocimientos, formal strategies of lived folk culture as related by doña Anita and Lily in interviews and informal conversations in the present, which grew the archive from the middle.

Including new conversations shifted this project beyond linear chronologies and disciplinary conventions into the implications of an archive of individual moments. In practice, the process of creating Chicana archives meant that we included a unique set of "priorities, assumptions, and inventions" (Otero, personal correspondence, December 3, 2018) reflected in terms of "genealogies of empowerment" (Levins Morales 2001, 25). Open-ended and rhizomatic rather than static chronological connections between present narratives and archival objects created space for Chicana multidirectional ethics.

Conocimientos exposed the formal ethical frameworks detailed below; their Chicana ways of knowing deliberately aimed to cultivate more horizontal knowledge relationships. This ethical mandate is not predicated in political or academic titles but reliant on status embodied in hierarchies of knowledge encoded in quotidian sunrise greetings or serving your neighbor. Beyond organizing the archive to create a reflexivity that allows divergent points of view, perhaps the most salient silences involve the Mexican ethical constructs that organize everyday life.

Questions of belief or observation, past or present, subject or object, and context or text spilled beyond neat boundaries to decentralize notions of authority—for example, Can ethics guide an archive? Who can speak authoritatively? What form does authoritative discourse take? These are dangerous questions that erode disciplinary integrity, for "when you affirm everything, you affirm nothing at all" (de Vries 2018, 10). As Tsing observes life within a World Wide Web, we can watch the archive "(re)compose and (re)group around different shared imaginings that require trust and vulnerability, and create reciprocal obligations. . . . Trust is differentiated, subjective, relational, temporal and variable" (De Vries 2018, 10). Additionally, "radical curiosity beckons." We "cannot be reduced to self-replicating interchangeable objects . . . instead they require attention to the histories of encounter that maintain the chain" (Tsing 2017, 143).

Consider the tale collection, a signature genre of folkloristic publication since the late eighteenth century. Presenting tales as static texts situated within larger classification systems and demarcating "relevant" context—these conventions of the genre enact a linear progression from the act of collecting to the act of analysis, metadiscursively constructing the editor as central authority on the tales and their significance. The genre itself of the tale collection exemplifies some of the key characteristics of Deleuzian arboreal hierarchies. And examination of the archive of materials stored in Lily's garage indicates that the early stages of this project were clearly shaped by these generic conventions (see fig. 3.4). Typed-up drafts of the stories, for example, were each presented following the same structure:

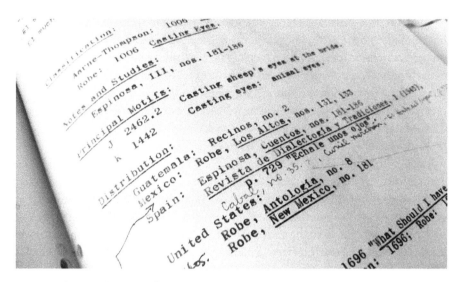

Fig. 3.4 Bibliographic notes from Lily Melton's archive of Sonoran folktales.

1. Title of the story in Spanish
2. Brief summary of the story in English
3. Complete transcription of the story documented through audio recording
4. The name of the storyteller
5. The town where the story was collected
6. The date the story was collected
7. Bibliographic information marking the classification of tale types, notes and studies, principal motifs, and distribution

It was the handwritten marginalia encountered in these same typed pages that first opened up new flows that did not fit cleanly into rigid categories structuring earlier iterations of the project. Interviews with Lily then sought out information about the role(s) she played in this research project, which uncovered stories about doña Anita's role in facilitating relationships so important to the initial fieldwork. This lead in turn generated new encounters with doña Anita at her house in Carson, California, in the present: not only Miriam's conducting an audio-recorded interview in July 2018 but also Lily and Miriam's visiting doña Anita's house in December 2017 in order to attempt to learn her expert tamale-making skills—to hilarious effect. Doña Anita's hands worked like haiku, a seemingly random spoonful of masa spread across the damp corn husk folded like origami. Lily and Miriam's laughter spilled alongside their blobs of dough that oozed out of the folded husks and fell onto the counter. Their tamales looked like *globos desinflados*, burst balloons, in comparison.

The outcomes mirror a larger purpose to enact a local recentering of power horizontally: power with, not power over. The remainder of this section focuses on conocimientos from doña Anita's July 18, 2018, interview (as noted previously, a parenthetical citation directs readers to the exact spot in an audio file). Her local voice led the research in the political work of valuing ethical perspectives that can be marginalized or rendered invisible in academic landscapes. The initial reason for the interview with doña Anita was to seek out information that could fill gaps in our knowledge about the Sonoran town of Rayón and her parents (both of whom not only hosted the fieldworkers in their home but also contributed to the archive as storytellers)—in short, to strengthen our understanding of the context of the stories that were collected in the past and the fieldwork encounters that generated them. The interview itself, however, disrupted dualistic categories of text/context so central to the genre of the tale collection in a way that led to new knowledge. During the interview, for example, doña Anita shared several stories with Miriam: an historia her grandmother used to share about a frog and a gold coin, an historia about an old woman who gives up her last bit of water and is rewarded by Saint Peter, and a recounting of her own experiences seeing an apparition of the Virgin in her backyard when she was eleven years old.

Notably, none of these stories were documented during the initial fieldwork expeditions in the 1970s; they were not represented in the archive of texts stored in Lily's garage. Rather, through the act of the interview and its subsequent transcription and translation by Miriam, the archive grew tangibly in its ongoing process of becoming, and notions of relevant context expanded beyond a unified and bounded local grounding in a singular time and place. When asked about her life in Rayón, Sonora, doña Anita collapsed the temporal plane and answered with vivid descriptions of her life in California. In Carson, California, in the present, she described a morning ritual of sociability she taught the neighbors: "porque doña Ana les ha enseñado" (2963.051973). As she and her husband sit in the sun drinking coffee, their neighbors greet them—"Good morning, doña Anita, don George, como amanecimos?" (1844.372608). Then doña Anita's husband George interjected that doña Anita has even taught "el trash man they come by, they stop and say 'Doña Anita, how are you?'" (2970.819048). With that example, she drew a connection between this social space and her life in Sonora: "En my town every morning si mi madre nos lo sende to go to the store to buy something," you would say good morning to every person you met, "to everybody!" (2934.537868). In this way she articulated the deliberate and time-consuming work of recreating northern Mexican social conocimiento, teaching her neighbors how to live in grace—in Southern California. She imparts the Sonoran knowledge of how to create civil space in urban areas to her neighbors. Doña Anita demonstrated "how knowledge of and from their everyday lives is the basis for theorizing and constructing an evolving political praxis to address the material conditions in which they live" (Acevedo 2001, ix).

Doña Anita also understood her life as one of working hard for her Los Angeles community, "por la gente" (3387.512744). She described how even as a widow with two children in California, she would wake up early in the morning on Saturdays to seek out food donations from local supermarkets. She would then load up her car with the food that the grocery stores were throwing away, long before there were city ordinances that allowed the practice. She would thus feed those in need out of the garage of her church. People came to know that she would gladly share food if they were hungry. Very successful people come up to her to thank her for helping their families when they were children, for answering the door with arms full of food when they knocked. As her personal wealth grew, she began to keep two refrigerators full of food so that she could help those in need, a practice that extends into the present.

Early in the interview, doña Anita recounted her childhood in Sonora as a time when people were healthy. But now, she lamented, children are born already sick: "porque never se enfermaba uno, nunca se enfermaba y ahora cualquier nino que nace, ya nace enfermo" (1545.473741). By way of explanation, she spoke of healthy food, cooking by comal on a fire, and offered this proverb she remembered hearing as a child: "La razon de los padres eran, decia: donde come uno comen todos" (1558.964535). This conocimiento speaks to more than sharing what you can, even if you do not have a lot. "One dish, one spoon" in Haudenosaunee philosophy teaches "lessons around consensus and cooperation" (Hoover 2017). Doña Anita's understanding of health relating to social balance provided a touchstone for the interview as a whole as she switched back and forth between recounting her experiences in both the past and the present, and asserting and enacting the values that have shaped her social worlds across time and national borders. We learn from doña Anita that the distinctions between past and present are less important than the bridge she is actively trying to create between them.

Doña Anita's ongoing praxis, to replicate social networks in California and to carry on the values of sharing resources with those in need, clearly informed her engagement with Lily—and by extension, the collection of fieldwork materials in the archive. When doña Anita asked her priest if she should send her children to Catholic schools, he said that real education happens in the home:

> "Padre, ¿sería necesario poner mis niños en escula católica?"
> "Me dijo no. La escuela esta en tú casa mi hija. Tú haz la vida de tus hijos. Tú eres la cabeza. Padre y madre tú los vas a formar." (581.323175)

He acknowledged not only that she functioned as both mother and father to her children but also that she was capable of "forming" them. Her authority and skill in all these contexts she considers especially poignant because she never studied past the first grade: "Escuela no tuve yo en México. Tuve hasta primer año namás de primaria" (1390.167075).

Her choice of words is another way doña Anita expressed her theoretical understanding of the project. Only twice did she use the word *cuento* or "story" to refer to the folktales or her own narratives. Once perhaps was because the interviewer couched the question using that term, and the second time it was couched before and after her preferred word, *historia*, or "history," so it may have been a simple strategy to vary word choice while retaining the meaning of *historia*: "Tambien la *historia* de mi tata David nos contaba muchos *cuentos* bonitos que es donde yo aprendí una *historia* bonita de la sandia" (2009.164626; emphasis added). She clearly marks her and her family's narratives as history to be learned from, not stories to be entertained by and disposed of. After telling an historia about an old woman, doña Anita said, "See how beautiful?" She continues in Spanish, "This is how one learns in childhood, the culture of education given by elders" ("Eso lo aprende uno con su niñez, la cultura de educación que le daban a uno los old people, la gente mayor"; 2721.216145). She further adds, "Nos enseñaban así" ("This is how we were taught"). Even though the interviewer consistently referred to the narratives as cuentos, doña Anita replied by calling them histories, and in her own words she defined the historias as conocimientos, as cultural transmission of knowledge across time.

Doña Anita met Lily while they were volunteering at the public school and forged the groundwork for Lily's husband's fieldwork:

> I approached her and I told her, "Ay, it gives me pleasure to meet you señora, even more because you speak Spanish!"
> "Me acerqué a ella y le dije, ay, me da gusto conocerla señora, y ¡más como habla español!" (1109.356553–1180.409615)

She remembers Lily saying in Spanish, "Your name Anita, look, I am Lily. I have a husband that is studying and he has to present a thesis of the history of precisely Sonora, Mexico." Doña Anita remembers feeling so happy to have a Mexican friend: "Ay! It made me so happy! We are not rich, your father knows, but they had big hearts, my mother and also my father, not because I'm telling you, but they had a lovely house above the canyon. La Santa Cruz is like that. And then I told her, go there to the pueblo and ask for Ramon Santa Cruz [her father], there he will give you what you need." Doña Anita also remembers visiting when Lily was there, saying she became family and left with friendship: "Si, pues un día que llegamos y llegaban mis hermanas tambien. Tu mamá ya la mirabamos como de la familia, y allí fue conociendo mi abuelita y a todos. Así vino luego y así se llevo una amistad." In this way, doña Anita taught us that those conocimientos forged in the past extend into the present.

The act of conducting interviews for this research generated new texts beyond the original archive of materials in Lily's garage, including the audio file and transcription that grounded this section. As Emily Callaci (2017) reminds us, texts are more than sources that fill gaps in our knowledge of the "facts" about a specific time and place. Texts become particularly productive sites for examining (and revealing) "the interplay of material, discursive, and social forms that give shape and substance" (11) to the narratives that carry the most authority. The voices and perspectives found in these texts elude reductionist and colonialist narratives of the research process, working instead to simultaneously "reveal the ad hoc labor of producing networks, moral communities, and solidarities" and "the work of power, hierarchy, and exclusion" (14).

## CONCLUSION

The implications of access and ease of interpretation in this vision might threaten chaos and missed deadlines. But if grounded in a decolonial imaginary, one finds ways to procedurally recenter Chicana labor, Mexican historias, and mothers' voices as scholarly. The difficulties with this essay's specific collaborative effort came every day that we had to face La Frontera, in this case the precipice between disciplines whose integrity depends on neutral positions and canonized forms. Specifically, the smoky mirror of cultural relativity that underpins ethnographic scholarship and resistance to universal truths serves to ground research within empirical frameworks that may act to privilege the powerful. In this way, cultural relativity (and curation) meant to protect may actually transgress ethics. The human rights and planetary rights being articulated in many genres, forums, and disciplines offer different conocimientos; and though experienced in different stages, these conocimientos are held in mycorrhizal common. Chicana scholars are asking us to choose sides, to not just identify agency but to make it transformative (E. Pérez 2003, 123). That our own experiences today were elucidated by the folktales in the collection and framed as historias by doña Anita returned us to an ethical understanding of Sonoran narratives' themes: locality, body, and unappreciated knowledge—while every disciplinary turn prevented interpretation of the stories as containing universal human truths. Yet doña Anita confirms why the historias exist: to teach us how to live in grace. For the sake of (re)creating an environment that is healthy and a society that is kind, she urges us to interpret her historias as a challenge to colonial ageist, patriarchal, and unethical norms.

Birth is messy. Reflexivity as a rhetorical exercise is not enough. We need to take a position that liberates women, migrants, children, and oceans. In discursive constructions that reject neutrality and authenticity, new practices of knowledge production are created, in which local voices, women's voices, impart a more mycorrhizal understanding of archive. The "scholarly"—and the disciplinary discourses that authorize it—needs to be reconceived so that it no longer serves to colonialize or canonize into silence. This chapter's effort to incorporate the local voices Chicana scholars point us toward continues to fail in many respects,[2] but we recognize that in that attempt we also learn to liberate, not just restate, folk knowledge.

Weaving doña Anita's own ethics and memories into the analysis of the research productively destabilizes hierarchies of authority and validates the unspoken ethnic and historical tension involved in how academics are and were perceived in provincial Mexico. Perhaps not surprisingly, many of the stories in the collection feature outsiders to the community and institutional authorities (e.g., priests and scientists) but invert their authority. Ultimately, through the words of doña Anita, we learn that local voices are not bounded by space and time; they can transcend borders, and historias hold the ethics relationship of a teller across time. What is at stake here is not merely an expansion of what gets recognized as "relevant" but also whose voices are (or are not) recognized as authorities and why.

## NOTES

1.  See Bock and Melton-Villanueva (2019) for additional discussion of the roles Lily Villanueva Melton played in the creation of this archive.

2.  For failure itself as a disruptive alternative to established notions of success, a willingness to fail in scholarly attempts, see Halberstam (2011).

## BIBLIOGRAPHY

Acevedo, Luz del Alba, ed. 2001. *Telling to Live: Latina Feminist Testimonios*. Durham, NC: Duke University Press.

Anzaldúa, Gloria. 2009. *The Gloria Anzaldúa Reader*. Durham, NC: Duke University Press.

———. 2015. *Light in the Dark = Luz en lo Oscuro: Rewriting Identity, Spirituality, Reality*. Edited by AnaLouise Keating. Durham, NC: Duke University Press.

Barker, Joanne, ed. 2017. *Critically Sovereign: Indigenous Gender, Sexuality, and Feminist Studies*. Durham, NC: Duke University Press.

Bauer, William J., Jr. 2016. *California through Native Eyes: Reclaiming History*. Seattle: University of Washington Press.

Bauman, Richard, and Charles L. Briggs. 1990. "Poetics and Performances as Critical Perspectives on Language and Social Life." *Annual Review of Anthropology* 19 (1): 59–88. https://doi.org/10.1146/annurev.an.19.100190.000423.

Bock, Sheila, and Miriam Melton-Villanueva. 2019. "Collaboration, Multivocality, and the Unfinished Story." *Journal of American Folklore* 132 (523): 61–73.

Briggs, C. L. 2007. "Anthropology, Interviewing, and Communicability in Contemporary Society." *Current Anthropology* 48 (4): 551–580. https://doi.org/10.1086/518300.

Callaci, Emily. 2017. *Street Archives and City Life: Popular Intellectuals in Postcolonial Tanzania*. Durham, NC: Duke University Press.

Deleuze, Gilles, and Felix Guattari. 1987. *A Thousand Plateaus, Capitalism and Schizophrenia*. Translated by Brian Massumi. Minneapolis: University of Minnesota Press.

de Vries, Patricia. 2018. "When Fungus Punched Anthropos in the Gut: On Crap, Fish-Eating Trees, Rhizomes and Organized Networks." *Rhizomes*, no. 34. http://www.rhizomes.net/issue34/devries.html.

Frink, Lisa, and Karen G. Harry. 2008. "The Beauty of 'Ugly' Eskimo Cooking Pots." *American Antiquity* 73 (1): 103–20.

Halberstam, Jack. 2011. *The Queer Art of Failure*. Durham, NC: Duke University Press.

Hammad, Suheir. 2004. "From Margin to Center." In *Word: On Being a [Woman] Writer*, edited by J. Burrell, xi–xiv. New York: Feminist Press.

Hoover, Elizabeth. 2017. *The River Is in Us: Fighting Toxics in a Mohawk Community*. 3rd ed. Minneapolis: University of Minnesota Press.

Johnson, Susan Lee. 2010. "Nail This to Your Door: A Disputation on the Power, Efficacy, and Indulgent Delusion of Western Scholarship That Neglects the Challenge of Gender and Women's History." *Pacific Historical Review* 79 (4): 605–617. https://doi.org/10.1525/phr.2010.79.4.605.

Kimmerer, Robin Wall. 2015. *Braiding Sweetgrass: Indigenous Wisdom, Scientific Knowledge and the Teachings of Plants*. 1st paperback ed. Minneapolis, MN: Milkweed Editions.

Levins Morales, Aurora. 2001. "Genealogies of Empowerment." In *Telling to Live: Latina Feminist Testimonios*, edited by L. del A. Acevedo, 25–32. Durham, NC: Duke University Press.

Lockhart, James. 1991. *Nahuas and Spaniards: Postconquest Central Mexican History and Philology*. Stanford, CA: Stanford University Press.

McDonough, Kelly S. 2014. *The Learned Ones: Nahua Intellectuals in Postconquest Mexico*. Tucson: University of Arizona Press.

Melton-Villanueva, Miriam. 2016. *The Aztecs at Independence: Nahua Culture Makers in Central Mexico, 1799–1832*. Tucson: University of Arizona Press.

Ortega, Mariana. 2017. "Decolonial Woes and Practices of Un-knowing." *Journal of Speculative Philosophy* 31 (3): 504–516.

Otero, Solimar. 2015. "Entre las Aguas/Between the Waters: Interorality in Afro-Cuban Religious Storytelling." *Journal of American Folklore* 128 (508): 195–221.

———. 2018. "Residual Transcriptions: Ruth Landes and the Archive of Conjure." *Transforming Anthropology* 26 (1): 3–17. https://doi.org/10.1111/traa.12120.

———. 2020. *Archives of Conjure: Stories of the Dead in Afrolatinx Cultures.* Chichester, NY: Columbia University Press.

Pérez, Emma. 1999. *The Decolonial Imaginary: Writing Chicanas into History.* Bloomington: Indiana University Press.

———. 2003. "Queering the Borderlands: The Challenges of Excavating the Invisible and Unheard." *Frontiers: A Journal of Women Studies* 24 (2/3): 122–131.

Pérez, Laura Elisa. 2007. *Chicana Art: The Politics of Spiritual and Aesthetic Altarities.* Durham, NC: Duke University Press.

Tsing, Anna Lowenhaupt. 2017. *The Mushroom at the End of the World on the Possibility of Life in Capitalist Ruins.* Princeton, NJ: Princeton University Press.

MIRIAM MELTON-VILLANUEVA is Associate Professor of History at the University of Nevada, Las Vegas. She received Ford Foundation and National Endowment for the Humanities (NEH) yearlong research fellowships, publishing in journals such as *Ethnohistory* on the methods that center Mexican indigenous women in historical narratives. Her monograph *The Aztecs at Independence: Nahua Culture Makers in Central Mexico, 1799–1832* (2016) demonstrates that the Nahuas maintained civic autonomy through local leadership, written language, and geographically distinct ritual cultures—despite centuries of colonial restrictions.

SHEILA BOCK is Associate Professor in the Department of Interdisciplinary, Gender, and Ethnic Studies at the University of Nevada, Las Vegas. Her research interests include the contested domains of illness experience, material/digital enactments of personal and community identities, the intersections between folklore and popular culture, and the values and challenges of cross-disciplinary collaboration. Her work has been published in the *Journal of American Folklore*, the *Journal of Folklore Research*, *Western Folklore*, the *Journal of Folklore and Education*, the *Western Journal of Black Studies*, the *Journal of Medical Humanities*, *Diagnosing Folklore: Perspectives on Disability, Health, and Trauma*, and *The Oxford Handbook of American Folklore and Folklife Studies.*

# PART II

Framing the Narrative

FOUR

—᠁—

# Afrolatinx Folklore and Representation

Interstices and Antiauthenticity

SOLIMAR OTERO

Folklorist Regina Bendix writes that the "search for authenticity is fundamentally an emotional and moral quest" (1997, 7). Her work *In Search of Authenticity* (1997) is a foundational study on the origins of the concept of authenticity in European philosophy, aesthetics, and folklore. It highlights important associations and meanings attached to authenticity: authorship, originality, and purity. Her thorough analysis of how romantic nationalism married authenticity to the development of folklore studies in nineteenth-century Germany and the United States resonates with how folklore as a field has understood its motivations and flaws (95).[1] A deeply reflexive study, *In Search of Authenticity* locates the desire for authenticity in the purview of the obsession with cultural purity and nationalism, as many societies struggle to find meaning in the face of the pluralities that modernity and postmodernity suggest. The work speaks volumes to today's resurgence of xenophobia, white nationalism, and patriarchal frameworks, couched in the language of authenticity, for creating social orders and values.

However, the search for authenticity is a kind of luxury. Contextual positioning with regard to social power, in terms of who can claim legitimacy based on cultural purity, makes all the difference in thinking through the role that emotion and morality may or may not play in the construction of the authentic. Certain subject positions, such as racial minorities, women, and members of the LGBTQI community, do not have the luxury of being granted the full personhood to claim authenticity. They can and often are the objects of a projected authenticity, but they do not hold the institutional power to be the sources of its verification or legitimization. Too often, the (re)construction of an authentic past or tradition is built on the violent subjugation of these groups as inherently flawed, fragmented, or suspect in regard to full subjectivity.[2] In creating new, creole religious traditions of connection through the experiences of colonialism, slavery, and sexual violence, the Afrolatinx traditions and communities explored here affirm a stance of antiauthenticity at the interstices of culture, place, and personhood.

This chapter discusses the cultural and social location of Afrolatinx religious and queer folklore as practices that defy discourses of purity. Building on traditions of cultural and racial admixture, Afrolatinx scholars, artists, and activists create new political kin through spiritual imagery. Rather than focus on policing authenticity, the works of Ana-Maurine Lara and Arturo Lindsay dig deep into everyday ritual practice as sites of antiracist outrage and empowerment. Lara's writing on Afro-Dominican queer spiritual modalities provides a road map to how Afrolatinx religious ontologies free up temporalities in ways that fight the colonialism of sensuality. Lindsay's evocative visual and performance art on Panamanian and African American experiences similarly brings to light how commemoration of ancestors is a necessary translocal site for creating solidarity between Latinx and African diasporic populations. Finally, the observations of the spirit medium Tomasa Spengler from Havana, Cuba, create on-the-ground routes to the worlds at the interstices that Lara and Lindsay evoke. All of my interlocutors theorize Afrolatinx futurities based on traditional histories of resistance found in vernacular religiosity. Their focus on finding common ground in the interstices of racialized experiences creates a much-needed dialogic space for those interested in combating inequality through the quotidian. Critical folkloristic practices pay attention to traditional spaces of antiauthenticity in art, literature, and spiritual life as a necessary kind of activism that resists silencing, homogenization, and appropriation.

## AUTHENTICITY, FOLKLORE STUDIES, AND "REALNESS"

In order to capture the differences in the discourses and purposes of authenticity that I am discussing here, I briefly turn to some of the existential debates surrounding the field of US folkloristics since its inception in the late nineteenth century. Many of the issues plaguing the search for folklore's identity stem from the move from what was a romantic nationalist European model to a decidedly pluralistic, sometimes more urban, and often immigrant-based subject of study (Newell 1888; Zumwalt 1988). The desire to locate a discernable authenticity in North American expressive culture fueled new kinds of romanticism, to be sure; however, the necessarily translocal, postcolonial, and diasporic nature of communities making up the "folk" and "folklore" created slippery subjects (Dorson 1976; Dundes 1989, 51–53).

There are striking similarities between how US folkloristics and the nation's political-public culture both struggle with determining the terms of inclusion, especially with regard to cultural and racial authenticity. Here, Barbara Kirshenblatt-Gimblett's questions about who needs authenticity and why are particularly useful to consider (Kirshenblatt-Gimblett and Bruner 1992, 304; Kirshenblatt-Gimblett 1998). Both the US body politic and the field of folklore reflect deep divisions that stem from a fear of a lack of a definable identity, the danger of being considered illegitimate. Kirshenblatt-Gimblett's concerns about staging authenticity mirror Nestor Canclini's work on the temporal flattening of Latin American Indigenous communities done by the museum's spatial narrative of cultural evolution (Canclini [1989] 2009, 2014). In many ways, the need to prove that folklore matters in the United States creates a similar desire for constructing a taxonomy and teleology for describing expressive cultures that are recognizable to a "scientific" epistemology.

Folklore studies in the United States has dealt with questions of academic and cultural legitimacy by both embracing and negating the notion of authenticity. Folklore as a discipline and practice negotiates innovation and tradition in ways that mark new genres, populations, and public cultures. From Richard Dorson's pronouncements of *folklorismus* or "fakelore" to considerations of virtual identities as folk expression, there is an obsession with finding, or at least negotiating, the "real" in the products of the imagination (Dorson 1976; Lau 2010). Much of this concern over the legitimacy of cultural expression and group identity is rooted in the uncomfortable proximity of truth to illusion, hypocrisy to sincerity (Bowman 1998, 138).

Our current political climate in the United States is obsessed, with good reason, with the battle over the meaning and place of the relativity of events, history, and communication of reality. The grab for economic and social power, in its most crass and brutal form, has created a space where the idea of authenticity, with its connotations of unalterable purity, becomes an inviting proposition. However, we must recognize that this desire for an easy and organic truth is deceptive in its simplicity and dangerous in its fast ability to create a template for social behavior and representation. Roger Abrahams's look at "creolian contagion" with regard to the plantation system in the Caribbean reminds us of how most populations, languages, and cultures in the world developed under economies and social conditions where authenticity was used as a barometer for whiteness, as well as a concept on which people of color's modes of play and resistance wreaked havoc (Abrahams 2003, 74–75). Relatedly, folklore studies have shown that these vernacular epistemologies of survival are both stigmatized by hegemonic social forces and treasured by the communities that hold them dear (Goldstein 2017; Zeitlin 2016). Then and now, who gets to decide who and what is authentic, according to which criteria, and to what ends?

Taking a cue from the wisdom generated by LGBTQI folk cultures, the concept and practice of "realness" is an illuminating interlocutor for understanding the power and aesthetics of simulating authenticity. "Realness" allows for a metacritique of the elusiveness of authenticity and the actual work that it takes to achieve its chimera. The vernacular concept of "realness" is explored in the seminal documentary of New York ball culture, *Paris Is Burning* (Livingston 1991; Butler 1993, 121–142; Poulson-Bryant 2013). Both as a category for walking in the balls and as an aesthetic to achieve, "realness" becomes a commentary on the normative weight of heterosexuality, whiteness, and economic success on all of us. As Dorian Corey succinctly puts it, "To be able to blend. That's what realness is. If you can pass the un-trained eye, or even the trained eye, and not give away the fact that you are gay, that's when it's real. Realness is to look as much as possible like your straight counterpart. The realer you look means that you look like a real woman. Or you look like a real man. A straight man. It is not a take-off or a satire. No, it is actually being able to *be* this" (Livingston 1991; emphasis in original).

Corey's framing of realness moves us into an ontological space. The act of performing realness for the artists at the balls or in the streets becomes an existential dilemma (Butler 1993, 130–131). However, the performability of realness in this context should emphasize the constructed nature of social conformability rather than reinforce an aura of legitimacy. What Corey and other drag queens illustrate about realness is the amount of work it takes to build its convincing nature, to exude a quality of being with complete confidence.[3] Realness exposes the process that makes it by uniting it to an endeavor of becoming that is both internal and external. Authenticity is situated in a process of validation that has at its root the problematic of taxonomy and verification. Realness plays off of authenticity's penchant for categorization yet also brings these essentialized qualities into question by working to recreate them. I am suggesting that the process of creating self, community, and culture for the sake of realness situates a critical understanding of this construction that authenticity seeks to elide.

*Paris Is Burning* has evoked critical sparring among theorists over the decades since its release (hooks 1992, 145–156; Butler 1993, 121–142; Muñoz 1999, 162–164; Bowman 1998, 135–138). Much of the debate centers on questions of access and representation and of gendered and racial authenticity in relation to the filmmaker, Jennie Livingston, a white lesbian, and the Black and Latinx ball community being explored in the film. Other popular representations of trans* and drag life such as the Puerto Rican documentary *Mala Mala* (Santini and Sickles 2014) and the FX television series *Pose* (2018) delve into the tensions between gay and trans* members of the community only hinted at in *Paris Is Burning*. For example, the frustration expressed by *Mala Mala*'s Max, a trans* male Puerto Rican, in not having access to testosterone on the island when estrogen is readily available, reveals the hidden shades of patriarchy and privilege that can operate in how medical authorities react to different trans* individuals.[4] In *Pose*, Blanca, the mother of the house of Evangelista and an HIV-positive trans* woman, is repeatedly thrown out of an all-male gay bar in Greenwich Village for being too Black, too Latina, and too fem (*Pose* 2018, season 1, episode 2, "Access"). Here, realness, like authenticity, has its parameters of attainment based on existing power structures that legitimize who can claim access to what identities and the costs of that claim.

The reality show *RuPaul's Drag Race* is perhaps the most pervasive example of working realness for fame, money, and in the show's parlance, "your legacy." Being legendary is an important marker of community respect based on performative expertise. The show's popularity has it running on its thirteenth season, with a global audience avidly involved in the selection of contestants and winners on social media. Hosted and judged by RuPaul Charles, international celebrity drag queen, episodes end with her universal call for self-acceptance: "If you can't love yourself, how in the hell can you love anybody else? Can I get an amen up in here?" Despite this claim for universal acceptance, the show has had its own difficult relationship navigating issues of class, race, trans* identity, and linguistic diversity (Poulson-Bryant 2013; Goldmark 2015).

The music video "Cover Girl," by RuPaul, illustrates a reflexive play with realness with regard to visual narratives of femininity, masculinity, and glamour. The song illustrates RuPaul's own sense of fluidity in relation to perception, desire, and reality. She sings,

> And when they see me, they want to be me, I am a fantasy.
> Cover girl, put the bass in your walk.
> Head to toe, let your whole-body talk.
> Cover girl, put the bass in your walk.
> Head to toe, let your whole-body talk.
> (Charles 2009a)

In this video (Charles 2009b), RuPaul performs femininity in a blond wig on the runway on top of a convertible, playfully teasing out the word *drag* for the audience. The chorus, beginning on the phrase *cover girl*, is repeated twice, with the second iteration being sung by an attractive African American man with no shirt, performing a butch masculinity. In some instances, the second chorus is also performed by a white drag king dressed like a gas station attendant and holding a gas pump, another nod to the performativity of gender being explored in the song. The lyrics, house music style, and imaging of the video open up spaces between realness and fantasy. At the center of RuPaul's provocation are the slippages she can evoke in racial, gendered, and sexual terms. The call to "let your whole-body talk" illustrates the polyphonic and embodied practice that is realness. The bass, inspiration, and epistemology clearly influencing RuPaul's pop manifesto of realness are rooted in Afro-diasporic Black swagger that emerges from a ball culture that is also entangled in Caribbean and Afrolatinx expressions of self-making (Kelley 1998; Gúzman 2008; Otero 2018).

The song continues, "Walk. Now walk. And what?" The lyrics are deepened here with their translation from the Spanish: "¿Y qué?" This question points to the ends of playing at authenticity. What are the eventual gains, losses, and meaning of such work? Here, I am reminded of Scott Poulson-Bryant's consideration of the un-say-ability of equating straight and gay African diasporic forms of culture, such as rap and drag (2013, 215, 218). Playing and working at queer realness can be at odds with Black and Latinx authenticities of femininity and masculinity, authenticities that are tied to nationalist longings that reinforce patriarchy, heteronormativity, and respectability. The murkiness of revolutionary reactions to women and LGBTQI participation in antiracist and liberation struggles only complicates the ways that realness and authenticity have intersected in especially African Diaspora, Caribbean, and Latino populations (Guerra 2010; Quiroga 2000, 19–20, 81–85; Anzaldúa [1987] 1999; Allen 2011; Lorde 1978; Ayorinde 2004; Glave 2003). Too often, the search for an authenticity becomes an essentialist tool for dividing members of communities sharing similar goals of obtaining political, social, and economic participation in civil society. The question, "And what?" / "¿Y qué?" reorients the audience to an enacted and action-centered approach to being and becoming real. This approach is deeply reflexive of the role that fantasy plays in creating modes to new realities and to metafuturities.

## FEMINIST AND QUEER FUTURITY AS ACTIVISM IN AFROLATINX SPIRITUAL EXPRESSION

Elsewhere I have thought through the ways that Afrolatinx drag and *oricha* cultures intermingle with regard to aesthetics, historical origins, and kinship making (Otero 2018). A central component holding these sister societies together is the understanding of the transformability of the human form. Queens, kings, mothers, and fathers are known in drag and santo houses for their ability to raise their kin and build communion through the spirit and art. There is an appreciation for incisive, skillful execution of traditional processes such as sewing, dance, and elocution that are vital components to the performance of drag and oricha religions.[5] The interstices between these communities emphasize that processes of self and world making (werk/*trabajo*), occur in a context of traditional antiauthenticity. In this case, authenticity necessarily evokes the cultural, historical, and colonial contexts in which it has been deployed to marginalize or silence hybrid and creolized individuals and communities.[6] In focusing on the artistry of multiplicity, Afrolatinx queer and oricha communities open up spaces of cohabitation that stretch the boundaries of personhood and gender. This slipperiness of subjectivity flies in the face of authenticity as a project of purity. Indeed, the inauthenticity that is tied to brownness, queerness, and tenuous materiality often manifests in the pathologizing of members of Afrolatinx queer and spiritual communities (Muñoz 2015, 209–210; Pérez 2016; Lara 2017a).[7] The ways that immaterial beings and occasional selves manifest as vital community members are at the core of how spirits, kings, and queens become active agents that resist, create, and live in hostile and often violent social conditions.

The very beings that manifest through bodies, gestures, words, and handmade art provide templates for expressing realness. Like RuPaul Charles, the orichas can walk in modes of becoming that manifest gender realness through the embracing of supposed oppositions. As Lydia Cabrera remarks in her personal notes on Yemayá, "Yemayá Ocutti . . .Yemayá tan macho como cualquier macho y tan hembra como lo de más / Yemayá Ocutti . . . Yemayá as macho as any macho and as feminine as all the rest" (Lydia Cabrera Papers, n.d.; translation mine). Yemayá Ocutti is a road of Yemayá, the maternal goddess of the sea, that can manifest in multiple ways through her followers.[8] Note how her fluidity between masculine and feminine realness mirrors RuPaul's penchant for playing with gender representation in "Cover Girl." In both cases, becoming feminine or masculine is a reflexive process that occurs on a continuum.

Afrolatinx LGBTQI and oricha-worshipping communities share historical and cultural interstices that solidify their ability to sustain expansive kinship practices. Whether it be in San Francisco, New York, or Havana, there are intersectional threads connecting the experiences and expressive cultures of santo and queer becoming in the context of racism, patriarchy, and homophobia (Beliso-De Jesús 2015; Conner and Sparks 2004; Fernández 2017; Thorne 2013). These connections highlight a kind of resistance and activism that rests on vernacular strategies of caretaking. In this manner, it makes sense that the maternal and awesome energy of the sea, Yemayá, becomes a site of inspiration, witnessing, and emergence.

Likewise, author and anthropologist Ana-Maurine Lara creates vivid representations of Afrolatinx queer spirituality through ocean imagery and conjure in her works *Erzulie's Skirt* (2006) and *Kohnjehr Woman* (2017b). The practices of conjure she explores in her writing resituate time, space, and materiality in a deep anticolonialism that suggests new historical imaginings that open up a space for personal liberation. Her writing is firmly located in the interstices, literally the sea, between African Diaspora, Latinx, Caribbean, and Afrolatinx experiences of creolized spirituality and queer sexuality. It disavows the call for authentic legitimization of her multiple communities through exclusion and classification. Rather, the voices, characters, plots, and texts Lara deploys suggest a collapsing of categories and traditions that reveal the possibility of alliance and mutual respect between communities of color, especially women.

Lara's sourcing of Dominican Vodou traditions through women's embodied knowledge illustrates yet another layer of the interlacing of Afrolatinx traditions through sensuality and the spirit. In *Erzulie's Skirt*, Micaela and Miriam are two Dominicans of Haitian heritage who work the cane fields, lose family members to racial violence, and love each other deeply. Their companionship is blessed through an intimate spirituality that is passed on through the generations, not uncomplicatedly with colonialism, patriarchy, and Christianity condemning and separating community members who try to keep these traditions alive (Lara 2006, 87–89). Secrecy is a necessary tool of physical and spiritual survival with regard to Miriam's and Micaela's religious and sexual lives. Their struggles are directly linked through spiritually recovered memory to the horrors of the slave trade. Consider the following passage:

> La Mar told of her place where two people lay with irons on their ankles. They gazed at each other across the darkness, despite the darkness, and their eyes shown like the stars. . . . Micaela watched as She appeared, beautiful and decorated, to reclaim her tortured children, to soothe their skin torn and mangled by the irons of slavery. She called to them: Come my children, rest in the folds of my skirt. She led them from the earth into her waters. And as quickly as she appeared, she disappeared, leaving her awake in the trails of her skirt. (160)

In this account, La Mar (the Sea) becomes a vehicle for Micaela recognizing herself in the eyes of her ancestors, slaves torn by shackles finding comfort in the ultimate rest of the ocean's skirt. The merging of the sea with the Haitian *lwa* of Erzulie also evokes a history of acceptance for LGBTQI practitioners of Vodou (Lescot and Magloire 2002; Danticat 2013; Conner and Sparks 2004). Significantly, this vision of La Mar appears to Micaela while she is getting ready to board a boat bound for Puerto Rico from the Dominican Republic. The passengers are all undocumented migrants with varying stories of distress and suffering. However, few survive the crossing of the Mona Passage, and those that do are taken as victims of human trafficking, including Micaela and Miriam (Lara 2006, 173–193). They survive an arduous bout of sex slavery and return to the Dominican Republic, reversing the dominant narrative of migration to the United States via Puerto Rico (Lara, personal communication, October 5, 2018).

Back in the Dominican Republic, Micaela and Miriam build a life for themselves, opening a small *colmado* (store) in the country for a Dominican Haitian community of cane workers and farmers. They entrust their knowledge of Dominican Vodou to a young woman, Yealidad, who inherits their power and the colmado upon their natural deaths. At the end of their lives, Erzulíe welcomes Micaela and Miriam into the folds of her skirt, into the imagery of the ocean. Miriam, upon taking her last breath in the colmado, "heard the pounding of the ocean beating out Erzulíe's song as she got closer to the waters" (Lara 2006, 7). The emergence of Erzulíe at this pivotal moment enacts the reciprocal relationship between devotee and lwa in Vodou. It illustrates an example of realness by accenting the process of transformation into an ancestor as understood by Afrolatinx religious imagery and folklore.

*Erzulíe's Skirt* also contains folk remedies for the soul and body. These emerge as short poems called *recetas para los vivos* that begin each section of the book. For example, for *espíritus perdidos en la noche* (souls lost in the night), one needs "Incienso de copal y mirra / Una escoba de palo / Un canto a Papa Legba / Pasar la escoba por los suelos de la casa, después pasar con el incienso" (Copal and Myrrh incense / A wooden broom / A song for Papa Legba[9] / Sweep the floor of the home with the broom, then pass the incense) (49). This *receta* appears in Spanish without translation in the novel. The linguistic code-switching also signals a move to the vernacular of folk belief. Lara invokes Papa Legba, a wooden broom, and the use of incense to indicate how Caribbean, African, and Indigenous sources inform this practice of cleansing the home.

In creolizing her recetas, Lara is eschewing the cultural politics of authenticity and providing a methodology for spiritual realness. Indeed, this and other recetas in the book evoke everyday practices that make up Afrolatinx women's healing traditions that occur in historically transnational interstices (Lara 2006, 3, 97, 109, 155, 171, 197, 227). These traditions include dream interpretation, talking to the dead, working with herbs, and reading signs in nature in order to allocate folk resources for the well-being of one's community (Tomasa Spengler, ethnographic interview, December 18, 2008; Manigault-Bryant 2014; Cabrera 1996). Lara frames her novel through these folk remedies in order to illustrate the centrality of women's vernacular practices in creating opportunities for healing, acceptance, and futurity. Thus, the evocation of such work in the book's context of human trafficking and racial oppression operates as a kind of activism. It unequivocally reaffirms Afrolatinx women's folkways of resilience, creativity, and resistance.

Another of Lara's works, *Kohnjehr Woman* (2017b), clearly situates the plight of Afrolatinx liberation within an inclusive African American framework. These narrative poems take place on a slave plantation in Virginia where a conjure woman, Shee, formerly accused of poisoning her masters in the Dominican Republic, arrives. Shee speaks through a mouth from which her tongue has been literally cut out. As Lara told me, "Shee's voice is a combination of English using Spanish phonetics, interspersed with made up language and Fon. Shee's backstory is that she was born in Dahomey, sold into slavery and ended up in Santo Domingo, and then fomented an uprising, had her tongue cut out and was then sold again to a Virginia plantation owner" (Lara, interview, September 28, 2018). The voice of Shee in the poems is meant to be read aloud, as "the [voice of the] kohnjehr woman is connected to your own" (Lara 2017b, vii).

Shee, with her broken yet powerful tongue, radicalizes the other slaves on the plantation, and some run away to freedom with her. Indeed, her first poem, "Odoldo Ees Deh Rehver," recreates the Yoruba word *odolodo* (bubbling river) in order to voice the unforgotten sound of her voice and the cultural source of her power, which are nonetheless forever changed by the history and violence of slavery. The plantation owner, known simply as He, also becomes a victim of Shee's magic and ends up getting shot by the river (69).[10] This reimagining of a shared Afrolatinx and African American past in the interstices of the imagination is full of pain, hope, and rebellion. I asked Lara about the cultural politics of doing this work. She responded that she is aware of "messing up the expectation of what Black women's bodies are supposed to do" (Lara, interview, October 5, 2018). This includes exploring Shee's own queer sexuality and her ability to use magic to motivate social action in *Kohnjehr Woman*.

Shee's presence on the plantation creates opportunities for the expression of folk knowledge and the building of kinship between an Afrolatina and African Americans. Without valorizing one set of traditions, language, or location as more authentic than the other, Lara allows for a futurity to be imagined in this mythical past setting. These alliances in the poems are based on very real shared traditions of vernacular healing and place making through the environment among African Diaspora populations in the Americas.[11]

The poem "Meadow Medicine" illustrates the creation of these bonds through the wisdom that links spiritual and natural worlds. It is written from the perspective of Samuel, a queer slave on the plantation who finds kin in Shee's being and knowledge. He expresses the creation of a multidimensional Black geography through the reinvention of the Virginia landscape when he "shares some secrets" (9). For example, he reveals that "at the praying ground" they "gather," and "there we turn the pot down" so that "no one can hear the sound" (9). He further describes how in the meadow, the oldest man "looks after the shoestring root," and the women make teas and baths out of "mullein leaves" and "chestnut bark, poke, collard roots, horehound, a lot of peach tree leaves" (9). Coming in from the fields with their stomachs empty and with scorching skin, this emerging Black transatlantic community remakes the Virginia landscape to serve their own needs of healing and spiritual communion. They collect leaves, herbs, and roots from the very land that they are forced to work to make productive. By creating an internal value to their labor, the men and women in the poem resignify the natural world as sustenance, as medicine that can also reshape space.

"Meadow Medicine" specifically places new and old traditions of African Di-aspora healing and root work in the North American landscape. The phrase *we turn the pot down* reminds one of the Bantú and Senegambian traditions found in Virginian slave archeology of placing cosmological designs at the bottoms of pots in commemoration of the creation of the universe and the ancestors (Ferguson [1992] 2004; Gómez 1998). The aforementioned herbs and plants, "chestnut bark" and "peach tree leaves," situate the reader in a ritual of cleansing that signals in-novation and the reworking of an American southern landscape. The meadow itself opens up the possibility of recognizing and rephrasing kinship and tradi-tion. It is a place where men and women take charge of caring for and therefore remaking the community through folk medicine. In positioning the formation of African Diaspora community within a natural landscape where rituals of healing take place, Lara asks us to imagine a past that carries its own vernacular codes of becoming that can be transported through tradition. Such a rendering of the past is often unverifiable through traditional archives and historiography.

This is why Lara's own critical writing on Afrolatinx "archives of imagination" asks the following key questions: "What if, just what if, we gave equal weight to that which cannot be controlled, clamped, ordered, tied down? Do our lives become less real?" (2017a, 5). These questions contextualize realness in regard to embracing forms of being, remembering, and telling that are not quantifiable. In doing so, Lara highlights how Afrolatinx communities do not easily fall into dichotomous taxonomies of race, nation, sexuality, and religiosity. She is asking the readers of *Kohnjehr Woman* to stay awhile in the meadow and to recognize its medicine as an antiracist guide for future work that can be done to shore up strength and resilience.

## ARTURO LINDSAY'S HEALING AND COMMEMORATIVE ART

Arturo Lindsay is a highly acclaimed Panamanian producer and scholar of Afro-Atlantic art (Lindsay 1996, 2013). Based for many years at Spelman College, he actively engages in fostering commemorative and healing arts at the interstices of African American and Afrolatinx shared cultural work. Like Lara, he reimag-ines pasts where religiosity brings African Diaspora communities together in the contexts of slavery, racism, and dehumanization. Paintings in his series "Celestial Dreaming" and the video performance piece *The Return of the Ancestral Messenger through the Door of No Return* situate Black souls at the center of reconstituting community through remembrance. These pieces constitute rituals of commemo-ration, rites of *mo juba*, as they are known in Yoruba-inspired religions, by naming and claiming the histories of those who have passed on. The imagery creates testaments to these individuals in ways that illustrate their realness as ancestors. Realness here operates from a frame of creative reconstitution, as in the Yoruba mo juba, of lives that still matter in a community's activated memory.

Lindsay's collaboration with African American playwright Ntozake Shange on the "Celestial Dreaming" paintings vivifies Black lives ended through violence in portraits of angelic constellations. The late Shange's project with Lindsay includes an unpublished collection of poems, "Smoke Voices: Interviews with the Spirits in the Art of Arturo Lindsay" (2017), that brings elements of recognition of the life histories of the inspirational spirits for Lindsay's creative vision of healing and kinship. The celestial journeys of spirits of murdered young Black men and women take the beautiful forms of hearts and patterns of light (see fig. 4.1). Lindsay related to me that this work situates a belief in reincarnation and return. Visually, it asks us to really confront the existential consequences of a deeply and blindly divided political and public culture. He emphatically remarked to me that his work, now more than ever, is "a challenge to not be self-righteous" (Lindsay, interview, July 25, 2018).

The artistic vision he holds of shared African American and Afrolatinx historical experiences, alliances, and tensions forms a contrapunto, a counterpoint. Lindsay sees the spirituality growing out of oricha worship, Palo traditions, and *espiritismo*, as well as the Black church, as intersecting conduits that can bring together communities of color in a time of stark disenfranchisement and hostility. *Compassion* is a term Lindsay used over and over again in our conversations about his life's work (Lindsay, interview, July 25, 2018). His visual art generates a powerful empathy, a call to acknowledge the active presence of Black and Afrolatinx lives. In "Celestial Dreaming," the angelic figures look back at the viewer in a manner that inspires recognition and witnessing. Holding this gaze requires work from the interstices, from a place of in-between-ness and connection.

Lindsay also physically moves us in a ritual of return from Portobelo, Panama, to Ile de Gorée, Senegal, in his video-performance piece, *The Return of the Ancestral Messenger through the Door of No Return* (2017).[12] In 2010, Lindsay was invited to enact a performance ritual for International Human Rights Day at La Maison des Esclaves. The piece I am analyzing here is a later creative work that was developed from that earlier installation. It represents a process of remembering and reactivation for Lindsay in an exploration of different mediums, audiences, and affects. The performance begins with a clip of waves breaking on the beautiful shore at Portobelo. A map is then shown on the screen, and a red line is drawn from Portobelo to Ile de Gorée. Lindsay's voice tells us that the piece is a "performance ritual" that takes place in three parts: Return, Reconciliation, and Healing. Lindsay provides commentary and narrative throughout the performance.

Fig. 4.1 Lindsay's *Spirits of Children Form the First Order in the Hierarchy of Angels*.

The next shot is of Ile de Gorée from the perspective of the ocean and stops at a still of a bird in the sky that recalls the Sankofa myth of souls returning to Africa. The sea's waves provide a visual and sonic background that acts as a bridge between geographic and temporal distances.

The Return portion of the performance piece brings us through the Sankofa imagery and the waves to the Door of No Return, the infamous last point of departure for those who suffered being taken as slaves to the Americas. Lindsay narrates and embodies the spirit that returns from Portobelo to the Door of No Return. The spirit wears what Lindsay calls "a punishment helmet" (see fig. 4.2) and carries a statue of a small child in one hand and a silver rattler in the other. In a detailed backstory, the piece shows Lindsay / the spirit coming through the castle's doors in search of his child and of revenge for his enslavement. It is important to note at this juncture that like with Shee in Lara's work, the spirit in this creative piece is not a metaphor but a catalyst for engendering healing and recognition of a shared history between Latinx and African Diaspora populations. Deepening the transcultural element of this connection, Lindsay's next words in the performance call out for the lost daughter of the spirit in three languages: "¿A

Fig. 4.2 Lindsay's *The Return*.

dónde está mi hija? Ou est ma fille? Where is my daughter?" We then see stills of
Lindsay / the spirit hunting through different portions of the castle, also shouting
in the colonial languages: "Who sold me? Qui m'a vendu? ¿Quien me vendió?"
The spirit continues to wander in stills that are now set to soft jazz piano music.

Lindsay then announces, "Reconciliation," and this word appears across the
screen alongside stills of the spirit with traditional Senegalese drummers and
dancers. We see and hear the ancestral spirit of return dancing and singing with
those assembled as an "act of reconciliation." The punishment helmet is removed
by one of the dancers, and the spirit / Lindsay is visibly freed and continues to
dance with the group. The contemporary jazz music playing in the background
becomes more energetic as the stills of dancing, singing, and drumming illustrate
a ritual celebration on site at the castle. The use of jazz and stills instead of actual
live footage of the ritual is an interesting and evocative choice. My reading of the
images and music indicates that Lindsay developed this creative piece out of a
ritual done in real time. Thus, the video-performance piece is a product of a larger
spiritual and communal process that must be respected. For the spirit, place, and
memory being invoked, the actual acts of return, reconciliation, and healing are
thus private with regard to their manifestation.

The final portion of the piece, the Healing, commences when a gourd of water is brought to the ancestral spirit. We see that Lindsay washes away the white paste that covers the spirit's face and body, explaining this as "a ritual act of purification." After the cleansing, the spirit is robed in a traditional Senegalese white gown and is then welcomed back home. Images of the performers and Lindsay's voice indicate the end of the ritual as a rejoiceful reunion that includes members of the audience joining the dancers, singers, and ancestral spirit. The sound of the saxophone brings the viewer to a final still of a setting sun over the sea as the piece closes.

The overall effect of Lindsay's video-performance piece is one of ritual return. It is a striking and solemn act that recalls the many Black lives lost across the ocean. The performance situates Lindsay in a kind of realness that evokes a memory of shared commemoration between Africa and Latin America. His embodied presence interrupts the space of Ile de Gorée in order to instill sensations of witnessing that accompany the sorrow and pain that are palpably locked into the very walls of the prison. The piece is metaphysical in its intent. Furthermore, the use of stills resonates with how ritual work in ethical folklore research is presented in partiality in respect to a community's wishes for sanctity and privacy.[13] It is placed within Afrolatinx and African Diaspora spiritual practices that resurrect ancestors in rituals intended for their inclusion in a community's present and future. Lindsay takes on the form of a returning slave-spirit so that a symbolic wholeness can be tasted, albeit briefly. His persona in the piece, like Lara's invocation of Shee, creates a historically imagined site where pasts can be revisited for antiracist work aimed at bringing together African Diaspora and Afrolatinx communities at the interstices of a shared legacy. Both Lara and Lindsay situate realness within spiritual identities that are multiple and enmeshed transnationally. The final portion of this chapter returns to everyday creative work by Cuban spirit mediums that is situated in similar terrains of Afrolatinx spiritual realness.

## CONCLUSION: DREAMING AND LIVING WITH THE DEAD, REALNESS

On an October morning in Mantilla, Cuba, my godmother, Tomasa, sits next to her *nganga*—an entity associated with Bantú ancestor worship in Cuba. She uses the *chamalongos*, discs of dried coconut, to speak to El Señor del Patio,[14] as he is known in our house. Tomasa turns to me and shares this experience about how El Señor first revealed himself to her in dreams: "All of the dead have given me their names in dreams. The first time that I saw him, El Señor, standing by the window, it frightened me so that I woke up. . . . And later. . . little by little I became adapted to it. But it isn't easy" (Spengler Suarez, interview and participant observation, October 5, 2008; translation mine).

Tomasa, as a Yaya Nquisi, an elder priestess of the Palo tradition, is well versed in talking to the dead. Her description of the process of dreaming the dead recalls Lara's and Linday's processes of resuscitating African Diaspora dead through the imagination. Tomasa's spirit guide, El Señor, acts like a father figure, a protector that serves as a resource for her and the spiritual community she serves. Also significant is the revelation of the dead's names in dreams. Naming is an especially powerful tool in conjuring reality and presence—thus, the revelation by El Señor signals a transference of power, kinship, and solidification of a mutual bond.

It is telling that the dead in dreams inspire a feeling of presence. They want to be seen, recognized, and called into being. This last point brings me to Tomasa's focus on developing spiritual sight and relationships with the dead as a process. She acknowledges her own fear at the first sighting of El Señor. But, poco a poco, she adapts to this new sensation and set of experiences. It is understood that embarking on a journey of proclaimed kinship with the dead is not easy, will challenge accepted standards of perception and reality, and will take time. This deceptively simple yet sage advice allows for there to be an individualized trajectory in determining one's dead. It also allows for there to be an opening for the sharing of similar experiences of dreaming and other kinds of interaction with the supernatural without judgement.

Tomasa's personal experience narrative at the site of a divination ritual brings me back to the consideration of realness in the works and practices discussed in this chapter. Talking to and dreaming the dead are situated in enmeshed practices that are woven together to make manifest the intangible essence of these guides. Whether it be Blanca from *Pose*;[15] Shee, Lindsay's ancestral spirit; or El Señor, Afrolatinx ancestors become accessible through multigenre creative practices that rely on community and remembering, practices that are ongoing and constantly revised for new purposes and audiences. These modes of enacting truths are not reliant on an outside verification of authenticity. Rather, their efficacy is intuitive and generative of further acts of commemoration and healing. The connections between Afrolatinx spirituality and queer realness is clearly located in a sensibility of transformation—transformations shared at historical, cultural, and spiritual crossroads that dare to envision bonds, imagine pasts, and forge a futurity of compassion and hope.

## NOTES

1. See also Abrahams (1993).
2. See, for example, Georg Wilhelm Friedrich Hegel's ([1837] 2004) determination of Africa as a continent without a history in *The Philosophy of*

*History*, a treatise that outlines the "spirit" of individual and collective action in the creation of history. Hegel asserts, "At this point we leave Africa not to mention it again. For it is no historical part of the World; it has no movement of development to exhibit" ([1837] 2004, 99).

3. This is indeed one of the takeaways that the character Stan from *Pose* offers us. His white, straight, and rich existence working for Donald Trump is nothing but a huge sham in the face of his love for trans* diva Angel (2018).

4. Here I would like to note the important work of Paul Preciado (2008) in formulating a pharmacological theory of gender expression and fluidity in *Testo Junkie*.

5. Joseph Cassara's (2018) novel *The Impossible House of Beauties* reimagines the early life of Angel from the New York Drag House of Xtravaganza, with detailed descriptions of gay Latinx life and spirituality.

6. See, for example, Cohen and Glover (2014).

7. See also Hufford (1995).

8. For a good *patakí*, a sacred narrative about Yemayá in this and similar roads that play with masculinity and femininity, see Cabrera (1980, 45–48).

9. Deity of the crossroads.

10. The river is a site of reckoning in Afrolatinx religious traditions such as Santería, Candomblé, and Palo.

11. See, for example, the encyclopedic *Ewé* by Pierre Fatumbi Verger (1995).

12. A video of the performance can be viewed on YouTube, posted by Lindsay on June 15, 2017, https://www.youtube.com/watch?v=VUx9JnZr1yU.

13. For more on this need for ethical considerations of ritual privacy and temporality in folklore research, see the work of Barre Toelken, especially "The Moccasin Telegraph and Other Improbabilities: A Personal Essay" (1995).

14. This translates loosely to "Sir of the Backyard."

15. The character of Blanca is partially based on Angie Xtravaganza, the mother of the House of Xtravaganza, whose multigenerational Afrolatinx drag family appears in *Paris Is Burning*. Angie Xtravaganza died in 1993 from an AIDS-related illness.

## BIBLIOGRAPHY

Abrahams, Roger D. 1993. "Phantoms of Romantic Nationalisms in Folkloristics." *Journal of American Folklore* 106 (419): 3–37.

———. 2003. "Questions of Criolian Contagion." *Journal of American Folklore* 116 (59): 73–87.

Allen, Jafari S. 2011. *¡Venceremos? The Erotics of Black Self-Making in Cuba*. Durham, NC: Duke University Press.

Anzaldúa, Gloria. (1987) 1999. *Borderlands: La Frontera*. 2nd ed. San Francisco: Aunt Lute Books.

Ayorinde, Christina. 2004. *Afro-Cuban Religiosity, Revolution and National Identity*. Tampa: University Press of Florida.

Beliso-De Jesús, Aisha M. 2015. *Electric Santería: Racial and Sexual Assemblages of Transnational Religion*. New York: Columbia University Press.

Bendix, Regina. 1997. *In Search of Authenticity*. Madison: University of Wisconsin Press.

Bowman, Ruth L. 1998. "Humbug and Romance in the American Marketplace." In *Exceptional Spaces*, edited by Della Pollock, 121–141. Chapel Hill: University of North Carolina Press.

Butler, Judith. 1993. *Bodies That Matter*. New York: Routledge.

Cabrera, Lydia. 1980. *Yemayá y Ochún*. Miami: Colección de Chicherekú en el exilio, Ediciones Universal.

———. 1996. *La medicina popular de Cuba*. Miami: Colección Chicherekú, Ediciones Universal.

Canclini, Nestor. (1989) 2009. *Culturas híbridas*. Ciudad de México: Delbolsillo Editorial.

———. 2014. *Art beyond Itself*. Translated by David Frye. Durham, NC: Duke University Press.

Cassara, Joseph. 2018. *The Impossible House of Beauties*. New York: Ecco.

Charles, RuPaul Andre. 2009a. "Cover Girl (Put the Bass in Your Walk)." Track 3 on *Champion*. New York: RuCo.

———. 2009b. "Cover Girl (Put the Bass in Your Walk)." YouTube, April 8, 2009. Video, 02:57. https://www.youtube.com/watch?v=KpDjc5yQRdw.

Cohen, Matt, and Jeffrey Glover. 2014. Introduction to *Colonial Mediascapes*, edited by Matt Cohen and Jeffrey Glover, 1–43. Lincoln: University of Nebraska Press.

Conner, Randy P., and David Hatfield Sparks. 2004. *Queering Creole Spiritual Traditions*. Binghamton, NY: Harrington Park.

Danticat, Edwidge. 2013. *Claire of the Sea Light*. New York: Vintage.

Dorson, Richard M. 1976. *Folklore and Fakelore: Essays Toward a Discipline of Folk Studies*. Cambridge, MA: Harvard University Press.

Dundes, Alan. 1989. *Folklore Matters*. Knoxville: University of Tennessee Press.

Ferguson, Leland. (1992) 2004. *Uncommon Ground*. Washington, DC: Smithsonian Institution.

Fernández, Alexander. 2017. "Odú in Motion: Embodiment, Autoethnography, and the [un]Texting of a Living Religious Practice." *Chiricú* 2 (1): 101–117.

Glave, Thomas. 2003. "Fire and Ink: Toward a Quest for Language, History, and a Moral Imagination." *Callaloo* 26 (3): 614–621.

Goldmark, Matthew. 2015. "National Drag: The Language of Inclusion in RuPaul's Drag Race." *GLQ: A Journal of Lesbian and Gay Studies* 21 (4): 501–520.

Goldstein, Diane E., ed. 2017. *The Stigmatized Vernacular*. Bloomington: Indiana University Press.

Gómez, Michael A. 1998. *Exchanging Our Country Marks*. Chapel Hill: University of North Carolina Press.

Guerra, Lillian. 2010. "Gender Policing, Homosexuality and the New Patriarchy of the Cuban Revolution, 1965–70." *Social History* 35 (3): 268–289.

Gúzman, Mañuel. 2008. "'Pa' La Escuelita con Mucho Cuida'o y por la Orillita': A Journey through the Contested Terrains of the Nation and Sexual Orientation." In *Puerto Rican Jam*, edited by Frances Negrón-Muntaner, 209–228. Minneapolis: University of Minnesota Press.

Hegel, Georg Wilhelm Friedrich. (1837) 2004. *The Philosophy of History*. Translated by J. Sibree et al. Mineola, NY: Dover.

hooks, bell. 1992. *Black Looks*. Troy, NY: South End.

Hufford, David. 1995. "Beings without Bodies: An Experience-Centered Theory of the Belief in Spirits." In *Out of the Ordinary*, edited by Barbara Walker, 11–45. Logan: Utah State University Press.

Kelley, Robin D. G. 1998. *Yo' Mama's Disfunktional!* Boston: Beacon.

Kirshenblatt-Gimblett, Barbara. 1998. *Destination Culture*. Berkeley: University of California Press.

Kirshenblatt-Gimblett, Barbara, and Edward M. Bruner. 1992. "Tourism." In *Folklore, Cultural Performances and Popular Entertainments*, edited by Richard Bauman, 300–308. New York: Oxford University Press.

Lara, Ana-Maurine. 2006. *Erzulie's Skirt*. Washington, DC: RedBone.

———. 2017a. "I Wanted to Be More of a Person: Conjuring [Afro] [Latinx] [Queer] Futures." *Bilingual Review / La Revista Belingüe* 33 (4): 1–14.

———. 2017b. *Kohnjehr Woman*. Washington, DC: RedBone.

Lau, Kimberly. 2010. "The Political Lives of Avatars: Play and Democracy in Virtual Worlds." *Western Folklore* 69 (3/4): 369–394.

Lescot, Ann, and Laurence Magloire, dirs. 2002. *Des hommes et dieux* [Of men and gods]. Creole, English subtitles, 52 minutes, Haiti. Watertown, MA: Documentary Educational Resources.

Lindsay, Arturo. 1996. *Santeria Aesthetics in Contemporary Latin American Art*. Washington, DC: Smithsonian Institution Press.

———. 2013. "Dancing *Aché* with Yemayá in My Life and in My Art: An Artist Statement." In *Yemoja*, edited by Solimar Otero and Toyin Falola, 187–196. Albany: State University of New York Press.

Livingston, Jennie, dir. 1991. *Paris Is Burning*. English, 71 minutes, United States. New York: Art Matters et al.

Lorde, Audre. 1978. *The Black Unicorn: Poems*. New York: Norton.

Lydia Cabrera Papers. n.d. Folder 11, "Orishas: Yemayá—Manuscripts, Notes, Notebook." Cuban Heritage Collection. University of Miami Libraries.

Manigault-Bryant, LeRhonda. 2014. *Talking to the Dead*. Durham, NC: Duke University Press.

Muñoz, José Esteban. 1999. *Disidentifications*. Minneapolis: University of Minnesota Press.

———. 2015. "Theorizing Queer Inhumanisms: A Sense of Brownness." *GLQ: A Journal of Lesbian and Gay Studies* 21 (2/3): 208–209.

Murphy, Ryan, Brad Falchuk, Brad Simpson, et al., producers. *Pose*. 2018. FX Productions.

Newell, William Wells. 1888. "On the Field and Work of a Journal of American Folklore." *Journal of American Folklore* 1 (1): 3–7.

Otero, Solimar. 2018. "In the Water with Erinle: Siren Songs and Performance in Caribbean Southern Ports." *Southern Quarterly* 55 (4):144–162.

Pérez, Elizabeth. 2016. *Religion in the Kitchen*. New York: New York University Press.

Poulson-Bryant, Scott. 2013. "'Put Some Bass in Your Walk': Notes on Queerness, Hip Hop, and the Spectacle of the Undoable." *Palimpsest* 2 (2): 214–225.

Preciado, Beatriz. (2008) 2013. *Testo Junkie*. Translated by Bruce Benderson. New York: Feminist Press and CUNY.

Quiroga, José. 2000. *Tropics of Desire*. New York: New York University Press.

Santini, Antonio, and Dan Sickles, dirs. 2014. *Mala Mala*. Spanish and English, 87 minutes, Puerto Rico, United States. New York: El Peligro, Killer Films, and Moxie Pictures.

Shange, Ntozake. 2017. "Smoke Voices: Interviews with the Spirits in the Art of Arturo Lindsay." https://static1.squarespace.com/static/59139f851b631b1476621629 /t/59876af1a5790a7d30d83f3d/1502046964948/Smoke+Voices+Proposal.pdf.

Thorne, Cory. 2013. "Saluting the Orishas in a Havana Gay Bar: Queering the Sacred and Secular in a New Gay-Positive Cuba." Talk delivered at the American Folklore Society Annual Meeting, Providence, RI, October 17, 2013.

Toelken, Barre. 1995. "The Moccasin Telegraph and Other Improbabilities: A Personal Essay." In *Out of the Ordinary*, edited by Barbara Walker, 46–58. Logan: Utah State University Press.

Verger, Pierre Fatumbi. 1995. *Ewé*. Rio de Janeiro: Grupo Companhia das Letras.

Zeitlin, Steve. 2016. *The Poetry of Everyday Life*. Ithaca, NY: Cornell University Press.

Zumwalt, Rosemary Lévy. 1988. *American Folklore Scholarship*. Bloomington: Indiana University Press.

SOLIMAR OTERO is Professor of Folklore at Indiana University in the Department of Folklore and Ethnomusicology. She is author of *Archives of Conjure: Stories of the Dead in Afrolatinx Cultures* (Columbia University Press, 2020) and *Afro-Cuban Diasporas in the Atlantic World* (University of Rochester Press, 2010). She is also coeditor with Toyin Falola of *Yemoja: Gender, Sexuality, and Creativity in the Latina/o and Afro-Atlantic Diasporas* (SUNY Press, 2013).

# FIVE

# Behaving like Relatives

## Or, We Don't Sit Around and Talk Politics with Strangers

RHONDA R. DASS

Leonard Peltier, a Native activist, stated in *Prison Writings: My Life Is My Sun Dance*, "I don't know how to save the world. I don't have the answers or The Answer. I hold no secret knowledge as to how to fix the mistakes of generations past and present. I only know that without compassion and respect for all of Earth's inhabitants, none of us will survive—nor will we deserve to" (1999, 230).

I must state upfront that I, like Mr. Peltier, do not have the answers. I can only speak from my perspective and perhaps contribute a bit to a better understanding of what it means to work with Indigenous communities in our pursuit of better understanding Native people and their folklore. Including and preferencing Native voices in the research of folklore seems to be something that has been overlooked and mishandled for a long time in our field. I had planned to look at the history of the work done by non-Native folklorists and to explain where and how we could incorporate critical folkloristics into our work with Indigenous communities. However, as with most plans, my path led me in a different direction.[1]

The direction I have chosen is to share with you a bit of me and what being a folklorist has meant for me. As a folklorist, I have found myself struggling to reconcile my academic training with my cultural heritage. On one hand, as a folklorist I have received a very thorough and prestigious training at the hands of some of the biggest names in our field. On the other hand, I have been taught by the most important people in my life, my ancestors, my relatives, how to be a good human being and how to be in the world. The divide in my path must be addressed to better delineate how we can be both respectful to Native communities and inclusive of Native folklorists within our academic ranks.

Early American folklore studies overlooked the collection and analysis of traditional practices from Indigenous communities of North America in keeping with the salvage paradigm that was prevalent during the foundational years of our field on Turtle Island. This institutionalized practice paved the way for modern methodologies that often neglect the postcolonial locality of Indigenous practices. The traditions of Indigenous people and the people themselves have had a vacillating relationship with American folklore scholars. While early practices were to ignore Native practices as they were not part of the salvage efforts, the scholarly lens would return periodically to Native people when it benefited the people collecting, applying the theories and methodologies that were developed for use with immigrant communities.[2] At times embraced and at others dismissed as having no relevance to a national narrative or culture, any attention paid to Indigenous communities has been from a less-than-stable paradigm that bases its understandings in cross-cultural comparison to European cultures only.

Additionally, Native people have become adept at deflecting researchers who approach them without appropriate connections to community members or any idea on how to approach a community and the commitment that is inherent in establishing a true relationship.[3] Access is limited, answers are by rote, or any information of value is carefully obfuscated or eliminated from interactions. In contrast to the standards of academia, Native cultural participants require a different set of legitimizing credentials, connect in ways that are culturally appropriate, and expect a higher commitment from researchers before they will participate in more meaningful levels of collaborations. Basing our work in Indigenous ways of knowing must foreground any work that we undertake as folklorists with Indigenous communities. We must also be willing to rethink our interactions with Indigenous communities and address the differences inherent in the work to date based on our historic neglect of these populations or interactions based only in a colonial understanding.

The place we must start the conversation is identifying what it means to be Native in America. It is a complex identity that is highly regulated legally and culturally, usually to the detriment of inclusivity and those pushed to the margins due to colonial practices. A claim to Native identity ultimately puts one in opposition to and outside of American culture and is seen as a political act if not a political identity. This claim can be based in either a political identity or an ethnic identity that has little to do with the modern Native reality but is based in a colonized past and is a sign of systemic racism that continues the process of assimilation of Native people into American culture.[4] This can be seen in the use of slurs and derogatory language demoralizing those in the present by references to the past, such as the use of the term *Pocahontas* to demoralize and disenfranchise claims of women or *Geronimo* in reference to claims of men. Colonizers and subsequent settlers were very successful in establishing the methods of erasure of Native people from a large group who could lay claims that superseded their own to desirable resources, mainly land. These methods were structured to allow for the continuous colonization of Indigenous people by their very own relatives. Once introduced, the systems of colonization and erasure continue to divide, push, and negate Native people from both the center and the margins of their own culture, and these systems are questioned only when those who once occupied what was perceived as a safe space find their own close kin falling into the cracks at the edges. Claiming a Native identity is therefore also contentious within Indian Country as we have picked up the colonial voice, a voice endowed with power that is recognized even among ourselves. We will use erasure to discredit someone or their ideas or to limit beneficiaries of what is perceived as limited resources. Because of their distance from reservation life and understandings embedded in the land, the larger diasporic Native existence is seldom seen as having a true claim to Native identity or ownership of knowledge that would be of use to researchers, and this existence is often not even noted when non-Natives speak about Native culture in America today. This narrows what is perceived as Native traditions and how they have truly been shaped by the colonizing forces that are still at work.

Let's clarify this a bit. One can be ethnically Native without being politically Native. One can also be politically Native without being ethnically Native. Or one can be both politically and ethnically affiliated without being embedded in Native cultural production. What makes Natives Native in America is not what researchers have paid attention to when conducting folklore research among Native people. What makes people Native in America is an understanding passed on from the federal government and complicated by the numerous interpretations and policies that have shaded that understanding. A complex system of colonization is overlaid onto Native communities and distorts the simple understanding of identity as being based in the landscape of our origins. Instead, this system creates a complex of nearly impossible restrictions that are based in biological understandings and reinforced by cultural practices and cultural constructs that slowly and continuously eliminate more and more people from that identity.

This is the system that is in place and that must be addressed to understand how Native people are in the world. This is the system that gets people to replicate their oppressors in order to survive culturally. Nowhere is this more obviously in need of our attention than in the examination of traditions and how they reflect the identity of Native people. We who are so versed in hybridity, diffusion, and the dynamism of cultural production target Native people who, in our trained opinions, reflect the "true" Native culture. However, what we are really doing is creating a reflection of our own views on Native culture in our interactions with Native people who fit our understandings, neglecting colonial realities of assimilation practices, and not with the larger Native presence. Folklorists own the research methodologies, undertaken from a colonizer's perspective, that further this agenda by identifying who is the "most Native" or that ideal tradition bearer as defined by a field constructed to examine the traditions of their own European ancestors. This further reinforces the systemic elimination of those at the margins and the diversity that is Native identity and existence. Folklorists must behave like relatives, or understand and preference an Indigenous worldview[5] in their dealings with Indigenous people, if we are to stop the replication of colonial assimilation techniques that stifle and marginalize Native people and continue the process of eradication of Native existence.

I am Anishinaabe. My family has been the victims of colonization in many ways, but one major result is that I did not grow up directly connected to community. My great-grandmother was taken away from her family when she was quite young to attend a boarding school. When she married a non-Native man rather than returning to her reserve, she was declassified as Native by the Canadian government. Due to her experiences in being taken away to school, our family learned to hide our Nativeness and "pass" as much as we can. Even though three of my four grandparents are Native, we did not openly participate in Native traditions. Only through the stories and teachings of my grandmothers did I grow in the knowledge of who I am and where my family came from. Our traditions were not something that was practiced in public. This, along with the disgraceful blood quantum system, places me not only outside of my Native community but also outside of settler culture in America. The very work that I strive to do has likewise been an instrument to disenfranchise my claims to my own heritage and leaves me conflicted as to my role in academia.

I am a teacher, a scholar, an activist, and a marginalized member of a diverse community. These roles are conflicting when brought to the academic world and create a situation where, despite any efforts, I will never completely be part of that world. To be Native is to stand in opposition to American culture. As a cultural institution, the academic institution epitomizes American cultural hierarchy. Standing against the academy is required to teach in the field of American Indigenous studies, requiring me to disrupt the academic world with my very presence. Having this standing, I am proud to not fit into academia, but it also is a very lonely place to occupy, knowing that I will never fit into the world that I aspire to be a part of.

As a person of mixed heritage, I work hard to understand my role as both a woman of Native heritage and a member of the academic community when it comes to the field of folklore. It is not a simple process or an easy one. Often I find myself off balance and not identifying with my true self[6] and what I know in my heart to be the way forward, distracted by the language and constructs of the academic world. It is a clear sign to me that I have lost my way when my language changes from talking from my perspective to a neutral voice that reflects none of my Indigenous heritage and training, even though it is the accepted academic voice. It shows I have lost sight of what it is to be a relative and to behave like one. How can I write a treatise on behaving like relatives when I do not feel as if I am behaving like one myself? I need to recenter myself and find my voice despite the requirements of the academic world and despite the ramifications for my academic career. This process negates my contributions to academia by speaking from outside the academic community and in a voice that is not seen as legitimate within academic circles.[7]

I must shift myself away from colonial influences just to write this missive. This also requires me to negate part of my own existence. I have to step away from my European ancestors; disconnect from my grandmother, who was the first person in her father's family to be born in the United States; step away from my Irish grandfather and his colorful past; and turn my back on part of my own folkloric existence. Embracing a Native identity tends to force you to choose between a Native and a non-Native presentation of self in the world. To truly hold to a perspective of decolonization, I must reject myself and who I am, or at least the half of me that identifies with anything other than Native. This dichotomous convention is also an artifact of the colonial past that holds tightly to the us-versus-them paradigm of Native existence. It makes me feel as if I have found yet another place where I do not belong. The choice of what I can and cannot embrace is often taken from me and assumed by people outside and inside my Native communities. This negotiation leaves me feeling disenfranchised in my pursuit of reconciling the various communities I am a participant in. I feel more like I am along for the ride rather than directing the path of my own life. Allowing those of us who straddle the lines between worlds to do so is often hard to understand for those who are squarely comfortable in their cultural milieus. Please bear with me as I struggle to present a Native concept[8] through a mixed voice to an unknown audience.

One of the first things I teach my students when we talk about writing is to know who your audience is. While I can assume an audience for this treatise, I cannot clearly know who will read it or how they will receive it. This is more of an Indigenous understanding[9] that transmitting knowledge is a very personal thing, and the one transmitting the knowledge has a responsibility to give it to ones who will honor it and use that knowledge appropriately. In the academic realm, we are trained to shout all we know as loud as we can to all who will listen. This is another issue that comes with any field of academic study outside of Indigenous studies that causes problems for Native academics. It is not how we would behave as relatives.

I intend more than a critique of what non-Natives have done, which would unintentionally but also inherently overwhelm and replace an Indigenous presence and voice in research about Native people. Instead, I intend to focus on what it means to behave like a relative, how we as folklorists can incorporate this Indigenous way of knowing as a basis for research in the field of folklore, and how we can incorporate our Native understandings[10] in the practice and theories of critical folkloristics.

To behave like a relative is to shift your perspective out of the colonial framework that does not allow you to exist as a whole person and embrace an Indigenous way of being and knowing about the world and yourself. This is not easy to accomplish in a colonial world, nor is it something you are automatically born into by virtue of Indigenous heritage. It is learned through our everyday existence with each other, through the interactions we have with all of our relatives—Native, non-Native, plant, and animal. It is presented to us by our Elders and embraced by those both young and old as they come to understanding in their own time. It is embedded in our folklore, and if studied properly, this folklore can lead you to a deeper understanding of what it means to behave like relatives without my words or intervention. It is in our stories, our art, our daily lives, and our way of being in the world. Behaving like relatives is a philosophical and cultural practice. It is embodied and lived knowledge of how to engage the world properly according to Indigenous peoples' understandings.

To behave like a relative is to embrace a new worldview that is as ancient as the landscape it is rooted in, a practice that is hard for even the most skilled researcher to do. The Indigenous worldview is not merely based in the land but is the land itself. It is the production of Native identity in that landscape that connects the past and future generations to the individual and the community as a whole. It goes against the comfort of the researcher to embrace this, as you must also embrace the reality of the changes in that landscape—the pipelines and highways, the high-rises and clear-cut land, the diverted rivers, and the trampled spaces where ceremonies were once held. You also need to see what our ancestors would see: Would they recognize this land? And you need to understand the changes and how that would affect them. It is to envision the future and whether we will recognize the land of our great-grandchildren.[11]

To behave like relatives is to know who you are in relationship to the people you are studying and respect your place in the cultural production. It means to relinquish the position of authority within your own work and allow the people you are working with to take the lead. It sometimes means that you must sit back and do exactly what you have been trained not to do or at least not do the things you expect you need to do to accomplish your research. I remember at the annual meeting of the American Folklore Society, held in Salt Lake City, Utah, in 2004, Barre Toelken explaining how he had "gotten it wrong," noting that he had not known who the narratives he was trying to collect had belonged to. It seemed a shame to me that he would spend fifty years with a group of Native people and not be told or not hear when he was told that he was on the wrong path. I believe that the intentions of my fellow folklorists are not nefarious or ill conceived, but I do know that they do not hear with a Native ear and therefore miss most of what is communicated to them by their Native collaborators.

Telling someone they are wrong is not in our cultural way of being.[12] We do not tell you, "No, you can't do that," in a direct manner, but we do so in many more subtle ways. Only when pushed to an extreme in which your actions threaten our way of being will we break with our ways and outright tell you no. This is seen as pointing at and highlighting someone's faults, something we traditionally do only through humor or other indirect methods. These ideational differences are usually not considered when researchers approach Native communities.

Behaving like a relative means taking the time to understand our own connection to the community and the individuals, knowing the relationship between individuals and where we fit with the ancestors and future generations. Behaving like a relative means knowing the family's history and aspirations and being aware that because of our position in the family we may not be privy to all of the family secrets at a particular stage of our relationship. It is also about knowing what may and may not be shared with outsiders—and having respect for those boundaries. Behaving like a relative is practicing and using the values of respect, reciprocity, and caring for not only the people of a community but also the folklore of a community.

There are many Native understandings that are not transmitted openly or told to everyone, and our traditional practices do not invite the unprepared and undedicated to the depths of our true understandings and ways of being in the world. We do not share them with outsiders as people in Western cultures share their political views with strangers sitting around in bars. Fully understanding and actually behaving fully as a relative would not further the aspirations of the average folklorist. Most folklorists will acquire access to only a refined set of understandings that are available for consumption by the general public. With the predilection of the academic world to be based in the advancement of careers on the sole activity of publication, this is an understandable defensive technique for Native communities to employ. However, it goes beyond the concerns of interacting with academics to a place within our worldviews that requires more from a person than what they receive. Behaving like a relative is at the heart of how we are in the world with all of our Native, non-Native, plant, and animal relatives. Behaving like a relative is what is required to understand our cultures and to be one of us.

It has always amazed me how many of my students are shocked by the lack of knowledge from some of the people in our Native communities. I have created a number of experiential learning opportunities for students—Native and non-Native—that will allow them to experience a Native learning environment rather than Native knowledge transmitted in a Western classroom learning model. They do not yet realize in their journey to behave like relatives the simple concept that knowledge—our knowledge—is meant to be shared in particularly Native ways and with particular individuals. This simple example clearly singularizes the problems inherent in interactions with Native communities by people who do not behave like relatives. The assumptions of ignorance on the part of the Natives rather than the critique of the methodology of the non-Natives are put forward and block a clear picture of traditions and traditional practices in our Native communities.

We also lose sight of what it means to be a relative. We have learned through colonization and multiple generations of assimilation practices to behave like Westerners, to forsake our own worldviews and traditional ways of being in the world. We have relatives that will sell you what you want of our knowledge. We have relatives that will trade knowledge for political power. We forget what it means to behave like relatives and are treated like nonrelatives by our blood kin. However, we are learning how to find our way back, and our relatives are treating us as if we will. It is also part of behaving like relatives to realize that each person is on their own path, in their own way, and to provide them with the opportunities to learn when they are ready for them and in their own time. So, when we do finally understand what it means to behave like a relative, we will be here waiting for us.

## NOTES

1. Please see the bibliography for a brief discussion on this important shift in direction.

2. It would be customary to provide examples and cite other people's work at this point in the narrative. However, with the intent of this work to be one that pulls us back toward an Indigenous way of being and based in Native understandings, it would not serve to go further into this topic. It is enough to mention that there are some that have done this, but it has been rare and not out of respect for Native ways of being. In addition, it has not been indicative of the methodologies or theories of folkloristics but rather indicative of individuals who came to understand the need to approach Native people in a different way.

3. In other words, they do not know how to behave like relatives and assume the responsibilities that come with that relationship.

4. The complicated understanding of Native identity is wrapped up in the identity politics of non-Natives, whom we call settlers. Again, to retain the focus of this missive to a needed one, I will leave this issue for a future conversation.

5. I use the term *Indigenous worldview* not only to express the idea of a non-Western worldview but also to represent the complexity of our Indigenous communities in all the vast array of distinct and complex understandings. Positioning myself within the communities and outside of them at the same time requires that I also distance myself for any specifics in this discussion. It is my attempt to speak out in a culturally appropriate way on how I see myself within all of my complex communities.

6. While complex, it is nonetheless how I view my identity, inclusive of all of my various community affiliations, my worldviews, and a unique blend of all my ancestors and what they have given me.

7. Expectations are inherent in "scholarly" work and set aside any cultural differences of language, thought, or worldview. This missive endeavors to become an example of breaking with that academic voice to be true to myself and my worldview.

8. This is to suggest not that there is a singular Indigenous epistemology but rather that, like me, we need to embrace the complex and multifaceted identity in all its messiness. This is a call to step away from the Western dichotomous us-versus-them understandings and toward an openness to the complexity of Native cultures.

9. While presented as a singular pan-Native idea, an *Indigenous understanding* is inclusive of any number of ideologies associated with an Indigenous people in a cultural context as being representative of cultural norms.

10. *Native understanding* is a synonymous term for *Indigenous understanding*.

11. For a great discussion of land and land issues for Native individuals, see Leanne Betasamosake Simpson (2017).

12. The term *cultural way of being* refers to the ideational tradition in the Anishinabek community that informs me through my socialization on how to behave when speaking out on any topic relating to Native people, particularly people in my communities. This singular perspective, while particular to Ojibwe people, is also practiced by other Native communities.

## BIBLIOGRAPHY

*Preferencing Native voices and Indigenous ways, it is complicated to not only create and use an instrument that is central to colonization but also place it in a document that is intended to break with the boundaries of colonization in the field. The decision to include a bibliography is intentional, as I struggle to position myself as both a Native person and a scholar. I include it here to claim my standing in both communities and to share my perspective on our field and its constraints on non-Western communications. The very act of including a bibliography became a political decision. My attempts to discuss these resources and views became a battleground that pitted Native voices against those in the folklore field. I wished to avoid this direct competition for attention and would direct you, dear reader, instead to the inclusion of the mixture that is at the foundation of my writing, offered here in a nonhierarchal alphabetical listing without judgment.*

Bronner, Simon J. 1998. *Following Tradition: Folklore in the Discourse of American Culture.* Logan: Utah State University Press.

———. 2002. *Folk Nation: Folklore in the Creation of American Tradition.* Wilmington, DE: Scholarly Resources.

Brunvand, Jan Harold. 1968. *The Study of American Folklore: An Introduction.* New York: W. W. Norton.

Champagne, Duane, and Jay Strauss. 2002. *Native American Studies in Higher Education: Models for Collaboration between Universities and Indigenous Nations.* Walnut Creek, CA: Altamira.

Child, Brenda J. 2012. *Holding Our World Together: Ojibwe Women and the Survival of Community.* New York: Penguin Group.

Dundes, Alan. 1999. *International Folkloristics: Classic Contributions by the Founders of Folklore.* New York: Rowman and Littlefield.

Gilio-Whitaker, Dina. 2018. "Settler Fragility: Why Settler Privilege Is So Hard to Talk About." Beacon Broadside: A Project of Beacon Press. November 14, 2018. https://www.beaconbroadside.com/broadside/2018/11/settler-fragility-why-settler -privilege-is-so-hard-to-talk-about.html.

Grande, Sandy. 2004. *Red Pedagogy: Native American Social and Political Thought.* New York: Rowman and Littlefield.

Moore, MariJo. 2003. *Genocide of the Mind: New Native American Writing.* New York: Avalon.

Paredes, Américo, and Richard Bauman. 2000. *Toward New Perspectives in Folklore.* Bloomington, IN: Trickster.

Peltier, Leonard. 1999. *Prison Writings: My Life Is My Sundance.* New York: St. Martin's.

Simpson, Leanne Betasamosake. 2017. *As We Have Always Done.* Minneapolis: University of Minnesota Press.

Wilson, Shawn. 2008. *Research Is Ceremony: Indigenous Research Methods.* Winnipeg: Fernwood.

RHONDA R. DASS is Director of the American Indigenous Studies Program at Minnesota State University, Mankato, which she founded in 2009. Her research focuses on the examination of cultural issues that highlight areas of conflict, collaboration, and cultural exchange. Her latest work looks at the production of identity through the personal narratives of Native American direct-action experiences.

# SIX

# Political Protest, Ideology, and Social Criticism in Wolof Folk Poetry

CHEIKH TIDIANE LO

African nationalist movements and cultural renaissance activists tapped into oral traditions to inspire new stylistic demarcations from Western literary canons (Falola and Ngom 2009). The Négritude movement is a case in point. With the influence of Euro-American folklore scholarship, folklorists and scholars of oral literature shifted their focus onto the artistic performance of African oral expressive cultures and generic classifications (Dorson 1972; Dundes 1999; Ben-Amos 1975; Finnegan 1997). This trend has not changed much until today, relegating folklore scholarship as a tool for proving African oral traditional literary or artistic worthiness in comparison to Western art and literary forms or to document the existence of certain genres such as epic narrative (Okpewho 1990; Barber 1997). This study seeks to push further the boundaries of this paradigm to examine how folklore plays a critical function in the everyday struggles of communities against poverty, oppression, exploitation, ostracism, and other subjugating institutions. As Jaco Kruger (2007) has shown, folk songs and poetry are critically important in African struggles and resistance against colonialism, apartheid, and other neocolonial and political regimes of oppression throughout the continent. This chapter extends that existing scholarship through the study of occupational songs and folk poetry in Wolof. I intend to problematize the dominant trends in folklore scholarship, calling for a more critical folkloristic approach that heeds basic ontological preoccupations of certain groups and their engagement with folklore today. I contend that folklore as a cultural production is neither an exotic field that needs safeguarding nor a demonstration of sophistry; instead, it is an expressive form on par with other forms capable of conveying the struggles and aspirations of oppressed and subaltern groups. To support this claim, this chapter draws from two categories of oral and written folk songs or poems that are effective communicative instruments and that address political and ideological concerns of contemporary Wolof society. The first category has been collected from occupational groups of fishermen in the northern part of Senegal. The second category is taken from poems written by local poets who often are errant and unknown individuals in the mainstream national and international academia. This marginalization is one of the rationales behind my choice to study their intellectual productions. This chapter contributes to documenting folkloristics' function as a tool of poetic resistance both between communities and the state and inside communities. After a brief presentation of African folklore scholarship, its orientations, and its agendas, I flesh out the emerging critical folklore theories, highlighting how they can aid in extending and complementing existing approaches in the field. In the final section, I analyze sample folk songs and poems and show how they are tools both of resistance against contemporary kinds of domination and for expression of the subaltern groups.

## CRITICAL FOLKLORE THEORY

The study of African folklore by Africanists has first been a reactionary ideology to the anthropological and philosophical allegations that denied civilization to Africans (Crowley 1969; Peek and Yankah 2004). The colonial project was first and foremost ideological, as it posited a theory that rejected African civilizational and cultural abilities. This agenda was designed to justify the civilizing mission and legitimize Western colonialism in Africa. In response to these assumptions, a group of younger intellectuals in Paris created the Négritude movement in the 1920s and 1930s for the promotion of African cultural heritage and the reaffirmation of the dignity of the black race.[1] European (more specifically, French) ethnological expeditions launched to collect African folklore and oral tradition were intended to prove the cultural backwardness of black people. It was imperative, then, to develop a counternarrative that would celebrate black aesthetics and pride through the revalorization of African folklore through written literature. Spearheaded by poets and writers in the francophone colonized nations such as Léopold Sédar Senghor and Aimé Césaire, this romantic, celebratory tone sparked disagreement among their anglophone counterparts, who adopted a more pragmatic approach, incorporating African symbolism and folklore in a more political rhetoric.

One of the leading theoreticians who critiqued the passive use of folklore as a pan-African reaction to colonial ideological and racial denials was Frantz Fanon. Inspired by Marxist and psychoanalytic theories, Fanon doubted the ability of folklore revival to respond to the European denial of African and black civilization. His criticism was clearly directed toward the Négritude movement, which he regarded as outmoded and sterile, arguing that the celebration of folklore was "totally incongruous with the colonial situation" (Fanon [1961] 2004, 171). Fanon was very skeptical of a type of folklore that does not help in the mobilization against the oppressive powers of Negro-African national communities. He deemed Senghor's Négritude as shallow and cut from the dire social realities of colonized or newly emancipated communities. He affirmed that "Negro-African culture grows deeper through the people's struggles, not through songs, poems, or folklore" (Fanon [1961] 2004, 170). Even in the period immediately following political independence, Fanon thought it was more urgent to work on national cultures rather than on a pan-African cultural revolution. For him, it is through the awakening of national consciousness that we can render expressive cultures relevant to the struggle, because that is the level at which "the storytellers who recited inert episodes revive them and introduce increasingly fundamental changes" (Fanon [1961] 2004, 174). In contrast to pan-Africanist ideologies, Fanon believed that any emancipation should begin at the local level and that folklore should be oriented to sensitize about the challenges besetting the communities. Folklore is meaningless and sterile unless it aids in the liberation of the nation and "the resurrection of the state" (Fanon [1961] 2004, 177).

Fanon's critical cultural theory echoes, if not derives from, Antonio Gramsci's Marxist theory of folklore. For both theorists, folklore to be relevant should challenge hegemonic institutions and liberate oppressed masses from exploitation and domination. Gramsci is more incisive in his theorization of folklore. For him, folklore is fragmented and operates below the popular culture level. To be effective, folklore should be moved into the critical consciousness realm. As Stephen Olbrys Gencarella put it, Gramsci "rejects folklore and common sense (or at least their reactionary elements) as parochialism that impedes maximum critical praxis and solidarity, but he does not call for their immediate eradication" (2010, 236). Fanon and Gramsci acknowledge that folklore is a constituent part of people's subculture; however, they consider it less relevant to political struggles against hegemonic forces if it is confined to reactionary celebration: "For Gramsci, overcoming reliance upon folkloric knowledge constitutes an early stage in the demolition of class inequality; this is why he indicts his fellow folklorists' admiration for the object of their study as misplaced desire, complicit in a system of oppression and hegemony that benefits the few" (Gencarella 2010, 237). Gramsci's critical theory is flawed by his evolutionary conception of human culture—he thinks in terms of stages in which folklore would be at a prelogical level (Beverly [1999] 2004, 138).

It must be clarified that neither Fanon nor Gramsci discards folklore as irrelevant, but they set some preconditions before it can reach critical consciousness.

Organic intellectuals, as opposed to popular wisdom agents, are to lead oppressed groups to reshape their folklore material to fit the current political issues of liberation. This standpoint intersects with what subaltern thinkers fear the most. Could subaltern groups speak for themselves, or do they need intellectuals or scholars from already hegemonic institutions to represent their voices? Folklorists or scholars engaged in the representation of communities' "expressive cultures need to be self-reflective and critically aware of their language choice and positionality to avoid replicating the hegemonic discourses that pay lip service to oppressed people's struggle" (Beverly [1999] 2004). As Beverly claims, "Folklorists' discourse manifests its own characteristic hegemonic tendencies in the aestheticizing of the experience" (Beverly [1999] 2004, 12). Other Marxist folklorists debunk the Gramscian approach that folklore is not sophisticated and critically reflexive enough to be a counterhegemonic discourse (Zipes 1984). In this regard, José Limón (1983, 45) claims, "Folklore actively contests the hegemony of dominant social orders and it does so in two modes. First, folklore has the capacity for direct contestation; that is, it can directly symbolize and 'name' the class enemy in the manner of political jokes and protest songs (Brennis 1993). However, and of greater interest, we are also told that folklore can also offer indirect contestation by its presence."

## WORK SONGS AND THEIR CONTEXT OF PRODUCTION

The Wolof are the dominant ethnic group in Senegal, representing around 46 percent of the population. Most of them inhabit the central west of Senegal. However, the Wolof language is the national lingua franca, spoken almost by 90 percent of the Senegalese. The Wolof society was traditionally a very hierarchized community, with several occupational groups called castes and a political organization formerly based on kingdom. The shift into European republican political organization has obliterated most of the traditional chieftaincies. However, certain considerations of traditional hierarchy are still celebrated by griots, or local memory holders, and often influence social interactions. Certain occupational activities are still tied to castes and are transmitted from generation to generation within those social groups. Blacksmithing, fishing, and music making are generally performed by traditionally known groups. For instance, most fishermen are Lebu, a subgroup of Wolof people. Similar organizations are shared by many neighboring ethnic groups of Senegal as well.

The occupational or work songs are created by unknown authors and spread across regions, with slight variations. The occupational songs under scrutiny here are essentially peasant songs and folk written poetry. Fishing songs or songs performed by Wolof fishermen bear similar traits, in addition to their use in public demonstrations or strikes as a form of resistance. Their audience is much limited, since they are often sung on boats at sea. Drawing from Mouhamadou Lamine Ndiaye's (2013) data collected from fishing and peasant groups, I expand the data with ethnographic field notes I took in 2009 and my exchanges with Mr. Ndiaye, who accompanied fishermen during their expeditions to record the performances or to elicit them verbatim once on shore. For the most part, he directly interviewed people and recorded his data through verbatim elicitation. Like the agricultural songs, these songs exhort fishermen to double their efforts and forget the pain of loneliness, away from their families. Fishermen can spend anywhere from a couple of days to several weeks at sea.

Folklore scholarship in Africa has aided little in the documentation of such instances in which occupational songs convey politically and ideologically charged messages. However, the function of folk songs and poetry as forms of resistance or reclamation is noted throughout Africa, especially in countries marked by violent decolonization processes or apartheid (Tsoubaloko 2016; Kruger 2007; Gelay 1999; Vail and White 1983). The second genre is what I call folk written poetry. Most of the time, such poets do not benefit from any form of recognition in academic institutions, since their literary canons and language differ from "modern literature." They use local languages and ignore the standard poetic techniques popular in world literature. The topics they engage with often directly address local issues, family, and other personalized subjects.

However, the poets use their texts to emit relevant criticism on a variety of questions, either by denouncing what they conceive as injustice or by advocating social reforms at large. Their poetic publications find outlets in short booklets or bound sheets published by amateur editing houses. They are occasionally published by NGOs and governmental agencies working for the valorization of indigenous languages. They are called errant poets because schools invite them to perform recitals. Despite this local consideration, such poets are not seriously taken to be professional writers in academia or circles of writers. They struggle to have their work published by domestic and international professional editing houses.

Folkloristics, as a discipline, should pay greater attention to such grassroots forms of folk or amateur literature, because they are grounded in local aesthetics and systems of value. They offer criticisms focused on real-life problems facing their community. For instance, fishing communities who have produced the corpus of songs in this chapter are confronted with border issues between Senegal and Mauritania. Recurrent confrontations are recorded, emanating from misunderstanding or violation of fishing regulations between the two countries. Frequently, casualties and homicides happened between the Senegalese fishermen and Mauritanian marine or coastal security agents. In 1989, Senegal and

Mauritania narrowly escaped war because of the tension between Senegalese fishermen and Mauritanian maritime guards.

The two governments constantly sign fishing agreements to appease the situation when it threatens to escalate. These political problems are apprehended differently by the fishing communities, who often lay the blame on both Senegalese and Mauritanian authorities. They also create a tense atmosphere of suspicion and contempt between maritime border agents and Senegalese fishermen. As Thomas Binet, Pierre Failer, and Andy Thorpe's (2012) sociological findings indicate, only around three hundred licenses are offered by the Mauritanian government, while thousands of pirogues illegally cross water borders to fish in the Mauritanian zone due to the increased transborder mobility of artisanal fishermen.

The next section examines these issues, showing how folklore can be a tool of resistance, reclamation, and parochialism. In both types of songs, part of the message is directed toward the internal members of the groups. The hierarchical forms of violence and organizational dysfunctions affecting the group's efficacy are pinpointed and condemned. Therefore, a critical view of folklore needs to attend to internal tensions within a given folk group, which amounts to what Richard Bauman (1971) calls the differential identity of the social base of folklore.

## FISHING COMMUNITY AND RESISTANCE

Senegalese fishing communities face a range of challenges in their daily activities. They lack the necessary tools, such as fishing gear and life preservers, and are confronted with expensive oil prices. These dire working conditions are reflected in their occupational songs, which can be interpreted as protest voices to change the status quo. Fishing, despite being the second source of national income, still lingers in an artisanal or rudimentary state. No significant innovations have been undertaken to modernize the sector. To this day, fishermen use traditional handmade and motor-powered boats, which are highly susceptible to weather hazards. The following song encapsulates the physical exertion the fishermen endure only to cast out and pull their fishing nets. The size of their boats often represents a real challenge for fishermen to work properly with their large nets:

| | |
|---|---|
| Mélal ni gayndé, gayndé njaay | Behave as a lion |
| Mélala ni gayndé, gayndé njaay | Behave as a lion |
| Mbaala day teer | It is only a net, it should land |
| Sunu mbaal day teer | Our net will forcibly land |
| Sunu mbaal kagn lay teer | When will our net land |
| 10h dafa wara teer | It should land at ten |
| Mélal ni gayndé, gayndé njaay | Behave as a lion |
| Mbaala dafa wara teer | It is only a net that should land |

The singer exhorts his coworkers to behave as lions—that is, to put extra effort into pulling back the nets, because time is running out. The customers and retailers go to ports or beaches to wait for the fishermen. Before 10:00 a.m., some of the fishing boats go offshore to sell their catch. This is the time when people usually go to the marketplace to buy foodstuffs including fish. Fish has a sociological dimension in Wolof society, because it is the staple meat that accompanies cooked rice. One of the threats to this resource is overfishing by foreign industrial fishing companies that are licensed to access the Senegalese fishing zone. With their sophisticated ships and tools, they become serious rivals to local artisanal fishing communities. Local fishermen navigate away into the neighboring countries' fishing zones without appropriate authorization, which creates additional problems with foreign maritime guards. Besides their direct or mediatized protests, songs offer them a platform to share their grief and express their sentiments in respect to their degrading working conditions.

In addition to the harsh conditions alluded to in the songs, the theme of violence among the fishermen arises frequently. It could be argued that the hardships they encounter in their activities create a strained environment where nerves get irritated very easily. As a result, group leaders and captains may exert violence over their employees or subaltern coworkers, ranging from insults to stigmatization. Through the songs, the victims attempt to sublimate such violence or simply denounce it. This long song illustrates the claim:

| | |
|---|---|
| Man de damay baayi mbaal | I am to abandon fishing |
| Mbaal de amul kilima | Fishing is not peaceful |
| Mbaal de amul raandma | Fishing has not yield |
| Saaga gudi, saaga beccëg | You are insulted night and day |
| Yuuxu gudi, yuuxu beccëg | You are yelled at night and day |
| Ass gudi ass beccëg | Dry up night and day |
| Mbaal de amul kilima | Fishing is not peaceful |
| Mbaal de amul randma | Fishing has not yield |
| Diri gare, diri gare | Pull the net out, pull the net out |
| Diri suba, diri ngoon | Pull night and day |
| Ass gudi, ass beccëg | Dry up night and day |
| Yuuxu gudi, yuuxu beccëg | You are yelled at night and day |
| Saaga gudi, saaga beccëg | You are insulted night and day |
| Mbaal de amul kilima | Fishing is not peaceful |
| Mbaal de amul raandma | Fishing has not yield |

The rudimentary nature of handmade boats accounts for why subaltern workers must constantly work to dry them up. The boats' sides are often low, which allows waves to pour seawater into them. To keep the boats afloat, some workers are charged with emptying the water and keeping them dry throughout the expedition. Any neglect in that task may sink the boat. To urge them to work hard, their bosses often subject them to humiliation by yelling at or insulting them. When open and direct protest may lose them their jobs, workers resort to poetic expression to depict the humiliating experiences they endure at sea. The poem is sung out loud to express the fishermen's disapproval of their working conditions. They are not just describing their plight; they raise consciousness among their colleagues who meet at sea. When another group of fishermen hears the songs, they are tempted to pick it up and perform it elsewhere. In so doing, they circulate the messages of the songs and encourage each other to mobilize. In Saint-Louis, Senegal, the fishermen often observe strikes and go to march on the street, brandishing red flags and singing those songs. Many times, they face the police, who struggle to disperse the angry mobs. The rhythmic patterns of *ëg* and *ma* ending alternately in most verses allow a certain musicality and easiness to be chanted in unison. Therefore, the songs are not just performed for the sake of enjoyment; they exert an energizing and mobilizing effect. The pain the fishermen share through the songs crystalizes into concrete street demonstrations and strikes that lead authorities to take action. As suggested by Gramsci and Fanon, occupational folklore facilitates the emergence of critical consciousness, because the songs performed by the fishers, for example, lead them to synergize their efforts around common goals. Such a strategy of covert resistance has started to be documented among African workers (Cohen 1980; Lombardi-Satriani 1974). However, unlike Fanon's claim for a national consciousness and state resurrection, the folklore forms examined here are only geared toward empowering self-bounded folk groups.

Another aspect of the predicament expressed through their songs is the exploitation to which powerful fishmongers subject them. After days or weeks of toil, they are often obliged to sell their catch at cheap prices to wholesale traders. The following piece is an illustration of a fisherman's resistance to an act of exploitation by a Waalo-Waalo, a trader coming from the northern province of Waalo:

| | |
|---|---|
| Jógal ma nax la | I can swindle you |
| Mano ma nax yaw | No you can't |
| Xalé bu tuuti man naa ko nax kay | I can swindle a child of course |
| Waalo waalo, walaatu dewlin | Waalo waalo a half oil liter |
| Leku ma ci ceebi, bullen ma niinal | I haven't eaten your rice, don't tarnish me |
| Naanu ma ci ndox mi, bullen ma tooyal | I haven't drunk your water, don't wet me |
| Xaala maala, ragal ya daw nañ | Xaala maala, cowards have fled |
| Ragal du dem géer | A coward does not go to war |

| | |
|---|---|
| Waalo waalo, walaatu dewlin | Waalo waalo a half oil liter |
| Xale bu góor mano ko nax yaw | You can't swindle a young man |
| Mane danaa ko nax yaw | I will swindle her |
| Xale lu mbaal xajal ko day doore | Watch out for the young fisherman, he is violent |
| | |
| Diri suba diri ngoon | Pulling morning and afternoon |
| Ngané danga ko nax yaw | And you want swindle him |

This song is a dialogue between a Waalo-Waalo and a fisherman. The former is ironically portrayed as swindler when he says he can swindle the profit of his interlocutor. He would not have shown his crooked intention in this way, but the singer wanted to creatively represent exploiters' understated agenda of usurping the profit of the fishing community. At the same time, the singer warns the Waalo-Waalo of a potential revolt that would destroy his scheme in the verse "Watch out for the fisherman, he is violent." From a Gramscian perspective, folklore offers a tool to challenge forms of hegemonic domination. *Waalo-Waalo* is a term that epitomizes the powerful economic businessmen who have a monopoly over the rice-irrigation sector in the northern part of Senegal.

One of the issues raised through the songs is the conflicting relationship that fishermen have with the Mauritanian maritime border patrols. As mentioned earlier, the transborder problem between Senegal and Mauritania reached its apex in 1989, entailing a heavy toll in both camps (Parker 1991). Since then, Senegalese fishermen and peasants have been at odds with Mauritanian border security services. The fishing community's songs are full of stereotypical and ironic images about the Mauritanians, known as Naar in Wolof. The tense relationship between the Naar, or Moors,[2] and the Senegalese dates back to the precolonial era and is reflected in different Wolof folklore genres, including proverbs. However, the occupational songs document the most recent perception of fishermen about the Moors. For instance, in the following song, the fishermen emit insults against the Moors by way of denouncing their violent and wicked treatment of arrested illegal fishermen:

| | |
|---|---|
| Naare way | Oh Moors |
| Ratatata tuy tuy tuy | Ratatata tuy tuy tuy |
| Cey naare way | Oh wicked maure |
| Ratatata tuy tuy tuy | Ratatata tuy tuy tuy |
| Sen —— | [an insult] |
| Yaw yaama sonnal | I am fed up with you |
| Ratatata tuy tuy tuy | Ratatata tuy tuy tuy |
| Naare way sa—— | Oh Moors, [an insult] |
| Yaw yaama sonnal | I am fed up with you |
| Ci gudi boy, ci beccëg boy | All day long |

| | |
|---|---|
| Man duma nelaw | I am sleepless |
| Te dootuma yaandoor | I no longer sleep at ease |
| Cey naare way | Oh you wicked Moors |
| Yaw yaama sonnal | I am fed up with you |
| Sama yaay yonni ma | I am sent by my mother |
| Yakam tima yaay booy jarul dara | She is in a hurry, the fish is cheap |
| Yaw yaama sonnal | I am fed up with you |
| Sa—— | [an insult] |

Some verses of the poem reveal that the maritime guards often use guns to shoot at them. In January 2018, a fisherman from Nguet Ndar of Saint-Louis was shot dead in a race between fishermen and the maritime guards (NdarInfo 2018). The ideophone of gunshots, "Ratata tuy tuy tuy," indicates that fishermen are frequently victims of gunshots when they reach the forbidden Mauritanian fishing zone. In the poem, the singer is indirectly stating that they are often killed for cheap fish that he is catching for his mother. This dramatic image is probably employed to alert the reader to the difficult experience the fishing community undergoes just feed the people, risking their lives at sea. In addition to the hazards of the weather, they are exposed to the gunshots of maritime security agents from the neighboring country.

The theme of slavery comes up in the fishing songs performed by fishing communities located at the northern part of Senegal, especially in Saint-Louis. In their continuous confrontation with Mauritanian maritime border officers, they relate their experiences by exaggerating them. Let's consider the following poetic excerpt:

| | |
|---|---|
| Bo dema ganaar | Whenever you go to Mauritania |
| ñoo lay jeema moom | They would enslave you |
| Nga dem nuwadibu | You go to Nuwadibu |
| Dañ lay jeme moom | They would enslave you |
| Teŋ laala leŋ | Teŋ laala leŋ[3] |
| Teŋ laala leŋ | Teŋ laala leŋ |
| Teŋ laala leŋ | Teŋ laala leŋ |
| Teŋa leŋa lenga leŋ | Teŋa leŋa lenga leŋ |

In real life, no fishermen have ever been reported to be enslaved in Mauritania. However, through this strong metaphor, they attempt to offer a portrait of their dire arrestation and custody conditions. The Mauritanian maritime security officers, as in any country, may put in custody fishermen who violate their legal fishing territory. Since the Mauritanian government provides licenses, those caught without authorization may be arrested and fined (NdarInfo 2018b). But through the songs, the fishermen raise their voices against the inhuman treatment they are given once arrested. They go so far as to compare it to slavery. Mauritania is one of the last nations on Earth to have abolished slavery, a practice that is deeply ingrained in their society. This may prompt the oppressed fishermen to use the term *slavery* to alert the public about the hidden form of bondage and oppression still going on there. Through folklore, the voiceless fishermen attempt to call other people's attention to their plight when arrested in Mauritania. Here, the songs, as Fanon conceives of folklore, are a critical medium of communication that addresses the fishermen's everyday predicament in their professional activities.

Through the performance of these poems, the Nguet Ndar fishermen of northern Senegal raise the awareness of other fishers elsewhere, creating a sense of community to muster their forces against the social injustice they encounter in their profession. The verses[4] about the violence they may express in cases of oppression and exploitation are often concretized through street demonstrations and damage to public infrastructure. In recent years, many strikes have been held during which fishermen brandish slogans of resistance, songs, and placards, engendering clashes with the police force. The most recent one occurred in 2017 in Saint-Louis (NdarInfo 2018a). Demonstrators wore red clothes and held insignias on which I could read, "Trop c'est trop," a French phrase that can be translated as "Too much is too much"; "Libérer les pêcheurs" ("Free the fishermen"), and so forth. The songs they sing at sea are often reiterated at the outset of their gatherings for strikes. The songs apparently can be recontextualized in real spaces of resistance as a means of mobilizing crowds, composed not only of fishermen but also of women and younger people. The performance of songs thus becomes a way of consolidating their sense of solidarity, the group identity of fishermen in times of hardship and joy. But more importantly, the songs serve to galvanize mobs of demonstrators in major fishing cities. When interviewed by the press, the 2017 strike leaders further elaborated on their reasons for protesting, explaining in a more direct way the resistance messages coded in their songs and slogans. For instance, an interviewee explained the circumstances that had led to the imprisonment of a couple of fishermen in Thies, the second-largest city of Senegal, before calling for their liberation. As Russell Kaschula, talking about the performances of contemporary poetry in West Africa, argues, "the thematic content of oral poetry has been broadened in order to reflect the important issues of the day, be they religious, political or social" (Kaschula 2001, xi)

## WRITTEN FOLK POETRY AND SOCIAL CRITICISM

The dichotomy between oral poetry and written poetry conceals overlaps and mutual enrichment of the two modes of poetic production in Africa. Folk poets may have varying levels of education in modern schools. Their major particularity is their attachment to their traditional roots and their interest in the challenges of their society as reflected in their production. Thierno Amadou Sall, whom I met in Bloomington, Indiana, in 2016, is an interesting figure in the folk poet group. He did not complete his high school degree, but he fluently writes in French. However, most of his poetic writing is in Wolof, and seldom in Pulaar, his native language. When asked about his choice of Wolof, he simply replied that it is the language of his audience. The difference between professional writers and the folk writers resides mainly in the use of indigenous language and the respect of Western literary canons. The folk writers often ignore the tenets of modern written literature and do not have a mastery of Western languages employed by African professional writers. It is true that they often seek wider recognition by having their work translated into French or English, but the basic structure and themes they develop differ from professional written literature. Their texts address issues ranging from family problems to marriage taboos, gender oppression, farming, and global governance. In their works, orality and literacy cohabit and supplement one another. Folk poets who are educated tap into literacy to write and archive their oral texts. I call them oral texts because they are generally destined to be verbally chanted or recited in front of an audience. *Taalifkat*, known in French as *poètes errants*, go from place to place, often invited, to recite their poems. During school events or literary meetings, they convene to share their poems. My first meeting with Thierno Amadou Sall occurred when he was invited to recite his poems at Indiana University. This international invitation was a privilege for him—most wandering poets are hardly known even in the elite circles in their own countries.

In one of his poems, Sall speaks in the name of the farmers when he denounces the disconnection between local farmers and the decision-making officials. Calling them intellectuals, Sall points out their ignorance of the farming world, which contradicts their pretention of being specialists in national agricultural development in the poem titled "Yow Yaa di Intellectuel" ("You the intellectual"):

| | |
|---|---|
| Mënuloo genn Dakar | You cannot go out of the city. |
| All bi ci say waxtan rekk | As for the bush, only through your mouth |
| Lanuy koy dégg | We hear about it. |
| Waaye man beykat bi | But me the farmer |
| Suma la soxlawoon | If was important to you |
| Dinga ma seetsi | You would visit me. |
| kow-kow nga ma jappee | You take me as a backward |
| soo nowoon s | Had you come to me |
| dina la mën diis samay soxla | I would've told you about my needs. |
| Xam nga lu ma tiis | Do you know My pain is: |
| Loo ma jappee ni sa bopp | You take me as your equal. |

This poem is a critical view on the armchair farming specialists who obtained their degrees in agriculture or related fields but who refuse to go out of the city and meet the fieldworkers on the ground. The farmer doubts that their theories are relevant to the farmers' needs. The poem offers a satirical picture of the widening gap between actual farmers and the intellectuals who pretend to be the problem-solvers from their air-conditioned offices in the city. Through this poem, the folk poet aligns himself with the voiceless and challenges the intellectuals who claim to represent the peasants but who are completely disconnected from their daily struggles.

In another poem, Sall goes on to criticize politicians and their demagogical electoral promises to the gullible people:

| | |
|---|---|
| Ngay falu | You are about to be elected |
| Dig ma ay geeji meew | And you promise me seas of milk |
| Ay geeji ganjar | And seas of gems |
| Nga xoymat ma ajjana | You make me think of paradise |
| Ma fal la, nga folli sama jamm | I voted for you, and you dismissed my peace |
| Ju neew ji ma amoon | The little peace I enjoyed |
| Rafle di ma nawal ay xiit-mbal | Now I am without clothes |
| Taxaawaalu doon sama ligeeyukaay | My only job is wandering |
| Wëraalu doon sama serign | Roaming around becomes my master |
| Ba may jangal saari am jot. | It even teaches idleness |
| Jamonoy pall dellusi, | Now election is up again |
| May nelaw | While I am sleeping |
| Di xandoor | Fast asleep |
| Di gent sama jammi elleg, | Till I dream |
| Nga fëg sama néeg | And you knock at my door |
| Yee ma, ma degg sa baat, | Waking me with your voice that I can hear |
| Gëna sangoo sama mbalaan, | I wrap myself in my cover |
| Naan la: "bukki, yappu amatul." | Telling you: "Hyena, no more meat." |

The poem includes a wealth of metaphors and symbolisms that capture the exploitation and political demagogy people are subjected to, with the form of resistance it insinuates. Using his own personal example, the poet offers a compelling picture of how politicians trick them and his strategy to unmask them. In the last verse of the poem, the politician is compared to a selfish hyena that eats the flesh of its victims—"Bukki yappu amatul," or "Hyena, no more meat." The state of slumber represents the gullibility he was in when politicians made beautiful but false promises to earn his vote. Once he realizes the fallacious basis of the political discourse, he begins to ignore them and calls them hyenas. Before elections, politicians go to the population with the most alluring rhetoric and promises, but once elected they become inaccessible. This ambiguous behavior is condemned indirectly in the poem, which can serve as sensitizing tool for the masses whose votes enrich bad politicians. The folk poem serves to denounce the continued exploitation by the elite political class. Folk poetry is a channel for poets to express social criticism of actions that they deem to be against social mores and values including national cohesion, dignity, and identity. Therefore, written folk poetry has a wider scope than oral poetry, as the former may often tackle issues of national interest, whereas the latter is generally preoccupied with immediate predicaments and concerns of the folk groups that produce the texts.

A shift from a focus on the aesthetic and performative dimension of verbal performances to a closer consideration of their political and discursive function could be a major disciplinary move in folklore scholarship (Bendix 1997). In a global society, marked by an increased social stratification and unequal distribution of riches, voices of marginal communities of all hues should be more clearly integrated into scholarly inquiries. Thanks to its proximity to folk groups, critical folkloristics could play a leading role in exposing the ontological preoccupation embedded in expressive cultures. Folk poetry, among other genres, is a spontaneous and handy tool of communication for occupational groups to assuage their labor hardships and, more importantly, to relay their concerns and protest oppressive systems. As suggested by Margaret Mills, the new critical perspectives in folklore see "verbal constructions of ourselves and others and the rhetoric that frames them as the products of particular historical positions (macro as well as micro) and the distribution of power within our social groups" (1990, 7).

In the global academic discursive regime, indigenous knowledge has tended to be regarded as raw data that need to be sifted through the lenses of scholarly voices. Even if it is inevitable for the self-reflexive scholar who examines indigenous texts to instill his or her own perspective, a keener sympathy about their ontological preoccupation and their own vision of their social struggles is key for any critical analysis. Folk groups produce their texts to reflect on the challenges of their community and time. Their texts are not simply artistic communication; they are ideological messages that consolidate or counter certain systems of practice or thought. Case studies of the peasant fishing songs and folk written poems demarcate themselves from the mainstream literary canons in terms of language and style without losing their artistic and thematic interests. Their modes of performance are intrinsically tied to the contexts in which producers and audience evolve.

The fishing songs are perfect illustrations. These folk groups do not differentiate artistic space from labor space or academic space from everyday space.

They work, sing, and reflect on issues that concern their activities, families, society, and the world at the same time. The artistic, didactic, and philosophical functions of their songs or poems coalesce and coexist. This is the reason why Jung wrote, "African folklore possesses a greater and more philosophical value that would appear at first sight. In the collective state of human society, it represents an aspiration to a state of things where the individual will have his due place" (quoted in Kruger 2007). To hear and understand their voices, the scholar should listen to their songs, proverbs, and everyday language. To Spivak's question of whether the subaltern can speak, these songs help us reply that they have never been silent. Through their songs and folk poetry, folk groups and individual poets formulate coded or clear messages to condemn social injustice, resist oppression, and denounce bad mores that ruin the social cohesion of their occupational and broader communities. Going down the streets with placards and patterned shirts, accompanied by songs, is their form of resistance against social injustice and exploitation. Songs are a politicized tool for contemporary occupational groups to reclaim their rights and urge for reformist decisions to support their well-being.

Perhaps there has not been enough attention on the part of professional scholars to show and share those voices in ways that would empower the folk producers of these discourses. Of the reasons that account for such disconnects between academic scholarship and folk knowledge systems, one could point out the format and method of articulating these discourses. Our disciplinary lenses through which we understand knowledge and discourse may differ from indigenous communities' epistemologies, but the basic preoccupation of denouncing injustice and resisting oppression remains the same: "That said, if critical research in folklore studies aspires to alleviate human suffering by drawing attention to limitations of certain ways of being and subsequently encouraging alternative ways of becoming, it cannot turn a blind eye to structures of oppression even within host communities" (Gencarella 2011, 262).

Folk literature in Africa is produced in African languages, not in inherited European colonial languages that are the lingua franca in academia and that neglect or marginalize knowledge systems produced in non-European languages: "Our indigenous literary resources are seen and treated, to a large extent (even locally), as second-rate materials" (Na'Allah 2018, 51). The gaps in folklore studies could be bridged through critical approaches that go beyond the celebration of artistic performance to address social differences and push the boundaries of academic parochialism. As stressed by Richard Bauman and Charles Briggs (1990, 60), "performances are not simply artful uses of language that stand apart both from day-to-day life and from larger questions of meaning." The critical study of folklore could further help in clarifying the impact of the embedded political messages of folk poetry on the broader social organizations in which it is produced and put in circulation.

## NOTES

1. A movement created by African students in French higher education to defend their rights.

2. *Moor* is translated from the French term *Maure*, which means the Arabized and Berber inhabitants of Mauritania. They have roots in the earlier Islamic Arabs who Islamized North Africa and part of Spain, called *Maurabitun* in Arabic or *Almoravids* in English.

3. Untranslatable ideophone, probably depicting wave sounds.

4. "Xale lu mbaal xajal ko day doore." ("Watch out for the young fisherman, he is violent.")

## BIBLIOGRAPHY

Barber, Karin. 1997. "Preliminary Notes on Audiences in Africa." *Africa: Journal of the International African Institute* 67 (3): 347–362.

Bauman, Richard. 1971. "Differential Identity and Folklore Social Base." *Journal of American Folklore* 84 (33): 31–41.

Bauman, Richard, and Charles Briggs. 1990. "Poetics and Performance as Critical Perspectives on Language and Social Life." *Annual Review of Anthropology* 19:59–88.

Ben-Amos, Dan. 1975. "Folklore in African Society." *Research in African Literatures* 6 (2): 165–198.

Bendix, Regina. 1997. *In Search of Authenticity: The Formation of Folklore Studies.* Madison: University of Wisconsin Press.

Beverly, John. (1999) 2004. *Subalternity and Representation: Arguments in Cultural Theory.* Durham, NC: Duke University Press.

Binet, Thomas, Pierre Failer, and Andy Thorpe. 2012. "Migration of Senegalese Fishers: A Case for Regional Approach to Management." *Maritime Studies* 1 (11): 1–14.

Brennis, Donald L. 1993. "Some Contributions of Folklore to Social Theory: Aesthetics and Politics in a Translocal World." *Western Folklore* 53 (2/4): 291–302.

Cohen, Robin. 1980. "Resistance and Hidden Forms of Consciousness amongst African Workers." *Review of African Political Economy* 7 (19): 8–22.

Crowley, Daniel J. 1969. "The Uses of African Verbal Art." *Journal of Folklore Institute* 6 (2/3): 118–132.

Dorson, Richard, ed. 1972. *African Folklore.* New York: Anchor Books.

Dundes, Alan, ed. 1999. *International Folkloristics: Classic Contributions by the Founders of Folklore.* New York: Rowman and Littlefield.

Falola, Toyin, and Fallou Ngom, eds. 2009. *Oral and Written Expressions of African Cultures*. Durham, NC: Carolina Academic Press.

Fanon, Frantz. (1961) 2004. *The Wretched of the Earth*. Translated by Richard Philcox. New York: Grove.

Finnegan, Ruth. 1997. *Oral Poetry: Its Nature, Significance, and Social Context*. Cambridge: Cambridge University Press.

Gelay, Betie. 1999. "The Peasants of Gojjam and Their Reflections on Contemporary Issues in Amharic Oral Poetry." *Aethiopica: International Journal of Ethiopian and Eritrean Studies* 2:124–43.

Gencarella, Stephen Olbrys. 2010. "Gramsci, Good Sense, and Critical Folklore Studies." *Journal of Folklore Research* 47 (3): 221–252.

———. 2011. "Folk Criticism and the Art of Critical Folklore Studies." *Journal of American Folklore* 124 (494): 251–271.

Kaschula, Russell H., ed. 2001. *African Oral Literature: Functions in Contemporary Contexts*. South Africa: New Africa Books.

Kruger, Jaco. 2007. "Songs of Struggle: Dominance and Resistance in Venda Ngano Song Narrative." *Journal of the Musical Arts in Africa* 4 (1): 1–27.

Lombardi-Satriani, Luigi. 1974. "Folklore as Culture of Contestation." *Journal of the Folklore Institute, Special Issue: Folklore Studies in Italy* 11 (1/2): 99–121.

Limón, José. 1983. "Western Marxism and Folklore: A Critical Introduction." *Journal of American Folklore* 96 (379): 34–52.

Mills, Margaret A. 1990. "Critical Theory and Folklorists: Performance, Interpretive Authority, and Gender." *Southern Folklore* 47 (1): 5–15.

Na'Allah, Abdul Racheed. 2018. *Globalization, Oral Performance, and African Traditional Poetry*. New York: Palgrave Macmillan.

NdarInfo. 2018a. "Marche des pêcheurs de Saint-Louis: La vidéo intégrale." November 3, 2018. https://www.ndarinfo.com/Marche-des-pecheurs-de-Saint -Louis-la-video-integrale_a23321.html.

———. 2018b. "Mauritane: 22 Sénégalais en garde à vue pour pêche illégale." August 23, 2018. https://www.ndarinfo.com/Mauritanie-22-Senegalais-en-garde-a-vue -pour-peche-illegale_a22649.html.

Ndiaye, Mouhammadou Lamine. 2013. "Wolof Occupational Songs." Master's thesis, Universite Gasbon Berger.

Okpewho, Isidore. 1990. *The Oral Performance in Africa*. Ibadan: Spectrum Books.

Otchere, Deborah. 2019. "Work and Happiness: Songs of Indigenous Ghanaian Fisherman." *Africa Every Day: Fun, Leisure and African Expressive Culture on the Continent,* edited by Kemi Balogun, Lisa Gilman, Melissa Graboyes, and Habib Iddrisu, 311–320. Athens: Ohio University Press.

Parker, Ron. 1991. "The Senegal-Mauritania Conflict of 1989: A Fragile Equilibrium." *Journal of Modern African Studies* 29 (1): 155–171.

Peek, Philip M., and Kwesi Yankah, eds. 2004. *African Folklore: An Encyclopedia*. New York: Routledge.

Tsoubaloko, Francois Haipinge. 2016. "Songs as a Tool of Resistance in the Namibian Path to Freedom." *Applied Science Reports* 6 (2): 122–126.

Vail, Leroye, and Landeg White. 1983. "Forms of Resistance: Songs and Perceptions of Power in Colonial Mozambique." *American Historical Review* 88 (4): 883–919.

Zipes, Jack. 1984. "Folklore Research and Western Marxism: A Critical Replay." *Journal of American Folklore* 97 (384): 229–337.

CHEIKH TIDIANE LO earned a PhD in folklore studies with a minor in anthropology at Indiana University. He is an adjunct visiting lecturer in the African Studies Program at Indiana University Bloomington. After several fieldwork trips in Saint-Louis, in his dissertation he examined the impact of UNESCO's World Heritage Listing on the Island of Saint-Louis of Senegal, focusing on intangible heritage forms. Parallel to this primary work, Lo's interests include expressive cultures in Senegal, particularly public celebrations as a technology of memory and identity politics. He also studies oral literature of Sufi and occupational communities through their songs and narrative texts in African languages.

SEVEN

—⟋⟋⟋—

## *Sugar Cane Alley*

Teaching the Concept of "Group" from a
Critical Folkloristics Perspective

KATHERINE BORLAND

As a classroom teacher, I am committed to inspiring a diverse student body to cultivate a folkloristic lens on social life. I am equally committed to encouraging my students from the very beginning to engage critically and reflexively with how and for whom we produce knowledge as folklorists. Diversifying our syllabi, as I have learned through years of teaching, is not simply a matter of presenting a variety of cultural expressions from an ever-increasing variety of groups. Neither is it a matter of including more authors of color on our reading lists, although there remains much work to do in this regard. It is also crucially about how we frame our discussions of difference within an analysis of power, history, and the production and consumption of knowledge.

I often begin my Introduction to Folklore classes by showing an amusing two-and-a-half-minute video produced by Folk Arts Everywhere (WeAreThe-Folk, 2010). The video offers a quick series of clips in which people of diverse ages, genders, races, and languages in various public and semipublic settings grapple with the question, Who are the folk? Responders move from utter confusion to oddball guesses to more serious answers—"Same culture, same religion," "Like-minded people," "My family, my folks"—to a quickening chorus of "Everyone." The final shot presents this well-known quotation by Alan Dundes: "Who are the folk? Among others, *we* are!" (1978, 20).

The Folk Arts Everywhere video introduces notions of difference into Dundes's expansive, present-and-future-focused definition of the social base of folklore,[1] but is it sufficient? In this chapter, I return to Dundes's (1978) widely taught essay to consider not only what he achieved for our field but also what he overlooked or obscured in that work.[2] Whereas "Who Are the Folk?" can be read as offering a form of intersectionality devoid of an analysis of power, we can incorporate the insights of Black cultural studies and postcolonial theories even in the introductory classroom to produce a more critical folkloristics for the contemporary world. In the Folk Arts Everywhere video, a middle-aged man seated at a casual dining place delivers the penultimate statement: "Everybody's the folk. I believe that. Everybody's equal." Like him, our college-age students may believe in social equality, but ample evidence to the contrary exists. How might our definitional concepts balance the impulse to celebrate our shared humanity with a commitment to advancing social justice in a profoundly unequal world? And given the predominantly white racial makeup of our professional discipline, how might instructors incorporate nonfolklore texts by authors of color into our classrooms in order to better address and attract a diverse student body?

One text that I have found productive in problematizing mainstream conceptions of the folk is Euzhan Palcy's ([1983] 2004) film *Sugar Cane Alley*. Based on Joseph Zobel's ([1950] 1980) memoir, a text that became emblematic of national identity on the island of Martinique, the film constructs an intimate rural lifeworld through songs, games, tales, and expressions of belief that contrast with the lessons of the colonial schoolroom. Simultaneously, the film visually and discursively interrogates what it means to identify as Black in a white-defined, white-controlled, racist colonial context. A performance-oriented reading of the filmic folklore in *Sugar Cane Alley* offers students a more complex understanding of the internal dynamics of group formation than the general contrast between an "oral" and a literate world that most literary and film critics discern in Zobel's work and subsequently apply to Palcy's adaptation. Through visual storytelling and aesthetics, Palcy creates a Caribbean imagined community that continually calls out systemic injustice.

Why turn to film to discuss folklore within a social justice framework? Many folklorists have contributed to our understanding of the mechanisms by which the voices of marginalized groups have been delegitimized. Carl Lindahl's (2012) essay on the legends of Hurricane Katrina comes to mind, as well as Barre Toelken's (2003) eloquent prologue to his collection of Native American folklore of the western United States. These texts are widely known and used in the folklore classroom, but to rely only on such texts conveys the idea to students that folklorists are the necessary white translators for the marginalized, a perspective that neither scholar referenced above would support. Given the lack of diversity in our profession, we need to look beyond the many excellent texts—both theoretical and ethnographic—that mostly white folklorists have produced in order to more effectively center marginalized perspectives in our teaching.

A brief review of the essay-length formulation of Dundes's "shared identity" thesis provides a baseline for understanding its noncritical version of intersectionality, which we, as faculty introducing the field to new students, can problematize through juxtaposing it with other theories of identity from both within and outside folklore studies. Dundes begins his argument by reviewing nineteenth-century European definitions of the folk as peasants.[3] Contesting the idea that folklore is rooted in a cultural past, Dundes focuses on its continuing relevance and function as "a socially sanctioned framework for the expression of critical anxiety-producing problems as well as a cherished artistic vehicle for communicating ethos and worldview" (1978, 9). This present-focused description and the examples from mainstream culture that Dundes provides to support his argument operate at a level of generality that ignores questions of stigma, difference, and exclusion.

By positing that the folk are *any group of people whatsoever* who share at least one thing in common," Dundes offers a definition that is both expansive and antiessentialist (1978, 7). Rather than focusing on groups defined by biological characteristics, Dundes highlights volitional and even part-time group membership. Since any one person participates in multiple groups, the relative importance to that individual of any one identification must be determined rather than assumed. Moreover, pointing to the phenomenon of code-switching, Dundes argues that identity is inherently flexible. These ideas partially align with notions of intersectionality developed by feminist scholars of color, critical race theorists, and postcolonial theorists (Anzaldúa 1987; Bell 1973, 1987, 1992; Collins 1990; Collins and Bilge 2016; Crenshaw 1989, 1991; Crenshaw et al. 1995; Delgado and Stefancic 2017; hooks [1984] 2000; Hull et al. 1982; Williams 1988), but Dundes ignores the power dynamics that allow some groups to define others in ways that reduce their capacity for self-expression. In a later essay that recycles much of the argument in "Who Are the Folk," he acknowledges two nonvolitional identity categories: sex and race. Nevertheless, he concludes by reasserting his notion that all groups constitute themselves through folklore in much the same way: "[Folklore] is actually one of the principal means by which an individual and a group discovers or establishes his or her identity" (1983, 259).[4]

Although other folklorists quickly contested Dundes's "shared identity" thesis by pointing out that many folklore genres presuppose substantial differences in identity between performer and audience (Bauman 1971; Abrahams 1981), these interventions did not take up questions of social inequality as a factor in group identity formation. Self-fashioning remained central to the verbal-art-as-performance orientation, a perspective that highlights performer agency.[5]

As Dundes and others were redefining the central concepts of the discipline, folklorists of color were identifying the potential distortions that researchers who were not members of the groups they were studying had introduced into their descriptions of those groups, particularly across differences that also constituted lines of privilege. Américo Paredes (1977), for instance, discerned the operation of social prejudice in many of the pronouncements by white Anglo scholars about

Mexican Americans and Mexican American culture. Specifically, he argued that these scholars' literal interpretations of spoken language often distorted speakers' messages by failing to understand nuance, metaphor, and humor as elements of a community's ways of speaking. This lack of linguistic competence combined with unexamined prejudice proved to be a lethal combination for scholarship on Mexican Americans.[6] John Roberts (1993) pointed out retrospectively that white scholars had often used interpretive frames that highlighted deviance and pathology to describe Black performance repertoires. Moreover, those scholars who focused on the folklore of mainstream groups might overlook differences in the repertoires of groups living outside the mainstream. For example, Patricia Turner (1993) recognized that urban legends circulating in the North American Black community were unlikely to be shared across racial lines, making them all but invisible to white folklorists and allowing Black community members to retain control over their meaning.

When Dorothy Noyes ([1995] 2016) updated the folkloric notion of group, she recognized difference, unequal access, and unequal influence as part of the collective display events that produce social imaginaries.[7] Subsequently, Noyes ([2006] 2016) pointed to intransigent power asymmetries that govern the contemporary world. In the contests among nations, she observed, richer countries continue to appropriate material resources from poorer countries, leaving them with "culture" as a compensatory but ultimately unsustainable form of wealth. She argued forcefully that folklorists can support the continuity of marginalized people's culture only by supporting their right to live and be heard. In these formulations, she draws inspiration from postcolonial writer-theorists, who recognize culture as the ground for life itself. Kenyan Ngugi wa Thiong'o (1993) puts it this way:

> Culture has rightly been said to be to society what a flower is to a plant. What is important about a flower is not just its beauty. A flower is the carrier of the seeds for new plants, the bearer of the future of that species of plants. If economic and political liberation are essential for our liberation, equally the liberation of our cultures, our feelings, values, outlook, are a necessary measure of the true extent of that economic and political liberation. Or put it another way: if culture is the product of the totality and continuity of our economic and political struggles, it is also a contributor, a reflection, and a measure of the success of those struggles (57).

For groups who have been stigmatized through a centuries-long experience of economic, political, and cultural domination, regaining initiative after a period of sterile imitation of foreign models, as Aimé Césaire ([1955] 1972) had already argued, remains a central and enduring challenge to maintaining and furthering group identities. Culture in this sense functions not simply as a means to express anxieties or project worldviews. It is the progenitor and sign of the ongoing struggle to reproduce and legitimate cultural difference within a system where such difference is consistently devalued.

Martinican writer-theorist Éduoard Glissant has developed the twin ideas of opacity and relation to propose a new way of valuing and acting across difference. For Glissant ([1990] 1997), Western European domination of groups regarded as "other" was motivated by a drive to understand them, to reductively render transparent what the Europeans initially found to be opaque. He proposes instead that people have the right to remain opaque to one another (and indeed to themselves). For Glissant, however, opacity does not prevent acts of solidarity, where new identities emerge from the networks formed through people acting and experiencing things in common. Postcolonial theorists, then, generally regard cultural identity as an ongoing assertion of difference against the attempts of others to define, determine, or contain it.

More recently, John Roberts (2008) has warned that the desire of some in our discipline to construct an apolitical, atemporal "grand theory" of vernacular creativity has compromised folklore's ability to draw productively from and to be taken seriously by newer academic interdisciplines, such as postcolonial studies, African American studies, and other ethnic studies formations. Scholars in these fields go beyond celebrating the marginalized to contest and dismantle the structures that reproduce relations of privilege and marginality in the first place. One powerful way of inserting an understanding of power into our understanding of group identities is the concept of intersectionality.

### INTERSECTIONAL IDENTITIES AS DEVELOPED IN FEMINIST OF COLOR AND CRITICAL LEGAL STUDIES

The idea of intersectionality emerged in North America in the 1980s in two overlapping contexts: feminist activism and critical race theory, a partner field to critical legal studies. On the one hand, activist women of color lodged a forceful critique against a feminist movement that perhaps unwittingly universalized a white, middle-class experience of gender oppression. The volume *All the Women are White, All the Blacks are Men, but Some of Us Are Brave* conveys in its title the erasure of marginalized groups within marginalized groups as an overlooked element in social struggle (Hull et al. 1982). In a similar vein, bell hooks ([1984] 2000) challenged white feminists' singular focus on gender oppression, because it failed to take into account the lived experience of Black women in the civil rights movement, who had engaged Black men as allies in a common struggle. A few years later, Gloria Anzaldúa's (1987) genre-bending work evoked the multiple and overlapping forms of oppression that the author's intersectional identity—Chicana, lesbian, working class, and bilingual—entailed. She argued that the key to personal liberation lay in embracing cultural fluidity and in recognizing that pure categories of identity are an ideological fiction that works to discipline and contain one's subjectivity.

Black legal scholar Kimberlé Crenshaw (1991) codified these ideas in the term *intersectionality*, which acknowledges the ways in which one's membership in different groups is not simply additive but creates different kinds of experiences, perspectives, and forms of oppression. Intersectionality recognizes that any social category—race, class, gender, sexuality, and so on—contains a multitude of incommensurable positions and experiences within it and that these categories work together rather than separately to construct relations of privilege and oppression.[8] An intersectional perspective, one that develops by centering the experience of the most marginalized rather than the most privileged members of a group, offers a more comprehensive and inclusive approach to social justice than one that is narrowly focused on a single issue.

The idea of centering marginal perspectives, of viewing problems from the perspective of those most affected by them, also offers epistemological advantages (Harding 1993). Recognizing that privilege carries with it a certain blindness to the perspectives of others, centering the marginalized perspective allows for the kind of reflexivity from which new, transformational thinking can occur.[9] If we recognize that Dundes's expansive definition of folklore develops from and engages a mainstream perspective, then we can also recognize that it might overlook or obscure the special dynamics that negatively affect groups who find themselves outside the mainstream.

As Black feminists were modifying the notion of multiple group affiliations by infusing an analysis of power into the concept, critical race theorists such as Derrick Bell and Richard Delgado were rethinking how legal structures of power affected people of color. Distressed by the lack of progress that the incremental approach of the civil rights movement had achieved, these scholars launched a forceful attack on the liberal idea of a level playing field, demonstrating that it masks continuing inequalities that replicate and exacerbate differences based on race, harming Black people as a group (Bell 1973; Delgado and Stefancic 2017; Crenshaw et al. 1995). Moreover, they argue that white supremacy, rather than being a social ill that exists in spite of the law, is ingrained in our current legal system. In order to transform a structure that privileges whiteness, they argue that the system should be reimagined from the perspective of the Black subject. Recognizing that this perspective has been available almost exclusively through the lens of white scholars and artists, critical race theorists imbue the task of telling a Black story of the Black experience with a sense of urgency.[10] In two widely read works, Bell (1987, 1992) pioneered the use of metaphorical fictions to uncover the enduring effects of racism on Black people. In her influential essay "On Being the Object of Property," legal scholar Patricia J. Williams (1988) powerfully combines personal and family memoir with a consideration of legal personhood to demonstrate the continuing legacy of slavery in the contemporary world. This emphasis on storytelling in critical race theory offers a productive overlap with the kind of folklore research that brings the perspectives of the marginalized into dialogue with mainstream perspectives.

To sum up, as Dundes worked to distance his concept of the folk from history in order to pursue a present-and-future focus, North American critical race theorists highlighted the enduring nature of inequalities, historically established before marginalized people were granted rights and personhood. While the folkloristic concept of group that we have inherited from Dundes and that we continue to promulgate in the introductory classroom stresses volitional identities forged through participation and performance, Black studies scholars focus on unchosen, stigmatized identities. Recognizing these identities as social constructions born of historical relations of privilege and oppression, these scholars nevertheless argue that they continue to matter in the ongoing replication of social inequality. Creating a more critical folkloristics in our classrooms requires engaging and incorporating these theoretical perspectives into our canon.

In the Caribbean context, many of these same ideas were developing in the twin effort to decolonize the majority world mentally and politically, an effort spearheaded by three generations of Martinican activist writers, among countless others around the world. In the 1930s and 1940s (the period represented in the film *Sugar Cane Alley*), against the background of a racist French colonialism, Césaire developed a transnational cultural movement he called *Négritude*. in dialogue with Senegalese activist and writer Léopold Sédar Senghor. The founders of Négritude recognized a philosophical and aesthetic connection between Africans and those living in diaspora despite their historical differences. For Césaire ([1955] 1972), Négritude was an affirmation of the civilizational values of the Black world in the face of a colonial educational structure that demanded assimilation to an exclusively white concept of civilization. His aim was to decontaminate the idea of Blackness and of African roots for colonized people as well as to recognize a shared historical predicament among people of African descent around the world. In *Black Skin, White Masks*, first published in 1952, the psychiatrist and revolutionary Frantz Fanon (1967) elaborated on how the demands to assimilate to a white model contributed to the Black subject's loss of a sense of a unified self. This fractured identity is manifested in Caribbean literature of the period as a kind of disabling madness. However, Fanon believed it was possible to resist this process by embracing a revolutionary, future-oriented Black identity as opposed to returning to some primordial precolonial ideal, a folklore, as some versions of Négritude had suggested. He states, "A national culture is the whole body of efforts made by a people in the sphere of thought, to describe, justify and praise the action through which that people has created itself and keeps itself in existence" ([1963] 1968, 233). Just as critical race theorists argued that the scholar should not just study structural racism but should work to dismantle it, Fanon argued that poets could not stand outside of the concrete struggle for the liberation of colonized and formerly colonized people.

Nielsen (2013) argues that the implied essentialism of the proponents of Négritude is a strategic one, used to instill pride in the group and counteract the debilitating effects of colonial relations on individual and group subjectivities. She points out that Fanon, like North American critical race theorists, recognized race as a social construction that nevertheless continues to have material effects in the world. Indeed, subsequent generations of Caribbean theorists have moved beyond the ahistorical and essentializing tendencies of Négritude to recognize and value multiple, intersecting cultural influences and to reject the idea, echoing Anzaldúa and others, that pure categories ever existed in the first place. Édouard Glissant, for instance, champions creolization, or intercultural borrowing, as producing positive diversity rather than being a sign of cultural degradation.[11] He argues, "Creolization is not an uprooting, a loss of sight, a suspension of being. Transience is not wandering. Diversity is not dilution" (2008, 82). For Glissant ([1990] 1997, 143–144), Caribbean identities are more fruitfully understood as relational—emerging from territorial mobility and the absorption of many cultural influences—rather than rooted in long association with a particular homeland, as discourses of indigeneity propose. Determined to replace the individual quest for identity with an understanding of the dynamically forming group, Glissant, borrowing from Deleuze and Guattari, argues that older ideas of relatedness based on the model of roots and branches should be replaced by a more rhizome-like conception of connectedness, not just for Caribbean people but also for those in the rest of the Americas and, indeed, the world. As I will show below, Palcy's ([1983] 2004) reworking of Zobel's story in the film *Sugar Cane Alley* simultaneously offers a positive, affirming image of rural Black identity, recognizes the different levels and sources of oppression within an already marginalized and oppressed group, and lays bare the unjust and unequal relations that continue to hobble cultural flourishing. It provides a way to discuss group identities for marginalized people both as positive and volitional and as unchosen obstacles to individual and group thriving. By offering a portrait of this complex reality to a broad audience, Palcy both affirms Martinican identity and invites a broader identification with and connection to the particularities of the Martinican case.

## THE PERFORMANCE OF IDENTITY AND FILMIC FOLKLORE

Folklorists have long understood the benefits of studying fictional and semi-fictionalized works, such as those produced by Thomas Hardy and Zora Neal Hurston, because they construct the ethnographic context for performances of folklore that is otherwise difficult to capture and convey (Webber 2015, 19, 68).[12] Fictional films permeate contemporary life, and the images they convey can exert a power over memory equivalent to that of lived experience (Zhang 2005). Thus, individuals searching for a sense of their own cultural identity may be as affected by filmic representations of heritage as by the practices of which they have firsthand knowledge.[13] In addition, students interested in learning about people different from themselves may form their associations based on characters they know only through film. Indeed, with practices of online viewing, the influence of film in constructing social imaginaries will only increase. In the context of fifth-generation, "root seeking" Chinese and Chinese diaspora directors, Juwen Zhang (2005) notes that directors take considerable license in deploying traditional symbols, practices, and story lines. He offers the term *filmic folklore* to identify these folklore-like performances, and he cautions viewers against taking filmic representations of the past as mirrors into a lost world or simply mining films for traditional motifs.[14] Instead, we must attend to how filmmakers adapt folkloric materials to the overall message they wish to convey. In other words, we can read a film as an interpretation of rather than a container for the folklore it presents. We can examine how a given director uses folklore as a vehicle for particular arguments, but, given the complex and polysemous nature of film, we can also examine the serendipitous effects of those choices as well.

I have used *Sugar Cane Alley*, Palcy's ([1983] 2004) film adaptation of Zobel's ([1950] 1980) memoir of growing up in rural Martinique, for over twenty years in my introductory classes and have found it to be a constantly generative text, as my students and I continue to discover new dimensions to this coming-of-age classic. Zobel's autobiographical novel was written within the tradition of Négritude, a philosophical, political, and literary movement, as I have mentioned, that was formed in reaction against the colonial-era erasure and degradation of the African roots of African-descended peoples. The novel quickly became required high school reading in Martinique, Guadeloupe, and Senegal. Unlike other authors of the period, Zobel aspired to a form of social realism that avoided direct political critique, relying instead on the compelling nature of the injustices he narrates to move the reader's conscience. Palcy grew up on the island and read the work at age fourteen; at twenty-eight, she returned from her studies in Paris to render the story in film. With the exceptions of Darling Legitimus, playing M'Man Tine, and Douta Seck, playing Médouze, Palcy relied on nonprofessional actors, who were recruited from the very neighborhoods the film depicts (Costanzo 1992). As these children play 1930s-era versions of themselves, Palcy inhabits the position of the film's protagonist, not by penning a scholarship-winning autobiographical essay, as the young José Hassam does, but by producing her own first film to critical acclaim.[15] Thus, through a series of textualizations Zobel's childhood experiences have become a collective story of Martinique.

The novel functions as a bildungsroman, following the young José from his rural childhood to his escape from poverty through schooling, which entails a physical journey from fields to village to colonial capital; it also depicts his formation as a writer, who ultimately uses his French literacy to conjure a Créole reality that contests disparaging white definitions of Black subjectivity. José benefits from the mentorship of an elderly cane worker, Médouze, who tutors him both on the importance of nature and on his ancestral history, as well as from the sacrifices his mother and grandmother make to ensure he is formally schooled. These "home" influences complement the lessons he receives from his teachers so that José is able to avoid developing the self-alienating, Black inferiority complex that Fanon (1967) identifies with colonial schooling. Written at a time when Martinique was gaining a measure of autonomy from France, Zobel's work expresses confidence that assimilation through schooling can positively transform the Black experience[16] (Kande 1994; De Souza 2002). Palcy's adaptation presents a more nuanced, intersectional understanding of the uses of and obstacles to formal education.

The thirty-three-year gap between the novel and film accounts, perhaps, for the difference in their ideological thrust. Critics agree that Palcy brings out the political implications of Zobel's memoir and provides a feminist lens to the story of a young boy's escape from poverty (Gaudry-Hudson 2003; Ebrahim 2002; Durham 1999; Haley and Warner 1997). Film scholars have generally focused on the changes Palcy introduces in her liberal adaptation of Zobel's text: she consolidates the novel's mother and grandmother into the figure of Ma'Tine;[17] she lengthens and deepens the influence that Médouze has on the young José;[18] she introduces the theme of mixed-race identity by inventing a mulatto character, José's friend Léopold;[19] she inserts an intersectional analysis by contrasting José's experience with that of his girlfriend Tortilla;[20] and she modifies José's own character from the passive experiencer to an active and sometimes rebellious figure in the film.[21]

Although Zobel's title indicates that his story is more communal than individual, and though he translates the rich oral dimensions of rural Créole life into his French-language novel, Palcy accentuates the communal aspects of the story even further.[22] In fact, she provides a dedication at the beginning of the film to "all the world's Black Shack Alleys," making a story rooted in the particularities of colonial-era Martinique stand for a broader socioeconomic reality. Thus, she challenges viewers to recognize the majority of the world's people, who continue to live in grinding poverty, as conscious subjects with distinctive values, desires, and aspirations that deserve to be recognized and cultivated. Moreover, she renders the lifeworld of Black rural workers through a set of rich and varied visual and verbal performances of filmic folklore. Film and literary scholars have generally viewed the folklore in both texts as functioning to evoke an oral world that contrasts with that of the schoolroom and have focused most specifically on the griot-like lessons of Médouze (Kande 1994; Durham 1999). Carolyn Durham, for example, quoting Guadaloupean novelist Maryse Condé, sees the chants, songs, charms, riddles, and tales as "a pedagogy of survival in a hostile environment" and Médouze's greater presence in the film as "a countervailing force to that of the school and French colonial culture, so that José is able to move from one geographic/cultural space to the other with the fluidity of a hybridized identity" (1999, 148).[23]

What film and literary critics miss in their broad and, we might add, outdated understanding of folklore as "orality" are the idiosyncratic and sometimes contrasting ways that Palcy deploys verbal and nonverbal folklore forms in her film. Consistently, the oral filmic folklore provides the vehicle for Black Shack Alley residents to recognize and name their oppressor. Rather than offering an escape from reality or a picturesque accommodation to a situation of injustice, the oral filmic folklore conveys straightforward resistance without the kind of coding or signifying that folklore and literary scholars would expect to see in the oral forms of marginalized groups (Gates 1988; Glissant 2008; Radner and Lanser 1993). In other words, the filmic folklore is more didactic and less playful than folklore collected ethnographically, allowing the viewing audience direct access to messages that might be shared only within the group in real-life circumstances.[24] A set of embodied practices complement the oral arguments, practices that accentuate the agonistic world of the sugar mills and that force a recognition of the materiality of the body as a central aspect of identity.[25]

The film opens with shots of a series of thirteen sepia-tinted photographic postcards as a visual metaframing of the dominant colonial narrative. The postcards depict daily life in 1930s-era Martinique and are accompanied by a jaunty ragtime melody, perhaps from a player piano. We see the bustling city of Fort-de-France, a white military regiment on parade, a line of people with baskets on their heads disembarking from a ship, a tranquil rural village, a large family of Black workers outside their thatch-roofed wooden house, and finally, workers cutting cane. The static, conflict-free reality evinced through this collection of snapshots, however, is immediately challenged in the first action scene, which begins with an aerial shot of the cane workers' living quarters. In a voiceover, the young José explains that summer vacation has begun, and the children are anxiously awaiting their parents' departure so that they may be free. Ma'Tine hoists her hoe to her shoulder and warns José not to do anything that will make her angry when she returns. He kisses her on the cheek, and she leaves with the other adults. José's companion, Tortilla, runs into the foreground, shouting, "They're gone," and the scene cuts abruptly to a medium shot of a mongoose and a black snake fighting in a cage. As the band of children yell excitedly, egging the creatures on, the camera angle shifts to contemplate the fight from behind their jostling bodies. Another cut shows Tortilla running to find José at the creek. She warns him of what he's missing and asserts she will claim his watch if the mongoose wins. José refuses, saying his friend Carmen has given him the watch, which he wears around his neck. José and Tortilla return to the fight, the mongoose kills the snake, Tortilla tries to grab the watch, and she and José roll wrestling to the ground.

Rather than providing a verbal example of folklore that would signal our entry into what literary critics have called the world of orality, the initial action of the film offers the visceral excitement of a traditional game.[26] The mongoose and snake are natural enemies, the one pitting his speed and agility against the other's venom. But the children orchestrate the deadly combat for their own amusement. The scene functions to underline for the viewer the apparently natural but unfair brutality of the world they are entering, as well as the fascination the children have with conflict. Thus, Palcy immediately challenges the colonialist, picture-postcard assumption that island life is harmonious in its variety, each one contented with his lot. That José and Tortilla imitate the animals in their own brief fight aligns them visually with this state of nature, where victory goes to the fiercest rather than to the most deserving. By the end of the day, the band of children have broken a bowl, Ma'Tine's only remembrance of her deceased daughter, and she beats José for it, in spite of Tortilla's making him a charm ("Three knots in a blade of grass, you'll be saved"). Although this charm and the magical chant that the other children have offered earlier are ineffective in warding off the beating, these gestures demonstrate a solidarity among the children that reassures José that he is not alone. Nevertheless, his "group" identity as enacted through folklore is an imperfect defense against injustice. Moreover, his participation is anything but volitional, as the Dundes definition of the folk implies. Instead, the group forcefully incorporates José into their project.

In the next scene, presumably the following day, we encounter a tableau of workers and managers in the cane fields. The managers are dressed in smart uniforms, are lighter skinned than the workers, and display their own internal ranking: one mounted on a horse gives an order to one astraddle a pony, who transmits it to a man on the ground, who yells the command, all within earshot of the workers. This visual representation of the caste-like structure of domination simultaneously renders it ludicrous. Concerned that the cane cutters aren't working quickly enough, one manager threatens to fine a man for peeing. After loudly defending himself, this worker begins a chant that simultaneously broadcasts his unfair treatment and synchronizes the workers, speeding up the work. The managers don't react, indicating that they don't understand or are invested in pretending not to understand Créole. This scene sets up a pattern in the film in which verbal folklore—songs, chants, tales, and legends—consistently expresses resistance to (usually) white oppression. In contrast to characters introduced later who live and work in nearby Fort-de-France, the cane workers speak loudly and angrily about the injustice they experience.[27]

At the same time, Palcy creates a strong contrast between the angry physicality of the workers in general and the more philosophical but equally bitter Médouze. First introduced as the workers line up to be paid, old Médouze is consistently shown bare chested with a cloth wrapped around his waist, African style. In this scene, against a background of workers loudly denouncing unfair fines and wage rates, Médouze peppers José with riddles that require attention to the details of the natural world. Later that evening, while the other male workers drink, dance, drum, chant, and wrestle in the darkness, José makes his way to Médouze's cabin, where the old man lies sleeping on a board. Médouze awakens, rises stiffly, pours himself a swig of rum, and then signals to José to move outside to the fire. There Médouze begins what appears to be a storytelling session with the characteristic "Cric?" "Crac!" call-and-response opening formula. But rather than producing the amusing tale José expects, the old man quickly shifts his tone, and he recounts instead his African father's account of the history of the abolition of slavery. Several critics have noted that Palcy transforms Zobel's version of this story to accentuate Black rebellion as opposed to white benevolence as the driving force for abolition.[28] The filmic and novelistic Médouze agree, however, in their analysis of the continuity of poor, Black oppression: "Nothing has changed. The whites own all the land. The law forbids them from beating us, but it doesn't force them to pay us a decent wage."[29]

From a folkloristic perspective, Palcy's use of a traditional opening formula—cric-crac—to deliver a revisionist history lesson is discordant.[30] Moreover, the scene strongly contrasts the chanting, drumming, fighting throng at the edge of the frame and the "oral tradition" that is transmitted dyadically at its center. The Médouze-as-griot analysis fails to capture the way that Médouze and José set themselves apart from the community of men in Sugar Cane Alley.[31] These men can be seen simply as a chorus, providing an "African-like" sonic landscape to the real (intellectual) action, and perhaps this is what the filmmaker intended, but they nevertheless transmit an embodied cultural knowledge that simultaneously contrasts with and supports Médouze's verbalizations. This throng knows their own oppression and lives anyway, exercising their creative and expressive capacities in the interstices of a system they cannot steer toward justice. In the film, José must literally push his way through these bodies in motion to get to Médouze, the tired figure of ancestral wisdom.

In one sense, Médouze represents the voice of Négritude. Yet even as she deploys Médouze to represent a valuable African inheritance that contrasts with the lessons of the French colonial schools, as Zobel had done in his text, Palcy dramatizes the limitation of positing African origins for Caribbean culture. At the end of their storytelling session, José fervently tells Médouze that he will go with him to Africa. Médouze, turning to address the camera, grimly replies, "Alas my child, Médouze will never go to Africa. Médouze has no one left in Africa." Turning back to José, he adds, "When I will be dead, when my old body is buried, then I will go to Africa, but I can't take you along" (Palcy [1983] 2004, 22:48–23:40; English subtitles). Thus, he reveals that their African homeland is the product of a cultural imaginary unsupported by a network of concrete, living relations. In the folklore classroom, we might pause to consider how Palcy stages the Caribbean-generated philosophical debates around an oral Négritude and a more embodied *créolité* in her staging of filmic folklore.

Médouze does die about halfway through the film. On this occasion, the cric-crac opening formula announces the communal commemoration of his passing. But the resulting performance strikes an altogether different note from Médouze's bitter history lesson. After José and the others discover Médouze's body in the cane fields at night, the scene shifts to a long shot of almost total blackness. Against this backdrop, the return of the individual searchers is marked only by the bobbing lights of their torches, as if a constellation had suddenly come to life. We hear the elongated summons of one speaker, "Eeeehhh Criic!" followed by the collective response of his audience, "Eeeeehh Crac!" and the darkness gives way to a firelit assembly in front of Médouze's shack. In sharp contrast to Médouze's stiff severity, a much younger eulogist accentuates his words with an assertive swagger, deploying humor and exaggeration to mark Médouze's passing:

> If he hid his body to die in the canefields, he did it so that we, his brothers,
> would not inherit his old sleeping board, smoothed by his old bones
> and the pipe that never left him, night or day.
> Mr. Médouze did not want his old brothers to inherit his bantam, defeated in
>     all its
> fights,
> or his barrels of gold and silver that Whitey gave him with a kick in the ass,
> saying, go on, old nigger, smelling of piss,
> saying, go on, old nigger, last generation after the toads!
> Eh Crac!
> (Palcy [1983] 2004, 52:38–53:20)

As in the earlier scene at Médouze's cabin, the embodied dimension of this per-formance produces a sense of collective belonging, a group vitality that contrasts with the speaker's verbal message about the indignities of life in the cane fields.[32]

If Médouze's greater influence in José's life offers an opportunity to explore Caribbean notions of identity forged through a struggle for Black self-definition, Palcy's insertion into the story of the friendship triad—José, Tortilla, and Léopold—allows for an exploration of questions of intersectionality. Moreover, when we consider the story in this way, we replace the singular focus on one child's journey out of the cane fields given by the bildungsroman structure of the plot to contemplate a more complicated group story in which José's success is not so tied to his own exceptionality.

On the first day back to the village school, as they wait in the corridors before class, a group of boys engage in an excited exchange of supernatural beliefs. Léopold, the mulatto student from the village, scoffs at the talk of zombies and witches. As the collective sharing continues, one child declares that white people are devils. Léopold challenges him, saying, "You don't know about whites. They've got everything. They don't need to become cats or dogs. Ask your dad if a cat or a dog sent him to work in a factory," and a fight ensues. In terms of the plot, this scene establishes Léopold's initial alignment with a white community that disparages Black knowing. Over the course of the film, however, Léopold chafes at his parents' attempts to keep him from playing with the other children, and he is ultimately disillusioned when his dying white father refuses to leave him his family name. By the end of the film, Léopold breaks into his father's sugar mill and steals the ledgers in order to prove the wage theft that the illiterate workers have long suspected. This is a very different use of schooling than José, the future writer, deploys. In place of an individual success story, Léopold enacts a sacrifice for his newfound group. In the final scenes, the fledgling revolutionary is led off, hands tied, to prison, but he is accompanied by a song that arises spontaneously from the workers who have gathered in solidarity with him:

> Martinique you suffer. Life is fading away.
> Young folk are regressing. The men and women are desperate.
> Yet we live simply. What we lack is money.
> And as for justice, don't even mention it.

The song continues as the scene cuts back and forth between shots of Léop-old being dragged behind a horse and the singing crowd brandishing their farm implements from behind a fence.

> When I crossed over the sea
> To see what was happening in Guadeloupe
> Their suffering is like ours!
> This deep-rooted misery in our guts

Who among us can tear it out?
How terrible it is
The people cry famine
Life has become impossible in this land
Yet life could be easy
Money and Justice are what is needed to end our suffering

Once again, the filmic folklore functions simultaneously to denounce injustice and offer, if not retribution, at least solidarity to its victim.

Léopold's fall offers a compelling counterpoint to the young José's rise. As Léopold adopts the perspective of the cane workers and receives their solidary embrace, José is on his way out of the cane fields, lured by a scholarship in Fort-de-France. Yet the two children are not simply mirror images. Even in Fort-de-France, José remains psychically free from the effects of white racism, as Palcy underscores in a scene at the movie theater, when Mademoiselle Flora, the ticket seller, reacting to a thief who gets away, curses Black people: "I tell you I hate them! How can I be proud of my color when I see those people fouling up every day. It disgusts me. Anyway, except for my color, I'm not Black. My character is white." A shocked José rebukes her, asking, "Why, for a trifle, are you willing to condemn all Blacks?" demonstrating that he has so far avoided the trap of identifying with his oppressor.[33]

Critics point to the strong and enduring support that José receives in his home environment, with its clear understanding of the external source of oppression, as offering a kind of protection against the corrosive effects of a colonial education (De Souza 2002). Palcy certainly focuses on this aspect of his experience. For instance, José's rural upbringing takes up fully two-thirds of the film, whereas his time in Fort-de-France is less fully elaborated. Moreover, the four or five scenes that take place inside various classrooms are far outnumbered by the lessons José accumulates in his everyday life. However, by interlacing Léopold's story with that of José, Palcy offers an additional option: even those who partially benefit from an oppressive system may recognize and seek to rectify injustice. Moreover, the film repeatedly caricatures school learning, as symbolized by literacy. For instance, in a scene early in the film, Ma'Tine brings José food wrapped in newspaper one evening. He proceeds to paste the newspaper onto their shack wall as a kind of decoration, and she asks him to read what it says. The scrap of paper is an advertisement for pills to improve one's breasts, clearly an absurdity for the old Ma'Tine, whose bones are always aching. The message is clear: literacy, in and of itself, offers no more wisdom than the oral and embodied forms these workers rely on.

That Ma'Tine brings José food at all offers a way in to the additional intersectional gloss that Palcy provides by contrasting José's trajectory out of poverty through schooling with the fate of his friend Tortilla. Also scholastically gifted, Tortilla performs well enough on her exams to be offered a chance at the same scholarship José eventually receives. Yet, in a poignant scene, Tortilla's father refuses her teacher's offer to take her to Fort-de-France for the scholarship exam, explaining that he has arranged for her to clerk at the post office instead.[34] Palcy is careful to show, however, that the difference that gender makes in the two children's lives is crosscut by other factors equally outside their control. As the eldest of a large and growing family, symbolized by her very pregnant mother, Tortilla invents elaborate descriptions with her younger sister of the dinners they claim to have eaten in a transparent denial of their own hunger. In the payday scene discussed earlier, while José happily riddles with Médouze, Tortilla and her siblings huddle around her worried mother at the grocery, as she asks for additional credit to buy a few necessities. The message seems clear. Tortilla's mother's inability to engage in family planning affects her daughter's life chances, suggesting that the cycle of poverty is not, as Ma'Tine repeatedly claims, due principally to other parents' refusal to stand up for their own children.

To conclude, *Sugar Cane Alley* offers a rich and accessible text for exploring how individuals and groups create and defend their identities with and through their expressive repertoires in situations marked by social inequality. Zobel's text offers students a portrait of the young artist's double escape from poverty on the one hand and from the alienating effects of colonial schooling on the other. Palcy's additions to this coming-of-age story offer an intersectional comparison of three children's life trajectories as well. Whereas the folklore in the film works to express a shared, collective identity among rural cane workers, one that is focused on resistance to oppression and that appears more difficult to maintain in the "modernizing" spaces of Fort-de-France, the rural lifeworld remains agonistic and riddled with injustice. As we work to develop a more critical folkloristics for the introductory classroom, Palcy's now classic film has much to offer. It provides an accessible way for students to engage a Black Caribbean social imaginary that contextualizes folklore within a profoundly unequal social world, and it offers opportunities to engage postcolonial and critical theorizations of group and identity alongside those developed in the field of folklore.

NOTES

1. This expansive definition was first enunciated in his edited textbook, *The Study of Folklore*, as "*any group of people whatsoever* who share at least one common factor" (Dundes 1965, 2; emphasis in original).

2. In his introductory essay to a posthumous collection of essays by Dundes, Simon Bronner (2007) points out that Dundes adopted a polemical style of

argument that often focused on overturning an accepted idea. This approach accounts for the power of his insights, but it also suggests a tendency to ignore those issues that complicate his thesis.

3. Why Dundes chose to counterpose his expansive definition to those of nineteenth-century European folklorists instead of grappling with North American definitions of that era is worth considering. William Wells Newell (1888), for example, in his essay announcing the formation of the American Folklore Society and its scholarly journal, adopts the past-orientation of his European counterparts in his fear that folklore is fast vanishing but identifies the cultural artifacts of four groups—the descendants of English settlers, American Negroes, American Indians, and Canadians and Mexicans (none of whom can legitimately be considered peasants)—as of special interest to North American folklorists. Newell's inclusion of non-Europeans as "folk" was met with controversy, and John Roberts (1993) argues that he promulgated a model that privileged the European folk and posited non-European groups as mere imitators, obscuring and pathologizing the African origins of African American vernacular creativity. Moreover, Newell maintained an elitist view of cultural production that contemporary folklorists reject. In his earlier collection of the folk games of American children, he asserts the proposition that folklore filters down from the "intelligent class" to more "rustic" populations, concluding, "It is altogether a mistake to suppose that these games (or, indeed, popular lore of any description) originated with peasants, or describe the life of peasants" (1884, 7).

4. Here, it bears pointing out that given the unequal nature of our society, jokes told by members of marginal groups whose targets are members of the mainstream do not function in the same way as jokes told by members of mainstream groups about members of marginal groups. Dundes did engage with issues of African American stereotyping and thinly veiled racism in his examinations of joke cycles such as the Wide-Mouthed Frog (1980) and, with Roger Abrahams, elephant jokes (1969). However, in both cases he interprets the folklore as an expression of mainstream (white) anxieties and does not engage a Black perspective.

5. See Sawin (2002) for a feminist critique of the focus on mostly male performers and masculine performance venues in early performance-oriented scholarship.

6. See also Paredes's (1971) examination of the attribution of machismo to Mexican and Mexican American culture.

7. For Noyes, the problem in the folkloric conception of group is that it refers to two distinct processes: "the empirical network of interactions in which culture is created and moves, and the community of the social imaginary that occasionally emerges in performance" (2016, 21). Whereas the second will often depend on the first, as, for example, the yearlong effort required of a Mummer's band or a Samba school creates the density of relationships from which an embodied unity in performance can emerge, these moments of unified collectivity are difficult

to sustain. Moreover, Noyes points out that the desire for social unity that is so fleetingly experienced in enactments of the social imaginary can paradoxically produce intolerance to aspects of the social body that are difficult to incorporate. Following Benedict Anderson ([1983] 2006), Noyes notes that regardless of the constructed nature of the social imaginary, it remains dangerously powerful, prompting those who identify with it not only to die but also to kill on its behalf. Here, of course, she is primarily engaging the notion of the folk as nation.

I would argue additionally that taking the Patum of Berga as the model for display events tips the analysis toward a notion of totalizing unity that is not the norm in festival performances generally, where participation may be highly segmented and compartmentalized, and where the intensity of engagement waxes and wanes rather than building to a moment of total inclusion leading to a dissolution of individuality as in the repetitive dancing of the Patum. An excellent classroom text that underscores the fault lines in collective enactments is DeBouzek and Reyna's (1992) video documentary of the Santa Fé Fiesta, *Gathering Up Again*. This film demonstrates how the languages both of collectivity and of "separate but equal" mask the continuing subordination of marginalized groups in display events. Interesting to note and discuss with students is the more recent history of the fiesta. In 2017, protesters disrupted the traditional Entrada, which reenacts Don Diego de Vargas's supposedly peaceful reconquest of the Pueblo Indians in 1692. In 2018, the festival organizing committee permanently eliminated the Entrada, acknowledging its divisive nature.

8. Black feminist theorist Patricia Hill Collins (1990) introduced the term *matrix of domination* to express the same idea. The matrix of domination arises out of historically determined intersecting systems of oppression operating through structural, disciplinary, hegemonic, and interpersonal domains. Thus, membership in certain groups positions individuals within a field of power that either promotes or constrains their expressive freedom. This positioning is multilayered and complex. For more on intersectionality, see Collins and Bilge (2016) and MacKinnon (2013).

9. This perspective is also present in W. E. B. Du Bois's (1903) notion of "double-consciousness," where the person subjected to oppression has an awareness of both his own perspective and that of his oppressor. For Du Bois, double-consciousness produces harm, whereas in contemporary intersectional scholarship it offers a critical, reflexive lens that produces a broader vision on social life.

10. More recently, advances in technology have allowed Black people not only to recount how everyday racism affects their lives but also to document racist structures and actions in real time. Unarmed Black motorists killed by police after being stopped for minor traffic violations, such as Walter Scott and Philando Castile, force the issue of police brutality into public awareness when the incidents are caught on video and circulated through the internet. The everyday, ingrained racism of white women "enforcers" was made suddenly apparent when two

different women, humorously dubbed "Permit Patty" and "Barbecue Betty," were documented calling the police to report Black people they deemed criminal in the San Francisco Bay area during the same weekend. Whereas these acts might formerly have been dismissed as exceptions to the rule, the internet circulation of these texts unleashed a slew of reports of similar incidents across the country where white women were often targeting Black children, accusing them of criminality. This accumulation of everyday acts of racism on the part of white women shifts the focus of responsibility from police to everyone. It also redraws the picture of the racist from the angry white man who shows up to white nationalist rallies, hands taped in anticipation of a rumble, to apparently innocuous women who deploy police as their weapons.

11. Indeed, folklorists have taken up this notion of creolization as a fundamental cultural process not limited to the Caribbean or New World mainland cultures. See Baron and Cara (2011).

12. Hurston, particularly, has gained posthumous celebrity status in the field of folklore. And yet she labored under exploitive conditions to collect the folklore of African-descended groups in her home community as well as in the Caribbean and New Orleans. Her dependence on her white patron and funder, Charlotte Osgood Mason, who had her own agenda for collecting and disseminating Black folklore, makes determining Hurston's own perspective on her work less than straightforward. For more on Hurston's negotiation of her various roles as an insider-ethnographer, see Hernández (1993).

13. Anderson's ([1983] 2006) initial theorization of nationalism as an identification with a social body too large to actually grasp in any meaningful way depends on the perception of a shared inheritance rather than engagement in a shared experience or practice.

14. Zhang (2005, 267) offers the practices of the Hollywood Indian as a negative example of this kind of folklore invented for film. Subsequent literature and film produced by Native Americans wryly comments on the effects of such stereotypes on Native viewers' understandings of themselves. See, for example, *Smoke Signals*, a film adaptation of Sherman Alexie's (1993) short stories, produced by Larry Estes and Scott Rosenfeld (1998) and directed by Chris Eyre.

15. José Hassam is played by Garry Cadenet. In 1984, reviewers of the New Directors Festival in New York City uniformly praised this first work, and Palcy subsequently became the first Black woman to direct a Hollywood feature, *A Dry White Season* (1989), a story set against the Soweto uprising in South Africa (Costanzo 1992). With a long list of credits in French cinema and television, Palcy's English-language oeuvre is characterized by an enduring engagement with Black history, culture, and self-determination.

16. Martinique was granted the status of an overseas department in 1946, with representation in the French Parliament, after which the standard of living for residents improved.

17. We learn early in the film that Ma'Tine's daughter has died, leaving her to raise José.

18. In the novel, Médouze dies before José has even entered primary school.

19. This character is based on José's friend Jojo (George Roc) in the novel, but his mulatto identity is a wholly new addition.

20. Tortilla represents a case in which aspects of a number of minor female characters from the novel are conflated to form a central supporting character who remains a fixture in José's life throughout. In this way, the contrast between their life paths is accentuated.

21. Christine Gaudry-Hudson (2003) points to the scene in which José takes revenge on Madam Leónce for making him late to school as the central example of José's greater agency. His plan (never realized) to go to the principal of his school in Fort-de-France to complain after his teacher has unjustly accused him of plagiarism is another important instance.

22. Palcy's characters often speak in creole, a dramatic and welcome departure from the novel, according to Marjorie Hall Haley and Keith Q. Warner (1997), who discuss the film's generative potential for the foreign language classroom. For a reading of the novel as a collective autobiography, see Pascale De Souza (2002). De Souza argues that for female protagonists in Caribbean novels of apprenticeship, schooling plays a much more ambiguous role in the successful constitution of the self than for male protagonists.

23. Sylvie Kande (1994, 35–36) argues somewhat confusingly that references to folklore in Zobel's work should not be extracted from the text and treated as folklore, by which she means specially marked utterances, because they constitute part of the everyday verbal repertoire of people living in primary oral environments. Instead, following Irele (1990) and Glissant ([1981] 1989), she argues that these verbal performances constitute and represent a mindset that opposes a collective understanding to that of the individual self of the writer and of Western culture. Referring to the novel, she points out that though the story's narrator admires his community's orality, he does not capture its poetics in his text.

24. Mimi Sheller's (2012) examination of early nineteenth- and twentieth-century travel writing, primarily of Jamaica and Haiti, identifies in those texts moments in which the controlling tourist gaze is disrupted by the returning gaze of the "natives," who assert their own agency to define the situation, leaving the visiting writers disconcerted. Whereas the characters in *Sugar Cane Alley* do not interact with cultural outsiders in the frame of the film itself, their outspokenness offers a similar challenge to white film viewers, who cannot misread the message.

25. For more on the materiality of the body in performances of identity, see Desmond (1997).

26. In the contemporary environment inhabited by the viewer, this opening scene is likely to raise disturbing questions about animal cruelty (the mongoose, even when triumphant, typically dies).

27. Noyes ([1996] 2016) has argued that those groups who are most marginalized are paradoxically most able to construct a distinctive set of cultural practices that preserves an alternative consciousness. See also Jacqui Alexander's (2006) *Pedagogies of Crossing* for an analysis of how spirituality may offer a space for self-definition for marginalized people.

28. The French government abolished slavery in 1848 throughout the colonies; however, several Black rebellions had occurred before that date in Martinique, and, of course, the Haitian rebellion of 1802 led to the establishment of the first Black republic. Palcy, speaking through Médouze, conflates these historical rebellions in order to undercut a version of history that depicts emancipation as a gift from whites.

29. Zobel's version is similar: "I remained like all the blacks in this damned country: the békés kept the land, all the land in the country, and we continued working for them. The law forbade them from whipping us, but did not force them to pay us our due" ([1980] 2004, 33).

30. The two other occasions in the film where the cric-crac opening formula is deployed are in the wakes for Médouze and Ma'Tine. In these cases, the lead speaker ironically celebrates the deceased's accomplishment in dying.

31. Note that this separate status was already introduced in the opening scene, when Tortilla has to find José and bring him to the children's game.

32. Kande (1994), working from Zobel's novel, interprets the contrast between Médouze and the eulogist as that between the African griot, whose art did not survive the Middle Passage, and the Caribbean storyteller, who has since become the emblem of a vanishing local oral tradition.

33. José's friend Carmen has an even more complicated relation to whiteness. On the one hand, he shocks José by admitting that he is providing sexual favors to his white mistress, in effect pimping himself. On the other, he mocks his mistress, implying that he is the one in control of the situation.

34. Moved by the injustice, José quietly passes his watch to Tortilla as a compensatory gift. The action parallels that of Léopold's father, who offers his son a plot of land and a ring as an inheritance but refuses Léopold's mother's plea that he recognize his son legally by giving him his surname.

## BIBLIOGRAPHY

Abrahams, Roger D. 1981. "Shouting Match at the Border: The Folklore of Display Events." In *"And Other Neighborly Names": Social Process and Cultural Image in Texas Folklore*, edited by Richard Bauman and Roger D. Abrahams, 303–322. Austin: University of Texas Press.

Abrahams, Roger, and Alan Dundes. 1969. "On Elephantasy and Elephanticide." *Psychoanalytic Review* 56 (2): 225–241.

Alexander, M. Jacqui. 2005. *Pedagogies of Crossing: Meditations on Feminism, Sexual Politics, Memory and the Sacred.* Durham, NC: Duke University Press.

Alexie, Sherman. 1993. *The Lone Ranger and Tonto Fist Fight in Heaven.* New York: Atlantic Monthly Press.

Anderson, Benedict. (1983) 2006. *Imagined Communities: Reflections on the Origin and Spread of Nations.* London: Verso.

Anzaldúa, Gloria. 1987. *Borderlands/La Frontera: The New Mestiza.* San Francisco: Aunt Lute Books.

Baron, Robert, and Ana Cara, eds. 2011. *Creolization as Cultural Creativity.* Jackson: University of Mississippi Press.

Bauman, Richard. 1971. "Differential Identity and the Social Base of Folklore." *Journal of American Folklore* 84 (331): 31–41.

Bell, Derrick. 1973. *Race, Racism and American Law.* Boston: Little, Brown.

———. 1987. *And We Are Not Saved: The Elusive Quest for Racial Justice.* New York: Basic Books.

———. 1992. *Faces at the Bottom of the Well: The Permanence of Racism.* New York: Basic Books.

Bronner, Simon. 2007. Introduction to *The Meaning of Folklore: The Analytical Essays of Alan Dundes,* edited by Simon Bronner, 1–35. Logan: Utah State University Press.

Césaire, Aimé. (1955) 1972. *Discourse on Colonialism.* Translated by Joan Pinkham. New York: Monthly Review.

Collins, Patricia Hill. 1990. *Black Feminist Thought: Knowledge, Consciousness, and the Politics of Empowerment.* Boston: Unwin Hyman.

Collins, Patricia Hill, and Sirma Bilge. 2016. *Intersectionality.* Malden, MA: Polity.

Costanzo, William V. 1992. "Sugar Cane Alley." In *Reading the Movies: Twelve Great Films on Video and How to Teach Them,* 161–166. Urbana, IL: National Council of Teachers of English.

Crenshaw, Kimberlé Williams. 1989. "Demarginalizing the Intersection of Race and Sex: A Black Feminist Critique of Antidiscrimination Doctrine, Feminist Theory and Antiracist Politics." *University of Chicago Legal Forum* 1 (1989): 139–167.

———. 1991. "Mapping the Margins: Intersectionality, Identity Politics, and Violence against Women of Color." *Stanford Law Review* 43:1243–1299.

Crenshaw, Kimberlé, Neil Gotanda, Gary Peller, and Kendall Thomas, eds. 1995. *Critical Race Theory: The Key Writings That Formed the Movement.* New York: New Press.

DeBouzek, Jeanette, and Diane Reyna, dirs. 1992. *Gathering Up Again: Fiesta in Santa Fe.* Quotidian Independent Documentary Film.

Delgado, Richard, and Jean Stefancic. 2017. *Critical Race Theory: An Introduction.* 3rd ed. New York: New York University Press.

Desmond, Jane. 1997. "'Invoking the Native': Body Politics in Contemporary Hawaii." *TDR* 41 (4): 83–109.

De Souza, Pascale. 2002. "When I Means We: A Reading of School in French Caribbean Apprenticeship Novels." *Studies in 20th and 21st Century Literature* 26 (2): 261–284.

Du Bois, W. E. B. 1903. *The Souls of Black Folk*. Chicago: A. C. McClurg.

Dundes, Alan, ed. 1965. *The Study of Folklore*. Englewood Cliffs, NJ: Prentice Hall.

———. 1977. "Jokes and Covert Language Attitudes: The Curious Case of the Wide-Mouth Frog." *Language and Society* 6 (2) :141–147.

———. 1978. "Who Are the Folk?" In *Essays in Folkloristics*, 1–21. Bloomington, IN: Folklore Institute. Reprinted in Dundes, Alan. 1980. *Interpreting Folklore*, 1-19. Bloomington, IN: Indiana University Press.

———. 1983. "Defining Identity through Folklore." In *Identity: Personal and Socio-Cultural: A Symposium*, edited by Anita Jacobson-Widding, 235–262. Atlantic Heights, NJ: Humanities Press.

Durham, Carolyn A. 1999. "Euzhan Palcy's Feminist Filmmaking: From Romance to Realism, from Gender to Race." *Women in French Studies* 7:155–165.

Ebrahim, Haseenah. 2002. "*Sugar Cane Alley*: Re-reading Race, Class and Identity in Zobel's *La rue cases nègres*." *Literature/Film Quarterly* 30 (2): 146–152.

Estes, Larry, and Scott Rosenfeld, prods. 2008. *Smoke Signals*. Directed by Chris Eyre. Screenplay by Sherman Alexie. A Shadowcatcher Entertainment Production. Burbank, CA: Miramax Home Entertainment. Distributed by Buena Vista Home Entertainment.

Fanon, Frantz. (1963) 1968. *The Wretched of the Earth*. Translated by Constance Farrington. New York: Grove.

———. 1967. *Black Skin, White Masks*. Translated by Charles Markmann. New York: Grove.

Feintuch, Burt, ed. 1995. "Common Ground: Keywords for the Study of Expressive Culture." Special issue, *Journal of American Folklore* 108 (430): 109–111.

Gates, Henry Louis. 1988. *The Signifying Monkey: A Theory of Afro-American Literary Criticism*. New York: Oxford University Press.

Gaudry-Hudson, Christine M. M. 2003. "'Raising Cane': A Feminist Rewriting of Joseph Zobel's Novel 'Sugar Cane Alley' by Film Director Euzhan Palcy." *CLA Journal* 46 (4): 478–493.

Glissant, Édouard. (1981) 1989. *Caribbean Discourse*. Translated by J. Michael Dash. Charlottesville: University Press of Virginia.

———. (1990) 1997. *Poetics of Relation*. Translated by Betsy Wing. Ann Arbor: University of Michigan Press.

———. 2008. "Creolization in the Making of the Americas." *Caribbean Quarterly* 54 (1–2): 81–89.

Haley, Marjorie Hall, and Keith Q. Warner. 1997. "Joseph Zobel and Technology: From Novel to Film to Classroom." *CLA Journal* 40 (3): 380–391.

Harding, Sandra. 1993. "Rethinking Standpoint Epistemology: What is 'Strong Objectivity'?" In *Feminist Epistemologies*, edited by Linda Alcoff and Elizabeth Potter, 49–82. New York: Routledge.

Hernández, Graciela. 1993. "Multiple Mediations in Zora Neale Hurston's *Mules and Men*." *Critique of Anthropology* 13 (4): 351–362.

hooks, bell. (1984) 2000. *Feminist Theory: From Margin to Center*. Cambridge, MA: South End.

Hull, Gloria, Patricia Scott, and Barbara Smith, eds. 1982. *All the Women Are White, All the Blacks Are Men, but Some of Us Are Brave*. New York: Feminist Press.

Irele, Abiola. 1990. "Orality, Literacy and the African Imagination." *Semper Aliquid Novi*, edited by Janos Riesz and Alain Ricard, 251–263. Tubingen: Gunter Narr.

Kande, Sylvie. 1994. "Renunciation and Victory in Black Shack Alley." *Research in African Literatures* 25 (2): 33–46.

Lindahl, Carl. 2012. "Legends of Hurricane Katrina: The Right to Be Wrong, Survivor to Survivor Storytelling, and Healing." *Journal of American Folklore* 125 (496): 139–176.

MacKinnon, Catharine A. 2013. "Intersectionality as Method: A Note." *Signs: Journal of Women in Culture and Society* 38 (4): 1019–1030.

Newell, William Wells. 1884. *Games and Songs of American Children*. New York: Harper and Brothers.

———. 1888. "On the Field and Work of a Journal of American Folk-Lore." *Journal of American Folklore* 1:3–7.

Nielsen, Cynthia R. 2013. "Frantz Fanon and the Négritude Movement: How Strategic Essentialism Subverts Manichean Binaries." *Callaloo* 36 (2): 342–352.

Noyes, Dorothy. (1995) 2016. "Group." In *Humble Theory: Folklore's Grasp on Social Life*, 17–56. Bloomington: Indiana University Press.

———. (2006) 2016. "The Judgment of Solomon: Global Protections for Tradition and the Problem of Community Ownership." In *Humble Theory: Folklore's Grasp on Social Life*, 337–370. Bloomington: Indiana University Press.

———. 2016. "The Social Base of Folklore." In *Humble Theory: Folklore's Grasp on Social Life*, 57–94. Bloomington: Indiana University Press.

Radner, Joan N., and Susan Lanser. 1993. "Strategies of Coding in Women's Culture." In *Feminist Messages: Coding in Women's Folklore*, edited by Joan Newlon Radner, 1–30. Carbondale: University of Illinois Press.

Palcy, Euzhan, dir. and screenwriter. (1983) 2004. *Sugar Cane Alley*. Produced by Jean-Luc Ormières. New Yorker Films Artwork.

Paredes, Américo. 1971. "The United States, Mexico, and Machismo." *Journal of the Folklore Institute* 8 (1): 17–37.

———. 1977. "On Ethnographic Work among Minority Groups: A Folklorist's Perspective." *New Scholar* 6:1–32.

Roberts, John W. 1993. "African American Diversity and the Study of Folklore." *Western Folklore* 52 (2/4): 157–171.

———. 2008. "Grand Theory, Nationalism and American Folklore." *Journal of Folklore Research* 45 (1): 45–54.

Sawin, Patricia. 2002. "Performance at the Nexus of Gender, Power, and Desire: Reconsidering Bauman's Verbal Art from the Perspective of Gendered Subjectivity as Performance." *Journal of American Folklore* 115 (455): 28–61.

Sheller, Mimi. 2012. "Returning the Tourist Gaze." In *Citizenship from Below: Erotic Agency and Caribbean Freedom*, 210–238. Durham, NC: Duke University Press.

Thiong'o, Ngugi wa. 1993. *Moving the Centre: The Struggle for Cultural Freedoms*. Portsmouth, NH: Heinemann.

Toelken, Barre. 2003. "Prologue: The Snail's Clues." In *The Anguish of Snails: Native American Folklore of the West*, 1–8. Logan: Utah State University Press.

Turner, Patricia A. 1993. *I Heard It through the Grapevine: Rumor in African-American Culture*. London: University of California Press.

WeAreTheFolk [pseud.]. 2010. "Who Are the Folk." Craft and Folk Art Museum. YouTube, June 23, 2010. Video, 02:23. https://www.youtube.com/watch?v=TKojQvdRtGI.

Webber, Sabra J. 2015. *Folklore Unbound: A Concise Introduction*. Long Grove, IL: Waveland.

Williams, Patricia J. 1988. "On Being the Object of Property." *Signs* 14 (1): 5–24.

Zhang, Juwen. 2005. "Filmic Folklore and Chinese Cultural Identity." *Western Folklore* 64 (3/4): 263–280.

Zobel, Joseph. (1950) 1980. *Black Shack Alley*. Translated and introduced by Keith Q. Warner. Washington, DC: Three Continents. Originally published as *La rue cases nègres*.

KATHERINE BORLAND is Associate Professor in Comparative Studies in the Humanities at Ohio State University, where she teaches folklore, global literatures, and social theory. With a focus on women and Central Americans, she has written books and articles about oral narrative, festival performances, dance, international volunteering, solidarity activism and arts, family folklore, and feminist ethnographic method.

# EIGHT

# movimiento armado / armed movement

### ITZEL GUADALUPE GARCIA

the last time jesús crossed the border he was dead. his mind was shutting down, his soul about to travel into the spirit world; he'd been a crossing people drugs and intentions all his life. finally, he was going home, leaving behind an 8-month pregnant and undocumented maricela who would not attend his burial. there was something so cruel about this, that his lover and the mother of his children would not cry atop his grave like they'd unfortunately imagined many times, that she did not have the privilege he now had as a dead man: his body, his buried, purpled abandoned body would finally cross the border legally.

my father's death was the continuation of colonialism in its attempt to murder indigenous latin america and with it ancestral memory. as a result, i found purpose in transforming the inherited and experienced trauma of the border into a method of autonomous healing through systems of decolonized spirituality. when my awakening began, the river, la frontera, began speaking to me, as it had spoken to gloria anzaldúa, *the border is an open wound,* she said speaking the truth of the border. and it is an open wound because there is an illness and aggressor. as a true child of the border i knew that wounding is to learn to heal, and to heal is to create medicine.

in this essay, i discuss the border wounds i carry and the medicine i have created. i argue that every body affected by the psychic field of the border is intrinsic in the actual healing of the border space and is a reflection of the river herself. she weaves her dreams and water through our blood and memory. she gifts to us the sacred knowledge we need to create for her liberation. we are the body of the river and our bodies are the source of wounding and medicine.

in the beginning, the river gave me a mother and a father. my mother was a healer. my father was a brujo. their magic was a sacred inheritance. but it was forbidden to me. colonialism turned all ancestral magic into guilt and demons.

colonialism transformed my father's ability to cross portals and understand water into a jesú cristo narrative, where my father was the main character. and my
mother maricela, the archetypal, all compassionate, suffering, nothing and sub-
missive mother. and who was i? but fluid in movement and body, my flesh so filled
with blood that i sang through my skin calling for a full moon.

### MY FATHER: THE MYTHIC SUN

my father left home when he was fourteen. he knew he could open portals to different worlds. he discovered his gift when he was young while he grew up in the
river, always wishing for the other side of rumored wealth and education.

the thick centers of the river had swallowed many who did not understand the
nature of portals. they got caught into the illusion of pacificity. the water could
not speak and warn them but it was a mistake to assume that she did not have a
language.

my father understood the language of water and the cycles of the river. he'd
always tell me that el otro lado would change our lives, he dreamed they'd finally
have what was promised to poor and brown people: education, money, status.
despite this, my father never taught me how to swim, i was a mermaid of the
shore despite longing for the other side like he did, i felt that in some ways this
incapacitated my ability to understand him, or understand my emotions about
him. he said we would make it out there, he'd always made it through, for me, for
mami. his voice coaxed me. i held on to these fantasies and superstitions of my
value and potential, never fully letting his intentions go.

i was ten when i lost him. my father was murdered by an american policeman.
he was beaten to death and then shot twice. he died of severe wounding to his
head. when the case went to court, racism, discrimination, and my father's illegal
status resurfaced. the first lawyer said he could not defend an immigrant. the
second lawyer was younger and hopeful.

i didn't understand anything. i had lost sense of self and faith. i knew nothing
of the world except that jesús was dead. he took with him the nerve-wracking
faith in a better future that i'd been nurtured by and held on to desperately to
provide clues about who i was. without a narrative of progress, i could not fathom
the world.

eight years after jesús's murder, i received a full-ride scholarship to the university of texas at austin, which placed me at the most unimaginable space ever:
the idea that i'd fulfilled my father's dream. i had made it through some magical
threshold. so i sought to share it with my father.

look! how much the pain of your death served me! look! i am exceptional. despite trauma, i thrive. my body like the river was filled with waters that were too

blue, too ready to be pregnant and spill over. the voices in my head said to look for my father, to quench my nostalgia.

so i did. i looked for the man who resembled my father the most in the whole university of texas. his name was jesús, just like my father. i would learn most of myself through falling in love with this boy who did not see me as equal. but he also did not see himself as equal to our peers.

jesús-boyfriend, just like jesús-father, would become both the dream and the aggressor. i saw him through toddler eyes of love. i subconsciously began to pick up where i had left off with my father, the first time i had felt abandoned. eventually, my relationship with jesús-boyfriend ended in my own confinement within the domestic space and confusing situations of rape that i could not discern. jesús-boyfriend became the provider, the male authority in my life, the punisher, the cross, the enforcer of the parameters of my material body.

i felt like i had entered the space of karma. i was halfway through her mouth without even realizing. eager to be eaten by her gaping, aching teeth. i had abandoned myself, my soul, my light had stayed stuck in my father and then jesús-boyfriend, the more light i gave the less of my soul occupied my body. and an empty body? is empty of purpose, therefore?

dead. a vessel cannot survive without light within. light cannot survive without a vessel. the ancient knew vessels were sacred, they respected the physical body. colonialism, however, attacks the body through dynamics of violence where the past merges with the present and dominates the future. in my imaginative mind, i believe there was a karmic state to this condition, i believe i have been here before. i remember the abuse, the mechanisms of manipulation. and i thought about past lives. maybe because seeing my mother, my grandmother, my great-great-grandmother, my great-aunts, my aunt, my cousin, go through abusive situations where male partners did not respect their bodies, their intelligence, their effort, their beauty, their magic, their sacred space all at the same time did feel like 500 years of past lives. my body was imaginative and experienced feelings as unrelated to temporality.

my body dictated my reality.

so i shut my eyes, when my ex-boyfriend-jesús stuck his fingers inside my vulva in the middle of the night without a warning, without permission, and i imagined myself in the mouth of karma. i stretched myself wide, my legs met the border of her teeth. my hands were tight around her uvula. and then to my wild surprise i said her name. i did what few do: i remembered.

i heard gloria in my mind, as an ancestor, as a guide, as a river-spirit manifested through words: *Coatlicue da luz a todo y a todo devora. Ella es el monstruo que se trago todos los seres vivientes y los astras, es el monstruo que se traga al sol cada tarde y le da luz cada manana. Coatlicue is a rupture in our everyday world. As the Earth, she opens and swallows us, plunging us into the underworld where the soul resides, allowing us to dwell in darkness.*

karma, coatlicue, the all-hungry, devourer of worlds and limbs and ancestral cycles, "do you sometimes find you eat too much and you just wanna, and you just wanna . . . purge?" i asked quietly, shy of myself.

in 2016, i took acid while riding a beat-down taxi cab with my then girl-friend krystal and my great mexican oaxacan healer and ancestral friend luisito, while we ate into a mango, laughing and giggling and speaking of nawales. we were on the way to meet jesús-boyfriend at some random japanese park in mexico city. i was twenty. and jesús-boyfriend and i were studying abroad together at the autonomous university of mexico city (unam).

as an outsider living in mexico city with no expectations, i entered true awareness of the space of deadness, of imaginative space, of mystery. the spirit world and what the ancestors would call nepantla, the in-between monster who converged memory and time, the third space.

mexico city is a point of universal movement, of luchas that are ancient and sacred in their roots, the presence of indigenous resiliency is everywhere. constantly, there is hope, as well as oppression and classist injustice, violence and racism, but there is hope. hope that is colorful and poetic and fluid. hope in young people with ancient memory and old people with youthful strength.

mexico city is an in-between space because it is portal to precolonial indigenous magic while existing in modern-day colonialism, neoliberalism capitalism. there is an interesting blend of past and future merging into the present. people of color of black and indigenous ancestry as well as indigenous revolutionaries and communities have maintained the in-betweenness by recreating ancestral memory through the abandoned/traumatized spaces capitalism has discarded. in mexico city, in-betweenness is a culture, it is a movement, it is a way to manifest through the margins and the blind spots of the capitalistic ego.

in my indigenous sociology class, i read a poem about the relationship i had to colonialism expressing that it was emotional, personal and reflected through the stories of my ancestors. the teaching assistant of my professor, pacheco, found my poem intriguing so he lent me a book, black skins, white masks by frantz fanon. my intellectual connection with pacheco was instantaneous. pacheco introduced me to luis and then to chanti ollin, an occupied space or squat, abandoned by capitalism rehabilitated to sustain art, resistance and indigenous memory.

at the end of my study abroad semester, chanti ollin was evicted unjustly from the autonomous home they had created under the pretense of arresting 3 people who were no longer living in the okupa. the night of november 22, 800 grenadiers broke through the windows and doors of chanti to evict the colectivo and detain

26 people, 5 were foreigners. one of them was deported. i was there for a week of barricade, but the struggle continued for weeks. the barricade was created by revolutionaries demanding the liberation of the community space with music, art and by educating the public of the corruption of then-governor miguel ángel mancera.

and then, chanti ollin passed on. i felt something leave the faces of my friends, but they continued walking creating more in-between spaces. because movement never ends, it just creates more waves. and chanti ollin was a casa en movimiento, a house in movement.

previous to taking acid, in the taxi, luis, krystal and i had discussed the mayan nawales, specifically the t'zolkin mayan calendar. according to luis, my nawal was ajpu, el vencedor de las pruebas espirituales. luis asked me if i could see any connection between myself and ajpu, the solar God: the father figure, the sun, the creative, el caracol y humano, la flor.

i said, let me see, in a small voice. my mind quickly flickering to the many times i'd felt guided by the sun, by my father, by the sunflower. i came from a pueblo con una fábrica de caracoles, they came from the gulf of mexico, as my pueblo was very close to matamoros, a coastal tamaulipan city. we simultaneously smelled of sweet and salty water, caught between the ocean and the river. when i was a toddler baby, i'd cut all the flowers of my grandmother's garden because they looked so beautiful. i knew it inside me that flowers were mine.

oh, my dad is the Tz'i, el perro what does that say . . . *el coyote, the law, the authority, the justice and faithfulness of order* . . . what does that mean luis, luis? i thought of all the times my father was arrested, jailed and harassed for disrespecting authority. he hated cops. he hated authority. he hated rules and laws. he knew he could make better laws.

luis?

when i was 13, i spent a whole summer blowing air through my mouth trying to emit vibration. my stepfather once told me, "only putas whistle in bars." my mother did not say a word.

but i knew he was lying.

because that night of magic, luis and i held hands under the obsidian sky and whistled together a song for our ancestors. a calling for universality. unconsciously, we called on the great coatlicue, on transformation, on death, on memory. on the spirit of the river. of the third space of magic.

luis's voice reminds me of the stability of cerros. it is smooth like a rock. when he speaks, his voice becomes a hand over my back stabilizing and maintaining my posture. to the mayan and nahua abuelos dogs were guides as our ancestors crossed the underworld, la región del misterio. many other ancestral cultures be-lieved in the psychopomp, like anubis, or thoth or hecate who guided persephone to hades. they were messengers and portals who knew el inframundo. por eso el perro es el nawal del t'zi, el guardian de la autoridad, de los cerros, de las leyes espirituales y mortales.

my whistle crosses over into the space where air becomes thick with invis-ibility. my whistle is sharp, high and directed, it travels like an obsidian arrow cutting the in-between space and allowing for the portal to open in midair. my whole body is an arrow. eyesight. focus. premonition.

luis's whistle is graver and thicker, where my whistle cuts space, he fills it. his vibration is dirt, blood and bridge, creating the ground for spirits to walk into.

the dog wants to say hi to you, Luis said, ending the ritual, the calling.

what?

el perro te quiere saludar.

behind me, there's a lady holding a wolf-like dog, black and white under the belly. he stares at me with human eyes, his body is tense under the leash

i blinked . . . i was already panicking. but before truly breaking down, i asked the lady the dog's name.

dante, she said.

when i was fifteen, i read dante's labyrinth. i was a child obsessed with hell, heaven and religion. to my high(er) mind, dante was a guide and a vessel. my fa-ther was like dante, like anubis, like hecate, my father had guided people through the river, through danger, through the river, thick and pregnant, he was a coyote. it made so much sense in my feeling and mind that i crumbled to the floor, holding my arms out to dante like i had waited ten years of my life.

the dog convulsed into my arms, he understood my sobs. i clung to his neck, to his fragility and tangibility. i ran my fingers through the black hair, to the absolute sense of security and magic of his spirit.

the lady said, i tried to keep him away from you, because we had passed you by several times, but he insisted. he fought me for you. and i don't really know why.

thank you, thank you, thank you, i couldn't stop whispering or crying until they left. every single one of my tears was years of oppression and pain leaving my body. like the moon, i waned, my body becoming empty of the red pain of losing my father. in one single connection, in one single release, my pain had been changed.

## MY MOTHER: THE MYTHIC MOON

today it is March 2020, i am twenty-four years old and finally closing a chapter of obsession with my father. as a woman, i spent my childhood and teenage years resolving a conflict with my paternal ancestry. should i spend ten more decades analyzing my mother?

symbolically, i embody my mother. symbolically my mother is my other half, my shadow and moon. by focusing on analyzing her, i also study the patterns deep within my psyche, and my connection to mother nature. this is a foreshadow of the future. the: before i am my own woman.

my mother looked exactly like the moon when she was pregnant with me. her skin was pale and everything about her round. when she was pregnant with me, the stars reached to embrace like stretchmarks in her belly. and my father, seeing so much beauty, plucked her from the sky. he stole her from her dusty tamaulipecan horizons and, like contraband, transported her through the underworld river so that i'd be born in the opposite side of her sky. in the pot-of-gold end of the rainbow, america gringa.

my mother never grew up from that age, she was nineteen when she gave birth to me. my mother, unlike my father, was to me an underdeveloped, one-dimensional vessel. she is my shadow because i could not (cannot) see her (i struggle to see her, i just feel her).

when our sun died, the moon was forced to find another sun. and this is truly where my mother and i will always disagree. she wanted to remain in shadow, underdeveloped and affecting me and my siblings through a mouthpiece masculine. which made my ideas of her project through a male, phallic false authority. i saw it that way, i saw her personality through the cracks of my stepdad's mouth, her willpower in his hands, her freedom in the distance of his voice. this sun outshone me, outshone my siblings and every one of my mother's functions as an independent being.

my stepfather's name was francisco. when i was eighteen, francisco tried to take my virginity. he'd rape me in different ways but would not take the social construct of female purity. and when i'd finally gain courage to speak to my mother about her mistaken sun, it would be years later. it was too late, i blame my mother for my discovery of her personality, and deep within that, i also blamed myself.

everything came like lightning shattering all past versions of myself and my body and my worth, fiercely reencountering me with my subconscious shadow and the messages i had received from my mother i had failed to see. my mother was communicating. i just had never paid attention. i did not speak her secret language.

mami's eyes were soft like an oso's. they are the color of honey under the sun. mami has the heart of a child, and when she laughs her heart comes out through her lips, lips as glossy as a porcelain doll's, and soft, like baby thumps. and when she giggles, her upper lip folds, disappearing into her gums. she has a gap between her teeth, and if you look closely, you can watch the air gently slip through the bridge, beating into thumps: a child heart, a spirit, a tiny, air rose. mami is so adorable. and sometimes, i just wanted to take her hand, soft as oven gloves, and lead her into her arms.

i wanted to soothe her insecurities. i wanted to tell her she could create her own reality, that she did not need a man, that she was the sun, that she just needed to let go of the darkness, the fear, the past conditioning of class, race and patriarchal notions. but i was mami's daughter, not her mother, or her teacher, and mami did not study the concepts i did, she did not go to university, she did not know who gloria was, she did not know what decolonialization meant, she did not know how her partner's brutal murder was part of a larger cycle of injustice, she had not traveled to mexico city, she had not connected with her ancestral past.

how could i reach her? i had years she had lost.

and when mami's eyes widen as i speak my truth, mami's child-heart experiences the terror of heartbreak, the pain we never surpass as children, the pain that keeps repeating and coming back to haunt us.

she says: you are a dog, just like your father. she says francisco is a saint. she says you're not my daughter anymore. you're a perra, just like me.

i didn't know who she was after that. of all the unnamable deities, of all the goddesses who had given birth to the earth, the flower, the rain, of all those womxn who had been spat at, insulted, destroyed, maybe i was all of them, especially my mother. rejected, discarded from her value as a human being.

the pain overwhelmed me, once again i was full. so in my fullness i learned to read tarot cards to speak to my mother, to understand her language, why she had withdrawn so deeply from my life. why i had withdrawn so deeply from her. i could not explain the distance, the gap within my heart. once again, this was the border: an illusion. physically i was whole, psychologically, spiritually and emotionally, i was falling apart into pieces. my soul was fractured and half-dead . . . this is what the tarot said.

tarot was the expressive and intuitive umbilical cord to my mother's silence and emotional unavailability. through tarot, i was able to practice my own introverted and insecure femininity, to practice what i had inherited through my maternal line to understand the silent shadow. through the archetypes, i discovered my own hidden beauty and treasures. my fullness became less overwhelming and more like transformative wisdom.

eventually, it was this maternal gift that healed me by allowing me to release, understand and transform the wounds of patriarchy, hyperviolent masculinity, class, race, and colonialism. tarot became my autonomous therapy and control over my trauma and healing and in this case political awakening, too. through symbols i learned to read what was blocked from me: my own

power, the high priestess, my own beauty, the empress, my own transformation: the death card.

intuition, psychic energy, and the way my body embodied elemental, wildish
nature completely transcended and transformed my education at a white university. and through that lesson, i understood that my mother, though respecting
my father's wishes of a white education, was much wiser than my father had ever
been. she'd been a bruja all along and through her poison and all the dreams she'd
interpreted for me growing up, all the times she'd cured me by crossing an egg
over my forehead, all her talk of santa muerte behind my grandmother's back. it
was all worth more than the scholarship i was awarded by ut austin.

but it did not matter because in my mind, i had lost her. my mother. the symbol
of my ancestry. just like i had lost my father.

### THE MYTHIC MOVEMENT: MEDICINE VESSELS

my mother blocked my number and erased me from all social media. she poisoned
my siblings against me. she assured everyone francisco was a saint. everyone in
the family chose to ignore all of my accusations against my rapist.

i became desperate, i fell into drug abuse and constant dream states where i
relived ancestral rape. sometimes, the rapists were white men. they excavated my
body for blood. i filled their skin with red, decorated them like homes with roses
and warmth and vitality. some other times it was my grandfather soliciting my
little sister's virginity, i'd surrender myself instead. other times it was my uncles.
most often it was my stepfather, raping me, then raping my siblings.

and then a different dream entered my subconscious. i remembered what i
was wearing, a long blood skirt my mother had sown for me. a black blouse that
turned my breasts pale. at this point, i was staying with her best friend, i was float-
ing without a home, having now broken up with jesús-ex-boyfriend and i'd fallen
asleep in my friend's bed, after another sleepless night.

i woke up in the dream and saw two beautiful, giant butterflies. they flew over
my head, awaiting my attention. one was blue, the other yellow.

they spoke to me through their hovering. i had created them. i was a mother. i
screamed, shouting in terror at what had escaped my body. the idea terrified me;
it was fantastical and vast and not understandable to me.

then the door of the room flung open, jesús-ex-boyfriend appeared, wearing
the same clothes as he had when we'd broken up.

i begged him, i screamed at him. look, look what i did, how did i do that?

they aren't real, it's crepe paper, see?

i was shocked, but the butterflies were still there. and like lightning i realized
the truth. stop telling me what is real and isn't.

they aren't real, though.

but they're *mine*. and it's my dream.

i stood up from the bed, the butterflies flew through the open space of the door, rushing out of the apartment. i ran toward them, my breasts coming out of the blouse, my legs sprinting bare, ripping through the bloodred skirt. for one glorious moment of bliss and wholeness, i felt freedom, absolute and soul liberating.

then i woke up.

today, i am twenty-four and when i interpret dreams for people i do readings for, i practice what my mother taught me. i viscerally feel the other. i viscerally connect and live through the other. i merge. i overflow. the river flows through me like wisdom.

working with tarot and my mother wound, i've learned that though i understand my father and mother, i sometimes cannot understand the woman i am birthing from the extremes of the border.

constantly, my reality is challenged by my inherited concepts of masculinity and femininity, romantic relationships, and oppression. these are the histories of my father and mother. whereas, i create butterflies. whereas, i desire freedom. and movement.

i birth butterflies because my soul is like a butterfly, fluidly fluttering between reality and dream world, transforming, and dying and migrating. and so that when i return to the border, i can bring spring and beauty and movement.

in reclaiming spirituality, i understand that just as my body is an extension of the river, the river is an extension of latin america. and that indigenous, long-memory, américa latina is a wave of ancestral memory (this is medicine) spilling all into the united states' border, with passion, with revolution, with vengeance (this is medicine), it is spilling her wisdom to heal the wound-boundary that is an illusion of capitalism. it is spilling through us and our symbols.

and though our beginning is small and maybe a little dark, with butterflies (and coyotes and other rebeldes), smuggling across the border a dream is who we are. is who i am.

ITZEL GUADALUPE GARCIA is a published writer, teaching artist, witch, and astrologer from the border of South Texas and Tamaulipas. She has a BA in journalism from the University of Texas at Austin. Itzel has performed her poetry, short stories, and astrological-spiritual theories around academic and community spaces from Austin to Corpus Christi to the border and Mexico City. Her dream is to weave healing in spaces of Latin American vulnerability.

# PART III

Visualizing the Present

NINE

—␉␉␉—

# Ni lacras, ni lesbianas normalizadas

Trauma, matrimonio, conectividad y representación
audiovisual para la comunidad lesbiana en Cuba

MABEL CUESTA

ABSTRACT

*This chapter explores writing the self, culture, and sexuality in Cuba through multiple voices. Mabel Cuesta relates trauma, firsthand accounts of repression, and liberation through the everyday interactions of women in the LGBTQI community in Cuba. She uses a sense of place and personal narratives to illustrate how vernacular life and on-the-ground cultural innovations in Cuba give a space, for lesbians in particular, to bear witness. She also discusses how contemporary organic and popular responses to homophobia, such as the music of Las Krudas Cubensi, suggest the continuation of a resilient and creative community.*

2018 (MABEL)[1]

Estoy en la sala de la casa de mi amigo Evelio. En cada regreso a Cuba voy a cortarme el pelo con él. Supongo que es una forma de dar sentido de continuidad, de recrear lo que era mi vida antes de marcharme. Como si no hubiera pasado nada. Evelio es peluquero desde que tenía veinte años. Adoro sus manos y el modo en que ha venido haciendo esto por más de tres décadas. Adoro el cómo conoce los ángulos de mi cabeza, los remolinos de mi pelo—un pelo que ha cambiado tanto en su textura, en su color; pero que resiste desde sus remolinos. Y adoro, sobre todo, el espacio de intimidad y reflexión que se crea allí en la sala/salón de su casa.

El escenario se repite cada vez. Somos entre cinco y diez mujeres. Hablamos de todo lo que sucede en el barrio y más allá. Evelio es una suerte de director de orquesta para nuestras voces. La suya, firme, recuerda que no sólo dirige la apariencia de nuestras cabezas, sino su interior. Lo que diga Evelio queda escrito en piedra. En definitiva, es su casa y en realidad no queremos molestarlo demasiado—no se vayan ir las tijeras a otro lado. Porque Evelio no teme gritar, vena del cuello inflamada, que él sí es maricón sin pedirle permiso a nadie. Que cuando todos andaban en el closet, él paseaba por las calles de Matanzas como si su vida fuera una vitrina abierta; dejando claro que no tenía miedo a tocar o a ser tocado. Evelio habla desde la autoridad de quien ha sido siempre consecuente con su deseo. Escribe en piedra lo que dice mientras juega con nuestras cabezas.

Es el verano de 2018 y venden en los estanquillos de prensa el "Proyecto de Constitución de la República de Cuba." Un proyecto que de manera formal será llevado a debate en los barrios a través de las conocidas organizaciones de masas (CDR y FMC)[2] y también a través de las circunscripciones y consejos populares (órganos base de la Asamblea del Poder Popular).[3] Pero ese proceso ya comenzó en la sala de la casa de Evelio. Sin permiso. Sin filtro. Sin maquillaje.

"Pues yo no estoy de acuerdo con que se puedan casar dos hombres o dos mujeres," suelta el anfitrión. Algunas caras, no solo la mía, ensayan un rictus. ¿Será una trampa? ¿Una línea de sicología inversa para hacer desatar la homofobia de las clientas? Oigo pensar a las chicas en la sala y me preparo a ripostar, a fin de cuentas no solo soy la segunda y quizás única homosexual que está presente sino que vivo en otra parte, otro país, y eso siempre facilita la retirada. Pregunto: "¿Que no estás de acuerdo? ¿Con la falta de derechos que has padecido toda la vida? ¿Me explicas?" Evelio explica. Dice que ya no hay valores, que ahora mismo, siento que efectivamente no tenemos derechos, hay mucho travesti atrevido navegando las calles de la ciudad. Que ya los maricones no son lo que eran. Que él siempre fue abierto, pero respetuoso; que no tiene ganas de ver cómo dos pájaros se besan en los parques ni menos dos tuercas;[4] que por favor dejen esas cosas para su casa; ¡que no necesita la ley! Escribe en piedra.

Otra chica, muy joven, quizás veinte años, se atreve y salta: "pues yo sí estoy de acuerdo, Evelio; a mi prima su madre la botó de la casa y si no hubiera sido por nosotros, ahora mismo andaría como vagabunda por la calle. Mi prima estudió, tiene un trabajo, es una persona decente. Y mi tía la botó. Mi tía tiene otra hija que es medio puta y se va a buscar extranjeros a la playa y a esa sí la quiere mucho. Pero a la tuerca la botó. ¿Hasta cuándo, chico? Yo si estoy de acuerdo. Que se casen y bien. Que se puedan casar y bien." Casi llora. Evelio calla. La sala calla.

### 1971 (NANCY)

Yo era una joven de 24 años, estudiaba, trabajaba como contadora principal del hotel *Capri*, estaba seleccionada entre los cinco mejores jóvenes del centro. Pertenecía al pelotón de comunicaciones de las milicias de tropas territoriales, fui fundadora de la FMC y los CDR.[5]

Un día llegaron a mi casa (estaba con certificado médico por una crisis sacro lumbar aguda); se identificaron con un carnet del DTI[6] y me arrestaron. Me encerraron en una celda en donde la única luz era un bombillo incandescente de 15 watt, un hueco para hacer las necesidades, una pila que goteaba y cuatro literas con unas sucias colchonetas sin sábanas en donde había una prostituta y una ladrona. El piso lo compartía con ratones que se cruzaban. En mi constante permanecer de pie, pegada a la pared, los sentía pasar por mis zapatos, eran grandes. La prostituta repetidas veces se daba palmadas en las nalgas y decía una frase que tenía tatuada en ellas. La ladrona me alertaba que tenía que comerme la comida que tiraban en una bandeja metálica por debajo de la puerta de la celda porque si no, me llevarían a otra celda peor—ella me hacía el favor de comérsela.

Allí perdí la noción del tiempo. No sabía si era de día o de noche ni si los alimentos que nos daban eran los del almuerzo o los de la comida. El tiempo fue eterno, vinieron a buscarme para interrogarme, me llevaron a una habitación que más que aire acondicionado, parecía un cuarto refrigerado. Yo llevaba un vestido corto, sin mangas, de poco escote como se usaba en aquella época. Estaban allí, vestidos con gruesos abrigos, un instructor llamado Mantilla y otro militar; éste último recostado a un archivo que golpeaba uniformemente con algo. Al rato ese ruido se hacía insoportable. Me miraban irónicamente. Me brindaron un cigarro, les di las gracias y les dije que yo no fumaba. Pregunté que qué pasaba conmigo y me dijeron que yo era homosexual y que tenía que decirles a cuántas personas más así conocía. Les dije que eso no era cierto, que habían ido a buscarme a mi casa, "¿con qué pruebas me acusan?"

El instructor me dijo que volvería a la celda y hasta que no dijera el nombre de otros que yo conociera iba a estar encerrada. Pasado otro tiempo—no sé si sería ya el día siguiente—me volvieron a llevar al cuarto refrigerado. Esta vez me dejaron sola por muchas horas y yo temblaba de frío; entonces volvieron a hacerme la misma pregunta "¿conoce usted a otros homosexuales? ¿dónde se reúnen? ¿a quién visita usted?" Les contesté "no conozco a ningún homosexual, no me reúno en ningún lugar y no tengo tiempo para visitas porque trabajo y estudio mucho." Volvieron a dejarme sola. Sentía mis manos y mis pies acalambrados de tanto frío, no sé qué tiempo pasó. Regresaron al rato con una mujer que me condujo a la celda de nuevo.

Cuando me volvieron a sacar de la celda, me llevaron a Cuba y Chacón; fue lo que alcancé a ver en el mojón de la esquina. Me iban a celebrar un juicio, pregunté "¿un juicio sin abogado defensor?" Era un salón grande con muchas sillas y un buró al frente en donde había un tribunal de tres militares (por supuesto vestidos de verde olivo); entre ellos una mujer. Un poco separado de ellos había un hombre vestido de civil, por su acento parecía oriental, era un testigo que ellos traían. Le preguntaron que qué tenía que decir de mí. Dijo "la vi salir en un carro con chapa

HK con extranjeros en donde también iba la hija de Rivas (el presidente del INIT[7] en aquella época). Quise decir que esa no era yo, que resulta que yo vivía en una casa de huéspedes en Paseo entre 13 y 15 y allí vivía también una muchacha muy parecida a mí y que este individuo se sentaba en Paseo a vigilarme y cuando salía ella me lo anotaba a mí.

Les pregunté, aunque no me dejaban hablar, si me estaban acusando de homosexual o de prostituta. No me contestaron y me dijeron que me podía ir, que luego me citarían.

Mi vida se convirtió en un infierno, estaba de certificado médico, pero ¿qué iba a hacer cuando tuviera que incorporarme al trabajo? ¿lo habrían comunicado allí? ¿perdería yo mi puesto? ¿mis estudios? ¿por qué me acusan de homosexual, de prostituta? Pasaron unos días y ya tenía que incorporarme a trabajar, llamé al instructor Mantilla y le pregunté si podía dar por terminado el suceso, me dijo que me presentara al día siguiente.

Al llegar al DTI me dijeron que iba a viajar, en el camino pregunté adónde me llevaban y me dijeron que el consejo de defensa social me sancionaba, por ser yo una "lacra social"; que me esperarían entre uno y diez años de privación de libertad—de acuerdo a mi conducta—que nos dirigíamos a la *Cárcel de Mujeres de Guanabacoa América Arias*. Lo perdía todo, absolutamente todo.

### LA CÁRCEL (NANCY)

Me dieron dos sayas y dos blusas de mezclilla azul, una sábana y una funda para la almohada de aspecto feo, piezas que habían sido blancas alguna vez. Una re-educadora me dio la bienvenida y me dijo que este sería mi hogar. En la puerta, una señora mayor me dijo muy bajito "cuando te pregunten di que mataste a tu marido." La otra mujer que me habló fue para preguntarme por qué estaba allí. No sé por qué se reían cuando respondía que había matado a mi marido.

Mi nuevo hogar tenía aspecto de almacén grande, con una puerta inmensa. Tenía un espacio al frente que había que cruzar para ir al comedor. Dentro había muchas literas colocadas a menos de medio metro—una al lado de la otra. Al final, los baños. Ahí puede haber habido unas 400 mujeres, sus causas eran variadas: asesinato, robo, traficantes, prostitutas, homosexuales. Era una cárcel mixta y las presas políticas estaban separadas. Comíamos en el mismo comedor; pero ellas primero que nosotras y otro tipo de comida. Si su comida estaba mala, las presas políticas hacían una protesta. Nosotras la tomábamos o la dejábamos. Protestar podía equivaler a terminar en el pozo—así le decían a unas celdas subterráneas, sin camas, con un hueco para las necesidades en donde castigaban a las que se portaban mal. Al otro día conocí a "Zapatico"; una muchacha joven y simpática quien se la pasaba en el pozo casi todo el tiempo. La vi ese día solamente. Por la mañana, todas salíamos para el patio con las pertenencias y la sábana y la funda porque se lo robaban todo.

Los días eran interminables. Como yo, había otras. Pero algo me resultaba muy curioso: el 99% tenía prácticas homosexuales y las prostitutas eran las parejas de las que estaban por asesinato. Cuando llegaba una homosexual le caían como hormigas a un dulce. Había que tener presente la sanción—un año o diez; hasta que termine su total reeducación. La que quería salir de allí al año no permitía que nadie se le acercara y mantenía una conducta intachable. La mayoría de las riñas tumultuarias eran por celos entre parejas.

Pasé los primeros días debajo de un árbol estudiando alemán. Me asustaban los pleitos entre ellas quienes fácilmente te involucraban para que te quedaras más tiempo. Allí conocí mucha miseria humana. Como me portaba bien y no era peligrosa, a la semana me sacaron a trabajar a una fábrica que había a unos diez metros del comedor. Se trataba de troquelar tapitas para los pomos de inyecciones.

La estancia en la *América Arias* sería de no menos de tres meses. Un amigo capitán fue a tratar de ayudarme y le dijeron que no se metiera en eso que le podían hacer un consejo de guerra. Mi familia hizo muchas gestiones y le dijeron en todas partes que tenía que cumplir mi sanción. Lo único que lograron fue que, por mi conducta, en lugar de estar tres meses estuviera solo veintidós días. Me pasaron para otra cárcel abierta llamada *Nuevo Amanecer*.

## CÁRCEL *NUEVO AMANECER* (NANCY)

Esta había sido la finca de Lecuona.[8] En la que fue su casa vivían las que tenían grandes condenas y no sé porque también ubicaban a algunas prostitutas. Había otras dos casas y una cabañita entre los árboles en los que Lecuona se inspiraba. Ahora le llamaban "el pabellón." Una vez al mes, las mujeres tenían derecho a unas horas de intimidad con sus maridos de la calle o presos—esta era una cárcel más abierta. Había una fábrica de confecciones de ropa, casi todas trabajaban en la fábrica. Allí trabajé alrededor de dos meses. El resto del tiempo fui profesora de matemática y español de la secundaria que funcionaba por las noches en aquel lugar.

A los seis meses me dieron un permiso de cinco días para salir a la calle, tenía tanto miedo que hubiera preferido no salir hasta que me tocara cumplir mi injusta condena. Con todo y mi buena conducta, cuando pasaron los primeros doce meses, hubo algunos problemas de orden administrativo y tuve que esperar quince meses para ser liberada.

De allí salí traumatizada, me regía la policía del pensamiento, no me atrevía a salir por miedo a que me fueran a llevar, porque sin ser una gente de la calle me sacaron de la casa y me hicieron cumplir quince largos meses, si me volvían a llevar eran dos años o "hasta su total reeducación: de dos a diez años."

Al salir me entregaron una carta para presentarme a trabajar que decía *sancionada por el consejo de defensa social a un año de privación de libertad* (quince meses). En otro renglón decía *lacra social, homosexual.*

## 2018 (MABEL)

La chica en el salón ha dejado un enorme silencio tras de sí. Quiero continuar con esta conversación. Aliviarla aliviándome. Quiero decirle que llevo años recogiendo testimonios de mujeres que fueron encarceladas, perseguidas, echadas de sus hogares y hasta de sus centros de educación por el solo hecho de ser lesbianas. Que la mayor parte de las mujeres a las que he entrevistado son, como su prima, muchachas decentes, trabajadoras . . . quiero decirle que este intento que hará la "Nueva Constitución" es de muchos modos positivo. Me angustia tanto verla tan triste que mi deseo se detiene ahí. No siento el impulso de decirle más, de explicarle que la consumación de este derecho contra el que hoy Evelio protesta, tiene motivos ulteriores; que los gestores e impulsores de su paso en la Asamblea Nacional no están tan interesados en la comunidad lgbtiq en sí misma sino en las repercusiones que tendrá la aprobación del matrimonio igualitario a nivel internacional y en el cómo hará ver a Cuba y a sus actores políticos "auténticamente preocupados" por el bienestar de la ciudadanía. Eso en el más esperanzador de los casos. Hay otro escenario posible. Uno en que realidad todo esto no es más que una gran cortina de humo.

Pero de cualquier manera hago mi intento. Algo estoy diciendo sobre lo trascendental, los derechos sobre los hijos, la propiedad, la legitimidad de que se establezca desde la letra de la constitución que el matrimonio no es exclusivo de "un hombre y una mujer" sino de "dos personas." Estoy en ello, bajándole nivel a la retórica académica y simplificando el mensaje cuando otra señora, quizás de setenta años, comienza a hablar. Dice "yo no entiendo mucho de ley, ni de derechos; pero mi hermana es doctora y allá por los años ochentas se tuvo que ir de Matanzas. Nuestra madre fue quien peor la trató. Mi sobrina, quien es ahora mismo una mujer de cincuenta años, siempre ha sido triste, reservada, como traumatizada. Ojalá mi hermana no hubiera pasado tanto. Ojalá mi sobrina hubiera sido una niña más feliz."

## 1981 (MIGDALIA)

No sabes la alegría que me da encontrarme con personas de mente abierta que no juzgan mal a otras por el comentario de un pueblo pequeño que era un infierno grande. Un pueblo al cual tuve que enfrentarme con la frente en alto, pues además del que fue mi marido, mi peor enemiga fue mi propia madre—que Dios la perdone y me perdone a mí por no haberla perdonado.

Nunca bajé la cabeza ante los comentarios de la gente, de los amigos de mi madre, pues fue ella la que más me empujó a mi amistad con M. Al acusarme de lesbiana (tuve que ir al diccionario para saber qué era eso) y hasta ese momento entre M. y yo no había más que una buena amistad y un gran agradecimiento de mi parte ya que me ayudaba con mi hija, quien era bastante cohibida en esa época.

Yo soy muy rebelde, rebeldía que nació de la necesidad de liberarme del cepo de mi madre, quien exigía mucho de mí; pero quien nunca me apoyó en nada. Fue mi más acerba crítica. Ella siempre fue muy liberal, pero no aceptaba que yo lo fuera. Mi madre tenía un grupo de amigas que, más tarde entendí, eran lesbianas: escritoras, poetas, etc.—no se si has oído hablar de L. C., poetisa de Holguín; era íntima amiga suya y así otras. Mi mamá fue la primera en acusarme delante de todos hasta el punto que consiguió que muchos colegas del hospital me manifestaran su apoyo pues no podían entender que una madre desacreditara a una hija que se había ganado el respeto de todos, no solo en el centro de trabajo sino en toda la ciudad.

Yo sentía una soledad espantosa, mi madre me separó de toda mi familia, trató de hacerlo con mi padre; pero nunca pudo. Mi padre y yo siempre fuimos muy unidos y él sí me apoyó siempre. Me casé con un hombre inmaduro y tuve una madre que era una víbora—que Dios la tenga donde la tenga que tener. ¿Qué envidiaba mi madre? Pues mi liberalismo. Ella hubiera querido ser así y no tuvo el coraje de hacerlo. Mi hija fue mi consuelo; pero en los primeros años—tal vez por la experiencias negativas de mi niñez y la forma de tratarme de mi madre—reproduje la forma de educarla que ella había usado conmigo. Fue M. la que me enseñó a cambiar mi actitud con mi hija, a acercarme más a ella. Ella me decía "no seas como fueron contigo, dale amor."

Tuvimos, M. y yo, una relación sana, llena de cariño, su apoyo hacia mí fue incondicional y eso en un momento dado me sirvió de mucho. Sin embargo, otros sembraron la cizaña en mi niña, su abuela y su padre trataron de separarla de mí; pero nunca pudieron. Ya cuando iba a casarse tuve que escoger entre mi hija y M. y escogí por mi hija pues me era muy difícil mantener esa situación.

Así que ya sabes más o menos la verdad de las cosas, sin tapujos ni arrepentimiento. Lo que he hecho en mi vida ha partido de mi pleno conocimiento y no creo haberle hecho daño a nadie con mi actuación, pues nunca fui una libertina, ni una persona chocante; pero sí exigí el respeto que yo daba a la sociedad y consideré que nadie tenía derecho a juzgarme.

Encontré en mi profesión el alimento que me hacía sentirme satisfecha de lo que hacía y di siempre lo mejor de mí y así lo sigo haciendo.

## 1988 (DAYSI, LA LACRA)

Ahí te va la historia de ser una lesbiana en una sociedad q te recrimina. . . .

Existía en la policía un sector que lo llamaban *Lacra Social*; el cual se ocupaba de perseguir y hacerles cartas de advertencia a quienes ellos consideran antisociales. Por ejemplo: homosexuales, prostitutas jóvenes que no trabajaban para el estado o no estudiaban. . . . Cuando salíamos a hacer vida social a un parque o a un cabaret o a alquilarnos en algún hotel; sencillamente éramos amonestados por el jefe de *lacra*. Nos abrían las habitaciones de los hoteles, nos humillaban y teníamos que marcharnos por el solo hecho de ser homosexuales, por reunirnos con los amigos. Sin embargo, en el mismo hotel podía haber grupos de heterosexuales con escándalos, broncas y hasta orgías que no eran molestados. Para nosotros no había ningún respeto. En las universidades cuando tenían conocimiento de que eras homosexual, buscaban el medio de expulsarte e igual en los centros de trabajo en donde no eras acogido.

Siendo joven y perseguida, a veces la policía me encerraba cuando me cogía en los parques con amigos. Me encerraban hasta por veinticuatro horas en donde el jefe de *lacra* me hacía desvestir en su oficina y muchas fuimos víctimas de abusos o manoseos. A mí, además, me pidieron que trabajara para ellos y así podría librarme de una condena de cuatro años. Ese trabajo consistía en darles información sobre los homosexuales, decirles quiénes eran. Al yo no acceder, se me acusó de contrarrevolución; por lo cual me retuvieron en la Seguridad del Estado.

Tras varios interrogatorios cada una hora, lo cual usaban como método de abuso sicológico, no pudieron probarme nada. Había agentes de ellos que se mezclaban con nosotros haciéndose pasar por homosexuales y nos proponían que pusiéramos carteles con propaganda en contra del presidente para ver si accedíamos y así condenarnos por "causa probable." Yo solo quería que me respetasen mi orientación sexual y lo dejé siempre muy claro. Muchas lesbianas se han acercado al cabo de los años y me han manifestado que ellas no tuvieron que pasar por eso; pero se les olvidó que tenían que reprimir su vida social y muchas hasta casarse lo mismo con gays que con heteros, tener hijos para tratar de pasar inadvertidas ante la sociedad, el centro de trabajo, su familia, los vecinos y principalmente para no estar en la mira del estado pues sabían las consecuencias que tenían que afrontar. Yo pasé por el desprecio de los vecinos, por los comentarios obscenos de los heteros, por las humillaciones aún en mi propia familia. Sentía que no tenía un lugar en ninguna parte del mundo y eso jodió un poco de mi existencia; aunque aún así pude resistir y defender mi identidad.

Con el tiempo y tanta persecución en los parques o locales en donde se reunían los intelectuales; después de atraparte varias veces y de perseguirte, te iban enviando cartas de advertencia y al tener varias en tu expediente, el resultado era

aplicarte *la ley de peligrosidad*[9] la cual actualmente existe y con la que te condenaban a cuatro años de prisión sin haber ninguna causa probable, tan solo por el
hecho de tener cuatro o más cartas de advertencia, por reunirte con otros homosexuales, tener pareja e ir a centros nocturnos con amigos, etc. . . .

Me aplicaron esa ley y me condenaron a cuatro años de prisión; los cuales
se redujeron a dos tras un proceso de apelación. En mi estadía en prisión pude
ver todos los abusos verbales y físicos contra las lesbianas. Tenías que trabajar
obligatoriamente; aún debajo del sol y hasta el cansancio pues ser una reclusa te
excluía de todo derecho si no eras capaz de someterte a sus reglas. Te privaban
de recibir tu aseo, de ver a tus familiares y hasta de algunos víveres que éstos te
enviaban. No podías sentarte ni tan siquiera con otra homosexual pues habría
consecuencias y como castigo te enviaban a una prisión de máxima seguridad en
donde se encontraban las personas condenadas por causas mayores: asesinatos,
violaciones, sabotaje, contrarrevolución, etc.

Fui enviada a esa prisión por no obedecer una regla que consideré abusiva.
Para mi sorpresa e ironía en este centro clasificaban a las lesbianas y todas tenían
que estar juntas en un destacamento de homosexuales pues no podían cohabitar
en destacamentos de heterosexuales. Es decir: en la calle nos condenaban por
reunirnos por tener parejas y aquí todas debíamos estar juntas como si fuésemos
un virus para los heteros. Salí al cabo de dos años y nueve meses y el estado
sería quien me ubicaría en un centro laboral. Ese centro tendría que ser algo así
como una fábrica, un puesto de mantenimiento o en los hospitales porque al ellos
haberme convertido en una *reclusa* o *presidiaria*, como aquí se estila llamarnos,
ningún centro me aceptaba para trabajar.

### 2018 (MABEL)

La señora que es hermana de la doctora ha terminado de contar, a grandes
rasgos, su historia. Yo he estado escuchándola y rumiando el relato de Daysi;
uno que escuché infinitas veces mientras crecía. Daysi es como una hermana
mayor a quien conocí justamente cuando salió de la cárcel. Daysi no quería comenzar a trabajar porque se sentía avergonzada por haber sido una reclusa, por
ser gaga, por ser demasiado andrógina; es decir "notablemente tuerca." Yo tenía
doce años cuando conocí a Daysi porque mi madre le ofrecía un espacio en casa
para venir a pasar las tardes y algunas noches. Era 1990 y aunque todo estaba a
punto de irse a un rumbo desconocido, todavía había que entrar a los cabarets
haciendo uso del formato de pareja heterosexual. De ese modo, "pájaros y tuercas" improvisaban divertidos pares. A veces el gesto era agotador y Daysi solo
quería estar en mi casa, al amparo de mi madre, quien sentía fascinación ante
todo lo prohibido.

Pienso en estas cosas mientras Evelio, por primera vez en mucho rato, decide contraatacar y a su modo excusarse. Evelio dice que claro que él entiende el propósito de la ley; pero que asimismo teme por los "beneficiarios." Teme que al sentirse aquellos amparados por el "gobierno," den rienda suelta a su imaginación y comiencen a ser "más" expresivos de lo que ya son.

Entonces decido que lo pondré al límite. Lo desafió con una invitación: "pues fíjate que Odalys y yo estamos contemplando la idea de casarnos la próxima navidad, cuando regresemos a despedir el año. Para entonces ya debe haberse oficializado la ley y queremos aprovecharla. Comprarnos una propiedad, celebrar con la familia nuestro amor. En definitiva nos casamos hace cinco años en Nueva York y no vemos por qué no hacerlo aquí. . . . Entonces, querido, ¿serás nuestro peluquero?"

Evelio sonríe, sabe que lo provoco y que empujo sus prejuicios con cierta tiranía. Dice que sí y que además lo haría no solo por mí, sino por Odalys, quien, como él, siempre ha sido muy abierta; pero a la vez muy decente.

ODALYS (1982)

Tengo diecinueve años y estoy lejos de todo lo que soy. No sé exactamente cómo he podido terminar aquí, al otro lado del mundo y en medio de este invierno. Leningrado es hermoso; pero no así los peterburgueses (no soy capaz de decir "leningradenses"). Me gustan las ciencias; pero no tanto como para estar tan lejos de mi familia, los amigos, aquel amor que me dejó temblorosa y llena de certezas por primera vez. Nada aquí me conmueve, solo ella y la amplia sonrisa de muchacha fresca y dulce con quien me tropiezo en los pasillos. Me mira. Nos hemos mirado varias veces en estos meses. Tenemos amigos en común: mongoles, vietnamitas, checos, chipriotas . . . con ellos solo podemos hablar ruso; pero entre nosotras creamos un espacio lúcido cuando todos se van y podemos contarnos la vida en español.

Ella tiene miedo y yo más. Ella tiene un novio que nos mira con sospecha. A mí ya se me conoce como deportista de alto rendimiento. No hablo mucho. No me apetece. En realidad es un ejercicio de control, de rebeldía. Sé que lo que digo podría siempre ser usado en mi contra. Creen que voy de interesante; pero solo tengo miedo. Estoy lejos de todo lo que soy. Todo lo que amo. Pero está ella.

Nos vamos de excursión a un pueblo de la frontera con Finlandia. Las muchachas deben compartir habitaciones y los muchachos lo mismo. Ella se apresura en decir: "yo comparto con Odalys." Su novio, que estudia otra carrera, no ha venido. La habitación tiene dos camas; pero cuando llega la hora de dormir ella se mete en la mía. Yo estoy temblando. Ella puede ser una espía. Ella está temblando. Puedo ser una espía.

Esto de cuánto sospechamos la una de la otra lo sabremos meses después. Cuando ya se ha peleado con su novio y se ha mudado a mi edificio, a mi aparta-mento en los dormitorios de la universidad. Cuando pasamos semanas sin dormir porque no podemos faltar a clases, ni sacar malas notas (nos regresarían a Cuba, nuestra misión aquí es la de representar dignamente a nuestro país); pero tam-poco podemos dejar de amarnos durante toda la madrugada. Ya no me siento lejos de nada. Ya quiero que su cuerpo sea para siempre mi territorio. Entonces tocan a la puerta.

La amiga que comparte habitación con ella, allá, en el lado opuesto de la uni-versidad, viene a decirle que su padre la ha estado llamando; que hoy lo ha hecho al menos cinco veces; que ella debe intentar comunicarse con él. Su padre es un alto comisionado del cuerpo diplomático cubano instalado en Madrid. Su padre nunca ha estado cerca, abandonó a su madre cuando ella era apenas una niña; pero desde que llegó a estudiar a la Unión Soviética la llama con frecuencia. Ella le dice a la amiga que no se preocupe, que si vuelve a llamar le diga que se cambió de edificio. Se marcha su amiga, un tanto decepcionada ante la respuesta recibida.

Me preocupo por un segundo y se lo comento. Ella desenfadada me besa y mete las manos en mi pantalón deportivo, me acaricia. Es insaciable. Yo respiro a través de sus dedos. Pasan casi dos años.

El padre llega un día a la universidad. Pregunta en la dirección de estudiantes internacionales dónde es el edificio de su hija y se presenta, buscándola. Le di-cen que hace mucho ya no duerme allí sino en el cuarto de su amiga Odalys, son inseparables. El padre indaga más sobre Odalys (carrera, edad, ciudadanía, dormitorio). El padre toca a la puerta de nuestra habitación.

Sorprendida ella, lo abraza y pregunta por qué no le avisó que vendría. Él me mira. Tengo mis pantalones deportivos, el pelo recogido, una camiseta blanca y unos tenis del mismo color. Todas las piezas que llevo son perfectamente ajust-ables a las del cuerpo de un muchacho. No siento deseos de serlo; pero me gusta esta apariencia confusa y mía. El padre se la lleva de allí con el pretexto de comer. Ella se viste y se va nerviosa.

Dos días después escucho que el padre ha pedido permiso para llevársela de vacaciones a Madrid. Ha pasado por el consulado en la ciudad y ha recogido su pasaporte y asimismo ha conseguido un permiso extraordinario de viaje. Todo esto me lo cuenta ella un mes después.

Me lo cuenta el día en que regresa de Madrid y el padre viene a mi habitación y recoge sus cosas. Me lo cuenta después que el padre se ha marchado. El padre que, sin que ella lo supiera, se las ha ingeniado para, una vez que la dejó instalada en su viejo cuarto, regresar al mío y decirme al oído: "si la vuelves a buscar te desaparezco en Siberia." Ella me cuenta de Madrid y me dice que volverá a tener relaciones con su novio. Me olvida durante el día, pero en las noches viene a llorar a mi cuarto. Yo tengo miedo. Decido regresar a Cuba y abandonarlo todo. Ahora sé que no soy capaz de dejar el nombre de mi país en alto.

## 2018 (DAYSI)

Sí, Mabe, se llama "red popular" es una especie de Facebook; pero cubano. Ahí te encuentras de todo. Compras, ventas, alquileres, productos imposibles de hallar en el mercado y también clasificados de gente buscando pareja. Hombres buscando mujeres; mujeres que buscan hombres; hombres a hombres; mujeres a mujeres. ¡De todo! La verdad nunca me imaginé que por 1 cuc[10] al mes, podría yo tener algo así. Vaya, no es que sea fácil tener 1cuc ni dedicárselo a eso; pero por lo menos es algo y recibes mensajitos y qué se yo, estás entretenida. De esa manera he tenido ya varias noviecitas, lo que pasa es que algunas están en La Habana y otras en provincias lejanas; pero ya tú sabes, algo es algo.

## 2019: NI LACRAS, NI LESBIANAS NORMALIZADAS

El investigador norteamericano Ted Henken, en su artículo "Cuba's Digital Millennials: Independent Digital Media and Civil Society on the Island of the Disconnected," analiza cómo la sociedad civil cubana se ha estado reconfigurando aceleradamente a partir de su entrada a las redes y cómo, a su vez, ello ha generado nuevas estrategias de pensamiento, comunicación y distribución digitales que han facilitado el debate de asuntos importantes y largamente silentes entre los ciudadanos. Para defender esta idea, presenta algunos datos relacionados con el pasado reciente y las expectativas de futuro vinculadas a dicha conectividad:

> These developments began with an increase in the number and diversity of Cuba's independent bloggers starting in 2004, followed by the subsequent growth of collective projects of citizen journalism since 2008. These phenomena have been fueled by the opening of Cuba's first public-access Internet cafés in June 2013, the possibility of accessing e-mail via cell phone for the first time in 2014, the establishment of 35 public Wi-Fi hotspots across the island in the summer of 2015, and the simultaneous spread across the island of "el paquete" (the packet), an informal digital data distribution system (Del Valle 2013). The continued expansion of the Wi-Fi hotspot plan, which reached 200 hotspots in September 2016, and the launch by ETECSA (the state telecom monopoly) of a pilot program to allow home Internet access for the first time to 2,000 customers in Old Havana in late-2016, along with its plans to offer Internet access via cellphone to paying customers for the first time in 2017, are bound to facilitate the growth and social impact of Cuba's independent media (Rodríguez Martinto 2016). (Henken 2017, 430–431)

Dejando por un momento los sustratos de trauma que aún aparecen en la sociedad civil cubana cuando se trata de discutir tanto la pertinencia de un estado de derecho para los sujetos lgbtiq como sus rizomas; parece igualmente sintomático que las lesbianas como grupo doblemente marginado desde su condición genérica, comiencen a atisbar ciertos hilos de esperanza a través de los intersticios que se abren para ellas en las redes sociales y otras formas de conectividad. El paquete semanal al que refiere Henken ha permitido, por ejemplo, que puedan disfrutar de series norteamericanas o europeas (*The L Word*, *Vis a Vis* y similares) en donde tanto los personajes como sus historias son eminentemente lesbianas.

Al plantear lo anterior no estoy suprimiendo estas mismas posibilidades y esperanzas para el total de la comunidad lgbtiq; pero es importante recordar que las lesbianas han sido víctimas no solo de marginalidad, silencio y falta de representatividad mediática en tanto mujeres sino también en tanto homosexuales. A nivel global, tanto las mujeres homosexuales, como las bisexuales y las trans, han sufrido de largas exclusiones dentro de los movimientos feministas y lgbtiq; dominando en el primero las figuras de mujeres burguesas heterosexuales y en el segundo, los hombres gays. Entre las más violentas exclusiones sufridas por este grupo se encuentra la de no ser representadas en campañas contra la violencia de género. Al respecto abunda la investigadora y activista cubana Mercedes García Hernández: "La violencia que sufren mujeres homosexuales, bisexuales y trans está totalmente invisibilizada en las campañas dirigidas a eliminar la violencia contra la mujer, pensadas desde la heteronormatividad hacia la mujer de pareja heterosexual, que siempre es violentada por un hombre: su padre, el marido, un amigo, etc." (Gordillo Piña 2016).

Me interesa entonces interconectar los testimonios de lesbianas cubanas de diferentes generaciones—esos que por casi diez años he venido recogiendo y de los que he presentado una selección aquí—con los sedimentos (productivos) de su trauma y las posibilidades de futuro que se presentan ante ellas al acceder a plataformas digitales diseñadas para la interacción social. Siendo que lo anterior ha globalizado, de manera simbólica, sus deseos y expectativas. Asimismo, me interesa presentar una conversación, muy somera en cuanto panorámica, sobre el trabajo del CENESEX,[11] la figura de Mariela Castro y el posible paso, vía referendo constitucional, de una legislación para el matrimonio igualitario. Finalmente propongo hablar de cuerpos lésbicos en consonancia con sus representaciones digitales y audiovisuales.

A día de hoy, las estadísticas sobre la violencia ejercida en contra de la comunidad lgbtiq, manifiesta en la discriminación laboral, el control sobre las cirugías de reasignación de sexo o el racismo siguen siendo "secreto de estado." Los investigadores cubanos y extranjeros que hemos asumido la tarea de examinar tales datos nos hemos encontrado con magnas prohibiciones. Incluso un bloguero

oficialista conocido en el ciberespacio como "Paquito el de Cuba," estuvo de-
safiando al gobierno en el año 2012 para que se incluyera en una encuesta para el
censo oficial a las familias homosexuales como alternativa a la composición del
hogar. La respuesta recibida fue negativa.

Atendamos entonces a lo que ha sucedido desde que en el 2006 Fidel Castro
pasara el liderazgo como primer secretario del PCC y del Consejo de Estado y
de Ministros a su hermano Raúl y éste a su vez intentara—apoyado en su hija, la
sexóloga Mariela Castro—hacer una suerte de saneamiento de imagen en cuanto
al modo en que lidia el gobierno con su comunidad lgbtiq. Nada verdaderamente
revolucionario le ha sucedido a este colectivo en términos de derechos. Hasta el
día de hoy, el matrimonio igualitario es sólo una promesa que sufrió una dura
estocada al quedar fuera de la nueva constitución aprobada en el 2019.[12] Asimismo, no hay derechos parentales, ni de reproducción, ni poder expreso a través
de representación gubernamental para parejas del mismo sexo o sujetos lgbtiq.

A la vez y problematizando más este asunto, no escapa a casi nadie la gran
ironía que constituye el hecho de que la comunidad lgbtiq cubana sea "visible"
nacional e internacionalmente a través de una representante del mismo poder
heteronormativo y censor que por más de cuarenta años la fustigó. Es decir, el
sempiterno poder de la familia Castro, esta vez representado por una mujer de la
próxima generación: la sobrina/hija Mariela Castro.

Si sólo indagamos con cierta seriedad, descubrimos que perviven aún ejerci-
cios de control policial, conocidos como "redadas" perpetradas con regularidad
contra travestis y trans en sus puntos de encuentro en La Habana. Siendo así, no
resulta difícil concluir que ese mismo poder de representación y legitimidad que
Mariela Castro propone desde el CENESEX, está entregando a los medios de
difusión un discurso pre-escrito y pre-aprobado por la nomenclatura poderosa
que en los sesentas condenaba a los individuos de clara preferencia homosexual a
los campos de concentración conocidos como UMAP;[13] en los setentas (testimonio de Nancy) los encarcelaba sin causa probable y en los ochentas los declaraba
"lacra social" (testimonio de Daysi).

Tomar el pulso de la comunidad lgbtiq en la isla con seriedad entrañaría el
gesto, con frecuencia olvidado, de escuchar las voces de quienes no están aso-
ciados al CENESEX. Además, habría que entender que ese "Centro," asociado
al Ministerio de Salud Pública (asociación que constituye en sí misma el más
elocuente de sus principios motores de saneamiento) puja por una normalización
y control de todos aquellos cuerpos que no respondan al modelo hegemónico
y largamente demodé que la tradición estalinista ha propuesto e impuesto a la
ciudadanía cubana. Como botón de muestra, hay que revisar los sucesos del 15
de mayo de 2019 cuando luego del frustrado intento de hacer constitucional el
matrimonio igualitario, el CENESEX—sospechosa y arbitrariamente—decidió

cancelar su habitual marcha por el orgullo lgbtiq. En respuesta, ciertos actores de la sociedad civil decidieron marchar libremente por el Paseo del Prado habanero. Dicha marcha terminó siendo reprimida por la policía ya que no contaba con los permisos pertinentes. Léase, los del CENESEX.[14]

La investigadora Frances Negrón Muntaner, ha venido anotando con acuciosidad algunos de los más significativos *modus operandi* del CENESEX y los ha resumido en su fundamental ensayo "'Mariconerías de estado': Mariela Castro, la comunidad LGBTQ y la política cubana":

> Si bien dentro y fuera de Cuba, la labor de Castro Espín se interpreta como una defensa radical de la comunidad LGTBQ contra el prejuicio, una lectura cuidadosa apunta a que su discurso está marcado por lo que podríamos llamar un fuerte "maternalismo" autoritario. Por ejemplo, en sus intervenciones en los medios de prensa y televisión, Castro Espín imagina las necesidades de los travestis en términos muy similares a los niños y adolescentes. El asunto no es, por ejemplo, que los travestis socialicen libremente y determinen como quieren ser (o no) representados políticamente. Más bien, según señala Castro Espín en un video de CENESEX titulado *Sexualidad, un derecho a la vida* (2005), a los travestis hay que "atenderlos," "escucharlos" y, sobre todo, "comprenderlos." (Negrón Muntaner 2016, 115)

Al margen de lo que plantea Negrón Muntaner, resulta difícil aceptar como legítimo el discurso que Castro Espín ha ido construyendo a través de declaraciones y entrevistas sobre democracia y diversidad. Cuando se apresta a declarar una igualdad de deberes y derechos para todos los sujetos que viven en la isla—con independencia de sus condiciones de raza, clase u orientación sexual—en realidad está enterrando todo aquello que pueda resultar ajeno a su propia idea de nación: una nación castronormalizada tanto para la ciudadanía *queer* como para la no *queer*.[15]

En un intento de argumentar lo anterior, quisiera detenerme en el dato de que entre el 2008 y el 2018, cada junio y como parte de la celebración de jornadas contra la homofobia, la directora del CENESEX bailó por las calles de La Habana una "conga" que como bien es sabido es un ritmo de carnaval.[16] El hecho de que sea "ese" el ritmo elegido para los desfiles del orgullo gay habanero, conduce a una breve digresión ya que impone recordar que los carnavales son desde la Edad Media un espacio creado por el poder para hacernos sentir liberados y realizados en un círculo bien delimitado y de corta duración (unos pocos días, una sola vez al año).

Entonces, no se trata solo de que Mariela Castro haya bailado durante diez años una conga de carnaval anual con la comunidad; sino de que quienes siempre estuvieron invitados eran exclusivamente aquellas personas asociadas *a* y convergentes *con* la agenda del CENESEX. Para confirmar todo lo anterior, hay que revisitar los sucesos del 15 de mayo de 2019. De igual modo, no puede desestimarse que las cirugías de reasignación sexual, continúen siendo autorizadas solo por Castro Espín, ni que sean exclusivamente concedidas a quienes se acerquen al centro que dirige.

Repasado lo anterior, interesa desembocar en las lesbianas cisgenéricas y en el cómo estos modelos de activismo normalizado no les reportan importantes beneficios, lo cual no significa que no haya grupos de ellas asociadas al CENESEX ni que no estén interesadas en la aprobación del matrimonio igualitario. Sin embargo, no es en torno a esos pequeños grupos ya alineados con el poder que propongo esta conversación, sino en torno a otros síntomas igualmente resistentes e interesantes.

### 2019: KRUDAS CUBENSI

Como otro brevísimo botón de muestra, retomo el aliento a través del dúo de *performers* conocido como las "Krudas Cubensi."[17] Para repensar con lucidez y equilibrio los escenarios en los que sobreviven las lesbianas en la Cuba contemporánea, en primer lugar hay que admitir que si bien persisten las condiciones de libertades a medias, homofobia de estado enmascarada tras el CENESEX, conexiones sociodigitales precarias y el excesivo control gubernamental vigente, hay también producciones culturales como la propuesta por las "Krudas Cubensi" que acusan recibo de ciertos desplazamientos imaginarios y fuertes quiebres del relato nacional. Aún si ese relato es producido por el CENESEX.

"Las Krudas" (como las llaman popularmente sus seguidores) son una pareja que en sus primeras apariciones (1999–2000) eran claramente identificadas como lesbianas cisgenéricas; sin embargo, en la medida en que han ido pasando los años y evolucionando personal y políticamente, se han desecho y resisten toda etiqueta con el fin de instalarse solo en el espacio de lo no conforme, lo *queer* por antonomasia. Cultivadoras del rap, el hip-hop y la poesía performática, comparten su tiempo entre las ciudades de Austin, Texas y La Habana. En la última década, han entrado y salido tanto de sus propios roles de género como de la isla con frecuencia y fluidez; lo cual deviene harto significante al decodificar los textos de sus canciones y sus poemas.

"Las Krudas" suelen presentarse más fácilmente legibles si nos acercamos a ellas desde un ángulo que las contenga como una de las más disidentes representaciones de "la revolución" y sus modelos de ciudadanía asignados a la mujer. Desterritorializados sus cuerpos y sus "patrias"; desafían, dinamitan y corrompen la ensayada castronormatividad. Aquella que se extiende desde la FMC hasta el CENESEX. En su prolífica producción audiovisual es posible establecer una macroidea que permea el resto de las que conformarían su no binaria ideología de género: el patriarcado es la más tóxica de las instituciones ya que contamina, controla y extorsiona la existencia de todo cuerpo alterno.

Otra vez, desde un afán de hacer un zoom de cámara al actual panorama de la nación lésbica cubana y dejando abierta esta discusión para un futuro libro, comentaré brevemente dos videos "krudos" que considero sintomáticos y productivos al deshacer esa voluntad marginalizante de los presentes actores del poder en la isla. Dichas producciones musicales son "Mi cuerpo es mío" (Kubensi 2014) y "En el solar" (Kubensi 2016). En el primero aparece la pareja reclamando autoridad para sus cuerpos; mientras en el segundo darán un paseo por los barrios y solares más pobres de La Habana.

En esos audiovisuales, las Krudas Cubensi enfatizan que (1) la revolución propuesta para las mujeres *queer* no tiene ninguna significación o contenido real para ellas, no las representa, y (2) hay otras cuestiones reales (siendo la pobreza la más importante de todas) en las que sí están más interesadas; pero de manera cotidiana y no como en esa conga con la que el CENESEX solía hacer un gesto anual de aproximación y aceptación a la comunidad lgbtiq en Cuba.

Me interesa discutir en conjunción estos dos materiales de las Krudas porque si bien en el primero se lee una intensión de carácter globalizador en tanto se denuncia el abuso y control sobre las mujeres en cualquier lugar del mundo; ya en el segundo hay un claro aterrizaje en La Habana de los pobres mientras aparecen sus cuerpos *queer* como parte legítima del paisaje.

En "Mi cuerpo es mío" se confronta a las históricas instituciones occidentales (iglesia y matrimonio): "saquen sus rosarios de nuestros ovarios/saquen sus doctrinas de nuestras vaginas/ ni amo, ni estado, ni partido, ni marido" (Krudas Cubensi); mientras en "El solar" lo confrontado es ya específicamente el gobierno cubano y la falta de recursos en las que viven las comunidades empobrecidas, especialmente las comunidades afrocubanas. En esta segunda producción, antes de comenzar la canción, aparece una dedicatoria textual en donde podemos leer "Habana, a ti te quiero de verdad"; cerrando toda alternativa de alejar el mensaje de su referente más inmediato: la ciudad de la que son originarias. Más tarde, la letra discurre desde la descripción de la vida social de un solar habanero "con sus colores, con su habitar, con su bullicio, con su lavar, con su chisme y su cooperar, ya la maraca empezó a sonar" hasta la real acusación de los estados de pobreza a la que están sometidos sus moradores "qué miseria, qué alegría, abierto los basureros, derrumbe de vertederos, dondequiera los mosqueros, *room for rent*, bicicleteros."

Resulta plausible argüir que la revolución "kruda" y "cubensi" es también el acto de hablar desde las intersecciones ya que, en su propio caso, los suyos son cuerpos atravesados por varias de ellas. Este par de artistas son negras, pobres, *queers* e inmigrantes en constantes viajes de ida y vuelta. Todo lo anterior concede a las "Krudas Cubensi" cierta *sui generis* autoridad al tener la posibilidad de comparar sociedades, formas de explotación y consumo, ideologías y representaciones imaginarias del poder. Dicha posibilidad queda traducida en sus textos en forma de denuncia que ataca tanto las formas de subyugación sicosociales como las instrumentadas por gobiernos y partidos específicos. Son raperas *queer* y desafían a las instituciones porque no les interesa cumplir el mandato para el que fueron asignadas. Son parte de otra conga; una con un ritmo enrarecido: ni lacras, ni lesbianas normalizadas.

### 2018 (NANCY)

Qué bueno que pueda ahora hablarse de estas cosas. En aquellos años yo no creí posible escribirte como lo he hecho. No me casaré con una mujer. Ya soy una anciana. Me lo quitaron todo. Nunca me pidieron perdón. Pero qué bueno que pueda ahora hablarse de estas cosas; solo te pido que no publiques mi nombre.

### 2018 (MABEL)

Evelio ya terminó de pelarme, de enjuagar el tinte a la chica que nos contó de su prima y de peinar a la señora que brevemente mencionó la historia de vida de su hermana. Él tiene esa capacidad para hacernos sentir atendidas a todas a la vez. Usualmente las que esperan lo hacen entretenidas. Sin embargo, estas horas han sido un tanto especiales. Él lo sabe, todas lo sabemos. Un silencio incómodo reina sobre la sala y una vez más decido romperlo a propósito de mi casi despedida. Les pregunto si han escuchado a las "Krudas Cubensi," casi al unísono me responden que no. Recuerdo entonces que las horas de conectividad (1.50 cuc por cada una) equivalen al 7.4 por ciento del salario medio mensual de un ciudadano cubano y que los videos de las "Krudas" solo pueden verse en youtube y que el dinero no alcanza más que para comer o escribir emails o chats a esos parientes que desde la diáspora envían remesas que facilitan la adquisición de dichos alimentos. Pienso también en que el otro modo de escuchar a las "Krudas Cubensi" sería en sus conciertos en vivo, esos que ofrecen tan esporádicamente en la ciudad de La Habana y que dichos conciertos no reciben ninguna promoción o apoyo en los medios de información masiva; esos que aún permanecen controlados por el gobierno.

Digo entonces desde la puerta: "la próxima vez que venga les traeré unos videos en una memoria usb, me encantaría que las escucharan, que me digan qué les parecen esas tuercas." Luego les digo adiós con la ilusión de poder contar esta historia alguna vez.

## NOTES

1.  Las cuatro voces que aparecerán a lo largo de este texto ofreciendo testimonios, corresponden a cuatro personas distintas. Tres de ellas (Nancy, Migdalia y Daysi) aparecen con seudónimos ya que han preferido mantener su identidad real oculta. Los cambios a nivel de estilo y vocabulario que el lector notará, están relacionados con el respeto que la autora de este trabajo ha concedido a sus diversas formas de expresión.

2.  CDR son las siglas para Comité de Defensa de la Revolución, organización de masas creada como sistema de vigilancia entre vecinos para proteger la Revolución en el año 1960. La FMC es la Federación de Mujeres Cubanas, creada en el mismo año con el objetivo de organizar a las mujeres y proveerlas con una serie de deberes y derechos en la construcción de la nueva sociedad.

3.  La Asamblea del Poder Popular, es la variante cubana para designar al Parlamento o Cámara de Representantes.

4.  "Pájaros" y "tuercas" es la manera despectiva con la que popularmente se designa en Cuba a homosexuales hombres y mujeres respectivamente.

5.  Siglas para las organizaciones de masas Federación de Mujeres Cubanas (FMC) y Comité de Defensa de la Revolución (CDR). Ambas fundadas bajo la dirección y apoyo del gobierno revolucionario en 1960.

6.  DTI siglas para Departamento Técnico de Investigaciones.

7.  INIT siglas para el Instituto Nacional de la Industria Turística, fundado también por Fidel Castro. En 1976, el INIT fue renombrado INTUR (Instituto Nacional de Turismo) y en 1994, aparece un ministerio dedicado a esta misma industria nombrado MINTUR.

8.  Ernesto Lecuona (1895–1963) fue un importante pianista y compositor cubano, quien se exilió en Estados Unidos en 1960.

9.  La popularmente conocida como "Ley de peligrosidad" en Cuba, es la Ley No 62 del código penal cubano aún vigente. La ley fue aprobada en 1987 y básicamente puede ser aplicada sobre sujetos que según los estándares del cuerpo policial, presenten una actitud "pre-delictiva." La ley en toda su extensión puede consultarse aquí: "Código Penal," *CEPAL*, Agosto 8, 2019, https://oig.cepal.org /sites/default/files/1987_codigopenal_cuba.pdf.

10.  "CUC" nombre con el que se designa a la moneda libremente convertible cubana y que por sus siglas en inglés corresponde a "Cuban Universal Currency." El salario medio de un ciudadano cubano es de 24 cuc al mes o 576 pesos cubanos.

11.  CENESEX es la institución asociada la Ministerio de Salud Pública que dirige Mariela Castro y que quiere decir en sus siglas: Centro Nacional para la Educación Sexual. Atención a la asociación entre institución asociada a la salud y el agrupamiento oficial de los sujetos lgbtiq en torno a ella.

12.  La ley de matrimonio igualitario no consiguió colocarse en la letra de la nueva constitución aprobada el pasado 24 de febrero de 2019. En el artículo 68 del

anteproyecto constitucional que se sometió a debate se preveía establecer que el matrimonio era una unión entre dos personas, sin precisar el género; pero frente el revuelo que causó esta modificación entre los sectores más conservadores de la sociedad (léase de diferentes iglesias protestantes), las autoridades finalmente optaron por una fórmula más imprecisa que no reconoce el matrimonio gay, aunque tampoco lo impide. La próxima etapa de este debate tendrá lugar en el parlamento cubano que tiene ahora un plazo de dos años para legislar sobre el matrimonio y someter la nueva ley a un nuevo referendo.

13. UMAP: Unidades Militares de Apoyo a la Producción. A ellas fueron condenados, para hacer trabajos forzados, cientos de homosexuales cubanos entre 1965 y 1968.

14. Más detalles de los sucesos del 15 de mayo son detallados en el artículo periodístico de Carlos Manuel Álvarez (2019), "Miedo, fiesta y represión: una pelea cubana contra el demonio," disponible en el siguiente enlace: https://elpais.com /internacional/2019/05/15/actualidad/1557934824_744776.html.

15. Utilizo el neologismo "castronormalizada" como parte de la hipótesis que aquí defiendo: la familia Castro continúa al poder ya que Raúl Castro se mantiene como primer secretario del Partido Comunista de Cuba (PCC) y dicho partido es el órgano rector de la nación; de modo que la figura del presidente Díaz Canel funciona sólo a nivel simbólico como una estrategia de ilusoria pluralidad. Dicha inmovilidad ideológica y de gobierno, facilita que las estrategias de normalización para un modelo único de ciudadanía que sesenta años atrás fueron instaladas desde las organizaciones de masas (FMC, CDR, MTT, etc.) puedan ahora ser desplazadas 'hacia' y recicladas 'desde' el CENESEX a través de una figura que no solo pertenece al clan familiar gobernante, sino que además detenta el control para establecer qué miembros de la comunidad lgbtiq son o no aceptables.

16. Como recién comentaba, el presente 2019 ha sido el único año en que la conga que acompañaba a las jornadas por el orgullo lgbtqi en La Habana no ha salido a celebrar con el auspicio del CENESEX.

17. Todo sobre las Krudas Cubensi (2019) en su página web.

### BIBLIOGRAPHY

Álvarez, Carlos Manuel. 2019. "Miedo, fiesta y represión: una pelea cubana contra el demonio." *El País*, Mayo 15, 2019, https://elpais.com/internacional/2019/05/15 /actualidad/1557934824_744776.html.

Henken, Ted A. 2017. "Cuba's Digital Millennials: Independent Digital Media and Civil Society on the Island of the Disconnected." *Social Research: An International Quarterly* 84 (2): 429–456.

Gordillo Piña, Lirians. 2016. "El silencio hacia las mujeres lesbianas y trans es violencia." Entrevista a Mercedes García Hernández. *SEMlac. Corresponsalía en Cuba del servicio de noticias de la mujer de Latinoamerica y el Caribe*, 2 de diciembre de 2016. http://www.redsemlac-cuba.net/diversidad-sexual/el-silencio-hacia-las-mujeres-lesbianas-y-trans-es-violencia.html.

Kubensi, Krudas. 2014. "Krudas Cubensi. Mi cuerpo es mio. Official Video. Odaymara/ Olivia/ La Real. Aiwey Tv." YouTube, 21 de junio de 2014. Vídeo, 03:41. https://www.youtube.com/watch?v=x-Pgwldfx8U.

———. 2016. "En el solar. In the building plot. Krudas Cubensi." YouTube, 26 de marzo de 2016. Vídeo, 06:46. https://www.youtube.com/watch?v=DoLCwU6gQXY.

———. 2019. krudascubensi.com. Julio 25, 2019. http://www.krudascubensi.com/.

Martínez-San Miguel, Yolanda. 2008. "Más allá de la homonormatividad: Intimidades alternativas en el Caribe hispano." *Revista Iberoamericana* 74 (225): 1039–1057.

Negrón Muntaner, Frances. 2016. "'Mariconerías de estado': Mariela Castro, la comunidad LGBTQ y la política Cubana." In *Nuestro caribe: Poder, raza y postnacionalismos desde los límites del mapa LGBTQ*, edited by Mabel Cuesta, 105–123. San Juan, Puerto Rico: Isla Negra.

MABEL CUESTA is US Latino and Spanish Caribbean Literature Professor at the University of Houston, Texas. She is a scholar, poet, and fiction writer. Among her extensive publications, her more recent works are *Lecturas Atentas: Una visita desde la ficción y la crítica a veinte narradoras cubanas contemporáneas* (Almenara, 2019), *In Via, In Patria* (Literal Publishing, 2016; Ediciones Matanzas, 2019), and *Nuestro Caribe: Poder, raza y postnacionalismos desde los límites del mapa LGBTQ* (Isla Negra, 2016). Her scholarly work has been widely published in peer-reviewed journals in Cuba, the United States, Mexico, Honduras, Canada, Brazil, Colombia, and Spain.

# TEN

# "¿Batata? ¡Batata!"

## Examining Puerto Rican Visual Folk Expression in Times of Adversity

### GLORIA M. COLOM BRAÑA

This chapter aims to explore the use of visual folk expressions by the multisited Puerto Rican community through a combination of physical and digital means to question the cultural and political status quo and create conversations in times of crisis. In September 2017, Hurricane María devastated the Puerto Rican landscape, leaving a trail of despair and consternation in its wake. The recovery efforts progressed slowly into 2018, but Puerto Rico had already been going through economic, ecological, and social upheaval in the preceding years. The economic crisis predates the hurricane by over a decade. The effects of economic turmoil have been compounded by ecological devastation such as the toxic ash storage in Peñuelas and beach destruction in Aguadilla, a growing identity crisis with the questioning of the Puerto Rican constitution in the US Supreme Court in 2016, the subsequent implementation of the PROMESA oversight board by Congress, and the fear of rapidly spreading diseases such as the Zika virus, among other issues clashing and converging in a cacophony of anxiety and instability. Digital forms of communication such as memes, hashtags, and viral videos interact with physical interventions in Puerto Rican spaces, providing dialogue between Puerto Ricans on the island and the ever-growing diaspora. Many of these events overlap each other in time, and the bombardment of information often becomes overwhelming. This chapter presents the events and reactions discretely in order to introduce and explain them, but they would often compete with each other for attention and action from an already beleaguered community. These case studies are based on observations of ongoing events throughout Puerto Rico during fieldwork trips between 2015 and 2017. I was able to observe the events described here firsthand as well as consume them through the news and social media. Even as this chapter is being published, the effects of austerity, ecological devastation, and neoliberal colonialism continue to dominate the Puerto Rican communities' attention, and quick-witted responses in both the digital and physical spheres emerge daily.

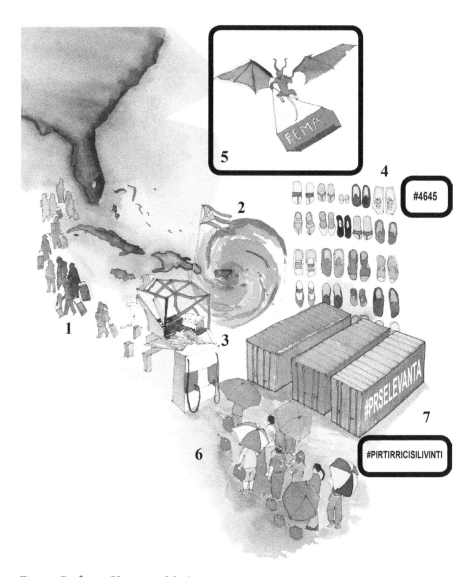

Fig. 10.1 Preface—Hurricane María.

PREFACE—HURRICANE MARÍA

1. The following illustrations were planned and painted by the author in tandem with their accompanying notes. These illustrations were designed to function as visual signifiers of the components of both digital place and physical space. Each theme is self-contained with a series of signifiers representing places, people, and events within the space of the same page. The digital aspects are surrounded by black digitally superimposed lines and text in order to differentiate the type of communication being presented. The accompanying notes are meant to be an interactive component that supplements the context of the images without superseding them.

2. Beginning with the passage of Hurricane María provides context for some of the events that Puerto Rico was going through in 2018, when this essay was being written. Emphasis is placed on the devastating effects of the hurricane and the community response through digital media to the state and federal governments' lackluster rebuilding effort.

3. Hurricane María, one of the most powerful hurricanes to strike Puerto Rico in the last century, crossed the entirety of the island on September 20, 2017. The recovery has been slow, and consternation has been mounting as the estimate of deaths due to the storm has increased exponentially from the official death toll of sixty-four that was established in the days after the storm to somewhere between three and five thousand according to the George Washington University and Harvard studies, respectively (Andrade et al. 2018; Kishore et al. 2018).

4. A display of shoes was presented in front of the state capitol building in protest of the lack of official recognition of a higher death count after the Harvard study came out on June 1, 2018. People brought a pair of shoes to represent friends and family members that died after the passage of the hurricane but were never considered to be included in the official list. Shoes were organized in rows, accompanied by candles, mementos, and photographs belonging to the deceased. The display, accompanied by the hashtag #4645, was already aimed to be viewed in person but documented photographically as well for Internet mobility and consumption (Bauzá 2018).

5. In August 2018, there was a rash of animal attacks, similar to the chupacabras attacks of 1995. The culprit was determined to be gargoyle-shaped cryptid in the coastal municipality of Barceloneta

(Primera Hora 2018). The sightings coincided with the discovery of missing FEMA supplies containers in different parts of the island (Robles 2018). Memes began making rounds addressing both issues, and some combined them in a logical manner.

6. The eternal lines for provisions after the storm's passage quickly became lines at the airport as the diasporic outflow increased due to the lack of job security and the destruction of houses and other buildings, as well as the ongoing austerity measures imposed by the Fiscal Control Board (Criollo Oquero 2018).

7. "Vernacular expressive culture can challenge structures of power, and at times like the present, those expressions acquire deeper relevance and urgency. Folk cultural practices, in this regard, are a form of clandestine and portable histories of defiant becoming" (Otero and Martínez-Rivera 2017). The state-sanctioned hashtag #PuertoRicoseLevanta, translated to "Puerto Rico Rises," was met with the sardonic parody #Pirtiricisilivinti, changing all the vowels to *i* in such a way that the message sounds parodic and ineffective as a reflection of the campaign itself.

Fig. 10.2 Digital and tangible spaces.

DIGITAL AND TANGIBLE SPACES

8. This project follows in the footsteps of those who challenge the idea of what constitutes a public space for communication and how these spaces can be defined in the context of social media in the translocal Puerto Rican community. This is done by looking at the interactions between the physical and digital spaces, particularly how each informs and changes the other.

9. Puerto Rican scholars have begun to produce writings about meme production as a form of mediating overwhelming situations in the last few years, the passage of Hurricane María marking a before-and-after dichotomy. Aziria Rodríguez Arce (2018) defended her master's thesis in comparative media studies at Massachusetts Institute of Technology, titled "Seizing the Memes of Production: Political Memes in Puerto Rico and the Puerto Rican Diaspora." The thesis focuses on the use of memes by island-located Puerto Ricans to vent frustration, diffuse tension, and communicate current events with the Puerto Rican diaspora, relating not only to the events surrounding the hurricane response but also to the effects of the federally appointed Fiscal Control Board overseeing the governmental budget and the colonial status of the island. Amanda Guzmán and Natasha A. Fernández-Pérez (2018), each completing their anthropology PhD at UC Berkeley, published a more popularly oriented article titled "In the Wake of Hurricane María, Memes Carry More Than a Little Truth," focusing on the use of memes by hurricane survivors to have a voice and to process unending frustration with the slow-to-nonexistent recovery effort as the months passed. The illustrations and scholarly notes provided in this essay are meant to continue this ongoing interdisciplinary conversation on Internet-based forms of communication through the lens of folklore.

10. The case studies illustrated and analyzed in this work are events and cultural reactions that were occurring concurrently. They represent some of the major events occurring in Puerto Rico with a primary focus on the time between 2015 and 2017, in the years before the arrival of Hurricane María. These events, often overlapping in time and space, occurred independently of each other yet share the basis of colonial struggle, digital space, and eventually online visual and textual vocabularies. The moment of meme creation is easier to pinpoint in cases such as the "batata" meme, which is based on a specific documented instance, than in others.

Often memes and interactions on the ground came to my attention once they had become viral, having spread exponentially while the specific moment of creation became disconnected from the process of spreading.

11. Digital media—particularly the two digital forms of communication highlighted here, the hashtag and memes—have been in direct relationship with the physical world, interacting through the photographic lens and changing the way in which people present themselves as well as the landscape for digital transferal.

12. The mural "Paz para la Mujer," translated to "Peace for Women," was painted on the side of a prominent overpass in the Santurce Barrio of San Juan, Puerto Rico, by the Moriviví Collective, a group of female artists who wanted to bring attention to violence against women in Puerto Rico. They purposely chose to depict bare-chested Afro-Latinx women covering their faces with butterflies coming out of their bodies, representative of the Mirabal sisters, who were assassinated in the Dominican Republic for standing up against the dictatorship of President Trujillo (Lugo Quijano 2016). The mural was quickly defaced by an unknown person or people who painted a rustic bra and pantie set in order to bring modesty to the mural (Saker 2015). In response, a group of women staged a series of performative acts by removing their tops and documenting it photographically for online distribution. The images spread through social media, especially through platforms such as Facebook and Twitter, where they were often censored and later contested by those sharing them. The artists later "censored" the murals with large-scaled pixilation while providing a photo exhibit of the topless activists standing triumphantly in front of the defaced mural. This incident formed part of an ongoing conversation challenging gendered norms, the treatment of women's bodies, and LGBTQI rights that continues into the present.

13. Robert Howard expressed the tension existing between the vernacular expressions of online communities and the institutional power to censor held by the companies hosting said sites (2015, 248–249). This tension is often evident in the censoring of works of art and of protest within sites such as Facebook. It can also lead to community members purposefully challenging the metrics used to establish what constitutes offensive material on digital sites.

14. Folklorists in the United States for over half a century have been using the principles of semiotics to analyze the transmittal of folk knowledge, mainly through the oral forms but also through others

such as performance and material analysis within the cultural context in order to better understand the messages being conveyed (Langlois 1985). These principles become crucial when formatting academic communication through a visual medium in such a way that the message is successfully communicated to the receiving audience.

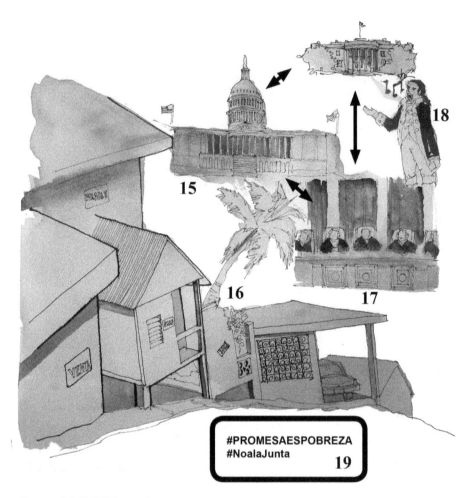

Fig. 10.3 PROMESA es pobreza.

PROMESA ES POBREZA

15. Puerto Rico has a long history of colonial rule, with four centuries of Spanish rule and over a century of American presence stemming back to the Spanish-American War of 1898 (Terrasa 1997). The colonial status of the island was semantically challenged in 1952 with the change of status to Commonwealth of Puerto Rico and the creation of a locally determined constitution. Puerto Rico was eliminated from the United Nation's official list of colonies on the provision that the commonwealth would have constitutional autonomy.

16. The bankruptcy of Puerto Rico's government took time to develop and was based on a series of loans that were becoming unrepayable, a constitutional provision obligating the commonwealth to prioritize debt repayment, tax-free bonds, the incapacity to declare bankruptcy, the removal of tax incentives for American factories, and refinancing decisions with hedge funds that ballooned the debt over 1,000 percent in a decade. The brunt of the economic downfall was reflected in the Puerto Rican housing market, which has been in a state of crisis since 2006, with roughly 18 percent of available houses vacant as of 2017.

17. The constitutional autonomy of Puerto Rico was challenged in 2016, just weeks before the creation of the Fiscal Control Board through a federal Supreme Court determination of the case *Pueblo de Puerto Rico v. Sánchez Valle* that Puerto Rico does not have own sovereignty to retry a person after they have served in federal prison, unlike the states (Ramos and Baerga 2016). Although it was a relatively minor case, there is concern among legal scholars that said ruling could jeopardize the limited autonomy granted in 1952 with the creation of the Puerto Rican constitution.

18. The Puerto Rico Oversight, Management, and Economic Stability Act, known by its acronym as PROMESA, was signed into law by President Barack Obama after receiving bipartisan support. The law requires a named Fiscal Control Board to approve the Puerto Rican government's budget with an emphasis on debt repayment (DeBonis 2016). Although the law protects the commonwealth government against lawsuits from bond holders, it puts the onus of repayment on Puerto Rican residents, focusing on austerity measures such as privatization of government services, lowering minimum wage in an already economically deprived area, and the slashing of retirement funds (Wicker 2016). On April 26, 2016,

Lin-Manuel Miranda, a New York composer and singer of Puerto Rican descent, used his fame from the successful Broadway musical *Hamilton* to campaign in favor of PROMESA. Miranda appeared on John Oliver's show, *Last Week Tonight*, to make a case for the bill as a viable alternative to bankruptcy.

19. "Promesa es pobreza" became a standardized slogan as well as a hashtag used by people opposed to the Fiscal Control Board. It was tagged on walls and used online along with less alliterative messages such as "#NoalaJunta."

Fig. 10.4 #yonomequito.

#YONOMEQUITO

20. In 2016, 89,000 people left Puerto Rico for the mainland United States. This number went up to roughly 281,000 in 2017 with the passage of Hurricane María (Cortés Chico 2018). Patterns of mass emigration had been occurring for years already.

21. People of every socioeconomic class have been leaving Puerto Rico since the beginning of the economic crisis in 2007. They have moved to different parts of the United States, often finding shelter and work with family and friends while they become settled in their new homes. Often, however, people moving to the mainland have ended up living in overcrowded motels for months on end, suffering from food insecurity, discrimination, and the lack of language skills to gain higher-paying employment (Wapa TV 2016).

22. The phrase *yo no me quito* or *no te quites*, translated respectively as "I do not quit" and "do not quit," are considered expressions of encouragement often used in Puerto Rico to connote perseverance and to encourage survival. The #nomequito hashtag campaign was initiated in early 2016 by Carlos López-Lay, a local businessman, as an inspirational tactic to keep moral up as austerity measures were being implemented. The campaign was well funded by private entities, and the hashtag often appeared on billboards and in ads and commercials (Pérez Cámara 2016). The backlash was swift. The message itself was vague (What were people quitting? What were people giving up on exactly?) and offered no solution to the larger economic and political structural problems at the moment, instead placing the onus of survival on the layperson. The main interpretation popularly held was that *quitarse* ("to quit") meant leaving the island. Many people who were leaving or had family who had recently left took it as a gaslighting commentary that to leave was to quit and therefore their identity as true Puerto Ricans was put into question.

23. #Yamequite, *ya me quité*, translated as "I already quit," was a response to #Yonomequito often used by members of the recent Puerto Rican diaspora in online arguments on the merits of staying in or leaving Puerto Rico.

26

24

28

25

27

Fig. 10.5 Black flags and doors.

## BLACK FLAGS AND DOORS

24. A collective of artists had painted the Puerto Rican flag using light blue, red, and white on the door of an abandoned building on Calle San José in Old San Juan in 2012 as part of a larger project. The collective repainted the flag in white and black on July 4, 2016, in response to the recently passed PROMESA in order to foster conversation (Artistas Solidarios y en Resistencia 2016).

25. The painted door immediately caught the attention of tourists, selfie takers, local residents, and the news. People began to interact with it in a more solemn way, leaving flowers, photos, and candles on the floor in the following days. The door also attracted unwanted attention and was defaced.

26. The painted door of San José is part of a longer tradition of politically motivated murals and graffiti, especially in the San Juan metropolitan area.

27. On August 13, 2016, tennis player Monica Puig won the first gold medal for Puerto Rico in the history of the Olympics. In celebration, many people photoshopped the door flag in triumphant gold to share online (Piñeiro Planas 2016).

28. The flag vocabulary has been adopted in protests, clothing, and mural art and as an avatar for Facebook users, among others.

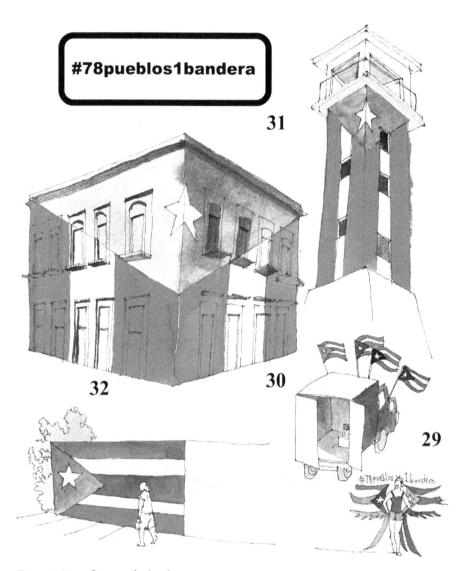

Fig. 10.6 More flags on the landscape.

MORE FLAGS ON THE LANDSCAPE

29. The Puerto Rican flag has a tumultuous history, going from a revolutionary symbol to being banned by the federal government to becoming the emblematic signifier of Puerto Rican cultural identity across the political spectrum. The standard red, white, and blue flag, based on the Cuban flag, is not without its own variations. Although the red stripes remain standardized, the blue triangle can come in three different shades depending on the political positioning regarding Puerto Rico's relationship to the United States. The pro-statehood flag has a rich dark blue mimicking the American flag's blue background. The more commonly used version of the flag, especially in state government buildings and events, has a highly saturated bright blue. The pro-independence version of the flag uses a light baby blue in the background.

30. Stores and street vendors began stocking up on flags, shirts, and apparel that reflected the new flag variations, including a version of the Puerto Rican LGBTQI pride flag, the gold Olympic medal variant, the different versions of blue reflective of political ideology, and the black resistance flag.

31. Héctor Collazo, an artist following in the footsteps of Artistas Solidarios y en Resistencia, began a campaign to mural paint the Puerto Rican flag in more traditional colors of sky blue, red, and white on the facades of buildings that were emblematic, historic, and abandoned in each of the seventy-eight municipalities of Puerto Rico (Ceneida 2017). Each of the paintings is signed with his Facebook and Instagram handles so that people can follow the progress of the mural work.

32. There is little information, however, on the legality of the mural work, which does not conform to historic property protection laws, or information on permission from the property owners (Junta de Planificación 2010). In order for his murals to stand out, Collazo specifically chose buildings that were already considered historically significant or emblematic of each town. Many of these buildings are anywhere from one to four centuries old, often from Spanish colonial times. They may be abandoned but are often registered as either local or national historic places, and any alteration, including painting, needs to go through a permit process.

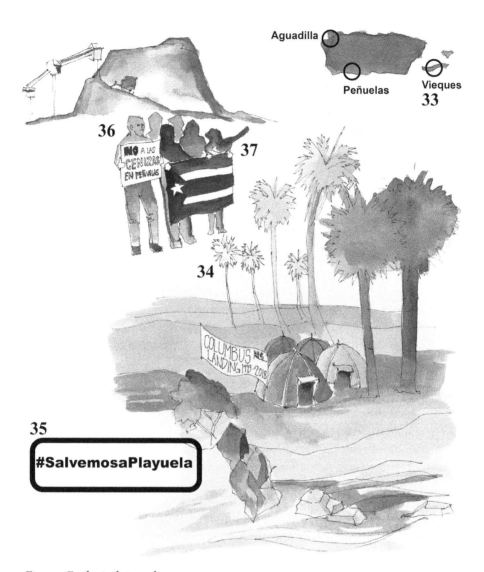

Fig. 10.7 Ecological struggles.

ECOLOGICAL STRUGGLES

33. There is a long history of protesting ecological damage framed in a
    decolonializing context throughout Puerto Rico. Catalina de Onís
    (2016) researched the performative cultural aspects of community
    activism throughout Puerto Rico with particular emphasis on the
    intersection between decolonizing initiatives and environmental-
    ism. De Onís researched protest movements in the island munici-
    pality of Vieques, which had served as a practice bombing range
    for the US military until 2003. The community of Vieques contin-
    ues to protest the perceived inaction by the US government in re-
    habilitating the heavily polluted landscape. Community members
    correlate the high rate of cancer on the island with the heavy met-
    als and other toxins that can still be found both on land and in the
    sea. They use creative means, such as combining site occupation
    with dance, performance, and sayings ("Estamos aquí pa' que tu
    lo sepas"—"We are here, just so you know"), with group solidarity
    to continue to address and bring attention to the ecological plight
    in Vieques (101). These principles are reenacted in and adapted to
    different sites and contexts throughout the island.

34. A long-standing struggle between developers and activists taking
    place in Playuela (Little Beach), Aguadilla, came to greater atten-
    tion in early 2016 as the development company geared up to begin
    construction on the Columbus Landing Resort on an ecologically
    sensitive beach (Cruz 2017). The project had begun the permit pro-
    cess in 1994 but had suffered decades of budgetary, planning, and
    permit delays; the company renewed their construction process
    in 2016. Protesters combined social media activism with physical
    occupation of the space, emulating the concurrent protests oc-
    curring in North Dakota by the Sioux people against the Dakota
    Access Pipeline projected to run near the Standing Rock Indian
    Reservation.

35. Activist movements were organized and led through Facebook by
    groups such as Salvemos a Playuela (2017) with updates on events,
    calls for action, and posts spreading awareness of the group's pur-
    pose. Signs and photos on the ground were prepared specifically
    for online dissemination.

36. Even as people were camping on the Aguadilla beach, other activ-
    ists were busy preventing trucks from depositing ash for storage in
    the town of Peñuelas on the southern coast of the island (Santiago
    Caraballo 2016). Half of Puerto Rico's energy is generated through

the use of petroleum, the residual ashes of which have to be disposed of. Protestors argued that the ashes were toxic and would
cause continual health problems as well as environmental devastation for the local community.

37. In both Playuela and Peñuelas, protestors interwove physical
manifestations at the contested site with constant use of social
media, using performativity for a mainly online audience in order
to dramatically extend the reach of their causes: "In many cases,
individuals on the outskirts, many of whom belong to minority
ethnic groups in the United States, 'adopt *unconventional* political
strategies and participate in protest politics'" (Martinez 2005).

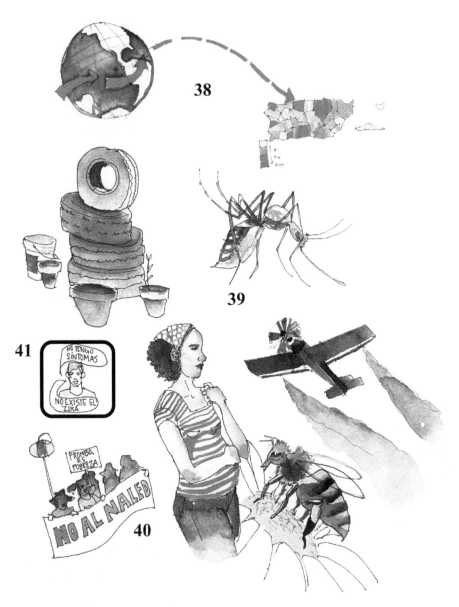

Fig. 10.8 Zika, fear, conspiracy theories.

ZIKA, FEAR, CONSPIRACY THEORIES

38. Even as ecological and economic struggles were being contested on the streets of Puerto Rico in 2016, the Zika epidemic that had traveled the planet's circumference finally reached Puerto Rico and was transmitted through the already prevalent *Aedes aegipti* mosquito. Previous years had already seen the quick spread of various strains of dengue fever and chikungunya. The new epidemic, however, was considered more insidious because it often had mild to no symptoms yet was correlated with microcephaly and other birth defects in the children born of infected mothers (McNeil 2016; Sun 2016). It was projected that one in five Puerto Ricans would become infected over the course of the year.

39. The proposed use of the insecticide Naled via plane dispersal caused as much and sometimes even more concern than the spread of the disease itself (Caro González 2016). Reports were coming in from South Carolina that the use of Naled had caused millions of bees to die (Yuhas 2016), prompting terror of an exacerbated ecological crisis in an already precarious ecosystem. A history of federal and military projects over the previous decades, including experimenting with the use of Agent Orange (US Department of Veterans Affairs 2015) and testing the contraceptive pill on Puerto Rican women (Briggs 2002), among other incidents, led people to be furious at their lack of voice in the decision to use a potentially dangerous chemical on the land. The concern about the toxic effects of Naled and the insidious effects of the disease propelled conspiracy theories to thrive, particularly regarding the disposability of Puerto Rican bodies as experiments to protect mainland US citizens from potential epidemics.

40. Dr. Rafael Joglar, an activist and biologist specializing in amphibians, told the newspaper during July protests against the use of Naled, "Los pilotos llegaron hace ya una semana y ahora llega el Naled. Esto es una declaración de guerra. No queda otro remedio que tirarnos a la calle a defender lo nuestro: biodiversidad, agricultura, salud . . . Patria." This translates to, "The pilots arrived a week ago and now the Naled arrives. This is a declaration of war. There is no other solution but to take to the streets and defend what is ours: biodiversity, agriculture, and health . . . Country" (Figueroa Cancel 2016).

41. NPR reported the following: "Yet health officials also say efforts to stop the spread of the virus are being hampered by mistrust, indifference and fatigue among residents, over what some view as just the latest tropical disease to hit the island" (Beaubien 2016).

Fig. 10.9 ¡Batata!

¡BATATA!

42. May 1, 2017, marked the first May Day commemorated in Puerto Rico after the implementation of the Fiscal Control Board (Caro González 2017). The impact of the austerity measures on daily life and people's consternation over the lack of accountability on the part of the government and major banks meant that this was also the biggest protest in decades. Before the day was over, there were broken windows, allegations of police brutality, and multiple arrests.

43. *Batata* (*Ipomoea batatas*), also known as yam or sweet potato in English and slang for a corrupt or ineffective politician, became the center of meme production and a lighthearted break from the politically charged context of the May Day protests in San Juan. A young man holding a sweet potato stopped in front of the Telemundo news camera and with a smile simply said, "¡Batata!" before continuing on his way. The moment was captured live on the news, filmed from a grainy television, and posted online. The sweet-potato-toting man immediately became a meme, with expression ranging from still images to parodic music videos (itsMaldow 2017). Both the image and a nine-second video clip were circulated throughout social media platforms even as dire news of arrests was streaming in. Eventually, simply typing the word *batata* without context or supplementing visual text was enough to evoke the entire meme.

44. People used their own cameras to document the ongoing events as combined bystanders, active participants, and witnesses.

45. The black-and-white Puerto Rican resistance flag was used as one of the protest symbols during the march through the Milla de Oro, the "Golden Mile" financial district in San Juan.

Fig. 10.10 Conclusion.

CONCLUSION

46. All of the events mentioned here overlapped at some point. The majority occurred simultaneously, crowding the newsfeeds on social media, competing for the attention of a beleaguered audience. The examples here do not cover all of the goings-on in Puerto Rico at the time, nor were the reactions universally in favor or against any single position. These examples constitute but a slice of the events that constantly cross the digital and physical spheres.

47. Each of the conversations presented in the case studies has continued into 2018. Hurricane María caused a temporary interruption in the prioritization of attention and resources, but over time attention has returned to ongoing economic, ecological, social, and political debates with the added weight of posthurricane rebuilding.

48. Case studies in folklore are often studied and treated independently with careful and pronounced analysis in order to gain as much cultural knowledge from the text as possible. There might be something to be gained by juxtaposing multiple examples of the somewhat overwhelming bombardment of media and events occurring simultaneously in a subaltern space of crisis. The events interrelate, inform each other, and affect people's responses to the intense stimulation they are experiencing.

49. "Latinx scholars are challenging Eurocentric frameworks of academia by highlighting scholarship produced by people of color or other disenfranchised communities in academia. In doing so they are also pushing against the norms of academic writing and products by using 'brown' epistemological frameworks and intellectual lenses" (Otero and Martínez-Rivera 2017). This chapter, with its combination of illustrations and supporting text, is part of an ongoing effort to experiment with the tools provided within folkloristics from the lens of a scholar researching her own community. The saying goes that an image can say a thousand words. It is now a matter of processing how image and text enrich and communicate with each other and their audience.

BIBLIOGRAPHY

Andrade, Elizabeth, Nicole Barrett, Uriyoan Colon-Ramos, Mark Edgerg, and
    Alejandra Garcia-Meza. 2018. *Project Report Ascertainment of the Estimated Excess
    Mortality from Hurricane María in Puerto Rico in Collaboration with the University
    of Puerto Rico Graduate School of Public Health.* Washington, DC: George
    Washington University.
Artistas solidarios y en resistencia. 2016. "¡La bandera está de negro, Puerto Rico en
    pie de lucha!" *8ogrados,* July 8, 2016. https://web.archive.org/web/20160719014138
    /http://www.8ogrados.net/la-bandera-esta-de-negro-puerto-rico-esta-en-pie-de
    -lucha/.
Bauzá, Nydia. 2018. "Llanto y mucha emoción entre los miles de zapatos colocados en
    el Capitolio." *Primera Hora,* June 3, 2018. http://www.primerahora.com/noticias
    /puerto-rico/nota/llantoymuchaemocionentrelosmilesdezapatoscolocadosenelca
    pitolio-1285721/.
Beaubien, Jason. 2016. "Puerto Rico's Efforts to Stop Zika Are Hampered by
    Mistrust." NPR, August 10, 2016. https://www.npr.org/sections/health-shots/2016
    /08/10/489433636/puerto-ricos-efforts-to-stop-zika-are-hampered-by-mistrust
    -disease-overload.
Briggs, Laura. 2002. *Reproducing Empire: Race, Sex, Science, and US Imperialism in
    Puerto Rico.* Berkeley: University of California Press.
Caro González, Leysa. 2016. "Fatal el Naled para las abejas." *El Nuevo Dia,* July 13,
    2016. https://www.pressreader.com/puerto-rico/el-nuevo-d%C3%ADa/20160713
    /281668254312541.
———. 2017. "Un 1 de mayo muy diferente." *El Nuevo Dia,* May 1, 2017. https://www
    .elnuevodia.com/noticias/locales/nota/un1demayomuydiferente-2316487/.
Ceneida. 2017. "#78Pueblos1Bandera: Ruta de las banderas." Adictos a Descubrir
    PR (blog), August 6, 2017. http://adictosadescubrirpr.com/2017/08/06
    /78pueblos1bandera/.
Cortés Chico, Ricardo. 2018. "El nuevo gran éxodo de puertorriqueños a Estados
    Unidos." *El Nuevo Dia,* June 24, 2018. https://www.elnuevodia.com/noticias
    /locales/nota/elnuevogranexododepuertorriquenosaestadosunidos-2430577/.
Criollo Oquero, Agustín. 2018. "Puerto Rico perdió 6% de su población tras
    huracán María." *Caribbean Business en Español,* March 9, 2018. https://cb.pr
    /puerto-rico-perdio-6-de-su-poblacion-tras-huracan-maria/.
Cruz, Ramón. 2017. "Playuela, protestas y permisos." *El Nuevo Dia,* February 22, 2017.
    https://www.elnuevodia.com/opinion/columnas/playuelaprotestasypermisos
    -columna-2294038/.
DeBonis, Mike. 2016. "House Passes Puerto Rico Fiscal Rescue Bill Ahead of July
    Cliff." *Washington Post,* June 9, 2016. https://www.washingtonpost.com/news
    /powerpost/wp/2016/06/09/puerto-rico-fiscal-rescue-is-poised-to-pass-house-as
    -july-deadline-looms/.

de Onís, Catalina. 2016. "'Pa' que tú lo sepas': Experiences with Co-presence in Puerto Rico." In *Text + Field: Innovations in Rhetorical Method*, edited by Sara McKinnon, Robert Asen, Karma R. Chávez, and Robert Glenn Howard, 101–116. University Park: Pennsylvania State University Press.

Duffy, Margaret, Janis Teruggi Page, and Rachel Young. 2012. "Obama as Anti-American: Visual Folklore in Right-Wing Forwarded E-mails and Construction of Conservative Social Identity." *Journal of American Folklore* 125 (496): 177–203.

Figueroa Cancel, Alex. 2016. "Protestan por la llegada del Naled a la isla." *El Nuevo Día*, July 21, 2016. https://www.elnuevodia.com/noticias/locales/nota/protestanporlallegadadelnaledalaisla-2222927/.

Guzmán, Amanda, and Natasha A. Fernández-Pérez. 2018. "In the Wake of Hurricane Maria, Memes Carry More Than a Little Truth." *SAPIENS*, May 16, 2018. https://www.sapiens.org/technology/hurricane-maria-memes-puerto-rico/.

Hinojosa, Jennifer, and Méndez, Edwin. 2018. "The Housing Crisis in Puerto Rico and the Impact of Hurricane Maria." Centro de Estudios Puertorriqueños. https://centropr.hunter.cuny.edu/research/data-center/research-briefs/housing-crisis-puerto-rico-and-impact-hurricane-maria.

Howard, Robert Glenn. 2015. "Introduction: Why Digital Network Hybridity Is the New Normal (Hey! Check This Stuff Out)." *Journal of American Folklore* 128 (509): 247–259. https://doi.org/10.5406/jamerfolk.128.509.0247.

itsMaldow [pseud.]. 2017. "¡BATATA! [Jingle] #ParoNacional—ItsMaldow." YouTube, May 5, 2017. Video, 02:19. https://www.youtube.com/watch?v=CJ30WDnWIQE.

Junta de Planificación. 2010. "Reglamento Conjunto de Permisos para Obras de Construcción y Usos de Terreno." San Juan: Oficina del Gobernador.

Kishore, Nishant, Domingo Marqués, Ayesha Mahmud, Mathew V. Kiang, Irmary Rodriguez, Arlan Fuller, Peggy Ebner, et al. 2018. "Mortality in Puerto Rico after Hurricane Maria." *New England Journal of Medicine* 379 (2): 162–170. https://doi.org/10.1056/NEJMsa1803972.

Langlois, Janet L. 1985. "Folklore and Semiotics: An Introduction." *Journal of Folklore Research* 22 (2/3): 77–83.

Lugo Quijano, Rocio. 2016. "Morivivi: cuatro artistas, un colectivo." *Merodea* (blog), October 26, 2016. https://merodea.com/women-we-heart/wwh-morivivi/.

Martinez, Lisa M. 2005. "Yes We Can: Latino Participation in Unconventional Politics." *Social Forces* 84 (1): 135–155.

McNeil, Donald, Jr. 2016. "As Zika Rages in Puerto Rico, Action Falters." *Seattle Times*, July 30, 2016. https://www.seattletimes.com/nation-world/as-zika-rages-in-puerto-rico-action-falters/.

McNeill, Lynne S. 2012. "Real Virtuality: Enhancing Locality by Enacting the Small World Theory." In *Folk Culture in the Digital Age: The Emergent Dynamics of Human Interaction*, edited by Trevor J. Blank, 85–97. Logan: Utah State University Press.

Otero, Solimar, and Mintzi Auanda Martínez-Rivera. 2017. "Introduction: Poder y Cultura: Latinx Folklore and Popular Culture." *Chiricú Journal: Latina/o Literatures, Arts, and Cultures* 2 (1): 6–15.

Pechio, Marcos. 2017. "La batata y usted: entrevista al Chico Batata." *La Marginal* (blog), May 5, 2017. http://lamarginalpr.com/la-batata-y-usted/.

Pérez Cámara, Jessica. 2016. "La campaña publicitaria que divide a Puerto Rico." *Univision*, February 23, 2016. https://www.univision.com/puerto-rico/wlii /entretenimiento/redes-sociales/la-campana-publicitaria-que-divide-a-puerto -rico.

Piñeiro Planas, Noel. 2016. "¡Boricua párate! Mónica ha ganado el oro." *El Nuevo Dia*, August 13, 2016. https://www.elnuevodia.com/deportes/otrosdeportes/nota /boricuaparatemonicahaganadoeloro-2230436/.

Primera Hora. 2018. "La gárgola ataca en Barceloneta." August 23, 2018. http://www .primerahora.com/videos/noticias/isla/lagargolaatacaenbarceloneta-249303/.

Ramos, Efrén Rivera, and Alexandra Sabater Baerga. 2016. "Derecho constitucional." *Revista Jurídica UPR* 85:431–435.

Robles, Frances. 2018. "Containers of Hurricane Donations Found Rotting in Puerto Rico Parking Lot." *New York Times*, August 10, 2018. https://www.nytimes.com /2018/08/10/us/puerto-rico-aid.html.

Rodríguez Arce, Aziria. 2018. "Seizing the Memes of Production: Political Memes in Puerto Rico and the Puerto Rican Diaspora." Master's thesis, Massachusetts Institute of Technology. https://cmsw.mit.edu/puerto-rico-seizing-memes -production/.

Saker, Gabriela. 2015. "Responden con los senos al aire censura a mural santurcino (galería)." *NOTICEL*, October 28, 2015. https://www.noticel.com/vida/responden -con-los-senos-al-aire-censura-a-mural-santurcino-galera_20170823090756513 /610593117.

Salvemos a Playuela. 2017. "Salvemos a Playuela—Posts." Facebook, July 20, 2017. https://www.facebook.com/salvemosaplayuela/photos/a.1169728286458167 /1288272474603747/?type=3&theater.

Santiago Caraballo, Yaritza. 2016. "Protestan en contra de proyecto turístico en Aguadilla." *El Nuevo Dia*, November 1, 2016. https://www.elnuevodia.com/noticias /locales/nota/protestanencontradeproyectoturisticoenaguadilla-2257673/.

Sun, Lena H. 2016. "Zika Is Expected to Infect 1 in 5 Puerto Ricans, Raising Threat to Rest of US." *Washington Post*, February 29, 2016. https://www.washingtonpost .com/national/health-science/zika-is-expected-to-infect-1-in-5-puerto-ricans -raising-threat-to-rest-of-us/2016/02/29/c1288e30-db62-11e5-891a-4ed04f4213e8 _story.html.

Terrasa, Gabriel A. 1997. "United States, Puerto Rico, and the Territorial Incorporation Doctrine: Reaching a Century of Constitutional Authoritarianism." *John Marshall Law Review* 31 (1): 55–93.

US Department of Veterans Affairs. 2015. "Herbicide Tests and Storage outside the US." Public Health. https://www.publichealth.va.gov/exposures/agentorange/locations/tests-storage/outside-vietnam.asp.

US Energy Information Administration. 2019. "Puerto Rico—Territory Energy Profile Analysis." November 21, 2019. https://www.eia.gov/state/analysis.php?sid=RQ.

Wapa TV. 2016. "¿Cómo viven algunos de los boricuas en el exilio?" YouTube, April 22, 2016. Video, 14:34. https://www.youtube.com/watch?v=LhSHgjrms6w.

Wicker, Roger. 2016. "S.2328—114th Congress (2015–2016): PROMESA." June 30, 2016. https://www.congress.gov/bill/114th-congress/senate-bill/2328.

Yuhas, Alan. 2016. "US Beekeepers Fear for Livelihoods as Anti-Zika Toxin Kills 2.5m Bees." *Guardian*, September 4, 2016. https://www.theguardian.com/environment/2016/sep/04/zika-mosquito-neurotoxin-kills-bees-livelihoods-beekeepers

GLORIA M. COLOM BRAÑA is a doctoral candidate in the folklore program at Indiana University. She is completing her dissertation on the cultural uses of modernist spaces, specifically traditional uses for open-aired carports in Puerto Rico. She did her bachelor's in environmental design at the University of Puerto Rico and has a master's in historic preservation from Columbia University and a master's in architecture from the University of Illinois at Urbana-Champaign.

# ELEVEN

# Forming Strands and Ties in the Knotted Atlantic

## Methodologies of Color and Practice of Beadwork in Lucumí Religion

MARTIN A. TSANG

Afro-Cuban Lucumí beadwork is highly symbolic of the religion it comes from, yet its presence has been lodged firmly in a seemingly secular and socialist milieu. Only scarce work has been carried out to date that helps us understand more fully this beadwork's symbolism and the attendant processes of making, knowledge production, and memory making. Beads and their making can offer a great deal to critical folkloristics and help us shift focus away from ethnographic and even museological forms of inquiry and exhibition; this shift in turn uncovers new data and illuminates interstitial and overlooked spaces of interaction and religion making.

In the song "Soy todo" by the popular Cuban music group Los Van Van, Mayito, the lead singer, notes the various natural and cultural aspects of Cuba and *Cubanía*, creating connections in the listener's mind between all things Cuban by multiple means, no matter who and where the listener is (Juan Formell y Los Van Van 2003). One verse contains the line "Soy los colores del mazo de collares," which explicitly refers to the beaded necklaces of the Afro-Cuban religion that can often be glimpsed around the necks of wearers in Cuba and the diaspora. Their presence often goes without comment, yet they signify so much. So well attributed is the wearing of a bunch of beaded necklaces to religious practice that the listener takes for granted what the lyric by Los Van Van signifies. This essay takes its cue from that which is commonly seen yet undervalued in folkloric and ethnographic research.

Intricate patterns of colored beaded necklaces adorn bodies and shrines; they are wound and stitched over sacred orisha implements and serve to visually encode the circulation and long histories that befit beadwork in circum-Atlantic expressions of sacred material cultures. Strands of glass beads fashioned by Lucumí (also called Santería or la Regla de Ocha) ritual artists are the flags of the orishas.

They perform a central role in rituals and celebrations and act as a living archive for transnational African-inspired ritual, memory, and identity. Wound and bound within these works are the entangled cultural stories and melded histories of European-, African-, and Asian-derived aesthetic practices. Some of these histories are not so immediately visible, yet in each finished, consecrated piece there are traces of global movement and connections that are as integral to its structure as the strings and knots that hold and bind. Communal beadworking in Havana's *ilé orisha* (houses of orisha worship) offers important sites and moments for religious instruction and social care. By focusing on beadwork as the veritable fulcrum of practice and knowledge, I seek to introduce a necessary conversation to the study of multiple and intersecting cultural traditions of color practice, and I argue that this conversation is foundational to theorizing the future of critical folklore methods. In addition to the potential impact that a focus on beads and spaces for beadwork in the Lucumí religion has on critical folkloristics, there are important lessons to learn about the long history of museum studies, which are connected to folklore in many ways. Jo Farb Hernández (2015) writes that the focus on folklore of museum spaces, their resources, and their personnel has been growing in recent years and manifesting in multiple ways. Hernández notes that exhibitions that use objects and ideas from folklore studies raise issues that are common to the discipline, academia, and other public-sector fields (62). A range of museum settings benefit from using folklore methods through object-oriented displays and the integration of new technologies, especially in audiovisual and interactive arenas. These inclusive tactics can also draw on different audiences, not only as visitors to the eventual displays and programming but also as new participants in their collection, creation, and pedagogy. In 2014 I participated in an initiative by the Horniman Museum and the Royal Anthropological Institute in London, United Kingdom, that led to the collaborative creation of a Lucumí beaded object made by an Afro-Chinese priest in Regla, Cuba (Tsang 2017). Through these measures and through concentrating on increasing diversity and inclusivity in the realms of both folklore and museum studies, foundational practices for both are in dialogue. The potential for expanding both fields is also creating opportunities for the exploration of religions such as Lucumí.

I explore the traveling biographies and itineraries of Afro-Atlantic beadwork through the making of these pieces, emphasizing the sacred, temporal, and transnational meanings and experiences of beads in terms of creating, wearing, and adorning, which are each physical facets of devotion. My central claim is that beads do far more than adorn: they act as portable storage devices for memory, as they contain and convey information about local and global flows of people, goods, and ideas, as well as organizing and categorizing Atlantic understandings of the spirit that have been greatly underestimated and academically overlooked.

This passing-over has occurred not only in the realms of folklore and the social sciences but also in economic and historical treatments of Afro-Atlantic religions, where they form a particularly rich source of inspiration.

Beads form part of everyday practice for thousands through their wearing and are present in significant ways in initiations and celebrations. By focusing on beads and especially the spaces where they are made, the ways they adorn bodies, and their aesthetic uses on altars and shrines, we can see that they are a form of connective tissue in ways that activate the beads as themselves living and having life-sustaining forces. This realization allows us to open up new avenues of conversation that center on the methods of understanding how ritual knowledge is transmitted in multiple ways and what other conversations can take place in these settings. I am interested here too in the ways that bead making contains graphic glimpses of Chinese and Afro-Chinese methods and ideas as handed down by practitioners and artists in Cuba and the diaspora. These ideas create spaces that do more than hint at the many ways that knowledge imparting and memory keeping are activated.

With these facets in mind, I discuss in this chapter the twofold connected aspects of beads and spaces for beading. Additionally, I broach Lucumí color theory in bead making, as color is easily unseen because of its ubiquity, and commonplace understandings of color in global and modern contexts can easily overlay the important and distinct correspondences ritual color plays in the lives of practitioners. By shifting our perception and recognition of color as a vernacular methodology and away from the narrower observation and descriptive purposes of color, we are able to apply these understandings in a useful way to folklore studies, providing bridges between diverse modes of investigation and fields of interest. I propose that color constitutes one of the foundational ways that orisha worshippers come to understand their spiritual purview, and by coloring in their otherwise transparent dimensions of belief, they transform their symbolic communication. Color, as evidenced in beading and its making, requires an understanding of it that brings about a new or distinct way of seeing, instructing, and learning in the ways of the orishas. As a corollary, culturally diverse memories are invoked and reconstituted in the elaboration of orisha beads, and practices of different and untold histories, especially of Chinese and Afro-Chinese attributes and knowledge, are encoded and layered in the resulting processes and products. I discuss here how the presence of the orishas is called through color and number combinations as much as it is through the dedication and *ashé* (spiritual life-force or power) raising rituals that accompany Lucumí beadwork. The importance of beadwork for adorning orishas and practitioners cannot be overlooked. Like cloth, stones, metals, shells, and much more, the employment of beads in orisha religions is consistent in its presence and acts as a conduit for creativity and invoking the spirit to be present and as close, intimate, and unwavering as a necklace touching the skin. Beads are present and have a unique role in all aspects of ritual life, including birth, initiation, death, and beyond. Beads are one of the orisha religions' most concrete and beautiful expressions of the divine through the hands of humans; they are generational and lasting expressions of bonds.

## THE BEADED AND KNOTTED ATLANTIC

The orishas are the central deities who are the foci for Lucumí beadwork. They comprise a large pantheon of deities originating from what constitutes present-day Nigeria and Benin, and they are actively worshipped in Cuba, as well as many other places including Brazil and Trinidad. There are further orisha diasporas around the globe, particularly in Europe and the Americas. Beads are made by worshippers in Cuba, Brazil, Nigeria, and many other locales,[1] quite often in communal settings; they are received in special ceremonies, are worn by initiates, and can denote titleholders and membership. In addition to body adornment, they cover ritual objects and are incorporated in shrines and altars.

The prominence of beads in Afro-Cuban religion can be historically traced across the Atlantic to the rich royal and social customs of the many Yoruba kingdoms, whose nobility and priests have been adorned and robed in beads for centuries. Akin Ige states that beads "are significant to the Yorùbá because they are believed to represent the glory of the gods," pointing to the many cultural and religious uses of beads: "The priests, chiefs, and traditional rulers (obá) of Ilé Ifẹ̀ wear kinds of beads that reflect their standing in the complex stratified Yorùbá society." Traditional marriage custom, still observed, states that a new bride should be adorned with beads around her waist, presumably as a sign of wealth, status, and fecundity, and that their absence "is regarded as outlandish and even abominable" (Ige 2010, 66–67).

Historically, beads for the Yoruba are essential as social markers, indexing prestige, status, and wealth, and they were made in West Africa for millennia. From the 1600s, West African trade was fueled by mass-produced beads made in Italy, France, and Bohemia, which catapulted their global trade, resulting in slavery, warfare, and colonialism. Through beads, vast fortunes were made across the globe, and the value of beads could be measured in the complex system of bartering, including for human lives. The social importance of beads is witnessed in existing literature through the inclusion of proverbs that speak of the beads as status markers and the epitome of wealth, beauty, and aesthetic elegance in daily and ritual use.[2]

Beads are an outward, physical symbol of living opulently, conspicuously signaling status and power, and they can be recognized as such within the various echelons of society. For the Lucumí, wearing beadwork is an outward sign of belonging and signifying adherence to multiple forms of worship, which, considering potential oppression, can be a daring act of resistance. Lucumí beadwork is not gendered, in that all genders wear all types of orisha-related beadwork. Lucumí beads are not deemed jewelry or only aesthetic adornment, as they have deep symbolic meaning that can be read by members of the community. The prominence of beads and their making creates key opportunities to develop critical methodologies in folkloristics, methodologies that explore the ways in which their making and makers, as well as the use and understanding of color in Lucumí ritual settings and objects, inform worldviews and create opportunities for expression, assistance, and connectivity.

Moreover, the act of beading, the practice of making orisha regalia and adornments, creates communal spaces of instruction where ritual and historical knowledge is discussed, debated, and reconstructed. The beading of items is a social affair, and I highlight these important moments in terms of other conversations that have happened during beading, ostensibly acting as sites of convergence for orisha and adherents that provide safe spaces for the discussions of important matters that are ancillary to the task at hand. In the Lucumí understandings of practice through beads and the employment of color theory, it is the dissemination and reconstruction of knowledge as a community effort that connects practitioners. Our more significant understanding of the pivotal role of bead practice given in these ethnographic examples reveals useful channels of inquiry for the broader field of folklore studies. In this vein, communication in these apprentice-type settings is foundational to the study and practice of material culture. I seek to revise the terms of engagement by putting the materials and people first, as beads connect the people and knowledge to each other. Through their colors and the communal discussions that are generated through these times together, beads can activate memories that are stored somewhere in the object or provoked in the mind and thus act as devices that instruct. Therefore, we can ask how much knowledge is transferred cognitively and discursively, and what knowledge is transferred by mimesis and mnemonic systems not necessarily or adequately expressed in words.

## AFRO-CUBAN RITUAL, COLOR, AND MEMORY

Lydia Cabrera (1970) provides us with a useful entryway for the discussion of color via her work on the importance of precious stones, *otán iyebiyé*, where she gives color correspondences for some of the most well-known orishas worshipped in Cuba:

> Cada Orisha es "dueno de un color," tiene un color emblemático. Fun-fun, el blanco, le pertenece a Obatalá. Elú, azul profundo, a Olokun; aféreré, azul

claro, a Yemayá. Eidé, lobedo, verde, a Ochún y a Orula. Pupo, rojo a Changó, a Agayú y a los Ibeyi. Popurusa, morado, a Ogún y a Ochosi. Awo pupo, owura, yeyé, amarillo, a Ochún y a Orula. Dudu, negro, Elegua y a Echu. Y todos entremezclados a Oyá. Los Orishas actúan en sus colores. Con ellos protegen a sus hijos y devotos en los Ileke-Orishas, collares de cuentas que tienen, como saben los adeptos de todas las sectas de origen africano, un gran valor místico.

Each Orisha is "owner of a color," each has an emblematic color. Fun-fun, white, belongs to Obatalá. Elú, deep blue, Olokun; afereré, light blue, to Yemayá. Eidé, lobedo, verde Ochún and Orula. Pupo, red, Changó, Agayú and the Ibeyi. Popurusa, purple, Ogun and Ochosi. Awo pupo, owura, yeyé, yellow, to Ochún and to Orula. Dudu, black, Elegua and Echu. And multicolored for Oyá. The Orishas act in their colors. With them they protect their children and devotees in the Ileke-Orishas, the necklaces of beads that have, as the adepts of all the sects of African origins know, a great mystical value. (13–14; translation mine)

While some of the color and bead correspondences reported by Cabrera may differ from today's practice and material record, Cabrera underlines the active influence of color in connecting the orishas and their worshippers. Colors are not merely decorative or emblematic; they have performative and generative actions that act as conduits for protection and form part of an exchange of knowledge and practice, based on non-Western sentiments of theological color representations. Lucumí rituals, initiations, and their attendant practices and embodied meanings are particularly reliant on and referential to color.

There are four primary colors in the Lucumí ritual spectrum: white, red, blue, and yellow. These four, which are described in that order in Spanish—*blanco, rojo, azul*, and *amarillo*—are the hued signatures of the four orishas who are indispensable in ordaining a priest or *olorisha*, independent of which orisha or *alagbatorí* a person is being initiated to. What's more, these colors appear in different ways and in various materials: cloth, paints, herbal extractions, and beads, as well as being referenced and praised in Lucumí songs and parables. There is a hierarchy among the four colors. Such a hierarchy codes the use of these colors during ritual, and their presence in sequences and patterns configures, activates, and directs Lucumí consecrations. A principal ritual song employed in the initiation process includes the following lines that delineate the seniority of the color white over red:

*Efun odo agba osun*
White chalk of the wooden mortar is the elder of red osun camwood[3]

*Egbon a wa dá ashé*
The elders give [their] ashé

*Efun ewa osun l'aburo*
White chalk is the elder sibling of the beautiful, red camwood

According to Roy C. Abraham (1981), *efun* is the white chalky substance used in the service of the *funfun* or white orisha, of which Obatalá and *osun* is a rosewood powder whose "sap dries to a blood-red resin" (490). The above song clearly indicates the seniority of white chalk over red camwood, which in turn instructs the patterns of color used and their order implemented in ritual. Color pigments made present through paints and natural materials distinguish the ceremonies between those of one orisha and another. Therefore, the process of initiation and consecration of any one orisha will be reliant on an ability to skillfully and correctly apply color in ritualized moments through the material means of paints, fabrics, and beads.

Colors present in the form of beadwork for the orishas are meant to be seen, worn, and displayed, both on orishas and on humans. Beads, when worn on the body or as part of a ritual display, act as spiritual affirmations and symbols of devotion and can signal multiple or layered meanings. Beadwork can be interpreted and read according to etic or esoteric logics such as adepts, as Cabrera calls them, often revealed in stages via the passing through and then participation in ritual and initiation practices. In the Lucumí religion, one may first encounter the orishas through viewing a person's necklace (fig. 11.1) or bracelet, whether proudly and overtly worn or just able to be glimpsed at the nape or at the wrist. The visual contact may not be meaningful or readable in the religious correspondence that the wearer intends, but to those who are familiar with the religion will easily identify the patterns and colors of necklaces, especially when more than one is worn at a time (see the *ileke* ceremony, below). Similarly, those who have undergone the lengthy one-year-and-seven-day priesthood initiation will wear the large multistrand mazos on the second or "Middle Day" as part of their debut process. The mazos worn represent the principle orishas consecrated during the initiation and form part of a ritual ensemble where the initiate is dressed in a ritual garment that reflects through color their tutelary orisha. Together, the cloth and beads indicate the presence of the orisha sacralized in the person, show the richness and power of the orisha through fine cloth and costly beads, and affirm the person's lifelong connection to their deity in the presence and reverence of the religious community.

## AFRO-CUBAN ILEKE

The practice of making beadwork and its subsequent ritual uses in Afro-Atlantic religions such as Cuban Lucumí ceremony are fruitful avenues for discussing folkloric methodologies of fieldwork in religion. Beads are known as *ileke*, which is a Yoruba-derived word used widely in the circum-Atlantic, and just like the West African name shared across countries and time zones, beads are anything but static. I argue that the unique positionality of orisha beadwork as both personal

Fig. 11.1 An olorisha or priest's inherited red-and-white Shangó ileke, photographed in Havana. The necklace uses "green heart" or "Hudson Bay" brick-red beads, which were made in Murano, Italy, between 1480 and 1830.

(work on the body) and public (visible as shrine ornaments and worn necklaces and bracelets) transgresses borders, and these positions are transportable modalities for religious pedagogy. My use of the phrase *knotted Atlantic* refers to the circuitous memories and complicated histories of and between the Antillean islands, waterways, and paths. Similarly, it refers to the charting and course of a person's life through ritual strategies, of which beads and their attendant ceremonies and applications are an integral part. The cartographies of beads, countries, colors, and deities create transformative moments in the lives of participants.

While Afro-Atlantic religions such as Lucumí are popularized because of semipublic events such as drumming and call-and-response singing, not to mention the more sensationalized ideas of sacrifice and possession, there are several sites of religious knowledge, praxis, and community engagement that have eluded both the researcher's eye and the broader public's. Ritual knowledge on the use and consecration of beads in orisha practices came with slaves from different ethnic groups such as Oyo, Egba, and Ijesha that are today shortlisted as Yoruba. For the Lucumí, the many orisha each have their own coordinates in colors and numbers of which beadwork becomes the primary visual reference point. *Ileke* is the Yoruba-Atlantic word for "beads" and is commonly used to describe orisha-beaded necklaces that play a sacred and central role in the physical attributes and practices of Afro-Cuban religion.

Beads not only are strung on a physical cord but also are a metaphysical chain that connects the person to their spiritual tradition. These necklaces and beaded objects embody coded messages and memory in their colors, patterns, and coordinates. Beads adorn shrines and bodies, linking the two and infusing both with ashé. They are artistic, and their making requires great skill; they are beautiful too, which echoes the Yoruba monarchy among which the orisha are counted. However, their ritual consecration and preparation and their context—the beads' necessary presence and performance in Lucumí space and time—create their core worth and significance.

The work of David H. Brown (2003) on the ritual power of Santería art forms provides a sensitive analysis of the fashioning and use of elaborate *collares de mazo*, large, multistring orisha necklaces used to adorn shrines and bodies, rigorously underscoring the many vital roles that beads play and perform. One such occasion of ritual bead visibility that I witnessed during fieldwork was during the *día del medio*, the "middle" or second day of the seven-day orisha priesthood ceremony where the brand-new orisha initiate, or *iyawó*, wears several ornate collares de mazo, signifying to the community that the person has been vested with the ashé of the orishas as represented in the assemblage of clothing, ceremonial "throne," and beads, which collectively and "proudly proclaim the consecration of an *oricha's* new child: a king, queen, or warrior" (191). Robert Farris Thompson

(1984, 95) aids my understanding of beads as bridges and links between Yoruba tradition and religious expression in Cuba, as he explains that the heavily beaded and sumptuous royal tunics appear in Cuba in a renewed form of the beaded garments worn by the sacred drums used ritually in Lucumí worship.

The ilekes or single-strand beaded necklaces are worn by initiates after rituals have been performed on both the person and the beads. The ilekes are made by initiated Lucumí bead artists and consecrated according to Lucumí religious practice to infuse the beaded object with ashé, or divine power and spiritual force for change. The beads become personal, sacred objects through their fashioning by practitioners and subsequent ritual action. These beads are worn to convey religious meaning and for their spiritual actions. Rogelio Martínez Furé (1961) makes a distinction between profane or unconsecrated ilekes and those that are consecrated, which are then called orisha ileke and which can "quiet an unruly spirit, cure sickness, or protect its owner from any [spiritual] current or [maleficent] work" (1961, 23; translation mine).[4] An olorisha, Jorge, who has been beading for more than forty years in Havana, explained that all beads made of glass, precious materials, or semiprecious materials are "reserved for the orishas, the kings, and queens of the religion" (Jorge Carrillo, interview, February 2018) and that devotees earn the right to be ornamented by beads through the agency of initiation. One of the first initiations often undertaken by Lucumí adherents is the ceremony of putting or receiving the beads. In preparing for such an event, as with other initiations that require them, the necklaces are specifically made for the person, often by commissioning a known orisha beadworker.

The ileke ceremony, known as "receiving the beads," which are called *los collares* in Spanish, is a particular initiation often undertaken upon first entry into the religion and occurs before one becomes an orisha priest. It is a one-day process followed by a week of wearing white clothes, in which the person becomes formally welcomed into the orisha house or ilé orisha by his or her orisha godparents and thus receives the protection and ashé of the orishas, in the form of the ritually prepared necklaces. While this is a ceremony that one can undergo when entering the religion and beginning a formal commitment, the diversity and variations found in orisha practice mean that this is not mandatory or standard. However, the receiving of beads, specifically necklaces, more or less features at some point in the initiation life cycle of a person and can occur in many ways, either standalone or integrated as corollaries to other rites.

As indicated above, the ileke ceremony is a weeklong process. The ceremony occurs on day one, and the new initiate wears white clothes for the following six days and observes some restrictions, which echo the commitment made when undergoing *kariocha* or priesthood initiation In so doing, the person becomes welcomed into the orisha house and receives the necklaces. The ileke ceremony

Fig. 11.2 Lucumí orisha ileke, counterclockwise from the bottom center: Eleguá (red, black, and white), Obatalá, Oshún, Shangó, and Yemayá (blue, crystal, and pink coral).

entails receiving a set of consecrated, single-strand necklaces that represent at least four orishas fundamental to the religion: Obatalá, Oshún, Shangó, and Yemayá (a fifth necklace, that of the orisha Eleguá, is quite often but not always given to the initiate at this time; see fig. 11.2). After undergoing the ileke ceremony, the person has the right and privilege of wearing the consecrated orisha necklaces of these five orishas. Within the sacred time and space of the initiation, the recipient receives the color-coded necklaces pertinent to these orishas, and this may be the first time that the specific colors pertaining to each deity become known to the person. From then on, through wearing them, colors can become connected permanently in the person's mind to the individual orisha, and the person can begin to recognize other significant instances of ritual color use. Therefore, from the beginning of a person's involvement and induction into the Lucumí religion, beads play a prominent role, and color initiates subtle yet deep forms of knowing that continue to expand and evolve throughout the person's education and ritual pursuits. As the relationship deepens, one may become an orisha priest through further initiations, at which time the orisha vessels of the major orishas are received, and further ceremonies are performed for the person to connect their head or *orí/eledá* to their orisha.

### CREATING THE BEADWORK: INTIMATE SPACES OF PRACTICE, INSTRUCTION, AND CONVERSATION

Beadworking is an ilé activity, bringing together disparate people to learn traditional beading techniques and the attributes of the orishas, to earn knowledge, and to seek spiritual and practical help. This chapter uses ethnographic data from Cuban fieldwork, including time spent with an Afro-Chinese priest and master bead artist, as well as members of the ilé who came together regularly to create and discuss beaded objects for worship. These meetings and spaces of practice show how, in the hands Afro-Chinese priests and ritual artisans, small, pierced pieces of glass become teaching and memory devices and how these practices catalyze the transmission of multiple forms and subjects of knowledge in meaningful and often intimate ways. Through this approach of focusing on the making and attendant discussions, we can better understand what happens in such spaces of bead practice that convey information on orisha theology and ritual discourse, especially in terms of color as an organizational principle and how such spaces and times for beading offer the opportunity for instruction in ritual ways and for practical and frank discussions on critical and sensitive matters.

A single-strand ileke or beaded necklace worn by initiates uses critical number, color, and pattern compositions, often comprising approximately four-millimeter glass beads that are sourced from manufacturers based in the Czech Republic. Italy and Bohemia have traditionally supplied many world cultures—including Native American and African beadworkers—with their supplies through lengthy and complex trade routes and unequal, transnational formations of power, wealth, and authority. These trade routes are especially and deeply implicated in the histories of colonialism and enslavement. Today, China and Japan also make beads that supply the world beadmaking communities. The necklace length may be approximately twenty inches, so they can be worn comfortably about the neck and are supposed to reach the navel. While some orisha ilekes documented in Cuba (see figs. 1 and 2) were more elaborate than others, all the Lucumí priests I interviewed about religious beadwork stated that these beads were not worn for aesthetic reasons or as fashion statements.

When speaking about beads and their ritual importance, several Lucumí participants whom I interviewed stressed the requirement of having these beaded necklaces made by initiated members of the religious community. Thus, beading is a necessary mode of religious devotion, expression, and pedagogy that requires ritual and mythological knowledge. One senior priest of the orisha Yemayá, Avelardo, stated that there was a religious protocol that needed to be fulfilled when making an ileke, as a ritual invocation to the orishas must be uttered when tying and knotting the finished necklace. Many priests agreed. One *madrina* or godmother to several initiates stated that she intones a special *mojuba*—an invocation for God, the universe, the ancestors, and the deities—every time she ties a necklace. She stated that such an action would be impossible for an uninitiated person to do, thus invalidating any necklaces that are for sale in the small *tiendas religiosas* (religious goods stores), where it cannot be verified that an initiate had ceremoniously tied the ileke for sale (Iyalorisha Carmen, interview, February 2018).

According to the priest, an *aleyo* or religious outsider who has not undergone the specified initiatory rites should therefore not be making these items, as they would not be able to effectively perform the religious incantations needed when closing the necklace, nullifying its prospective use and future consecration as an ileke. Through these invocations that are required in the proper fashioning of the sacred, the beaded ileke are connected to the power of chant in other global traditions, including Native American sand painting and Buddhist mandala making, which is accompanied by mantra. Many priests continue to make their own necklaces for ceremonies rather than buying them premade in the botanica or religious goods stores (fig. 11.2), as priests agree that it is unlikely that the commercially available ilekes would have been made following the necessary ritual protocol.

Beads are devotional and symbolic gestures of outward (and inward) expression of the Lucumí religion. Thus, the beads used in Afro-Cuban religious practice have a value that is not intimately connected to the secular economy or solely a means for aesthetics, embellishment, or adornment in the name of art or beauty. Furthermore, through their ritual preparations and the considerations that are placed in the making, wearing, and handling of beads, they are regarded as being more than their physicality. Beads co-opted into creations for the orishas can be thought of as having biographies (Kopytoff 1988), and they have itineraries (Joyce and Gillespie 2015), the latter fitting both their industry and making as beads and their employment as orisha beadwork.

## INVENTIONS AND TRADITIONS: AFRO-CHINESE BEADWORK

During fieldwork in Cuba, I was able to document the household orisha bead *talleres* (studios) of two Afro-Chinese priests, whose insights help advance our understanding of Cuban religious racialized identities. Chinese and other racialized Cuban presences are often discussed in terms of Fernando Ortiz coined word *transculturación* (transculturation; see Ortiz, Le, and Malinowski 1991), which is the meeting and amalgamation of disparate European, African, Asian, and indigenous cultural products and processes that form a unique and unifying Cuban identity. The master beaders Pablo and Jorge supply many ilé orisha, *babalawo*, and foreign practitioners with beadwork. The commissions made by both artists were incredibly varied: from exquisite Aña drum aprons or *banté* that contained mythic scenes and abstract designs, beaded gourds, vessels, horsetail fly whisks, staves or canes, and more, to large numbers of single-strand ileke for initiations and the multiple-stranded collares de mazo, very large and ornate bunched necklaces comprising thousands of beads that are worn on particular occasions by initiates and are draped on orisha vessels during ritual feast days, anniversaries, and other celebrations. Both beadworkers also employed assistants, who would undertake special projects after proper training, and both master beadworkers and their assistants, whose work would often occupy many hours of each day, would be helped in some form or other by members of the religious household, extended family, and visitors. During my research tenure, there was a rotating core of helpers who, depending on skill, time, and desire, would sort beads, string them, sew cloth linings, and perform other tasks ancillary to the making of beaded objects. Much like the lead bead artist and those who assist in the making processes, the individual beads that are collected, tied, and knotted into the service of the orishas become microcosms of the larger ilé orisha. Beads and ilekes are the material contingent to the worshippers who gather and create them. Through their making, spiritual power or ashé is raised, condensed, and channeled into these objects, eventually secured there through the ceremony, and mirrors the ways and functions of the ilé orisha in its entirety.

The community members who lend their hands to beading efforts can be involved in thin and thick engagement, meaning that their participation is largely self-determined, and some may be central or supportive to the beading process. What struck me during these hours were two things: the instruction of knowledge, techniques, and practices that were discussed as being of Chinese origins and the ancillary topics discussed lying outside the tasks at hand. Both leading beaders spoke of their conscious adaptation of Chinese forms and aesthetics that they applied to their work. Jorge, who had been beading consistently for over thirty years, was trained by a Chinese Cuban initiate, who, in turn, adopted many beading, sewing, and placement techniques common to Chinese embroidery and tapestry making, for which his family was historically renowned. Both ritual beaders described the importance of creating beadwork in the "correct way," which upheld tradition through the processes employed

of fastening and securing beads, and through bead color and number correspondences, and they also spoke of the ways that they could be creative in
terms of bead sizes, shapes, textures, and items chosen to be beaded. Chinese
artistry and methods are embedded in the ilé orishas that rely on and commis-
sion such beadwork, making for often unknown Asian influences in beadwork
otherwise thought of as resolutely African in its making. Asian iconography
runs throughout Lucumí materiality: the vessels that house the consecrated
elements of each orisha are often of Asian design, and wooden and ceramic
statues are also employed in shrines and represent divination narratives or
essential parables, called *patakín*.

The materiality is important, but the ways that the time is spent in these communal practices is as important as—or from some vantage points, more important than—the final beaded object, which may be exhibited only on brief ritual
occasions. The balance between practice and finished product highlights a critical
symbiosis between the two, as they bring together people, materiality, and the
spirit in ways that are balanced and reciprocal. In these capacities, beads and
their creations are memory-storage devices for racial and ritual knowledge that
are transferred not only cognitively and discursively but also without words, by
mimetic action as mnemonic systems that are significant tools of communication
and knowledge sharing. Lucumí religious beadworks are mnemonics that flatter
the deity in bold representations of beauty and seniority through the employment of scarce, expensive, and precious resources, and they function as extended
tools for communication in two ways. Within the Chinese Cuban practices of
beadmaking, many beads made of ivory, coral, jet, amber, mother-of-pearl, and
other materials have been repurposed for orisha work after being handed down
by generations of mixed Chinese and Afro-Cuban heritage. Malas, Buddhist
prayer beads, and secular jewelry have been dismantled and used to make necklaces, bracelets, and collares de mazo, which create moments of conversation
when the pieces are displayed or worn. These pieces, while relatively few, become
physical devices for discussing ethnic and religious interactions that go beyond
our understanding of syncretism as it has been applied in anthropological and
folkloric studies as a cornerstone of Lucumí practice. Instead, these materials of
mixing and memory can be considered as part of a process I deem "interdiasporic
cross-fertilization" (Tsang 2016). First, the making advances understanding of the
processes by which the deities and their adornments are fashioned or come to be
born, allowing individuals to glimpse the inner workings and habitual practices
of communities of orisha worshippers. Second, the use of these materials to communicate generational and spiritual knowledge through their ritual functions
underscores the representational ability and functions of orisha material culture.
The making of beads, the wearing of them on the body post-initiation, and the

dressing of gods and altars create deep connections that develop a transformative understanding of aesthetics and praxis.

## CONCLUSION

Instruction and learning of bead techniques, being communal, open up spaces for communication and conversations that are not easily had in other spaces of ritual action and celebration. Thus, the countless hours spent beading and being present in beading spaces sheds new light on the ways ritual knowledge and assistance are scaffolded and couched by these practices and conversations. Participants are engaged in spiritual activity and have a platform to express creativity, to offer their labor, to interact on many levels, and to receive advice and assistance through relevant discussions during production. Critical folkloric studies provide ample opportunities for the study of both beadwork in the Lucumí religion and the negotiated fields of assemblage and creativity that add further rich dimensions in the multiple and meaningful ways that materiality can frame the preservation and promotion of memory and ritual knowledge in other, yet-untold venues.

## NOTES

Fieldwork research for this chapter was made possible by financial support from the Ruth Landes Memorial Research Fund, a program of the Reed Foundation.

1. Within the wider Yoruba-Atlantic universe, excellent examples of Brazilian candomblé ileke and other *orixá* beadwork can be found in *Obaràyí: Babalorixá Balbino Daniel de Paula* (Mariano et al. 2009). For Yoruba beadwork in Nigeria, see the work of Fagg (1980); Armstrong (1981); Beier (1982); and Pemberton (2008).

2. See, for example, "Eniti o so ileke pari aso" (Owomoyela 2008, 258), a proverb that is translated as "The Person who adorns himself with beads has done the ultimate in self-beautifying."

3. These are parts of a song that is used in the initiation of a new priest; they are part of oral memory and communal instruction, as they are learned while participating in the ordination of the initiate. The translations to English are mine. The ritual vocabulary of the Lucumí religion presents specific challenges in translation resulting from centuries of remembering and alteration, over time losing important tonal inflections found in the principally Yoruba language and etymology from which it derives. Yoruba language is polysemic, and thus there are multiple ways in which individual words can be translated according to accent and stress.

4. From the Spanish "aquietar un espíritu discolo, que curar a un enfermo o proteger a su dueño de cualquier corriente o trabajo" (Martínez Furé 1961, 23).

## BIBLIOGRAPHY

Abraham, Roy Clive. 1981. *Dictionary of Modern Yorùbá*. London: Hodder and Stoughton.

Armstrong, Robert P. 1981. "Yorùbá Beadwork." *African Arts* 15 (1): 21–22.

Beier, Ulli. 1982. *Yorùbá Beaded Crowns: Sacred Regalia of the Olokuku of Okuku*. London: Ethnographica in association with the National Museum, Lagos.

Brown, David H. 2003. *Santería Enthroned: Art, Ritual, and Innovation in an Afro-Cuban Religion*. Chicago: University of Chicago Press.

Cabrera, Lydia. 1970. *Otán iyebiyé: Las piedras preciosas*. Miami: Ediciones C.R.

Fagg, William Bueller. 1980. *Yorùbá Beadwork: Art of Nigeria*. With a foreword by Bryce Holcombe and descriptive catalogue by John Pemberton. New York: Rizzoli.

Hernández, Jo Farb. 2015. "Folklore in Museums: Issues and Applications." In *Putting Folklore to Use*, edited by Michael Owen Jones, 62–75. Lexington: University Press of Kentucky.

Ige, O. Akin. 2010. "Classification and Preservation of Ancient Glass Beads from Ile-Ife, Southwestern Nigeria." Glass and Ceramics Conservation 2010. Interim meeting of the ICOM-CC Working Group, Corning, NY, October 3–6, 2010. Hannelore Roemich.

Joyce, Rosemary A., and Susan D. Gillespie. 2015. *Things in Motion: Object Itineraries in Anthropological Practice*. Santa Fe, NM: School for Advanced Research Press.

Juan Formell y Los Van Van. 2003. "Soy todo (Ay Dios amparame)." Track 3 on *En el Malecón de la Habana*. Cuba: Timba Records.

Kopytoff, Igor. 1988. "The Cultural Biography of Things: Commoditization as Process." In *The Social Life of Things*, edited by Arjun Appadurai, 64–91. Cambridge: Cambridge University Press.

Mariano, Agnes, Aline Queiroz, Dadá Jaques, and Mauro Rossi. 2009. *Obaràyí: Babalorixá Balbino Daniel de Paula*. Salvador, Brazil: Barabô Design Gráfico e Editora.

Martínez Furé, Rogelio. 1961. "Los collares." *Actas del folklore* 3:23–24.

Ortiz, Fernando, R. J. Le, and B. Malinowski, B. 1991. *Contrapunteo cubano del tabaco y el azúcar*. La Habana: Editorial de Ciencias Sociales.

Owomoyela, Oyekan. 2008. *Yoruba Proverbs*. Lincoln: University of Nebraska Press.

Pemberton, John. 2008. *African Beaded Art: Power and Adornment*. Northampton, MA: Smith College Museum of Art.

Thompson, Robert F. 1984. *Flash of the Spirit: African and Afro-American Art and Philosophy*. New York: Vintage Books.

Tsang, Martin A. 2016. "Yellow Blindness in a Black-and-White Ethnoscape: Chinese Influence and Heritage in Afro-Cuban Religiosity." In *Imagining Asia in the Americas*, edited by Zelideth María Rivas and Debbie Lee-DiStefano, 13–33. New Brunswick, NJ: Rutgers University Press.

———. 2017. "The Power of Containing and the Containing of Power: Creating, Collecting, and Documenting an Afro-Cuban Lukumí Beaded Vessel." *Journal of Museum Ethnography*, no. 30, 125–147.

MARTIN A. TSANG is Cuban Heritage Collection Librarian and Curator of Latin American Collections with a secondary appointment in the Department of Anthropology at the University of Miami. Martin is a cultural anthropologist who has researched the Chinese indentured presence in Cuba and Asian influences in Afro-Cuban religious practices. He has published about Afro-Cuban religious writing conventions and continues to explore Afro-Atlantic connectivity and circulations through materiality, especially the uses and movements of beads and beadwork in Lucumí religion. Martin is an initiated Lucumí priest and specializes in making Afro-Cuban beadwork, which has been widely exhibited.

# TWELVE

## Of Blithe Spirits

### Narratives of Rebellion, Violence, and Cosmic Memory in Haitian Vodou

ALEXANDER FERNÁNDEZ

This chapter examines the performance of spirit possession in Haitian Vodou, with a comparative exploration of violence related to the Haitian Revolution and the Vodou possession rituals performed therein. For this work, I use *violence* to describe the voluntary physical and psychic vulnerability that possession priests or worshippers expose themselves to in order to oblige possession by the spirits, or *lwa*, as an integral aspect of Haitian Vodou. More specifically, this chapter unpacks the obscured analogies of possession and how the body is both subject and object of religious action. Attending to language tropes arising during possession rites, metaphors of spirit mounting and riding call attention to the violent nature of ritual trance such that the body of the possessed, like a horse, must contend with the will of the lwa. I unpack the term *violence* in relation to Haitian Vodou and revolution because it is a concept all too often glossed as having solely negative connotations and as anathema to sacred and social stability. Folklore and vernacular understandings of violence as deployed in Haitian Vodou add to the larger narrative of the important work that violence can do in historically, culturally, or metaphysically situated perspectives.

Vodou ritual sacrifice and possession conducted in 1791 was the cosmic catalyst from which the Haitian Revolution was mapped, and it eventually resulted in the abolition of slavery and an independent Haiti in 1804 (Desmangles 1992). Vodou's emergence as the ritual linchpin of the Haitian Revolution necessitated acts of violence in two ways: first, through ritual animal sacrifice and, second, through spirit possession. Though these vital elements of the Vodou ceremony performed before the Haitian Revolution at Bois Caïman are revered by adherents as its propelling effort, they deserve further intimate dissection for academic disambiguation. The anagogic and mystical momentousness of possession and sacrifice cannot be dissociated from this investigation, therefore explicating the phenomenological uniqueness of aforesaid rebellion and the ethnocide it abolished. I argue that the memory of these historic events that resulted in the formation of the first Black republic in the Global South informs and infuses contemporary ideas and practices of Haitian Vodou.[1] This chapter unpacks how such an integral and popularized national legacy, as well as the forms of violence it encompasses, continues to shape the religious identity and sociocultural consciousness of Haitians on the homeland and their diaspora.

Drawing on the theoretical framework of Karen Richman (2005) and building on theories of bodily performances, resonating with Ioan M. Lewis's (1989) concept of religious belief as embodied worship, I discuss the nature and perception of Vodou possession and its associated tropes of mounting, action, and violence, invoking an understanding of this phenomenon in relation to bodily hexis and religious encounter. My work here addresses the lacuna that exists in the current literature on the subject of Vodou possession, positing that further investigation is required to understand the junction of the body and performativity that are core foci in the execution of Haitian Vodou religion. I examine the tropes and vocabulary of Vodou possession, address recurring subjective misconceptions, and offer a novel approach to understanding the corporeal and the spiritual through the lens of possession.

The methodology for this chapter is based on a qualitative, ethnographic, and anthropological research design, incorporating both primary and secondary sources of data. I use these social science frameworks because they allow for the incorporation of religious, historical, and ethno-social tenets in combination and are sufficiently robust for the data to be adequately interrogated. Furthermore, the deployment of these methods directly informs the study of the vernacular that is folklore.

One source of primary data are the interviews conducted with lwa in the heads of Vodou priests in possession, a somewhat rare approach that is incorporated in my investigation for two important reasons. First, it foregrounds the relevance and respect that the practice of possession holds within Haitian Vodou itself, discursively entrained as being one of the major keys to the success of the Haitian Revolution. It is therefore used here as a connector of religion and revolution to explore ideas of violence in both. Second, possession, which has been understood traditionally through the metaphor of a spirit riding or mounting a horse (human being) and recently through the development of cohabitation or transcorporeality, continues to be extremely prevalent in contemporary Vodou worship, and both these means of understanding are simultaneously used to describe possession in this work. By using this source of data to focus on experience as a means of narration, this investigation offers a voice and a positionality that incorporate practitioners and their deities, as well as an opportunity to explore their methods of remembering history and mythology.

## DIVINE PANTOMIME

Historically, the scholarship presented on ritual possession in Haitian Vodou has misconstrued this phenomenon as hysterical dramatization, a product of the individual's own psychoses expressed through the bodily enactments of fanaticism connected directly to their historicity of class struggle and rebellion. Writing in 1946, Dr. Louis Mars, professor of psychiatry at the Institute of Ethnology, Port-au-Prince, Haiti, described Vodou possession as not only a mental crisis but also a product of the disequilibrium that Haitians struggle with as a result of their sociopolitical past. Later, in 1982, as a guest professor of psychiatry at Fisk University in Nashville, Tennessee, Mars admitted to his misdiagnosis and emended his original observation of thirty-six years prior: "The first observations made on Vodou possession in Haiti have been gathered by doctors who used Western clinical models to diagnose Vodou. Little by little, we realized that we were mistaken and made the necessary corrections" (Saint-Lot 2003, 51). It is important to note that the absence of a tangible divinatory canon or oracle, similar to the agents of oracular interpretations found in Afro-Cuban Lucumí or Santería, puts emphasis on ritual possession, making it extremely prevalent in contemporary Vodou worship as the sole transmission of divine doctrinal intervention.

## SPIRITS OF REBELLION

The Haitian Revolution historically began on August 14, 1791, with a Vodou sacrifice of a black boar by the *houngan* (Vodou priest) Dutty Boukman at Bois Caïman, Cap-Haitian, Haiti, a sacrifice offered to the fiery female spirit, Erzulie Dantor. From there, incited by the ceremonial sacrifice and provoking directives set out by Dantor, insurgents sacked the surrounding towns and cities, slaughtered members of the oppressing classes (James 1949, 79–80), and launched the rebel slaves to what is historically recognized as the only successful slave revolt in Western history, a revolution fought by slaves and spirits with a belief reinforced and inspired by Vodou spirituality and magical artillery. It is a prominent chapter in the history of slave legacies that virtually every Haitian, whether in Haiti or in its diaspora, acutely and proudly accepts (McAlister 2002, 204). Markel Thylefors (2009) describes this juncture as important not only for gaining an independent Haiti but also as a pivotal moment in cementing Vodou as a religion in the formation of the country's national identity. Furthermore, Vodou, or "Revolutionary Vodou," as Thylefors deems it, incorporates national patriotic symbolism such as the red and blue of the Haitian bicolor (Thylefors 2009, 74), embedding religion deeply in cultural politics and vice versa.

Leslie Desmangles (1992) writes that racial discrimination reached its apex in Saint Domingue when the French Revolution broke out in France in 1789 (29), and with mounting slave rebellions, Vodou became intrinsically linked to resistance, struggle, and defiance. It was this agency, confirmed and reinforced by Vodou rituals of spirit possession, that encouraged enslaved Africans on Saint Domingue to actively shape their lives, in spite of the imposition of dominating colonial ideologies and other brutal practices of the ruling classes. It also served to counteract a tacit system of wholesale, hegemonic cultural revisionism. Hence, the role of Vodou spirit possession has been central not only within the parameters of a religious framework but also within a broader, more pragmatic cultural context that allows for the continuity of African thought and praxis in Haitian society and its ability to form and inform the lives of Africans and their descendants in the Caribbean and other diasporas. In so doing, religion is recast in a transformative and dynamic light, bringing about deep social reform and demonstrating potent tools for action and change.

Benjamin Hebblethwaite and Joanne Bartley (2012) characterize Haitian Vodou as the hereditary spiritual tradition of African descendants in Haiti. Known as Vodou in official Haitian Kreyòl orthography and also in academe, it is more commonly referred to by practitioners as *sèvi lwa* (serving the lwa) (Ramsey 2011, 6). The lwa, colorful spirits or deities that comprise the Vodou pantheon, inhabit a realm between humanity and the isolated or absent supreme God, *Bondye*. Richman (2005, 22) notes that initially Vodou referred solely to a genre of ritual music and dance, and that with time outsiders and a growing number of metropolitan and itinerant worshippers modified the term to refer to the religion as a whole. Richman states that while such usage is thought of as "foreign," it is now widely accepted yet still relatively alien to many in the rural areas where people, more often than not, described their religion in terms of being Catholic and also "serving the spirits."

Vodou, much like its Afro-Cuban Lucumí and Afro-Brazilian candomblé sister traditions, can be described as a religion with roots tapping several different regions and ethnic groups of Africa, condensed into a coherent and porous theology in Haiti along with other local and European religious and cultural elements. Of these diverse African geographies, two important areas stand out for being highly influential due to their massive involvement in the slave trade in Haiti: Dahomey (today, the Republic of Benin) and the Congo (Hebblethwaite and Bartley 2012, 2). Greatly impacted by the colonial impositions of Roman Catholicism, which was enforced by French colonialism on the island, Vodou thrived as a subterranean current, publicly surfacing only within carefully veiled symbolic and coded appearances through the hybrid agencies of syncretism and creolization. A commonly cited example of this is the everyday, embodied expressions of Haitian Catholicism that become Africanized or creolized, resulting in lwa being worshipped through the outward veneration of Catholic saints.

Claudine Michel (2002, 28) cogently explains that Vodou presents ethics, life lessons, and "thematic modalities" that possess and imbue transformative power through narrative, oral myths, call-and-response songs, acts of healing, and especially the possession performance of the lwa. Roger Bastide (2003, 57) notes that the Haitian Revolution witnessed and was marked by the emergence of many Haitian folk heroes, who are credited with inducing and spearheading the slave revolts in the northern parishes. These charismatic figures are remembered and venerated in Vodou rituals and are associated with the pantheon and action of a family of spirits called the Petro lwa (described as hot spirits), a creole term for the "nation" of Vodou spirits of central African or Congolese origin. Petro spirits are characterized as being "hot-tempered and volatile, given offerings of rum mixed with ingredients such as coffee, hot pepper, blood, and gunpowder" (Métraux et al. 1972, 73). This vital link between action, violence, and religion is shown in the collective memory and the dissemination of the narrative that slave revolts were inspired specifically by the Petro lwa. It can be argued that these deities become spiritual embodiments of violence (Métraux et al. 1972, 39), born out of the resistance and rage of Africans who valiantly fought against slavery (Desmangles 1992, 33). Furthermore, this family of fiery spirits emerged out of a transatlantic dislocation, the brutal displacement of Africans from their homeland, and the prolonged terror and violence associated with the Middle Passage. The Petro lwa were nurtured in secret on the island, their rituals performed during late-evening hours; they provided a moral force and potent ally, helping form a matrix of cohesion and solidarity necessary for the plotting against Napoleonic forces.

## THE SPIRITUAL AND SPIRIT-FULL FORMATION
## OF THE FIRST BLACK REPUBLIC

Following the 1791 sacrifice of the black boar in Bois Caïman, the success of the revolution rested on an ethos of infallible spiritual strength and guidance. Such a coordinated tactic may have been as successful as it was only by having clearly defined symbolic strategies. Vodou, as the key binding force and source of a symbolic call to arms for a geographically disjointed people under a common cause, resulted in a paradigmatic shift redolent of an exceptionally turbulent and historical passage in the often cited "New World." This discourse is defined as *mythos* by Patrick Bellegarde-Smith and Claudine Michel (2006). For these authors, mythos affords a framework for the aforementioned initial violent act and is a term used to categorize memories that shaped Haiti's national identity during the colonial and postcolonial periods (27).

The initial sacrifice of the black boar was conducted to preserve the lives of those itinerant freedom fighters. The choice of the animal to be dispatched was specifically made for its metaphoric embodiment of secrecy. We learn from Vodou songs that recall and commemorate these religio-historical events what the boar signified, that "just as the swine looks to the ground so should their mission be carried out covertly" (Hebblethwaite and Bartley 2012, 177). Participants in the sacrifice understood that this was a powerful message speaking of the necessity to practice secrecy in order to be victorious—the offering of the boar and the spilling of its blood being the catalyst through which their own lives would be spared. Animal sacrifice here can readily be seen as a human substitution and serves to redirect violence into "proper" channels (Girard 1977, 10). By incorporating the sacrifice as scapegoat and as model for a secret methodology of resistance, the struggle for independence was fought not only on a physical level but also on the spiritual and metaphysical planes. In some measure, the act of spilling the blood of the boar fastened in the minds and imaginary of those assembled, and through their ensuing underground networks, the idea that the lwa not only bolstered the rise to power but also had an active role in it themselves. By supplicating the lwa, the enslaved Africans found the ritual embrace with which to catapult what would be a monumental insurgence. The hot and fearsome lwa Ogou Feray, patron of iron and war, possessed the war hero Dutty Boukman, and his fiery and equally ferocious consort, Erzulie Dantor, "rode the head of" (possessed) a *mambo* (female possession priestess). Together, they formed a perfect alliance in the monumental task at hand, breaking down the infrastructures of bondage using temerity and sheer, brute spiritual force.

These supernatural entities also provided enduring models of identity in the face of colonial and catechistic attempts by the plantocracy to eliminate personhood in the physical and spiritual makeup of African slaves in Haiti. The notion of the person as a symbol of and for human consciousness as inherited through Vodou is distributed throughout the body (Bellegarde-Smith and Michel 2006, 2). Modes of suppression of the Black body or identity have taken many forms and are another measure of violence. Karl Marx (1967) speaks of the fact that the labor of the many transforms itself into the capital of a privileged few—in this instance, the bourgeoisie or, rather more aptly named, the plantocracy, a term designating the privileged otherness of the dominant, landowning elites. These ruling classes owned the factors of production—that is to say, not just the machinery but also the slaves themselves. Marx argues that an essential aspect of this effort involved the process of dehumanizing African slaves in order to fit this capitalist regime. This was carried out by various means, including the deconstruction of the African past, creating a tabula rasa or blank slate by which Black people became expendable, less-than-human beings. Blackness was devalued and reified against the notion of whiteness. Skin color was schematized and had the effect of further inculcating notions of humanity, or rather the lack thereof. Mythologies of the Black person were also promoted in order to bring about the idea that slaves were naturally part of the economic and social order, making them less than human. When humanizing qualities were removed from the Black body, it became socially acceptable for physical and symbolic forms of violence to be committed. Vodou was the invisible element that sought to turn these ideologies on their head as well as being a method of healing for said violence. As a means of spiritual reconciliation and an African system of religion and thought, Vodou imbued the African slave with a restorative sense of self and personhood. In so doing, Vodou needed to deal with experiences of violence, allowing for what could be deemed a "grammar of violence" that I suggest helps explain the place and performance of ritual violence contained in Vodou practice.

Through the performance of Vodou—specifically through possession, which incorporates violence in a novel, positive way—there is the ability to reinstate a lost past and alleviate geographical isolation from the homeland by providing a temporary yet recurring transmission and communion with power and knowledge. Possession also creates a break for transformation to happen. As rites of passage do, possession offers a temporally powerful and affective experience that happens in magical time when in ritual circumstances. The practice of Vodou, often covert, introduced a system of internal adaption—a system of thought that allowed the space for change in the social order of Haiti. It enabled a system of orientation of the mind and body in line with a creolized African thought and action.

FROM THE HORSES' MOUTHS: UNDERSTANDING
POSSESSION AND POSSESSION AS UNDERSTANDING

The lwa of Haitian Vodou are a complex site of collective meanings. Lwa possession in the ritual framework of Vodou has a vital and important duty: the lwa inform their adherents in the ways of being. They become in this sense road maps for actions to be taken, and they are physically responsible for the myriad of results and outcomes that may be experienced by the devotees, bound within their mythologies, clear signs of human emotions, and notions of African exigencies and performance. To echo Clifford Geertz (1973, 141), symbols and religious systems, in which the lwa can be included, are strategies for encompassing situations. In this manner, through ritual possession, the lwa are able to maintain a deep and abiding connection between devotees and their home, Guinen, a mythologized idea of an African homeland. By coming in the heads of devotees, the lwa make a transatlantic journey via the *poto mitan*, or central post of the *hounfor* (temple), from Africa (Brown 1991) across the seas. This creates a sacred link between African ancestors, their traditional systems of thought, and New World pragmatisms. Through these interactions and spiritual journeys, the lwa's divine intervention is made continuously present in the lives of Vodou practitioners. The lwa, who come with specific characteristics and ways of being, inform Vodounists in likely, everyday scenarios and offer various options and solutions for social, political, and emotional tensions. The lwa as embodiments of action are thus examples of behavior that mirrors everyday realities, serving as guides for stratagems in the quotidian lives of Vodou practitioners and adherents.

In a discussion on spirit possession, Mary Keller (2002) analyzes possession as a "discursive space of theology" (34). Such a position refutes the need to question possession as "real" or "fake." Instead, Keller proposes an "instrumental agency" that further positions possession in the multitude of forms of spirits, ancestors, and divine entities as "paradoxically powerful," culturally relevant, and increasingly important in the wake of global capitalism (124). Rather than concentrating on arguments of validity or the "reality" of Vodou possession and its spirits, which adds little to the use and position of such bodily performances, Lewis (1989) foments a case for their serious consideration by stating, "I do not proceed to contest the validity of their beliefs, or to imply, as some anthropologists do, that such beliefs are so patently absurd that those who hold them do not 'really' believe in them" (127). Rather, Lewis argues that possession has several important and central sociocultural roles in the religious frameworks of those who practice it. My treatment of the subject of possession directly reflects on and concurs with Lewis's approach. It is important to engage in discourse from an ethnological and phenomenological perspective that allows for discussion of how the body experiences different moments of religious practice.

## AN ETHNOGRAPHIC ACCOUNT OF HAITIAN
## POSSESSION AND AN INTERVIEW WITH THE LWA

It was the evening of October 4, 2016, Little Haiti, Miami, Florida. Assembled in a familial atmosphere, an enthusiastic group of individuals, both *vodouisant* (Vodou initiates) and lay folk, members of the Sosyété San Francois, eagerly waited to see the lwa, through whose divine intercession a tribute was being offered to the family patron, San Francois/Saint Francis. They were in the hounfor of a close friend, colleague, and grassroots Haitian Vodou historian, Houngan Asogwe Jean-Antoine, at the time well into a very youthful seventies, for which he credited the spirit of his deceased mother, who herself lived to an also very youthful 102 years old. Hopeful that Jean-Antoine and I could follow up on a previous conversation about an interfaith analysis we kept postponing on possession as violence in Afro-Cuban religions and Haitian Vodou, I planned for a long evening observing and taking special note of what could be seen as violent gestures during spirit possession. Jean-Antoine had extensive knowledge of the importance of Vodou's role in the Haitian Revolution and how the rituals performed can be seen as violent. He had also done considerable research on gender transformations and violence through the lens of spirit possession in Haitian Vodou, something I have classified in my current work as *trans-spirit gender-bending*, a theory where I posit that during possession, specifically in Cuban, Haitian, and Brazilian spirit possession cultures, there are visible manifestations depicting physical transsexualizing pantomime enacted by the possessed priest. My interactions with Jean-Antoine began after a "coincidental" encounter at a *misa espiritual* (spiritual-medium gathering) I conducted in my home in Miami in early 2012. After witnessing spirit possession as practiced in Cuban spiritual traditions, and one of his own guides having "come through," Jean-Antoine's curiosity was the basis for a strong friendship that flourishes even after his passing in December 2017.

Jean-Antoine's spiritual lineage and family, his *sosyété*, links him to a direct descendant of the Vodou family responsible for the sacrifice officiated to Erzulie Dantor at Bois Caïman in 1791. This particular *rasin* (root) of Haitian Vodou, originating in the northern Haitian region of Cap-Haitian, migrated south to Jacmel, presumably to avoid extermination at the hands of not only the French armed forces but also an envious, rival sosyété. After greeting the gathered members of this prestigious Vodou family, I asked Jean-Antoine if I could assist in the preparations as the night progressed. His response came in the form of a gentle gesture, tapping my nape and inviting me to take my place among the congregation and enjoy the evening—a friendly "Chita! Jwi!" ("Sit! Enjoy!"). As the songs of praise began and the ritual libations were performed, I could feel the *kouran espirityèl* (spiritual currents) circling the *peristil* (Vodou temple space). I followed Jean-Antoine's graceful gestures as he opened the ceremony, the sacred choreography of Vodou libations performed around the poto mitan, accompanied by assisting the priests in a sacred choreography dance for the divine.

Once he had finished the lengthy ritual salutations and genuflections required at the start of all Vodou ceremonies, Jean-Antoine's body, in a state of temporary inertia, began to convulse and jolt in an eloquently maneuvered pantomime enacting stern and ardent movements. The arrival of Erzulie Dantor both abruptly awed and silenced the assemblage. Loud tonalities, simultaneously resembling impassioned laughter and buoyant laments, echoed from her (his) slightly clenched lips, camouflaged behind an alluring leer and haughty laughter. Erzulie's piercing gaze fell on the muster of faithfuls, scrutinizing, surveilling. The affable flock watched in a venerating stupor as tears began to cascade solely from Erzulie's left eye. It is a belief in Vodou that as the matriarch who ruled the Haitian

Revolution, Erzulie Dantor's tears constantly remind her children of her sadness for their grief and sufferings. In contrast, her contemptuous laughter resonates with trenchant reverberations predicting the demise of her devotees' adversaries.

Once Dantor possessed Jean-Antoine, she proceeded to make her ritualistic libations—pouring and drinking rum at the foot of the poto mitan. She greeted the elders and the general collective, and much to my astonishment, she piercingly directed her gaze at me and then uttered in a stern yet motherly tone, *"I know what you come to find gason Alexander. I have that which will quench your thirst, but I need the support of the host of the event in question."* Granted, my level of anticipation escalated to immeasurable heights, as I had no idea where Dantor intended to take me or what "thirst" was to be quenched. The attendees excitedly dressed Dantor in an elaborate navy-blue dress, copiously adorned with red lace, then wrapped her head in a blue-red *mouchwa* (headscarf) and handed her a machete set ablaze with Florida Water, a bottle of rum, and a cigar.

Now draped in ritual attire, Dantor affixed her gaze on one of the women sitting in the circle of mambos, tauntingly approached her, and, taking a robust gulp of her rum, sprayed the drink over the mambo's head. She placed her machete on the woman's right shoulder, and as if a puppet pulled by its strings, the woman began to tremble like a leaf in a strong gale. Moments after, rising from her seat in wading movements, brusquely lifting the rim of her long skirt, and placing her arms akimbo, Ogou Feray had entered the priestess. Again, the attendees rushed to dress the lwa in ritual garments. For Ogou, a khaki military uniform, adorned with authentic honorary US Army medals over the left breast of the blazer, a rapier replacing the more common machete, a pipe, a bottle of rum, and a red mouchwa were the regalia that gave flair to this warrior-spirit's performance.

After a brief ritualistic promenade, abandoning some traditional ceremonial obeisance, Ogou approached me and directed me to follow him to a *badji* (inner sanctum or altar room) away from the crowd. As Ogou and Dantor harmonized and reconciled their respective territory—female spirits stand to the left of male entities in Haitian Vodou—only one *badjikan* (badji attendant), who spoke English, was allowed to remain in the room for the purposes of translation. Sitting in hallowed communion with these two spirits, unsure of what conversation would transpire, I listened as Erzulie was given first discourse: **"My children had suffered long enough. My womb agonized from their cries. When Ogou called me to arms, I accepted his recruitment to take ordnance on behalf of my progeny. I accepted the sacrifice of a black pig and as its warm blood flowed, so did my rage against the oppressor. . . . I tied up my dress and took a dagger to my bite. My gaze became reddened with fury and I devoured the enemy with the swiftness of my sword. I tell you gason; Ogou's machete was no match for me"** (Erzulie Dantor, October 4, 2016).[2] Segueing from Dantor's statement, Ogou spoke of his own participation in the sacrifice at Bois Caïman: *"I stood by her side, but it was Erzulie who wreaked havoc on the white man. I watched her consume the souls of the moribund and delight as the despot's blood emptied from his body. As the sacrificial swine had been sectioned off and its parts taken to the sites indicated through the ritual, so were the thoughts and bodies of the adversary divided. They could not gather themselves long enough to formulate a plan of action that would restrain our revolt. One bloody hand washed the other, and both washed the face of indignation"* (Ogou Feray, October 4, 2016).

Most Western cultures define possession as a spiritual invasion, a bodily violation of sorts, usually violent, unholy, and bizarre. Understanding these spiritual infiltrations as truth is challenging at many levels for the Western mind. Therefore, the notion that Vodou possession is a welcomed, joyous, and enriching experience can be thought provoking indeed. An essential element of Vodou is the construction of a relationship between the devotee and the lwa. This relationship, by no means transitory or ephemeral, involves the extensive exploration and intensive trust established between deity and believer. During the ceremony, the houngan and mambo chant incantations that invite the lwa to possess and speak through members of the sosyété. Many of these songs are taunts to provoke the spirit to come and defend their characters. There are theocratic degrees of possession in Vodou, a hierarchy or spiritual echelon of sorts. A visit by the lwa through possession is described as the climax or "apogee of any *sèvis* (service, ceremony) wherein the priests are the bodies through which the lwa speak and communicate with their participants" (Richman 2005, 199). It is important to note that not every initiated head is susceptible to or capable of withstanding possession. These "heads" receive and transmit the peripheral "currents" of the spirits. This phenomenon was explained to me by Jean-Antoine as *lwa vète*—the spirit behind the mortal veil.

In Vodou, possession is regarded as a rapturous, freeing experience, expressed through welcomed fits of spirit occupancy. This state of accepted divine custody disentangles identity boundaries otherwise made adamantly inflexible by the constraints of social status, gender, and race—another defense for putting society on the *qui vive*, on the alert, as Vodou practitioners endearingly refer to the interactions with their deities. As seen in the above vignette, possession allows for a brash elderly man to embody the satirically coquettish and fiery female spirit of war and love, Erzulie Dantor, and for an older, somewhat frail woman to become a suitable horse for the warlord spirit, the fearsome Ogou Feray.

### BEYOND BOIS CAÏMAN

In the Haitian Revolution, it was a Vodou possession ritual that incited the slaves to muster the courage necessary to revolt against the oppression of the French.

Accepting and rejoining with that essence of divergence became the motivational element of the slave animus. Houngan Dutty Boukman, the horse for Ogou in the 1791 ritual of insurgence, has become a national hero, popularized by song and verse. Relatively few practitioners and fewer Haitian scholars remember the name of the female officiant and horse for Erzulie—Marinette-Corrine Edaïse—which does not surprise Patrick Bellegarde-Smith, who notes that she is but one of a number of women ignored in Haitian historiography; only wives and consorts are typically remembered (Bellegarde-Smith and Michel 2006, 83). The lwa Ogou in all of his many aspects, and particularly as Ogou Feray, can thus be seen as more than a spiritual avatar; he is also a nucleus of many different symbolic qualities necessary for successful battle. Syncretized in some lineages with St. James the Greater, Ogou is venerated as leader, liberator, national hero, and the spiritual general of the Haitian Revolution. Ogou and Erzulie were present at every stage of the design of the revolution—Ogou as the owner of iron and the munitions of war and Dantor as the ferocious maternal authority—which led to the "tempestuous guerrilla activities of the slaves whose overt passion to end slavery terrorized planters" (Desmangles 1992, 148). These possession performances of Ogou and Erzulie collapse time and space, bringing historical events to vivid, living color. Through the combination of two distinct forms of violence, that of the positive and transformative possession itself and that which is relayed through the possession, exists an active and dynamic aspect of Vodou that spurs and inspires ideas by example of transformation and liberation.

More than three hundred years ago, a new Haiti emerged with the spiritual aid of the lwa. While transformation is inevitably turbulent, the violence of the revolution encompassed both a physical plane and a spiritual one. While Haiti today is different from Haiti in 1791, it is not detached from that time because of its Vodou. Although Vodou is still publicly shunned by a portion of Haiti's population, especially with recent interventions by foreign Christian movements to convert the populace, many if not the majority of Haitians synchronously practice some form of Catholicism and Vodou worship. Vodou art and symbolism in the form of murals depicting sacred iconographies are popular in the public milieu. The names of the spirits are known to virtually all, and possession is a recognized and respected part of ritual and sacro-social discourse.

## HUMAN HORSES AND SPIRIT MASTERS

In Haitian Vodou, there are a plethora of *nasyon lwa* (spirit nations), including male, female, and ungendered entities. Some examples are Marasa (childlike twins), Petro (hot), and Rada (cool), and some are even exuberant and obscene, as seen in the family of Ghede, which can dance in the head of the *hounsi* (spirit servitor). As mentioned earlier, the individual that experiences possession is described as being a horse for the lwa. These unique vocabularies of possession and metaphors of mounting are crucial for our emic understanding of the violent nature of the practice. Vodou possession as an act of violence is contextualized within metaphors of the spirit as a powerful and dominating entity, mounting or riding the body of the person, penetrating, coming into, descending upon, and causing an altered state wherein the quotidian personality of the individual is temporarily displaced by that of the deity. Violence is therefore expressed as the struggle by the infiltrating spirit to dominate the guest host, arbitrarily contracting with the individual's incarnate spiritual essence first, then coproducing a unique layer of agency that I identify as the *dance of two souls*. Ritual violence and violence as ritual can be seen or interpreted as a form of dance in many different historical and cultural instances. These performances and practices can include mock battle or even forms of martial arts such as Brazilian capoeira.

An initiated individual can experience multiple possession by different lwa over the course of their lifetime, even during one isolated ritual episode. However, one specific lwa will eventually be identified as the owner of the head. It is through this guiding lwa that the person may then undergo initiation rites to become a houngan or mambo, consecrating the person as a ritual specialist (*Kanzo Asogwe*), thus beginning their training in the service of the lwa. The guiding lwa is called the person's *mèt tèt*, or master of the head, furthering the metaphorical narrative of the person as *chwal*, or horse, culminating in their ability to speak and communicate with participants and in possession occurring through dominance of the body by the lwa or master.

Another term that can further build on our understanding of how violence is registered in possession is *bosal* (Bourguignon 1991, 17), literally "wild" or "untamed." A person that has not been through the ritual preparations to become a houngan or mambo is deemed bosal (savage), and, just like riding an untamed horse, experiences of possession in this state are viewed as untrammeled, fierce, and even dangerous. The rites of priestly initiation include steps to temper the person for possession—breaking in the wild horse, if you will, and allowing the head to be danced or ridden by the lwa in less violent and erratic ways. While possession in Vodou has its integral place in established ritual and is a requirement in many ritualistic settings, it can also happen involuntarily and within the larger sociocultural sphere, sometimes without announcement.

### A BROADER PERSPECTIVE

In West Africa, the Oyo-Yoruba maintain several metaphors of possession that were part of the seed that resulted in the efflorescence of Haitian Vodou.

Anthropologist J. Lorand Matory (2003) explains that the possession relationship between the person and the spirit is implicit in the Yoruba verb *gùn*, meaning "to mount," which refers to what a rider does to a horse. The term also refers to what an animal or a brutal man does sexually to his female partner (422). The Haitian Kreyòl cognate for *gùn* is *monte*, which encodes "the same three referents—sexual penetration, horsemanship and spirit possession" (423). This word has a long and established history of usage by worshippers in Haiti, Nigeria, Cuba, Brazil, and elsewhere.

Vodou, including its ritual practice of spirit possession, is a way of dealing with both violence and memory. Vodou spirit possession offers a framework through which important historical acts and the narratives that surround them are remembered and incorporated into a living, collective memory. Possession is an exciting aspect of Haitian Vodou religion that examines multiple layers of meaning in terms of violence: the violence of possession is not seen as destructive; it is instead envisaged as a process that results in something positive. Through possession, there is a disintegration and reintegration of the self that emphasizes the connection between ephemerality and materiality. Be it communing with the divine, prescribing agency, or acting as a pressure valve in a global society where tensions need to be released, possession effectively turns on its head the commonly held notion of violence as something antisocial or anticultural, with only negative and destructive outcomes, to be isolated and expelled. To such a degree, Vodou ritual possession incorporates a form of violence in its ritual and symbolism for the betterment of its followers. There is an extensive and ongoing discussion by several scholars hypothesizing that there are systems of spirit possession that function as a means by which marginalized individuals, women in particular, are able to have a voice through trance that would otherwise be denied to them.

Listening to what is spoken and performed in possession and being mindful of the positionality of the *sevite* or vodouisant as both protagonists and audience effectively and poetically affords a voice to the spirit itself. Possession can thus be seen as a bridge to understanding and assimilating the past and to applying lived examples to contemporary situations. Often the lwa will recall the events of the past to instill guidance and to aid the sevite in decision making at crucial and challenging times. In this manner, Vodou and its practices, including sacrifice and possession, are ways of balancing both violence and memory. It is the goal of this chapter to explore a multilayered and nuanced approach to explore the power of possession not only as violence but also as the interplay between violence, memory, and ritual.

Pierre Bourdieu (1991, 17) states that societies are based fundamentally on relations of power and capital, which appear in various forms—economic, political, social, and religious—and this dynamic lies at the very core of dominance and violence. It is the inception of social capital that allows for the means of acquiring other modes of capital; hence, those that own the forces of production can acquire the means to dominate in religious settings, thereby reinforcing the stronghold of the dominant group and exerting will over the oppressed. When placing Bourdieu's concepts in conversation with Haitian and religious practices, it can be argued that the colonizer's monopoly over social capital and the means of acquiring more capital allowed for the plantocracy, and other European elite, to compose a superstructure or hierarchy in which African slaves and Vodou occupied the lowest sociocultural levels. Bourdieu stresses that it is not just economic or land capital that produces this superstructure. The relations of domination are social positions imbued with varying degrees of social and religious capital, of networks and contacts that form the social space in which this capital is circulated within clearly defined and regulated boundaries. This reproduces and perpetuates existing relations of domination. What makes this idea even more interesting is the fact that these forms of domination, because of the way they are enforced by every social means, including religious ones, are in fact disguised or naturalized so that they do not seem to be a system of oppression; rather, they are just the natural order of things and a fact of unquestionable everyday existence. In Bourdieu's terms, this is described as the notions of *habitus* and *doxa*, where "power secures itself" (87).

## AYIBOBO! CONCLUSION

The established institutions of imposed European religion and education sought to enforce Western thoughts and ways of domination, coupled with the tabula rasa or erased history of the African past. However, these ideologies were met by internal resistance in the form of Vodou. Haitian Vodou was the antidote to hegemonic cultural capital and the violent acts that were inculcated to dehumanize the Black body. While the African body arrived in Haiti with few if any tangible objects or possessions, there existed strong African religious and social memories and practices that prevented the erasure of notions of African identity. The religion—or rather, religious movement—that formed Vodou sought to protect and empower the African person in the new continent and continue to inform a worldview that was wholly African in origin. This vernacular strategy of violently remembering has been critical to the overall resiliency and efficacy of the tradition. African slave workers were able to mobilize their own capital, as explained by Bourdieu's (1991, 24) theoretical scheme of fields, in an effort to either defend or subvert the legitimacy and hegemony of existing practices—the status quo—and the meanings systematically assigned to them. In this way, while Catholic imagery was imposed as part of a system of reeducation in dominance, these practices were symbolically subverted in meaning and given alternative attributions according to preexisting African thought. This alternative symbolic capital was then able to accumulate as more and more persons came to identify with these symbols in the same countercurrent way, and thus a movement was born.

Terry Eagleton (1991, 39) comments specifically on what Bourdieu (1991) calls *doxa habitus* as being the kind of stable, "tradition-bound social order in which power is fully naturalized and unquestionable" (Eagleton 1991, 47), so that no social arrangement different from the present could even be imagined. Vodou troubles this notion of the established that is above reproach in society and that "goes without saying," and it does so as an empowering tool in such a way that it was able to harness a particular kind of symbolic capital appropriate to the field. Thus, in turn, Vodou became legitimate—a power that is implicitly (covertly) rather than explicitly (overtly) endorsed.

Despite being the only country that was able to win its own independence by a slave revolt, Haiti is the poorest country in the Western Hemisphere. And although we know that many take great pride in Vodou's role in gaining freedom, the religion has also been charged with being antimodern and an obstruction to linear progress, so much so that in the immediate aftermath of the January 2010 earthquake, several leading newspapers ran copy in which Vodou became the primary scapegoat for the country's negative experiences (Ramsey 2011, 22). This dichotomy would be the ideal basis for future research in anthropology, religious studies, folklore studies, and related fields, especially the ways in which possession and networks of Vodou practitioners form and inform Haiti's social and cultural milieu.

## NOTES

1. While the term *Global South* can often have economic and political connotations when uniting countries located in Asia, Africa, Latin America, and the Caribbean, I use it here to focus on Latin America, the Caribbean, and Africa hemispherically and away from Euro-US-centered intellectual and methodology-generated paradigms.

2. Bold and italics express communication with a divinity in possession being quoted.

## BIBLIOGRAPHY

Bastide, Roger. 2003. *Social Origins of Religion*. Minneapolis: University of Minnesota Press.

Bellegarde-Smith, Patrick, and Claudine Michel. 2006. *Haitian Vodou: Spirit, Myth, and Reality*. Bloomington: Indiana University Press.

Bourdieu, Pierre. 1991. *Language and Symbolic Power*. Cambridge: Polity.

Bourguignon, Erika. 1991. *Possession*. Prospect Heights, IL: Waveland.

Brown, Karen McCarthy. 1991. *Mama Lola: A Vodou Priestess in Brooklyn*. Berkeley: University of California Press.

Desmangles, Leslie G. 1992. *The Faces of the Gods: Vodou and Roman Catholicism*. Chapel Hill: University of North Carolina Press.

Eagleton, Terry. 1991. *Ideology: An Introduction*. London: Verso.

Geertz, Clifford. 1973. *The Interpretation of Cultures: Selected Essays*. New York: Basic Books.

Girard, René. 1977. *Violence and the Sacred*. Baltimore: Johns Hopkins University Press.

Hebblethwaite, Benjamin, and Joanne Bartley. 2012. *Vodou Songs in Haitian Creole and English*. Philadelphia: Temple University Press.

James, P. I. R. 1949. *Les Jacobins noirs*. Paris: Gallimard.

Keller, Mary. 2002. *The Hammer and the Flute: Women, Power and Spirit Possession*. Baltimore: Johns Hopkins University Press.

Lewis, Ioan Myrddin. 1989. *Ecstatic Religion: A Study of Shamanism and Spirit Possession*. London: Routledge.

Marx, Karl. 1967. *Capital*. New York: International.

Matory, J. Lorand. 2003. "Gendered Agendas: The Secrets Scholars Keep about Yorùbá-Atlantic Religion." *Gender and History* 15 (3): 409–439.

McAlister, Elizabeth A. 2002. *Rara! Vodou, Power, and Performance in Haiti and Its Diaspora*. Berkeley: University of California Press.

Métraux, Alfred, Hugo Charteris, and Sidney Wilfred Mintz. 1972. *Voodoo in Haiti*. New York: Schocken Books.

Michel, Claudine. 2002. "Vodou in Haiti: Way of Life and Mode of Survival." *Journal of Haitian Studies* 8 (1): 98–109.

Ramsey, Kate. 2011. *The Spirits and the Law: Vodou and Power in Haiti*. Chicago: University of Chicago Press.

Richman, Karen E. 2005. *Migration and Vodou*. Gainesville: University Press of Florida.

Saint-Lot, Marie-Jose Alcide. 2003. *Vodou, A Sacred Theatre: The African Heritage in Haiti*. Coconut Creek, FL: Educa Vision.

Thylefors, Markel. 2009. "'Our Government Is in Bwa Kayiman': A Vodou Ceremony in 1791 and Its Contemporary Significations." *Stockholm Review of Latin American Studies* 4:73–84.

ALEXANDER FERNÁNDEZ is a cultural anthropologist whose research takes a novel approach to the study of the sacred ecologies and possession cultures of Afro-Atlantic religions. Alex holds high-ranking titles as an initiated priest and ritual specialist in the Afro-Cuban Lukumí and Palo Mayombe traditions for over forty years. He currently teaches for the Department of Religious Studies and the Department of Global and Sociocultural Studies at Florida International University.

# PART IV

Placing Community

# THIRTEEN

# "No One Would Believe Us"

## An Autoethnography of Conducting Fieldwork in a Conflict Zone

### MINTZI AUANDA MARTÍNEZ-RIVERA

In August 2016, I returned to Bloomington, Indiana, after spending my summer in Mexico doing fieldwork. One day I had lunch with a close friend, the brilliant Dr. Maria Hamilton Abegunde. During our lunch, we shared our recent stories of conducting research in conflict zones. She had just returned from Juba, South Sudan. From that conversation, Abegunde, an award-winning writer, wrote a poem that merged our stories of fieldwork. That poem became part of an award-winning compilation of poems based on her experiences in Juba. Her poem, our poem, has helped me process some of the things that I have experienced while doing fieldwork, as well as helped me understand why we—researchers and scholars—do what we do. Parts of her poem are interlineated throughout this piece in order to help me tell this story. The complete poem is at the end.

The truth: we can't tell people that what we fear most is what we've already lived

On a sunny and peaceful Saturday in early June 2009, I was returning home after buying some popsicles in Angahuan's main plaza. As part of my yearlong dissertation research, I had been living for three months in this community in Michoacán's Sierra P'urhépecha, Mexico. As I was leaving the main plaza, a large PFP (Federal Preventive Police) convoy drove without stopping through the middle of Angahuan. The cars of the convoy were all black pickup trucks with the PFP logo and had large machine guns mounted on them. Each car transported at least ten men (two or three sitting in the cabin and the rest on the truck beds); all of them were dressed in black with their faces masked and held machine guns or rifles. The convoy and its trajectory were designed to intimidate. Knowing that the streets were no longer safe, I hurried home, in case something happened.

A week before, Angahuan's police had apprehended a group of woodcutters from a neighboring community who were illegally cutting trees in Angahuan's forest. This time, however, instead of surrendering the woodcutters to the authorities in nearby Uruapan (Angahuan's head municipality), as was common practice, Angahuan's political leaders decided not to turn them in.[1] As it turned out, one of the apprehended woodcutters had political influence in his town, which put pressure on the state to send the PFP to Angahuan to force his release.

A couple of days after the first convoy scouted Angahuan, another PFP convoy entered town, stopped in the main plaza, and began shooting into the air to frighten people. The nearby elementary school was in session and full of children. The communal loudspeakers began announcing that families should go get their children, as the PFP was attacking and taking the children away. Panic ensued, and after a brief, violent encounter between the *comuneros* (residents) and the PFP, the comuneros apprehended ten soldiers and two trucks and held them hostage for some hours. A larger PFP convoy arrived as backup shortly after and surrounded Angahuan, blocking all exits from the community. Almost a thousand members of the PFP were deployed to Angahuan. My host family's home is just outside the town's main entrance, by the main road, so we were outside the blockade. From our home, we could see the PFP blocking the entrance to town; neither comuneros nor the press trucks that arrived could go in. The streets were devoid of the usual children playing and running around, and radios, which normally blast music during the day, were silent. A tense silence blanketed the community. For safety reasons, my host mother made all the young women stay inside the house, even while the young men sat outside intently watching and trying to hear what was going on.

Most of the commotion took place in the main plaza, which we could not see or hear from our house. We learned about it later from neighbors and relatives. After the initial altercation, communal leaders began negotiating with commanding officers and talking to the press to spread the news of how the PFP had barged violently into the community, putting children's lives in danger. Later that night, the comuneros reached three agreements with the government: that it (the government in general) could not enter the town proper without the community's permission,[2] that the government would provide an ambulance for the community to take their sick and injured to nearby hospitals (a request that had been denied for years),[3] and that the government would mediate, once and for all, between communities to clarify their borders. By the end of the night, the comuneros freed the soldiers, and the PFP left town.

While events like the one I just described did not occur every day, they were not uncommon. Images and stories of massacres (executed by either drug cartels or the state government), local shootouts, dismembered bodies, femicides, and people disappearing while traveling through the Sierra were everyday news. In this regard, Michoacán, like many parts of Mexico, can be considered a conflict zone. By *conflict zone* I mean "any locality where there is a reasonable chance of medium- to large-scale hostilities breaking out at any time" (Dareff 2010, n.p.; see also Hoffman 2003; Tavanti 2005; Wood 2006). And while it's been more than ten years since the war on drugs began, the end is nowhere in sight, and the violence is still rampant.

Living through unrest and violence while researching opened a different line of questioning and reflection for me: What is the impact—on oneself, our research, and our field—of conducting research in a conflict zone? How can researchers prepare for this type of research and reality? Why do we researchers not talk about the dangers of fieldwork? This essay, while not trying to answer these questions, does seek to challenge us to think about the dangers and perils of doing fieldwork, especially when doing so in a conflict zone.

> A mother and child snatched off the street by men in black clothes, black masks, hiding behind black windows, in a black car. With machine guns. In daylight while we are buying milk.

Drug trafficking and drug production in Michoacán go as far back as the 1930s, when poppy was cultivated in the Tierra Caliente region adjoining the state of Jalisco (Astorga 2012). In addition, because of the size and importance of the Lázaro Cárdenas port, Michoacán became an important transit area for drugs coming from South America. Throughout the ensuing decades, Michoacán has been home to different cartels; it is most recently the territory of Los Zetas, La Familia Michoacana, and Los Caballeros Templarios (Fuentes Díaz and Paleta Pérez 2015).

During the eighty years of the PRI's (Revolutionary Institutional Party) government control, cartels paid hefty fees to government officials so they could operate (González 2009). In return for the government turning a blind eye, cartels respected the civilian population, and in some stateless areas of Mexico, they served as a de facto government, offering resources and employment; building roads, schools, and health clinics; and providing other public services. The silent agreement between the cartels and the government ended with the election of Vicente Fox from the National Action Party (PAN) in 2000. As the state began to interfere with the cartels' business plans and models, cartels had to diversify their products and services. In addition to producing and transporting illegal drugs, cartels began extorting civilians (e.g., charging civilians and business owners "protection" fees for their homes and business, as well as farmers for their crops and land),[4] engaging in illegal woodcutting and mining, and importing illegal Chinese products[5] (Fuentes Díaz and Paleta Pérez 2015). In 2006, when President Felipe Calderón officially declared the war on drugs, the last remaining agreements between the cartels and the state ended, and the local and state order was shattered, immersing the country into chaos.

The official escalation of violence in Michoacán began in September 2006, when members of La Familia Michoacana threw a bag of severed heads onto a club dance floor in Uruapan to announce their presence and send a warning to rival cartels. From then on, dismembered bodies became a common sight (bodies were and are left in plaza and cars, on rooftops, and near schools, highways, or other public spaces). Two weeks after assuming the presidency, President Felipe Calderón deployed over twenty thousand solders to multiple states, including over seven thousand operatives to Michoacán alone. Since it began, the war on drugs has claimed between sixty thousand and one hundred thousand lives in Mexico, per some estimates.[6]

In the case of Michoacán, violence escalated exponentially after military forces were deployed. La Familia Michoacana and the Zetas were fighting among themselves for control of the state and fighting against the military. Moreover, corruption at the state level was so rampant that in May 2009, the federal government orchestrated a raid of mayor government officials throughout Michoacán without informing the state government (Noel 2015). By 2010, most of the leaders of La Familia had been captured or killed, and by 2011, the remaining members formed Los Caballeros Templarios. By 2013, Los Templarios had gained control over most of the state, and the government (both federal and state) seemed incapable of stopping the violence. Currently, Michoacán does not have one principal cartel, but smaller cells, such as Los Viagra, Los Templarios, and La Nueva Generación, which are constantly fighting for territory.[7]

In many regards, Michoacán is a stateless state. Civilians trust neither the government nor government officials. Different groups "patrol" cities, towns, and roads, but nobody knows who they are. While some cities, such as Uruapan, do not have a police force (they were disbanded because of corruption), police forces from other parts of the state have orchestrated massacres, tainted evidence, and routinely violated citizens' human rights. The most recent massacres executed by the state were in Apatzingán (eight civilian casualties) and in Tanhuato (forty-two civilians and one police officer died) in 2015 (Human Rights Watch 2015).[8]

> A man refusing to open his door for anyone who does not have a key to get in
> and saving himself and his daughter that night from being shot to death.

Angahuan is a small P'urhépecha community of 5,773 inhabitants located in the Sierra P'urhépecha. The people of Angahuan are familiar with surviving violence and destruction. During the first half of the twentieth century, Angahuan was destroyed at least three times. The community was burned down during the Mexican Revolution (1910–1920), again during the Cristero Revolts (1926–1929),[9] and a final time during the eruption of the Paricutín volcano (1943–1952). Because

Angahuan is located on a plateau that overlooks the valley where the volcano emerged, the lava never reached the town, but the ashes caused considerable damage.

The last twenty years, and especially the last ten, have been very hard for the people of Angahuan. As drug cells monitor the traffic going up and down the Sierra, putting up blockades, charging for transportation and protection fees, and stealing cars, the road between Uruapan and Angahuan has become dangerous. However, because Angahuan's population is subjected to the stereotypical negative reputation of being "violent and savage Indians,"[10] cartels and the government tend to leave the community alone.[11] Consequently, cases of external violence (outside factors affecting the community) have been less frequent than cases of internal violence (domestic and family violence, fires, murders, and other forms of localized violence). However, the rise of internal violence is tied to the rise of external violence. Violence from the war on drugs has contributed to an increase in tensions, alcoholism, prostitution, and general violence inside the community. Shoot-outs between community members, partly fueled by alcohol, have increased. People in Angahuan have also been killed (most murders are never solved) or have disappeared. In June 2009, one of my research collaborators, César, was brutally killed in a nearby community. The reasons remain unknown, and the culprits were never apprehended. Another research collaborator, Víctor, disappeared in 2015. His whereabouts are still unknown, but he is presumed dead. Sometime after this disappearance, a former communal leader also disappeared, and he is also presumed dead. In September 2017, a fight between local rival factions for control of the communal political organization erupted in armed confrontation, leaving multiple people injured and one person dead.

In juxtaposition to an atmosphere of violence, cultural practices have acquired even more significance in the community, making the study of expressive cultural practices particularly relevant. As John McDowell (2000), David McDonald (2013), and other scholars have documented, expressive cultural practices, such as music and rituals, are particularly necessary and crucial in conflict zones and during times of extreme violence, as they may help communities mediate and process violent situations. In the case of Angahuan, it is particularly noteworthy that over the last ten to fifteen years, older celebrations have resurfaced (e.g., *pastorelas*, which is a dance performed by young women during Christmastime), new ones have been added (such as graduation ceremonies and quinceañeras), and older ones have expanded in scope (such as celebrations tied to the cargo system[12] and weddings). Moreover, in the years that I have been conducting research in Angahuan, cultural events have rarely been canceled, despite widespread insecurity and tension. In fact, it is during those times that cultural practices acquire extra relevance and importance.

I began this chapter by describing the afternoon of tension between the PFP and the people of Angahuan. That day, as in other cases when the community is at risk, men, women, and young people worked together to defend their community. Members of the Council of Elders and the members of the political cargos quickly took charge of the situation, keeping order, negotiating with government and military authorities, and presenting their case to the media. Meanwhile, women prepared food so everybody would have energy for the long night ahead. In situations like this, people in Angahuan pool their resources, be it wood, water, or cooking ingredients, and provide the labor to prepare food to feed large numbers of people.

That day, very few people could be seen walking around the community, and those who did were visiting each other to garner more information about what was happening and to make sure that everybody was safe. As my host family's home is at the entrance of the community, young men came to the house to see the PFP's blockade and discuss the situation. In this regard, the routine practice of visiting, which the community uses to stay engaged with one another and to ensure one another's well-being, was utilized as a communication network that, in addition to serving as a community-wide safety check, effectively disseminated information that could be strategic to the town's defense. Angahuan, like other small communities, may be fragmented and at times divided, but when the whole community is threatened or in danger, people work together for the common good. As demonstrated by the PFP's arrival in the community, in cases where the community is attacked or threatened by outside forces, most of the community will unite.

> The whisper that marks us as different, foreign, and vulnerable to being cheated in the market place. Or slapped while walking down the street alone.

Conducting fieldwork is by no means a safe enterprise. It transforms your life in unpredictable and unexpected ways. Fieldwork, traditionally conceptualized as an in-depth, long stay in a foreign community, is androcentric and imposes ideas of what "good" fieldwork should be, forcing researchers to make unhealthy and unsafe decisions for the sake of proving that they are good enough to do research.[13] Most researchers who struggle or suffer misfortunes during the fieldwork process—such as sexual harassment, rape, and other physical, emotional, or mental harm—tend to stay quiet for fear of being considered weak or not good enough. This silence is especially common for women, people of color, and members of the LGBTQI+ community. And even though it's become more common to read about the personal experiences of researchers while conducting fieldwork, there are still some topics that we shy away from.[14] We do not openly talk about violence, danger, rape, death, how we had to change our research project because it was not safe, or how we were sexually harassed or assaulted. When scholars do write about the dangers of conducting fieldwork, it is often merely a footnote, a small part of a chapter, or an epilogue. More importantly, people get uncomfortable with these discussions, to the point of shunning researchers or telling them to "get over" whatever happened to them. This is not to imply that conversations regarding the dangers of doing fieldwork have not happened; examples include Lee's (1994) *Dangerous Fieldwork*, Mazurana et al.'s (2013) edited volume *Research Methods in Conflict Settings: A View from Below*, and Behar's (1996) *The Vulnerable Observer*. But we still need to be more open about the dangers of conducting fieldwork in general. Why was I not trained to face the dangers of fieldwork? Why don't we (fieldworkers) openly talk about the challenges we face, specifically regarding safety and security?

During graduate school, faculty would talk about some of the most common challenges of fieldwork: adapting to a new environment, health complications, exhaustion, loneliness, establishing rapport, and so on. Some even talked about how they had to change their research plans because of security or health concerns. However, most of those stories never made it to the final product: the publication. I knew that some of my professors had done research in conflict zones, but they decided not to talk about the violence (be it political, racial, or physical), with the result of creating an idealized community on paper. I can understand this decision-making process and have felt pressured to do the same and not speak about the violence.

I have grappled for a long time with the decision to tell the stories that I am currently sharing. In my dissertation, only four pages of my conclusion dealt with Angahuan and Michoacán as a conflict zone. A large part of my ethical struggle was that I did not want to contribute to negative stereotypes that exist regarding Mexico, P'urhépecha people in general, and Angahuan in particular. Many people outside of Mexico, especially in the United States, see the country as a land filled with bandits, drug cartels, and villainous and savage people—essentially as a land ruled only by violence. Inside Mexico, people in nearby cities or mestizo communities describe P'urhépecha people as savage Indians, backward and uncivilized. I am always concerned that my work will be seen as either contributing to those stereotypes or remaining shallow for not "correctly" describing the relevant dynamics, practices, and realities of P'urhépecha communities. We are caught between Oscar Lewis (1961, 1968) and Robert Redfield ([1956] 1989).[15] I am constantly weighing my work against two fundamental questions: How do we ethically talk about stories that illustrate a particular reality without contributing to negative stereotypes? How do we create a balance so that we can showcase the complexity of human relations, practices, and lived experiences?

Another important part of my decision to not talk about the violence until recently had to do with the violence as such. How do we talk about stories that we want to forget or that we do not want our loved ones to hear about? How do we ethically talk about the fieldwork experience, its dangers, challenges, and rewards? I grew up in Michoacán; therefore, I was and am familiar with the social-political-economic dynamics that lead to violence among communities in the area (both related and unrelated to narcos). As Lorena Ojeda Dávila (2017) describes in her book *Celebración, identidad y conflicto*, some P'urhépecha communities have century-long feuds. However, I was not intellectually or methodologically prepared to deal with the level of violence that began after 2006. Notwithstanding the violence, I was determined to do my fieldwork and to collect my data, as I had been told that I had to do, even if this meant taking unnecessary risks and prioritizing my data over my own safety.

> No one would believe the instructions we leave with those who love us: If I
> don't contact you tonight, call the embassy. If I am crying when I call you,
> change my return ticket even if it doubles the price of the trip.

Since I began conducting research in Angahuan in 2006, I have always lived with a well-known and respected family, the Gómez Santacruz family. Na Juana and Ta Emiliano have ten children, and I am the same age as their older daughters, which helped me integrate into the family. Moreover, my own parents and siblings have gone to visit and stay in Angahuan, so both families have created strong familial bonds through me. Through the years I have been integrated into the community as a member of the Gómez Santacruz household.[16] While this means that my data and experiences in Angahuan are heavily influenced by the fact that the community treats me as a member of this family with the corresponding implications of being a single female member of the community, it also means that there are spaces in the community that I am not allowed to enter or conduct research in, such as the more political, male-driven spheres. As I began to conduct fieldwork, violence in the area escalated, and I could document as a firsthand witness the impact of violence on Angahuan's cultural fabric.

The roads in the P'urhépecha Sierra have always been somewhat dangerous. They are not well made, so car accidents are common and in most cases result in fatalities. When I began to conduct fieldwork in Angahuan, the community did not have cell phone reception. Therefore, when I was in the community I could not communicate at all with my family. For security reasons (such as traveling safely through the Sierra), I would send a text message to my parents as soon as I was leaving Uruapan and going up to the Sierra. A couple of days later, I would send a text message as soon as I arrived back in the city. By 2009, Telcel (Mexico's largest cell phone company) had installed an antenna in the community, which

facilitated communication with my family. By that time, the violence had escalated, and car accidents were the least of the dangers faced while traveling on the
road. One day in 2009, for example, as I returned to Angahuan, a group of men
had closed the roads going up the Sierra. This is a common practice meant to halt
the agricultural transportation industry. When that happens, some people decide
to wait until the roads open again, others try to take alternative routes, and others
cross the barricade on foot and try to find transportation on the other side. The
problem with the barricades is that you never know who set them up, whether it's a
group protesting the government or narcos. On a couple of occasions, I decided to
risk crossing the barricade on foot. This was not the safest or wisest decision, but I
justified it to myself by always sending text messages to my loved ones, and I was
always fortunate enough to make it home safe (to either Angahuan or Uruapan).
I continue the practice of sending text messages to my family and loved ones so
that they know at all times where I am. I will text when I leave a place and when I
arrive at a destination. If I do not text them every day, they know that something
has happened. With few exceptions, I text every day.[17]

Inside Angahuan, I was and am relatively safe. Because I am a de facto member
of the Gómez Santacruz household, people knew me and, when I was out and
about in the community, kept tabs on me. But one night, my host mother had a
nightmare that I had arrived crying and hurt at the house. In her dream, I had
been raped. Fortunately, it was just a nightmare. However, after that my host
parents asked me to be even more careful—to arrive home before sunset and to
not be alone at night around the community. Even during the day, if one of the
daughters was available, they would ask her to go with me, so I would not walk
alone. On the few occasions that darkness fell as I was conducting an interview,
someone would go looking for me so I would not return home alone. Wanting to
stay safe and trusting their instincts, I happily complied with their safety rules.

During my yearlong stay in Angahuan, from 2009 to 2010, I was constantly
torn between sending reports to my parents (who lived in Puerto Rico at the
time) and staying quiet about some of the events I witnessed. Despite my silence
on the community's situation (or perhaps because of it), my father would read the
local newspapers daily, trying to stay abreast of local goings-on and to gauge how
safe it might be for me. When the altercation with the PFP happened in June 2009,
I decided not to tell my parents. That week was particularly hard, as one of my research collaborators was buried on the same day that the PFP invaded Angahuan.
Unsurprisingly, when I spoke to my parents a couple of days later, my father had
read about the incident in the news, and my parents wanted me to come home.
I had to seriously consider what to do. At the end I decided, and promised my
parents, that if violence continued to escalate, I would leave. Fortunately, the violence did not escalate further at the time, and I was able to continue my research.

When I returned to Angahuan in the summer of 2011, violence had escalated, and I could feel the tension in the air. In April 2011, the comuneros of Cherán, another P'urhépecha community in the Sierra, had risen up in arms against the government and the drug cartels (mainly the illegal woodcutters).[18] The people of Cherán were tired of being bullied by both the government and the drug cartels, and after a couple of comuneros were killed, they took matters into their own hands. The people of Cherán closed the borders of their community, expelled the state government and police officials, organized auto-defense groups, and created their own form of government based on their *costumbres y tradiciones* (customs and traditions). Consequently, the drug cartels had to find another forest to steal wood from. Rumors circulated that the illegal woodcutters were going to move to Angahuan's lands and start cutting down its wood reserves. When I arrived in June 2011, the tension in the community was palpable, as Angahuan's comuneros were readying to fight if the illegal woodcutters decided to start cutting Angahuan's forest.

Widespread corruption in the military contributes to a general sense of insecurity and mistrust in the region. After the incident of June 2009, the military was banned from entering Angahuan, but in July 2011, they entered the town to apprehend a comunero. I was returning home from the main plaza when the convoy entered the town. They saw me walking by the road; they stopped in front of me, asking for directions. The commanding officer began to flirt with me. No one else was nearby. I was defenseless and terrified. I gave them vague directions and ran home.

As violence increased in the area, tensions likewise rose in Angahuan and its neighboring communities. All of us were and are living in a constant state of hyperawareness. What where some of the strategies that I used to be safe? I followed the communal rules (where I could go and to whom I could talk), my family's rules (letting them know at all times where I was), and my Angahuan family's rules (be home before nightfall and try not to walk alone). I also never had anything of value on me. I did not use any flashy jewelry, I left my laptop at an uncle's house in the city, and I had a simple bag where I carried my camera and recording equipment. And while I do not blend physically into the community (I am tall for a woman in the area, I have lighter skin and curly hair, I wear glasses, and I have a body shape more common to the Caribbean), I tried to appear as unassuming as possible and not draw unnecessary attention to myself. These were some of the precautions that other local young women also made and make. And despite all these precautions, I have been groped and sexually harassed, and in one case one of my host brothers had to get a drunk relative, who was being aggressive, away from me. With everything going on in the area, I was and am fortunate that nothing worse has happened to me. But the danger was and is always there, especially because women are snatched from the street and disappeared (which I have seen happen).

I have also made decisions regarding when to go, or not go, to Angahuan and move around the Sierra. During the academic year of 2017–2018, I lived with my parents in Pátzcuaro, roughly two hours away from Angahuan. And even though I was still in a conflict zone, Pátzcuaro is safer than Angahuan. My yearlong goals were to conduct fieldwork and write my book. And while other projects took precedence over my book manuscript, violence hindered me from going to Angahuan as much as I wanted to. Every time I started to organize my trip to Angahuan, something would happen: there would be a shoot-out in the community, narcos would take over the roads and close the main entrances of main cities and towns (Pátzcuaro included), and there was a wave of femicides in the area. I chose my safety over my professional goals.

Living in a conflict zone transforms you, even if you are there for only short periods of time, like in my case. You become constantly aware of your surroundings. If you are in a room, building, store, or bank, you immediately scan the place to locate exits as well as potential hiding places, and you scan people for potential allies in case of an emergency. You learn to read spaces and atmospheres. Something happens to spaces just before violence is about to erupt. It's difficult to describe, but it feels like electricity. And everyone knows that something is about to happen. That is when you know that you have to go home or find a safe space. Violence also becomes part of the landscape. One day I heard one of my cousins in Uruapan giving directions to my uncle: "Papá, you know that corner where X was killed? The store is on the next corner." Places are now known for their shoot-outs, or if someone was killed there, a body was dumped there, or someone was "picked up" at that particular spot. At this point, everybody in Michoacán has suffered, one way or another, because of the war on drugs and state-sponsored violence.

Something that I want to point out is that even though I have family in the area (my parents have returned to live in Michoacán), and Michoacán and the P'urhépecha Sierra is home, I can leave. As a researcher and university professor who lives and teaches in the United States, I have the option of leaving. My family in Angahuan, Uruapan, and Pátzcuaro do not have that option; that is their home. I can take a break from the violence, but they cannot.

Before the summer of 2011, I had not noticed how much I was holding my breath and how stressed I was. When I arrived in Puerto Rico to spend a couple of weeks with my parents, I was surprised to feel relief as I felt the stress leaving my body, and I became aware that I was emotionally drained. And now that

I am living in a new city in the United States, after a year in Michoacán conducting research and writing, I have noticed that I am still hyperaware of my
environment—even though I am in a safe, small city, and I am living in a nice
part of the city, I feel safe and relaxed only when I am inside my apartment.

No.

No one would believe us.

That we love what we do so much that despite threats of being disappeared we
   return because changing the world requires more than research and theory.

In the more than ten years that I have conducted fieldwork in Angahuan, I remain
in awe of, if no longer surprised by, the resilience of the human spirit in times of
conflict and how, even in the darkest of times, we find ways to laugh, love, and
enjoy life. Based on my experience and research, cultural practices and human
interactions are two essential elements that ensure our survival as communities
and cultures. And it was because people in Angahuan brought me into their community, protected me, and made sure that I was safe, that I have been able to do
the work that I wanted to and could do.

Before I conclude, I want to recognize that I know of colleagues who were
in "safe" areas, as well as researchers who took as many precautions as possible,
and horrible things still happened to them. Key informants, people whom
we trust and rely on, have been known to rape or sexually harass researchers. Folklore is a discipline that prides itself for creating deep and personal
relationships between researchers and research collaborators, and as such, it
could lead the way in humanizing the fieldwork process. However, folklore
needs to be more open about the dangers of conducting fieldwork—especially
for women and members of the LGBTQI+ community—and provide support
to victims of research violence. We talk about protecting the people that we
conduct research with, but we also need to talk about protecting and supporting our researchers.

In addition to the different strategies that I used to stay safe on a daily basis,
I had exit strategies in place, in case something happened. I wrote my fieldwork
journal in such a way that if something happened to me, at least my story would
not be lost, and I had multiple digital copies of my data. I was constantly aware
that I could die or that something could forever alter my life, and to be honest, I do
not know which option scared me more. I tried to make each day count, not just in
terms of collecting data but also in terms of living life to the fullest. Because even
with all these challenges, I loved my fieldwork experience. I love the people that
I connected with and the family that adopted me. Even with all these challenges,
no, I would not change what I do.

FIELD WORK
Maria Hamilton Abegunde
*For Mintzi Martínez-Rivera*

The truth: We can't tell people that what we fear most is what we've already lived.

A mother and child snatched off the street by men in black clothes, black masks, hiding behind black windows, in a black car. With machine guns. In daylight while we are buying milk.

A man refusing to open his door for anyone who does not have a key to get in and saving himself and his daughter that night from being shot to death. Like the man next door who wanted to be a good neighbor.

The man who looks at us too long when we walk down the street when we forget to not speak English.

The young boy who points his AK in our faces because it is the thing he is trained to do.

The dreams that we will be raped or hanged or put in a box.

The whisper that marks us as different, foreign, and vulnerable to being cheated in the market place. Or slapped while walking down the street alone.

No one would believe the instructions we leave with those who love us: If I don't contact you tonight, call the embassy. If I am crying when I call you, change my return ticket even if it doubles the price of the trip.

If they say they can't find my body, dream me so I can tell you who buried me. When you hear their names as you wake in the morning, promise you will hunt them in their sleep. Lock them in dimensionless REM where their screams strangle them.

No.

No one would believe us.

That we love what we do so much that despite threats of being disappeared we return because changing the world requires more than research and theory.

What we don't even say to each other: one day we may be asked to be the sacrifice. But every moment we are away from home, we pray that someone else is braver.

NOTES

1. In most cases, the trespassers come from Nuevo San Juan Parangaricutiro, a nearby community that has significant political and economic clout in the state.

2. Despite this prohibition, a military convoy entered the town to apprehend a comunero in July 2011.

3. A couple of weeks later, I saw the ambulance that was given to Angahuan, an old and out-of-service ambulance that was falling apart.

4. Some estimates say that just in extortions, cartels made over $189 million in 2012 alone (Paleta Pérez and Fuentes Díaz 2013).

5. Fuentes Díaz (2015) and Fuentes Díaz and Paleta Pérez (2015) argue that another factor that influenced cartels' shift in business models was NAFTA and the neoliberal economic market, as cartels had to diversify their business to remain competitive. In this regard, cartels became neoliberal enterprises.

6. For a detailed analysis of Mexico's war on drugs, please refer to González (2009), Grayson (2007), Maldonado Aranda (2013), and Walser (2008).

7. To some degree the violence between the cartels is increasing. During the summer of 2019, dismembered and mutilated bodies were found almost daily in Uruapan, left in public places, such as overpasses, roundabouts, plazas, and so on, with messages warning their adversaries and asking forgiveness from the civilian population. Sometimes the bodies were arranged in ways that look like grotesque and gory art displays.

8. As of the writing of this piece, during the government of the current state governor, Silvano Aureoles Conejo (in power since 2015), many communities and social movements and organizations (especially in indigenous communities) have suffered violent repression from the state government—in many cases leading to massacres. Even with the increase in violence among the different cartels, the governor has also been adamant to admit that the state is currently a conflict zone or war zone.

9. On both occasions, only the church and the *iurhixu* (convent) were left standing.

10. I have heard this negative stereotype about the people of Angahuan, and about other indigenous groups, from many mestizos in cities or from mestizo communities in the area. Regional newspapers also use negative adjectives when reporting events from and about indigenous communities.

11. Unfortunately, this unspoken truce has recently been challenged, as cartels have infiltrated the community. I was recently informed that in May 2019, a shoot-out between two rival cartels broke out in the community, as members of one of the cartels were hiding in the community.

12. The cargo system is a civil and religious form of organization that facilitates planning and distributing labor and economic responsibilities in a community.

13. Female scholars in anthropology, education, psychology, and other fields who conduct fieldwork-based research have started to write about the challenges

and dynamics of conducting research in male-driven spaces or following a research model that does not consider the realities and dangers that female scholars face while conducting fieldwork. For some resources, see Berry et al. (2017), Evans (2017), Gurney (1985), Nash et al. (2019), Pante (2014), Theres Kloß (2016), and Williams (2017).

14. An excellent example of current publications focusing on the dangers of fieldwork is the blog series curated by Beatriz Reyes-Foster and Rebecca Lester (2019) in collaboration with the Anthropology of Mental Health Interest Group.

15. Both scholars, in very different ways, contributed to existing stereotypes regarding Mexico as a land filled with violence but also with beautiful landscapes (that are ravaged by violence), millennia-old cultures (that sometimes are nonsensical), and peaceful or violent people. Lewis (1961, 1968) in *The Children of Sanchez* and more so in *La Vida*, presented his concept of culture of poverty where he argues that people who live in conditions of poverty create a culture that feeds into that poverty by creating a cycle that people cannot escape. His work contributed to portraying Mexicans and Puerto Ricans as people that are victimized by their own backward culture. Redfield ([1956] 1989) in *The Little Community* presents an analysis of the peasant community of Tepoztlán, in central Mexico. His idyllic portrayal of this community also contributes to an alternative stereotype of Mexico as an Edenic area composed of beautiful landscapes and peaceful people.

16. While I do have responsibilities in the community—I have been a godmother in celebrations and financially contributed to communal events—my integration is partial, as I will never be seen or treated as a full member of the community.

17. During the summer of 2016, as I conducted research in Angahuan, a huge storm destroyed the cell phone tower, so the community lost all cell reception. I had to find one of the last remaining land lines in the community to let my family know that I had made it safely to Angahuan.

18. For more information on Cheran's case, please see Ojeda Dávila (2015).

BIBLIOGRAPHY

Astorga, Luis 2012. *El siglo de las drogas: El narcotráfico, del porfiriato al nuevo milenio.* México: Editorial Grijalbo.

Behar, Ruth. 1996. *The Vulnerable Observer: Anthropology That Breaks Your Heart.* Boston: Beacon.

Berry, Maya J., Claudia Chávez Argüelles, Shanya Cordis, Sarah Ihmoud, and Elizabeth Velásquez Estrada. 2017. "Toward a Fugitive Anthropology: Gender, Race, and Violence in the Field." *Cultural Anthropology* 32 (4): 537–565.

Dareff, Scott. 2010. "Researching in Conflict Zones: An Abkhanz Example." *REECAS Newsletter.* Russian, East European and Central Asian Studies, School of International Studies, University of Washington. http://depts.washington.edu /jsishelp/ellison/2010/spring-summer/dareff-conflict. Page no longer available.

Evans, Anya. 2017. "The Ethnographer's Body Is Gendered." *New Ethnographer,* February 14, 2017. https://www.thenewethnographer.org/the-new-ethnographer /2017/02/14/gendered-bodies-2.

Fuentes Díaz, Antonio. 2015. "Narcotráfico y autodefensa comunitaria en 'Tierra Caliente,' Michoacán, México." *Ciencia UAT* 10 (1): 68–82.

Fuentes Díaz, Antonio, and Guillermo Paleta Pérez. 2015. "Violencia y autodefensas comunitarias en Michoacán, México." *Íconos: Revista de Ciencias Sociales* 53:171–186.

González, Francisco E. 2009. "Mexico's Drug War Gets Brutal." *Current History* 108:72–76.

Grayson, George W. 2007. "Mexico and the Drug Cartels." Foreign Policy Research Institute. E-Notes. August 2007. https://www.fpri.org/enotes/200708.grauson .mexicodrugcartels.html. Page no longer available.

Gurney, Joan Neff. 1985. "Not One of the Guys: The Female Researcher in a Male Dominated Setting." *Qualitative Sociology* 8 (1): 42–62.

Hoffman, Danny. 2003. "Frontline Anthropology: Research in a Time of War." *Anthropology Today* 19 (3): 9–12.

Human Rights Watch. 2015. "Mexico: Police Killings in Michoacán. Evidence of Extrajudicial Executions in Apatzingán and Tanhuato." October 28, 2015. https:// www.hrw.org/news/2015/10/28/mexico-police-killings-michoacan.

Lee, Raymond M. 1994. *Dangerous Fieldwork*. Qualitative Research Methods Series 34. Thousand Oaks, CA: Sage.

Lewis, Oscar. 1961. *The Children of Sánchez: Autobiography of a Mexican Family*. New York: Vintage Books.

———. 1968. *La Vida: A Puerto Rican Family in the Culture of Poverty—San Juan and New York*. New York: Vintage Books.

Maldonado Aranda, Salvador. 2013. "Stories of Drug Trafficking in Rural Mexico: Territories, Drugs and Cartels in Michoacán." *European Review of Latin American and Caribbean Studies* 94:43–66.

Mazurana, Dyan, Karen Jacobsen, and Lacey Anfres Gale, eds. 2013. *Research Methods in Conflict Settings: A View from Below*. Cambridge: Cambridge University Press.

McDonald, David. 2013. *My Voice Is My Weapon: Music, Nationalism, and the Poetics of Palestinian Resistance*. Durham, NC: Duke University Press.

McDowell, John. 2000. *Poetry and Violence: The Ballad Tradition of Mexico's Costa Chica*. Urbana: University of Illinois Press.

Nash, Meredith, Hanne E. F. Nielsen, Justine Shaw, Matt King, Mary-Anne Lea, and Narissa Bax. 2019. "'Antarctica Just Has This Hero Factor . . .' Gendered Barriers to Australian Antarctic Research and Remote Fieldwork." *PLoS ONE* 14 (1): e0209983. https://doi.org/10.1371/journal.pone.0209983.

Noel, Andrea. 2015. "Where Mexico's Drug War Was Born: Timeline of the Security Crisis in Michoacán." *Vice News*, March 12, 2015. https://news.vice.com

/article/where-mexicos-drug-war-was-born-a-timeline-of-the-security-crisis-in -michoacan.

Ojeda Dávila, Lorena. 2015. "Cherán: El poder del concenso y las políticas comunitarias." *Política Común* 7. http://dx.doi.org/10.3998/pc.12322227.0007.007.

———. 2017. *Celebración, Identidad y Conflicto: El Concurso de Zacán y el Año Nuevo de los Purepechas de Michoacán*. Morelia, Mexico: Facultad de Historia, Universidad Michoacana de San Nicolás de Hidalgo, Fondo Nacional para las Culturas y las Artes, El Colegio de America, and Editorial Morevalladolid.

Paleta Pérez, Guillermo, and Antonio Fuentes Díaz. 2013 "Territorios, inseguridad y autodefensas comunitarias en localidades de la Meseta Purépecha de Michoacán, México." *Revista Margenes* 13 (10): 62–68.

Pante, Ma. Bernadeth Laurelyn P. 2014. "Female Researchers in a Masculine Space: Managing Discomforts and Negotiating Positionalities." *Philippine Sociological Review* 62:65–88.

Redfield, Robert. (1956) 1989. *The Little Community and Peasant Society and Culture*. Midway reprint. Chicago: University of Chicago Press.

Reyes-Foster, Beatriz, and Rebecca Lester, eds. 2019. *Trauma and Resilience: Anthro{dendum}* (blog). In collaboration with the Anthropology of Mental Health Interest Group. https://anthrodendum.org/author/trauma-and-resilience/.

Tavanti, di Marco. 2005. "Chiapas Cross-Cultural Focus Groups: Doing Research in Dangerous and Culturally Diverse Contexts." *Sociologia e ricercar sociale* 75–76:1–12.

Theres Kloß, Sinah. 2016. "Sexual(ized) Harassment and Ethnographic Fieldwork: A Silenced Aspect of Social Research." *Ethnography* 18 (3): 396–414. https://doi.org /10.1177/1466138116641958.

Walser, Ray. 2008. *Mexico, Drug Cartels and the Merida Initiative: A Fight We Cannot Afford to Lose*. Backgrounder Executive Summary No. 2163. July 23, 2008. Washington, DC: Heritage Foundation.

Williams, Bianca C. 2017. "#MeToo: A Crescendo in the Discourse about Sexual Harassment, Fieldwork and the Academy (Part 2)." *Savage Minds* (blog), October 28, 2017. https://savageminds.org/2017/10/28/metoo-a-crescendo-in-the-discourse -about-sexual-harassment-fieldwork-and-the-academy-part-2/.

Wood, Elizabeth Jean. 2006. "The Ethical Challenges of Field Research in Conflict Zones." *Qualitative Sociology* 29 (3): 373–386.

MINTZI AUANDA MARTÍNEZ-RIVERA is Assistant Professor of Anthropology in the Department of Sociology and Anthropology at Providence College. Since 2005, she has conducted research on the P'urhépecha culture of Michoacán, Mexico, spending most of her time in the community of Santo Santiago de Angahuan. She has published articles on the indigenous rock movement in Mexico, indigenous popular culture, and the use of food as decorations. She is currently working on her first manuscript, *Getting Married in Angahuan: Creating Culture, Performing Community*.

FOURTEEN

## "La Sierra Juárez en Riverside"

### The Inaugural Oaxacan Philharmonic Bands
### Audition on a University Campus

XÓCHITL CHÁVEZ

This is a Cahuilla and Serrano Ancient Ceremonial Blessing. Where
ceremonial tobacco is used. The blowing of tobacco to the directions of North,
East, South, West, upward direction, below direction, and to the center. This
ancient Ceremony preceded the opening of the Ceremonial House
(Big House), the ceremonial center of gathering, in Cahuilla and Serrano
Indian villages. Many villages were located in what is now Riverside,
California. By sharing this ceremony with everyone here today at the
University of California, Riverside, it is the intention of our people to
welcome this Inaugural Oaxacan bands event in a good way.

KIM MARCUS AND MALLORY MARCUS
(CAHUILLA AND SERRANO)[1]

Opening with the Cahuilla and Serrano ceremonial prayer for the Inaugural
Oaxacan Philharmonic Bands Audition (fig. 14.1) sets the grounds for this
chapter by addressing the question, What can the study of folklore reveal about
vernacular strategies of belonging, survival, and reinvention in times of trouble?
The prayer invokes the topics of indigeneity and how Indigenous communities (both within and beyond US political borders) have been disregarded not
only in spaces and institutions such as the university but also in debates about
immigration and the construction of "Mexican" identity and in ethnographic
research. The production of the philharmonic bands audition and the writing of
the chapter were done with a methodological approach that I call *Sincere Collaborative Intention* that is based on a framework of ethics and commitment to the Oaxacan migrant community regarding how knowledge is produced and represented
in academic literature (Brown and Strega 2005). Since 2005, I have accompanied

Fig. 14.1 Kim and Mallory Marcus of Cahuilla and Serrano nations offer a ceremonial open blessing at the Inaugural Audición de Bandas. Photo by Irais Cardenas.

several Oaxacan migrant community-based organizations to witness, assist in creating, and participate in various cultural performances across Oaxacalifornia (Kearney 1995). This long-standing accompaniment with the Oaxaqueño community fostered the basis of trust in planning a community-oriented program at the University of California, Riverside (Tomlinson and Lipsitz 2013).

The present chapter documents a historic event, the Inaugural Oaxacan Philharmonic Bands Audition, organized by the author, Dr. Xóchitl Chávez, the first tenure-track Chicanx assistant professor at the University of California, Riverside's Department of Music, in collaboration with four pioneering Zapotec philharmonic community-based bands active in Los Angeles.[2] Held on January 27, 2018, this public concert was the first of its kind at a university campus in the United States to showcase Oaxacan community band practitioners, ranging from migrants to fourth-generation musicians. Bringing Banda Santa María Xochitepec, Banda Yatzachi el Bajo—Los Angeles, Banda Nueva Dinastía de Zoochila, and Maqueos Music Academy to the campus had a reciprocal transformative effect on the Oaxacan bands, the local Latinx community, and the university. The focus of this chapter is threefold: (1) it highlights the importance of community-oriented programming rooted in a sincere collaborative intention, such as when I produced the first Oaxacan Bands Audition at UC Riverside; (2) it applies a translocal[3] and feminist lens to document the role of intergenerational and gender representation in the Oaxacan wind band musical tradition;[4] and (3) it presents the making of this community-oriented event.

This historic event showcases the vast musical repertoire and caliber of the Zapotec community from La Sierra Juarez de Oaxaca in California since the 1970s, which features multiple generations of musicians and community-based efforts (Chávez 2017). The theme of the Inaugural Oaxacan Philharmonic Bands Audition was that of *pioneros*, pioneers. The four invited bands laid the foundation for Oaxacan music to become part of the soundscape of Los Angeles based on the translocal networks and relationships through which musical scores, instruments, and pedagogy continuously flowed back and forth throughout Oaxacalifornia. Through these exchanges, younger generations of Oaxacan youth are able to reaffirm their cultural identity at rehearsals and public performances. The music heard at the open-air concert is not taught in the public school system here in the United States (or in the public school system in Oaxaca). Instead, it is taught in the community by recognized musically inclined community members in autonomous migrant-led public spaces (Fox 2005). With forty years of perseverance and dedication, community leaders teach fellow *paisano/as*[5] and youth how to read and play music in backyard patios, driveways, or small rented spaces. According to my ethnographic research, which includes the creation of a register of Oaxacan philharmonic bands, there are forty bands in California. Today, there are twenty-five active Zapotec philharmonic community-based bands in Los Angeles County, whose vast repertoires include waltzes, marches, danzón, mazurkas, and paso dobles, among other genres (Chávez 2017). The very presence of these philharmonic bands shows their resiliency, organization, community membership, and dedication to maintaining their cultural identity. Having been able to work closely with several Oaxaqueño communities over the past decade, my motivation behind this event is to work in solidarity with the Zapotec philharmonic bands and foster a bridge to the university so that expressive cultural practices can be recognized and demonstrated by community members. This type of event allows for a sense of community and belonging in institutional spaces where Indigenous communities are not always represented.[6] The capacities of these bands to perform and incorporate Indigenous rhythms into European styles of music is not only noteworthy but also a testament to their resilient cultural and political history.

BACKGROUND

Nearly every town in the sierra regions of Oaxaca, Mexico, has a community wind band. This strong tradition of wind bands in Zapotec and Mixe communities can be traced back to the turn of the twentieth century while Mexico was forging a

national identity after the 1910–1921 revolution. Following a military-style structure, brass bands were implemented in each capital city throughout Mexico in
the attempt to ensure civic loyalty (Heath 2015; Chávez 2017). Although it is not
completely clear or documented how wind and brass instruments were first taken
to the extremely remote communities in the sierra region, each Indigenous community formed an all-male philharmonic band to play for their religious and civic
events throughout the year.[7] Today, nearly every community also has an *escoleta*,
a community-based music school sponsored through either family donations
or the municipality, which teaches children how to read and play music during
evening and weekend classes.

### Audición de Bandas en Oaxaca

The vibrancy of Indigenous community-based bands continues to ring for both
religious and civic celebrations year-round. One particularly important duty of
the community-based band is to provide community service, *gozona* (Zapotec),
during the town's patron saint feast day celebrations. Neighboring town bands are
invited to participate in a five-day gozona by playing music for various rituals and
activities related to the feast celebration. At the culmination of the patron saint
festivities, traditionally on the last day, an *audición de bandas* (a large public concert) is arranged on a basketball court or public square where each visiting band
sets up in different corners for a friendly showcase to display their best musical
repertoire. Other than each band member, the only other person to know what
songs will be played is the master of ceremony (a representative of the town's municipality), who announces the titles of the musical pieces and the order in which
they will be performed. There are two phases to the audición de bandas. The first
phase focuses on the interpretive quality of each band's repertoire through three
rounds of music—customarily, the first piece of music must be a march. The remaining rounds of music may highlight various genres including waltzes, over-
tures, fantasies, and other musical arrangements. After each community band has
played their best repertoire, all of the bands convene to form one monumental band
to mark the second phase. Once all of the bands meet collectively in the middle
to perform a mutually agreed-upon repertoire, which may include a march, danzón, or *son*, they end with the Oaxaca state anthem, a waltz entitled "Dios Nunca
Muere." True to the popular spirit of these musical events, no trophies or awards
are given—it is the applause of the audience that marks the people's favorite band.

### Formation of Oaxacan Bands in Los Angeles

In the chapter "Booming Bandas of Los Angeles: Gender and the Practice of
Transnational Zapotec Philharmonic Brass Bands," I write in further detail about
the formation of Oaxacan bands in Los Angeles (Chávez 2017). In the 1980s, many

Oaxacan migrant groups began to form binational organizations and Hometown Associations (HTAs) based on common shared identities (ethnolinguistic, racial, location of origin, religion, etc.) as a response to ethno-racial discrimination. The first two adult all-male bands to form in Los Angeles were Banda Santa María Xochitepec and Banda Yatzchi el Bajo—Los Angeles, followed by Banda Nueva Dinastía de Zoochila and a youth band representing San Andrés Solaga.[8]

Building on Jonathan Fox's (2005) concept of "mapping migrant civil society," my work on Oaxacan philharmonic bands documents the spatial distribution of rehearsal locations of the bandas Oaxaqueñas in Los Angeles, thus continuing to chart migration patterns to the city by specific Indigenous communities. Many of the bands are located in the neighborhoods of Koreatown and Midcity and host the rehearsal locations of other community bands. These neighborhoods are located in very congested areas, and as demographic shifts occur, finding a rehearsal venue that is an affordable space and conducive to the cacophony of sound has proved difficult. Many musicians stated that when going to banda practice they ran the risk of having the police called on them—a situation that many could not afford due to their precarious legal status. Today, bands still struggle to secure a stable rehearsal location. Several bands make arrangements with homeowners and rent their garage space for a set period of time; they then move to another in efforts to avoid criminalization. In an attempt to have a permanent site, band members of Yatzachi el Bajo actually dug out the basement in the current director's home in Koreatown. By using vernacular architecture, they created a music space for weekly practices. Another example is Maqueos Music Academy—through monthly donations from families, the music school holds daily rehearsals in a converted cinder-block warehouse soundproofed with blue and gray cardboard egg cartons located in Midcity. Banda Nueva Dinastía de Zoochila, located in Lynnwood, remodeled the garage of one of the founding directors to better soundproof, added a small window air conditioner, and painted the name of the band on the wall in order to have some sort of permanent space for rehearsals. These three examples speak to the geographic location of community-based bands and the type of place-making that Oaxacan migrants have been carrying out in the last decade.

### The Sierra Juarez in Riverside Vignette

In the spring quarter of 2017, the then chair of the Department of Music at UC Riverside, Dr. Leonora Saavedra, asked me what my research plans were for the 2017–2018 academic year and whether I had any programming events that I'd like to propose. After sharing my research agenda, I shifted my demeanor, and with a big smile I stated, "Since coming to UC Riverside, I noticed the architecture of the performing arts building and how the height of the structure creates a nicely curved shell that would provide perfect acoustics for an outdoor concert. I have this dream of collaborating with a number of the pioneering Los Angeles Oaxacan community-based wind bands to organize the first audición de bandas, open-air music concert. This music event would showcase the strength of intergenerational Zapotec bands in southern California. Additionally, this public performance would foster an educational pipeline with migrant community members and the university." Dr. Saavedra, who is also familiar with Oaxacan wind bands, asked, "How many bands are you thinking of inviting?" After some thought, I stated, "For this inaugural event, let's start *small* with four bands, which would collectively bring around one hundred forty musicians."

With a serious look and yet with a grin, Dr. Saavedra responded, "One hundred and forty musicians. Four bands. How many audience members do you anticipate will come?"

Quickly estimating the numbers in my head, I declared, "Including just the family members of the musicians, that number will easily reach around four hundred to four hundred fifty people." My department chair replied, "Great, create your budget for the event and present it to me as soon as possible." Ecstatic about the possibility of this historic collaboration and keeping in mind that January was six months away, I began to make phone calls to the pioneering Zapotec band directors in Los Angeles. Having collaborated with Oaxacan migrant communities across California and Oaxaca, Mexico, for nearly a decade and a half, I made efforts to follow customary Oaxacan protocol. First, I respectfully requested a community meeting with each band's leadership. Once a date was agreed on for me to visit, I prepared an information packet in Spanish for each member with the invitation to the Inaugural Oaxacan Philharmonic Bands Audition at the University of California, Riverside. Recognizing the significance of the specific community gathering, I also consulted with well-known band directors and composers in Oaxaca and in California to ask for their mentorship to ensure that the first audición de bandas Oaxaqueñas was organized in a community-oriented fashion and as closely as possible to the public concerts in their pueblo. These binational consultations bolstered my ability to communicate the necessary directions to the university's performing arts production manager with the specific needs for the musicians and a sense of hospitality during the event.

## COLLABORATION AND MENTORSHIP

In late August 2017, I reached out to each band director: Maestro Ernesto Cruz of Banda Santa María Xochitepec; Maestro Ali Guzmán of Banda Yatzachi el Bajo—Los Angeles; Maestra Jessica Hernández and her father, Maestro Porfirio

Hernández, of Banda Nueva Dinastía de Zoochila; and Maestro Estanislao Maqueos of Maqueos Music Academy. I requested a meeting with each band to formally present an invitation in Spanish on university letterhead outlining the Oaxacan Band Audition. It is extremely important to practice not only linguistic fluency but also cultural fluency in any interaction when collaborating with community.[9] Over the years, I had been allowed to accompany community leaders to meetings in California and in community councils in Oaxaca—this was the moment when I had to ensure I respectfully presented myself in front of the community leaders and bands. Following Oaxacan community protocol, upon arriving at a rehearsal, I waited outside to be called in. Once allowed into the meeting space, I made sure to shake the hand of every musician and family member present in the room, followed by sharing hard copies of the formal invitation.

Graciously, I thanked them for allowing me into their rehearsal and for their time, and I made sure to state my positionality as a non-Oaxaqueña before my professional identity as a cultural anthropologist and ethnomusicologist—I am a daughter of an immigrant campesino from Chihuahua, and my mother is of US Native heritage from northern New Mexico. This bicultural and bilingual background profoundly frames the ways in which I interact and collaborate with communities in terms of activism and public programming. I shared that I had witnessed a number of audiciones de bandas in the Sierra Juarez during the patron saint feast day as well as in Los Angeles for the celebration for Saint Cecilia, organized by Maestro Maqueos. In following my own methodology of sincere collaborative intention, I stated that this opportunity to have the first Oaxacan Philharmonic Band Audition on a university campus in the state of California was significant and I would ensure that every step would follow the guidelines of an audición de bandas in Oaxaca through their guidance and with the collaboration of recognized maestros in Oaxaca.

In the months before the event, I jotted down notes during in-person conversations with Maestro Porfirio Hernández and Maestro Estanislao Maqueos about the overall structure and preproduction of the audition. I asked each maestro to recall their memory of how the band auditions were held in the pueblos and asked whether there were any observations that I may need to work on with the university production manager to replicate the setting as best as possible. Interestingly, both LA-based directors asked me who was going to be the master of ceremony. They recommended that I select an elder who spoke Zapotec and Spanish and who was familiar with the audición de bandas. Both of the maestros agreed and suggested that I co-emcee with English translation, so university and non-Spanish speaking audience members would understand the cultural context and significance of the event (and not just think this was a "show"). After some discussion with band directors regarding whether they had community members that would be willing to serve as lead master of ceremony, Señor Mario Luna of Santiago Zoochila from Lynnwood, California, agreed to work with me.

Taking their recommendations, I began to think about the audición de bandas in Oaxaca. I recalled a particular linguistic style and intonation that the masters of ceremony performed. Fortunately, I had the privilege to meet the only female band director from Oaxaca, Maestra Leticia Gallardo-Martínez of Santa María Tlahuitoltepec (Mixe), and the well-known composer Maestro Andrés Reyes (Mixe) in 2014 in Los Angeles. Through WhatsApp and Facebook voice messages and calls, Maestra Leticia and Maestro Andrés tutored me in writing the appropriate verbiage in Spanish and English. Once I provided the program script to Señor Mario Luna, I had another round of tutorials with Maestro Andrés in Oaxaca over WhatsApp phone conversations in order to properly learn the linguistic intonation and speaking pace for announcing the songs. This practice of consultation and rehearsing with the maestros in Oaxaca and California was an important step, as it demonstrated my commitment to and respect for their communal traditions.

Lots of enthusiasm was generated about the inaugural audición de bandas at UC Riverside within the Oaxacan migrant community as well as in Oaxaca. When Zapotec composer and maestro Olegario Robles visited California,[10] after a brief conversation during a community event and learning about the efforts of multiple bands and families involved in the historic audition, he proposed to compose the *marcha oficial*, the official march, for the event. This march is played when all the bands gather into one monumental band and play together to signify the unification of all the Indigenous communities present. In early December 2017, I received a Facebook message with several attachments from Maestro Olegario. The message contained the sheet music for each instrument, collectively placed together—it was the score for the official march, entitled "La Sierra Juárez en Riverside, CA." Over a phone call, Maestro Olegario shared with me that he had named the official march "The Sierra Juárez in Riverside, CA": "It is an honor to share my musical knowledge and culture with the Mexican community born in the United States. This event is a significant moment for the Oaxacan community to gather at a university setting. I put a lot of energy into composing the song because I want people to be surprised when they hear the complexity of our music and what better place than at the university in Riverside where new generations of philharmonic bands continue to transmit their customs and traditions."[11]

The occasion, the location, and the people involved in the audition became Maestro Olegario's inspiration for the march. His statement marks the recognition of *los del otro lado*, the Mexican community abroad, and the intergenerational aspects of the philharmonic bands that are actively participating as cultural bearers of musical traditions. Implicit in Maestro Olegario's words is the call for

Fig. 14.2 Image of Performing Arts courtyard filled with musicians and audience members. Foregrounded is the sheet music for "La Sierra Juárez en Riverside, CA" (march), written by Zapotec composer Maestro Olegario Robles, who was inspired by this intergenerational gathering and specifically wrote this score as a dedication to the inaugural Oaxacan Bands event at the University of California, Riverside. Photo by Leo Pena.

Indigenous communities to be recognized for their musical contributions, particularly at educational institutions (fig. 14.2). Not only did the official score contain profound cultural significance, but the music event as a whole moved some participants to share their feelings of resiliency, intergenerational continuity, identity, and empowerment. The following section highlights a few examples of emotions evoked among elders and second-generation Oaxacan musicians and audience members at this historic gathering.

### INTERGENERATIONAL CULTURAL TRANSMISSION AND GENDER REPRESENTATION

Motivated by the larger-than-expected turnout, with over eight hundred people in attendance, co-emcee Sr. Mario Luna shared a few words in Zapoteco during the opening remarks and then provided the following Spanish translation: "Muchas gracias a los representantes de la universidad por estar con nosotros he dicho agradeciendo a los papás por el esfuerzo de los niños para que permitan que sus niños aprendan nuestra cultura Oaxaqueña y que no les de vergüenza en donde quiera que se paren que les digan que son de Oaxaca que no les de vergüenza señores. ¡Somos de Oaxaca y con orgullo! Tenemos que levantar la frente y decirlo con orgullo que ¡somos Oaxaqueños y esta es nuestra cultura y música!"[12] Looking out into the audience, I could see pride on the faces of many of the Oaxacan community members as they applauded Sr. Mario's words. To hear the Indigenous language of Zapotec from the Sierra Juarez resonating throughout the university's courtyard was an unabashed, powerful linguistic statement, which was particularly needed during the xenophobic Trump administration.

Within the ranks of the 140 musicians collectively seated in the center of the courtyard in a U-shaped configuration were children and adults representing over forty years of migration, community formation, and cultural transmission. Maestra Jessica Hernández succinctly described the setting as "es bonito ver un niño de 5, 6, 7, años tocando con una persona ya de 60–70 años en la música y ver esa continuidad y preservación de la música y es algo bonito."[13] For some young musicians, playing in the philharmonic band can be a family tradition, but for nearly everyone it is a way of claiming community membership abroad and asserting an ethnic identity. For Maestra Jessica, participating in the community-based bands allowed her to bilingually (in Spanish and English) articulate her identity as an Indigenous woman:

> I still struggle with my cultural identity sometimes. I consider myself a very cultural person, I can't even imagine what kind of identity issues other people have, because as an Indigenous person it is different. You know, people classify us as Mexican, but still being identified as Mexican still doesn't fully identify us. Mexican culture has a very unique culture—people think that because we're Mexican we are Mariachi or Banda Sinaloense. Being Oaxaqueño it's a whole other thing, an Indigenous identity that people still don't understand. I think now that Oaxacan culture is being exposed at this university level, at this academic level, it's again only the start of so much more to come.

A number of young Oaxacan female musicians grew up assisting their fathers during the formation of the philharmonic bands in Los Angeles. Maestro Estanislao Maqueos founded the Maqueos Music Academy, which is located in the bustling center of Koreatown (Los Angeles). The academy offers classes multiple times a day, and he depends tremendously on his eldest daughter, Maestra Yulissa Maqueos. Maestro Maqueos reflected on the importance of incorporating young musicians into leadership roles: "En mi caso tengo a mis hijas que ya estan tomando el liderazgo y también es una de las cosas que está pasando en la academia donde yo estoy y estamos dando oportunidad a nuevas personas—a

Fig. 14.3 Maestra Yulissa Maqueos directing the Maqueos Music Academy band, "Huapango de Moncayo." Photo by Alma Catalan.

los nuevos jóvenes para que ellos sigan estudiando que hagan lo que nosotros ya no pudimos hacer."[14]

In addition to studying music with her father, Maestra Yulissa graduated from California State University, Los Angeles with an undergraduate degree in music. Maestra Yulissa is the second Oaxaqueña female director to hold an undergraduate degree from a California public university.[15] To demonstrate her capabilities as a conductor, Maestra Yulissa chose to direct a piece that was first played in 1941 and directed by the renowned Mexican music conductor Carlos Chávez.[16] While the majority of the pieces presented at the audition were written by Oaxacan composers, the Maqueos Music Academy played a crowd favorite, "Huapango de Moncayo," written by Mexican composer Juan Pablo Moncayo. This composition is considered by many as the second national anthem of Mexico. Maestra Yulissa Maqueos adeptly directed the band through the beloved musical national symbol of Mexico as one of three women directors highlighted in the inaugural music event at UC Riverside (fig. 14.3). A moving aspect of the audition was the sight of these women directing individual pieces for their respective bands and then directing again when the bands formed one monumental band. It is only recently that male directors have begun to share the podium with women, in many cases their daughters and or nieces. To ground this poignant visualization of women musicians directing was to see Sra. Ofelia Guzmán, one of the first women brass band members in California (a forty-plus-year alto saxophone veteran), sitting within the ranks of 140 intergenerational musicians and representing her community, Yatzachi el Bajo.

Maestro Porfirio (Banda Nueva Dinastía de Zoochila) recognized the educational contributions of two other young band directors as a result of their attainment of the advanced degrees in music education, while also preserving their identities by stating, "A mí lo que me gusta es, por ejemplo Jessica y Ernesto son hijos de Oaxaqueños, entonces eso es lo que me da gusto. Me sorprende y me siento orgulloso de que ellos son hijos Oaxaqueños graduados de la universidad y de música, porque Ernesto es maestro de música y Jessica es maestra de música . . . y me da gusto de que les guste nuestra cultura y ellos sin haber nacido allí lo están tratando de sacar adelante." This quote points to how youth are becoming the transnational bearers of Indigenous cultures, creating epistemologies to teach future generations of Oaxacan youth. Second-generation Oaxacan musicians have demonstrated great musical capacity and leadership across California and in Oaxaca, participating in community-based and professional events. Since the formation of Oaxacan brass bands in California in the 1970s, women have moved through music ranks. Granted, they were not always supported, but each step demonstrates an example of persistence and astuteness in how each woman musician has broken down a cultural barrier (Chávez 2014).

## TRANSFORMATIVE IMPACT TESTIMONIOS

The following section speaks to how significant the Oaxacan band audition was for youth and elders in Southern California. One week before the event, amid the finalizing preparations, a former UC Riverside student sent the most moving email (Martinez 2018):

> Hello Professor Chávez, my name is Hernan Martinez and I am a recent Alumni from UCR, graduating last summer (2017). This is in regard to the event that you are hosting along with the other faculty involved for the Oaxacan Philharmonic Band Audition, I truly just want to say thank you, thank you along with others who are involved with this, to bring such an event and to bring all the bands together. As a son of undocumented parents from the State of Oaxaca who are Indigenous Zapotecs, it truly brings me happiness to see this event coming together and especially at my Alma Mater. As an Oaxacan who has been highly involved with the Zapotec community back in Los Angeles, I was really fascinated to hear and it touches me to know that this event will happen. So once more I really thank you for all your effort and I am excited along with my family to see this spectacular event, I really look forward to the bands playing Oaxaca state's anthem of "Dios Nunca Muere" as I identify the

most with this song. Once more, thank you Professor Chávez from me and my
family, and congratulations along with the faculty involved for creating this
magnificent event. I hope to see you all soon on the 27th of January.

Hernan's email foregrounds the relevance of the event and the students' aspiration to see themselves and their cultural practices represented on their campus.
Days before the event, UC Riverside students of both Oaxacan and non-Mexican
heritage began to reach out and ask how they could volunteer with any preparations. Before I knew it, there was a team of one hundred volunteers. From the core
group of volunteers that worked with me early on, I appointed specific lead roles
to carry out tasks the day of the event. Reflections on the transformative impact of
the Oaxacan band concert came in a steady stream. UC Riverside undergraduate
alumna Karla Hernández who assisted as a lead volunteer in the preparations and
who is a member of Banda Nueva Dinastía de Zoochila, said, "After participating
in the event, walking through the performing arts courtyard feels different. You see
people using that space now for performances, to practice, sit by the plants that were
added right before the event . . . I never thought I would see *my community* play our
music and share Oaxacan traditions on campus." Her words mark the importance
of space, empowerment, identity, and being visible at her university campus within
the larger context of being of Mexican and Indigenous in Southern California. Part
of the reciprocal transformative effect is that the performing arts courtyard has
changed—it was transformed, *abrió un camino*, from a once unaesthetically pleasing
space to a vibrant living space for fellow university students and colleagues to use.[17]

Given the number of people in attendance, there was an overarching senti-
ment of how transformative the event was for the university. Several university
colleagues and students directly approached me to comment that they had never
seen so many people from the community on campus and that this music event
was a true community event. Mexican-heritage students and faculty stated that
they felt like they were in Mexico, where you could feel the energy coming up
through the cement. One of the most moving public reviews about the band
audition was by Professor Emeritus Robert Garfias (2018) of the University of
California, Irvine, ethnomusicologist. On his Facebook page, he posted a detailed
account of the audición de bandas on January 29, 2018, the day after the event:

> Yesterday I had a very powerful emotional experience. I went to UC Riverside
> for the Oaxacan Band Audition. There are about 25 Oaxacan brass bands in the
> Los Angeles area. Four of them participated in the event at Riverside. This was
> all arranged by Dr. Xóchitl Chávez of UC Riverside. Most of the people there
> were Zapotecs from Oaxaca, with a few Mixes present as well.
>
> Each of the four bands played one piece then was followed by another band
> and so on until each band had played four pieces. Many of the pieces were quite

challenging and the bands were made up largely of high school age youths and younger, sprinkled with a good number of seniors. At the end of the single pieces they then combined into one colossal band of 140 musicians and played another three or four pieces. The intonation was very impressive and virtually no false notes. Clean precise playing. There were some speeches in Spanish and in Zapotec. I am myself an American born Oaxacan Mestizo felt very much a part of this. My father was from Tehuantepec, Oaxaca and although he has now been dead for more than 50 years, I still remember his fierce Oaxacan pride. So being surrounded by all this Oaxacan music so many of the *sones* sounding like those of Tehuantepec and surrounded by the people, I was very powerfully affected.

At the end of the playing of the four bands together, they all together started to play *Jarabes*, for dancing, one hour continuously and all from memory. One trumpet player would deftly cut into the very last notes of one Jarabe and by the first beat they were all playing together even in a different tempo and meter. They kept this up for an hour. I was flabbergasted. Such a display of integrated community. That so many had this shared repertoire was amazing. I was finally in tears. Would that my father could have heard it.

Dr. Roberto Garfias, an astute ethnomusicologist, vividly describes the complexity of the Oaxacan music and the overall structure of the music event. He rightfully points to the intergenerational aspect of the bands and marks his own positionality by evoking his father's memory. He also asserts his own sense of belonging with his heritage at the university. The most poignant act of resilience and transformation was when the bands played together for an hour so that the audience could take center stage and dance.

CONCLUSION

In our Department of Music meeting the following month, Dr. Bryan Adams made an enthusiastic statement, saying, "Finally, someone used the courtyard space for what it was made for—public events. The Oaxacan band event was an example for the rest of the departments at this university to see as a 'true community collaboration and community-oriented program on campus.'" The Inaugural Oaxacan Philharmonic Band Audition at the University of California, Riverside on January 27, 2018, was transformative. It was founded on trust and solidarity, but more importantly, it arose out of sincere collaborative intention between the Oaxacan communities of Los Angeles and the University of California, Riverside. The vision was to showcase the robust musical tradition from Oaxaca and highlight the trajectory (survival) of this cultural expression being maintained by second (even up to fourth) generation Oaxacan youth in California.

The proliferation of Oaxacan philharmonic bands in Los Angeles challenges threats of erasure and criminalization. Participating as a band member or as an audience member reaffirms one's ethnic identity in a time of xenophobic rhetoric and policies. At this music event, young women directors took the podium and energetically demonstrated their capacities as accomplished conductors, leading 140 musicians through intricate musical pieces. What made this concert on a university campus so impactful was its reciprocal transformative effect in producing the event—the power exchanges that took place in the contact zone in the production and during the event. The cultural exchange that took place was a process of educating the university performing arts production team away from Western styles of music performances and to learn how to accommodate community-oriented gatherings. The overwhelming support of students of Mexican Indigenous heritage who came out to help host visiting guests and welcome them to their campus validated the need for programming that makes them feel part of the campus. Likewise, the bands began to see and develop language to articulate their value and the type of treatment they should receive as artists. This was the largest community-oriented event that the College of Humanities, Arts, and Social Sciences has ever held, and there was an overwhelming response by community members being present on campus.

## ACKNOWLEDGMENTS

A special thank-you to Dr. Rosa Ficek and Dr. Adrian Felix for their editorial suggestions for this chapter.
Los directores, comités y familiares de las bandas: Banda Filarmónica Santa María Xochixtepec, Banda Yatzachi el Bajo—Los Angeles, Banda Nueva Dinastía de Zoochila, y Banda Filarmónica Maqueos Music.
A los maestros en Oaxaca: Maestro Olegario Robles, Chimalhuacán, Edo. De México.
Profesora Leticia Gallardo Martínez, Santa María Tlahuitoltepec Mixe, Oaxaca.
Maestro Andrés Reyes, Santa Cruz Ocotal Mixe, Oaxaca.
Maestro Eduardo Díaz Méndez, Jaltepec de Candayoc Mixe, Oaxaca.
A sincere thank-you to the numerous student volunteers for their hard work, but most of all for the tremendous support of Marlen Rios-Hernandez, Karla Hernández, Adareli López, and Claudine Avalos.
I am grateful to various colleagues, administrators, and centers at the University of California, Riverside:

Dr. Leonora Saavedra, Reasey Heang, Kathleen DeAtley, Sarah Nosce, and Greg Renne
Sandra Martínez and Dr. Ademide Adelusi-Adeluyi

Henry James Vasquez and Kim Marcus
College of Humanities, Arts, and Social Sciences Dean's Office
Native American Education Program
Office of Diversity, Equity, and Inclusion
Latin American Studies Program
Center for Iberian and Latin American Music
California Center for Native Nations
Chicano Latino Student Programs
Media and Cultural Studies
Department of Ethnic Studies

## NOTES

1. This opening prayer was written by Mr. Kim Marcus (2018) and sent to Dr. Xóchitl Chávez, to read out loud to the public right before the blessing on January 27, 2018.

2. The use of *pioneer* in this article is translated from the Spanish usage of *pionero/as* in earlier interviews and conversations with elder musicians and founding directors of Oaxacan brass bands in California (Chávez 2017). According to the *Merriam-Webster* online dictionary in English, *pioneer* as a noun is defined as "a person who is among the first to explore or settle a new country or area." As a verb it signifies the first to develop or apply a new method or activity. The use of the word *pionero/as* in reference to the Oaxacan philharmonic brass band music tradition in California represents a person who works toward the preservation and diffusion of Indigenous cultural practices. In Spanish, *pionero/as* is widely used among the Oaxacan community to emphasize a movement among Indigenous migrants who are fostering cultural spaces for new generations (Tapia 2018). It does not carry the same colonial connotation as in academic English.

3. I use the term *translocal* not only because of the continuous circulation of people, ideas, and materials but also because of the relationships and actions forged across political borders and within California (Rouse 1992; Glick-Schiller and Levitt 2006; Goldring 2002; Waldinger and Fitzgerald 2004).

4. Gender representation is undergoing major transformations as Oaxaqueña women take on more visible and significant roles as musicians and directors.

5. *Paisano/as* is a term used often by Oaxacan community members in Spanish to signify a person of the same state or town.

6. UC Riverside has two vital centers that provide support for students: Native American Student Programs and Chicano Student Programs. However, Indigenous Mexican and Central American students do not always feel comfortable in these spaces, as the dominant identity may be US territory Native communities or Mexican/Latin American mestizos.

7. According to my ethnographic interviews with Zapotec elder musicians ranging from sixty to ninety-five years of age in the two towns of Santiago Zoochila and San Andrés Solaga, Oaxaca, nearly everyone played by ear or learned to play by ear. It was not until the early 1980s that a music program was implemented at the Center for Social Integration (CIS)—an Indigenous boarding school in the nearby town of Zoochogo—where Maestro Ismael Méndez began to teach music courses and pedagogy and to form the next generation of music teachers. Maestro Ismael's teachings left a significant impact on music education in Oaxaca and in California. A few of the pioneering band directors in California were students of Maestro Ismael Méndez at one point and implemented his pedagogy with second-generation Oaxacan youth in Los Angeles.

8. Yatzchi el Bajo would later become the first band in Los Angeles to admit women. The first women in the band were mothers and wives of band members. See the documentary *Booming Bandas of Los Angeles* (Chávez 2014).

9. I also designed and printed six hundred bilingual programs in Spanish and English for the audience (Chávez 2018).

10. Maestro Olegario Robles continuously travels between the United States and Mexico working with Oaxacan community-based bands and has served as the musical director for Jenni Rivera's band.

11. Most audiciónes de bandas are held in parks, rented halls, or parking lots in Los Angeles.

12. "Thank you to all of the representatives from the university who are here with us. I want to thank all of the parents for their efforts with their children in allowing us to teach them about our Oaxacan culture, so they may never be ashamed of who they are wherever they live. That they declare, 'We are Oaxacan and proud!' We have to lift our heads and say with pride we are Oaxacan and this is our culture and music."

13. "It is amazing to see children five, six, or seven years of age playing alongside a person that is sixty to seventy years old in the band and to see that continuity and preservation of Oaxacan music. It is very beautiful."

14. "In my case, my daughters have taken on the leadership roles. That is one of the things that is happening at the music academy that I direct—we are giving opportunities to new people, to the youth so they may continue to study, an opportunity that many of us did not have."

15. See Chávez (2017) for a discussion of Maestra Jessica Hernández as the first Oaxacan woman director in California.

16. See Leonora Saavedra (2015) to read more about Carlos Chávez.

17. The subtext here is that I had administrative struggles when requesting repairs and cleanup of the cement floor in the courtyard with the dean and chancellor. Once I publicly announced at a Native American advisory board meeting that this event had garnered lots of press, as well as confirmation of live broadcasting via online and local radio, engineers and design teams begin to contact me.

## BIBLIOGRAPHY

*Secondary Sources*

Brown, Leslie, and Susan Strega. 2005. *Research as Resistance: Critical, Indigenous, and Anti-oppressive Approaches*. Toronto: Canadian Scholar's Press/Women's Press.

Chávez, Xochitl, dir., prod., ed., and videographer. 2014. *Booming Bandas of Los Angeles: Oaxacan Women and Youth as New Cultural Bearers of Philharmonic Brass Bands*. Available as "Booming Bandas of LA." Vimeo, April 7, 2015. Video, 06:22. vimeo.com/124352598.

———. 2016. Review of *The Inevitable Bandstand: The State Band of Oaxaca and the Politics of Sound*, by Charles V. Health. *Yearbook for Traditional Music* 48: W1–W2.

———. 2017. "Booming Bandas of Los Angeles: Gender and the Practice of Transnational Zapotec Philharmonic Brass Bands." In *The Tide Was Always High: The Music of Latin America in Los Angeles*, edited by Josh Kun, 260–266. Berkeley: University of California Press.

———. 2018. Program notes. Oaxacan Philharmonic Bands Audition/La Primera Audición de Bandas Filarmónicas Oaxacaqueñas. University of California, Riverside, January 27, 2018.

Fox, Jonathan, 2005. "Unpacking 'Transnational Citizenship." *Annual Review of Political Science* 8:171–201.

Garfias, Robert. 2018. Facebook comment sent via personal correspondence, January 29, 2018.

Glick-Schiller, Nina, and Peggy Levitt. 2006. "Haven't We Heard This Somewhere Before? A Substantive View of Transnational Migration Studies by Way of Reply to Waldinger and Fitzgerald." Center for Migration and Development Working Papers Series 06-01, Princeton University, Princeton, NJ, January 2006.

Goldring, Luin. 2002. "The Mexican State and Transmigrant Organizations: Negotiating the Boundaries of Membership and Participation." *Latin American Research Review* 37 (3): 55–99.

Heath, Charles V. 2015. *The Inevitable Bandstand: The State Band of Oaxaca and the Politics of Sound*. Lincoln: University of Nebraska Press.

Kearney, Michael. 1995. "The Local and the Global: The Anthropology of Globalization and Transnationalism." *Annual Review of Anthropology* 24:547–565.

Marcus, Kim. 2018. "Cahuilla Prayer." Electronic correspondence sent to author. January 26, 2018.

Martinez, Hernan. 2018. "Thank You." Electronic correspondence sent to author. January 20, 2018.

*Merriam-Webster*. s.v. "pioneer." Accessed September 3, 2020. https://www.merriam-webster.com/dictionary/pioneer#:~:text=1%20%3A%20a%20person%20who%20is,pioneer.

Nájera-Ramírez, Olga. 1994. "Engendering Nationalism: Identity, Discourse, and the Mexican Charro." *Anthropological Quarterly* 67 (1): 1–14.

———. 1999. "Of Fieldwork, Folklore, and Festival: Personal Encounters." *Journal of American Folklore* 112 (44): 183–199.

Paredes, Américo. 1977. "Ethnographic Work among Minorities: A Folklorist Perspective." *New Scholar* 6:1–32.

Rouse, Roger. 1992. "Making Sense of Settlement: Class Transnationalism, Cultural Struggle and Transformation among Mexican Migrants in the United States." In "Toward a Transnational Perspective on Migration: Race, Class, Ethnicity, and Nationalism Reconsidered," edited by Nina Glick Schiller, Linda Basch, and Cristina Blanc-Szanton. Special issue, *Annals of the New York Academy of Sciences* 645 (1): 25–52.

Saavedra, Leonora. 2015. *Carlos Chávez and His World*. Princeton, NJ: Princeton University Press.

Tapia, Ruben. 2018. "Música de pioneras bandas indígenas de México resuena en recinto Universitario." Radio Bilingüe, July 13, 2018. http://radiobilingue.org /features/musica-de-pioneras-bandas-indigenas-de-mexico-resuena-en-recinto -universitario/.

Tomlinson, Barbara, and George Lipsitz. 2013. "American Studies as Accompaniment." *American Quarterly* 65 (1): 1–30.

Waldinger, Roger, and David Fitzgerald. 2004. "Transnationalism in Question." *American Journal of Sociology* 109 (5): 1177–1195.

*Interviews*

Adams, Bryon. Interview by author. Riverside, CA. January 31, 2018.

Hernández, Jessica. Interview by author. Lynwood, CA. July 10, 2018.

Hernández, Porfirio. Interview by author. Lynwood, CA. July 10, 2018.

Méndez, Ismael. Interview by author. Oaxaca City, Mexico. March 20, 2014.

Reynoso, José Luis. Interview by author. Riverside, CA. January 27, 2018.

Robles, Olegario. Interview by author. Riverside, CA. December 25, 2017.

XÓCHITL C. CHÁVEZ is Assistant Professor at the University of California, Riverside, in the Department of Music. She is a scholar of expressive culture and performance, specializing in Indigenous communities from southern Mexico and transnational migration. She was a recipient of the University of California President's Postdoctoral Fellowship (2014–2016) and a Smithsonian Institution Postdoctoral Fellow (2013–2014). Her current work on second-generation Zapotec brass bands in Los Angeles investigates how women and youth now fill the ranks of musicians and new leadership.

# FIFTEEN

# Hidden Thoughts and Exposed Bodies

Art, Everyday Life, and Queering Cuban Masculinities

CORY W. THORNE

This exploration began after several years of ethnographic research on a ranch in suburban Havana (2010–2011 and ongoing), where I set out to understand creativity in everyday life, underground economies, and the shifting experiences of queerness during an era of increasing tolerance (and in some circles acceptance) of LGBTQI+ identities in Cuba. The ranch, several interconnected homes hidden in a rural section on the edge of the city, was previously the site of underground gay parties during the era when LGBTQI+ identities had to be deeply hidden and creative in order to avoid harassment and persecution. I began with a focus on three gay men who lived at the ranch and who organized the parties, and I continued with their extended queer family, aiming to tell stories of queer life that were otherwise ignored, invisible, and in many ways seemingly untellable. These lives, along with many other members of the subaltern, are encapsulated by queer theorist José Muñoz: "To be cognizant of one's status as an identity-in-difference is to know that one falls off majoritarian maps of the public sphere, that one is exiled from paradigms of communicative reason and a larger culture of consent" (2000, 68). This essay blends folkloristics and queer theory, giving evidence of Muñoz's statement while helping combat against it.

Telling these stories is an act of revealing and critiquing our understandings of a core folklore concept: everyday life. Likewise, it is a critique of how queer theory is commonly framed and understood in relation to a very narrow experience of the everyday: white, Global North, and privileged. While folklorists and queer theorists both seek to better address issues of social justice and inequality—through documenting, telling, and interpreting stories of difference—we likewise face limits to that understanding, especially when we write for audiences who experience Global North whiteness mostly as the center instead of the periphery, thus limiting our ability to see and communicate a true diversity of ways of being. I speak of myself when I critique these limits. As a gay, white, cis male Canadian academic, I have spent most of my life sheltered from experiencing or understanding the world beyond the dominant Global North. My friends in Havana, however, revealed to me some of the limits of my imagination, thus encouraging me to examine the ways in which hegemonic cultural imaginaries divide, control, and even hide these systems of power from us.

My critique of queer theory and the Global North conflation of sexual act as identity is in part inspired by my concerns with marking, such as with the diversity that leads to the ever-lengthening acronym of LGBTTI2QQSA—an acronym that represents not only increasing acceptance and awareness of sexual diversity but also increasing divisions within Global North identity politics. Just as José Quiroga (2000) examines the labels *gay* and *out* in terms of how they function in Latino America versus the Global North, I struggle with terms that might be used in the Global North to mark the identities of some of my research participants: gay, trans, *pinguero* (sex worker), scam artist, thief. None of these terms are suitable. Some of them are offensive. White affect limits our vocabulary and our ability to understand why. How are the terms *gay* and *pinguero* performed or rejected by men in Cuba who sell their bodies or their time to Global North tourists—tourists who are chasing encounters with hypersexualized, racialized, exoticized, politicized, marginalized Cuban men?

When Quiroga (2000, 8) critiques the ways in which the North "provides theory for the South's cultural practice," I ask, How do these tourists interpret their own experiences, as they categorize and theorize the identities of their hosts into Global North gay identity politics or queer theory? How do the narratives of tourists from the North differ from those of their hosts in the South? Whose voice gets heard? Which voices still need to be heard? These same questions underpin Quiroga's description of a tourist postcard image—a photo of two shirtless men on a Havana balcony, with the door behind them partly ajar: "Those bodies that used to be inside the rooms that lead to those balconies were *Cuban*, while their appearance in the balcony itself allows for their new configuration as (Cuban) *gay* males" (11). Bodies that were once rejected by the state are now desired by capitalism; bodies that not so long ago were tortured and imprisoned for deviant sexual activities are now advertised and manipulated for the tourist gaze. However, the individual narratives—the identities that are attached to these bodies—continue to be suppressed, hidden, and erased.

My critique of folkloristics and our approach to everyday life is influenced in part by Harris Berger and Giovanna Del Negro's (2004) *Identity and Everyday Life*, where they encourage us to question the neo-Romantic leanings of some approaches to contemporary folkloristics (e.g., *everyday* as a replacement for Romantic Nationalism), and they likewise critique the framing of everyday life as distinct from "special events"—another example of how un/marked categories enhance and limit our ways of seeing. Many of my research participants tell stories of everyday life that involve MSM (men who have sex with men) sex work or theft, but the labels *gay*, *prostitute*, and *thief* automatically erase the complexity, morality, and individuality that exist within their everyday, unmarked, unheard personal experiences. Likewise, these narratives are not fully formed into what we might label *personal experience narrative*, which are too "everyday" and thus are unmarked and unheard. The labels—marked categories—are a piece of Global North hegemony that encourages maintaining distance from the seeming mundaneness of everyday life in the South. The North frames the South in an attempt to erase and to control. By critically engaging with the everyday and by examining the power of un/marked categories, we can begin to escape from this Global North hegemony.

In 2018, after randomly meeting visual and performance artist Giorge Michel Milian Maura (on an afternoon while walking along the Rio San Juan *malecón*, as a tourist with my husband), I began to fret over my inability to adequately explain the lives of my friends in Havana. Looking at Maura's paintings, alongside a painting that I purchased in 2011 in Cienfuegos (Luis Alberto Pérez Copperi's *conflicto almado*), I became distressed. These artists were visualizing exactly what I was struggling to write, on a level to which I can only aspire. These artists have escaped the limitations of un/marked categories by focusing on the visual—using imagery to examine superimposed snippets of text (such as *conflicto almado*, *TESTOSTEROMANIA*, *MACHO*, *BARON*, and *MAS-CU-LINO*) and combining it with humor and the surreal so as to tell the untellable. Everyday life is reframed and marked as performance.

Through ongoing conversations with both artists, I've attempted to explain their works in relation to what I observed and experienced during my time at the ranch, as well as through continuing conversations with several Cuban friends who contributed to my fieldwork. This is a form of reciprocal ethnography, by a folklorist who envies the wisdom and aptitude of these and other artists to concisely and accurately reveal a depth of knowing that is elusive, anarchistic, and empowering. By viewing ethnography through these specific artists, I hope to meld the phenomenological power of surrealism with the pragmatic limitations of ethnography. This is still, however, an interpretation that is shaped through my own experiences and aptitude, but it is ultimately a responsibility with which they (Maura, Copperi, and my research participants) have trusted me. I thank them for their time and assistance, and I hope that I do their stories justice. These stories will be explored in greater depth and from additional perspectives in forthcoming publications, part of a critical queer ethnography of Cuban everyday life.

CONFLICTO ALMADO: ARMED CONFLICTED SOUL

*conflicto almado* (fig. 15.1) is the image of a Cuban revolutionary soldier who fails to embody the goals of the revolution. His body is exposed on a stage, yet his face is hidden. The artist, Luis Alberto Pérez Copperi, has cut up an English-language brochure that advertises an all-inclusive tourist beach resort and pasted it onto the soldier's face. The text of the brochure is partly hidden by a painted clown smile. His face and identity are masked, even while he stands naked on a stage, covering his genitals with his hands. This is a soldier without any physical armor, whose personal identity has been stripped in the way we frequently view military conscripts and good communist citizens, but he also disidentifies. He is a capitalist subject, forced into giving his body to the communist nation and then timidly stealing it back so as to sell its masculinity to foreign tourists for personal profit and survival. On the window ledge behind him, there is a plastic toy Cuban soldier—indicated by the red star on its chest—and it is aiming a rifle at the real soldier's head.

When I first met Copperi, he was sharing a small gallery with a friend, selling "Art of Resistance" in Cienfuegos, on the south side of Cuba. The space is on a side street on the edge of José Martí Park and within view of one of Cienfuegos's core tourist destinations, the 1887 Tomás Terry Theater—a reference to a Spanish businessman and slave trader and a representative of the official narrative of Cubanidad. The gallery was filled with smaller works containing scenes of everyday life that combine the ordinary with the surreal while hinting at confrontation. Many of his works, however, most of which are done with printer's ink on craft paper, are promoted and sold through the Cuban Art Space, part of the Center for Cuban Studies in Brooklyn, New York. Typically black and white with small splashes of color and occasionally layering materials (assemblage), these paintings use metaphor to create social critique and to document nonlinear histories, discussing Cuban life while disidentifying with hegemonic narratives of Cubanidad.

With an uncritical glance, the viewer might read it as *conflicto armado*, "armed conflict." However, the title is a linguistic metaphor meant to engage the viewer: *almado*, referencing armed conflict but fusing it with *alma*, soul. Contextualizing this painting within contemporary Cuban everyday life and juxtaposing the experiences of military conscription, communist propaganda, and patriotism against the pervasive underground economies as they relate to sex work or sex tourism, masculinities, and stigmatizations, I translate it as "armed conflicted soul." By writing the title in lowercase, Copperi suggests that this is not a singular or specific Armed Conflicted Soul; rather, it is an experience that moves beyond the individuality of proper nouns. It is not a singular or isolated experience but a

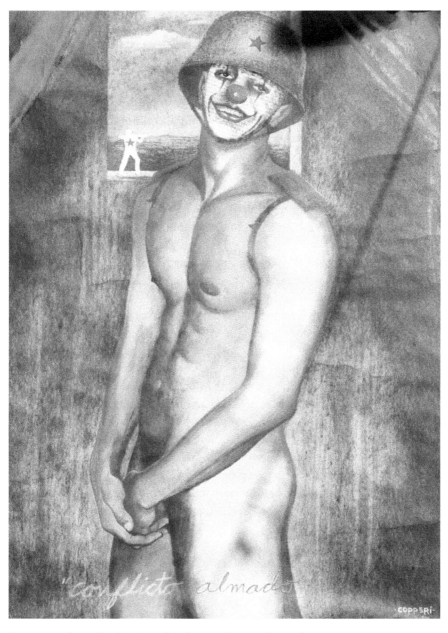

Fig. 15.1 *conflicto almado*, printer's ink on craft paper / mixed,
20 × 27 cm, c. 2011 © Luis Alberto Pérez Copperi.

visualized structure of feeling that speaks more closely to contemporary everyday life in Cuba. The painting stands as an example of Muñoz's reconfiguration of Raymond Williams's structures of feeling, forcing the viewer to question the role of white affect on their interpretation of the narrative (Muñoz 2000), intentionally blurring and disrupting so as to encourage viewers to examine their own limitations of experience. It is a feeling that we examine through deep contextualization of experience during our quest for humble theory (Noyes 2016).

When I asked Copperi about the potential danger of selling subversive and openly critical paintings, he explained that in the art world, it is the viewer that creates the interpretation. Drawn in by the military clown on the naked body of a sex worker who is poised on a stage with red velvet curtains, I began to interpret it as the visual representation of everything that I need to say about sex work, sexuality, and the surreal experience of doing ethnography in contemporary queer Havana. Over a series of conversations, I tested and developed my interpretation of this and other paintings—seeking Copperi's affirmation. By juxtaposing diffuse elements of Cuban everyday life, Copperi forces his viewers to question. My reading is based on Yunieski.

In my field notes, I have a collection of experiences that I group under the name Yunieski. It is a Russian-sounding name, commonly found among young Cuban men, reflective of the thoughts, dreams, and propaganda that led to a generation of parents teaching a generation of children Russian language and culture, under the belief in a more prosperous Cuban-Soviet future. Yunieski is the name that I use to characterize the experiences of multiple research participants (from 2010 to 2017) while constructing anonymity. While every individual deserves to be recognized for their unique and diverse stories and experiences, I use this composite approach for three reasons: (1) when documenting activities that are illegal or deeply revealing of personal morality, protecting identities is essential; (2) by using composites, I am able to incorporate dangerously personal elements of individual stories while adding a layer of protection beyond mere pseudonyms; and (3) by focusing on the emergent patterns of individual experience, I hope to give my readers a greater sense of eidos—the experienced essence of everyday life (Berger and Del Negro 2004, 25). Art is eidos. Ethnography seeks to translate eidos. Yunieski is my understanding of eidos in the context of queer male Cuban everyday life during this time frame.

Yunieski is a male sex worker, born near Guantanamo, who was identified in high school as being smart and hardworking and an excellent candidate to train in a specialized branch of the military. After moving to Havana, and after being outed as homosexual, he found himself without a home, an education, or a family. Having arrived in the city without a residency permit (vernacularly and derogatively labeled *Palestino*—an illegal migrant within one's own country),

Yunieski cannot work in any official or legal capacity, nor can he access his meager food rations guaranteed to all Cubans through the popularly revered and reviled Libreta de Abastecimiento (the ration supplies book).

As with Copperi's representation of this situation, Yunieski served his government and the revolution, and now he puts on a smile to sell his body. Yunieski is a pinguero, a category of sex worker, primarily MSM, that emerged after the collapse of the Soviet Union and the subsequent blow to Cuba's fragile economy (Hodge 2014; Stout 2014; Allen 2007, 2011). As imports and subsidies dropped and food shortages intensified, the government of Cuba opened the country to greater tourism while acknowledging the ideological dangers of Cuban-tourist interactions. As noted by Jafari Allen (2007, 185), "He [Fidel Castro] held that to embark on tourism as a development strategy was, in fact, like making a pact with the devil. . . . The re-emergence of tourism and related sex work hearkens back to pre-revolutionary structures of feeling. This includes contending with a tourist gaze that casts people of the South, especially blacks, as objects of their pleasure." As shown through ethnographic data and as summarized by G. Derrick Hodge (2014, 442), the development of the tourist sector rescued the Cuban economy and "brought social segmentation and differentiation, intensified racism, increase in property crime, a resurgence of erotic labor, and porous ideological borders."

Just as experienced by the soldier in this painting, Yunieski is a beneficiary of the tourist gaze, and he discovered that while his queer identity excluded him from the full realization of his revolutionary duties, his expert performance of an imagined Cuban masculinity would entice gay tourists and drastically improve his economic condition. The income from a few hours of sex work is approximately equal to the monthly salary of a military or government worker. It also has additional benefits such as access to leisure, fashion and brand-name clothing, tourist spaces, and non-Cuban media; it helps one build a sense of escape and cosmopolitanism, gaining worldly knowledge beyond the confines of state media. It creates a feeling of control over one's life and greater optimism for the future.

Yunieski was successfully negotiating these conflicting yet interconnected identities when I first spotted him hanging out with fellow pingueros at a cafeteria on Twenty-Third Street in Vedado, the center of Havana's queer community. He was showing his friends a series of photos of himself dressed as a military police officer. Intrigued by this performance, I arranged for an interview, and he explained to me that he was trained in the special police forces to work with male sex workers, kind of like a liaison to protect tourists from robbery, watch out for pedophilia, and monitor the drug trade. Perhaps sensing my suspicion or testing my ambitions, Yunieski arrived at the interview with two identity cards. The first was the standard *carné de identidad*, with his name, address, and photo—evidence that he was the person that he claimed to be. The second card, however, was a police ID with a different name and with his own passport-sized photo glued on over the original. He told me that he had lost his own card but that a fellow officer had lent him one so that he could make a new copy, and he suggested that perhaps I could help. Would I be willing to make a digital photo of this card, edit it, and put it on a USB stick so that he could go to the local photo shop and print a new one?

As a friend of a friend, Yunieski understood that I wasn't a tourist but rather that I was living with and writing about a group of gay and queer individuals in suburban Havana. He was testing me and testing his story. This story was well rehearsed and was his tool for gaining trust from strangers. By identifying as a hypermasculine man in uniform who is trustworthy but mysterious, he was performing for his expectation of the gay tourist gaze. It often worked. I bumped into Yunieski several times over subsequent visits, on the street, in bars, and at Mi Cayito, the "gay" beach in La Habana del Este, thirty kilometers east of the city. I last saw him in person in 2015, and in 2017 some of his friends told me that he was once again in prison. He was caught robbing an elderly male German sex tourist. Early in 2020, he sent me a Facebook message. He was in Ecuador, following the path of thousands of Cubans attempting to migrate to the United States. Eight months later—I haven't heard from him since. Yunieski's body was for sale, but his true face was hidden, and, just like *conflicto almado* / armed conflicted soul, he disidentified with the identities imposed on him.

In their multigenre, multijournal, interdisciplinary web text, Jonathan Alexander and Jacqueline Rhodes (2012) examine queer rhetorics and disidentification while using a black-and-white American army recruitment film that purports to introduce high school males to the physical training and the challenges of military duty. The narrator's script is serious but campy: "It's rough and rugged. You've got to be able to take it. Your body's got to be able to take it, because service means new physical demands on strength and endurance.... You got to be able to... carry heavy loads, do hard manual labour, use your body skillfully, be ready for instant actions... be prepared for anything and everything" (slithis 2007). The video opens with and later repeats a scene of two young men, naked and showering together. Near the end (at minute 2:20) the text "subliminal seduction????" is superimposed onto the original, scrolling across the screen in bold red. It is up to the viewer to create the interpretation. Do they agree with the narrator's suggestion?

Citing Judith Butler (1993) and Muñoz (1999), and referring to this video (slithis 2007), Alexander and Rhodes (2012) explain how disidentification deals with the recycling and rethinking of encoded meaning so that it not only situates individuals as both within and against certain hegemonic discourses but also moves beyond code breaking to render the unthinkable as it is held by the dominant society. Disidentification not only shows how the recruitment video is simultaneously homoerotic and representative of homophobia; it also shows the experience of simultaneous embodiment of inclusion and exclusion. It is an experience that is recognized by every queer individual, and it is the primary feeling that is visualized in *conflicto almado*.

As demonstrated by L. B. Blume and Rosemary Weatherston (2018), queer pedagogy through art invites (dis)identification both within and beyond queer communities, "activating in their viewers a complex, relational process of identification and disidentification that also undermines the boundaries between margin/center, subject/object, fluid/stable, universal/particular, self/other, and aesthetic/academic" (72–73). Queer images and performances (referencing multigenre art forms that include paintings, performance art, and poetry readings) interfere with and intervene in the production of normalcy that is central to many educational and institutional systems (74). Queer art encourages viewers to deconstruct and reexamine their own gendered and sexualized identities—encouraging (dis)identification as a tool of self-realization.

When I first saw *conflicto almado* hanging high up above various paintings and souvenirs in a Cienfuegos gallery (Galeria Maroya), I thought it was a confusing but powerful image. It visualized much of what I was then observing as part of my fieldwork in Havana's gay community but was struggling to understand and to explain beyond uncomfortable etic and hegemonic perspectives of Cubanidad. Gay everyday life was quite different from the dominant narratives. Luis Alberto Pérez Copperi's *conflicto almado*, however, became my tool for understanding disidentification and the lives of Yunieski.

### TESTOSTEROMANIA: MACHO: BARON: MAS-CU-LINO

*TESTOSTEROMANIA* (fig. 15.2) is a hypersexual and surrealist queer fantasy of Cuban male gym culture. With emotionless expressions, it shows twelve men, two of whom are assistants entirely masked as a harlequin and a clown, and a nurse—a white body with a red cross on his arm, distributing muscle injections. Four of the bodybuilders are using dumbbells, and one is doing sit-ups. One is standing with the nurse and injecting into his shoulder while another is measuring his biceps. One man is flexing for himself in front of a mirror, and deep in the background there is a voyeur—naked, watching, and masturbating in the shadows. The exposed bodies are marked as hypermasculine and hypersexual, but the hidden faces suggest a struggle with or even rejection of such markings; they struggle to find their place within Global North identity politics.

The harlequin and clown are distinguished by their tight-fitting checkered and striped bodysuits and painted masks that hide their expressions. Most of the bodybuilders are wearing skin-tight bikini briefs, all of them with clearly

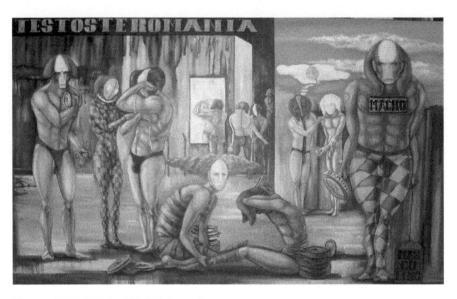

Fig. 15.2 *TESTOSTEROMANIA*, acrylic on canvas, 70 × 41 cm,
2012 © Giorge Michel Milian Maura.

defined bulges. Instead of masks, however, they have playfully anthropomorphic
heads—possibly bulls or Tauruses but possibly puppy dogs, who are serious but
not aggressive. The man with the syringe in his shoulder is dreaming of lollypops
("How sweet life will be once I have the perfect body"), and while it appears to
be steroids, it could easily be peanut oil (commonly and dangerously used in
Cuba for muscle injections to achieve instant narcissistic satisfaction). The largest man, in the foreground, has a red heart tattooed on his shoulder, a sign with
"MACHO" hanging on his hairy chest from a string in his mouth, a dumbbell
in one hand with the word "BARON," and a solid block held by a string in the
other with the word "MAS-CU-LINO"—words that are used interchangeably
in Cuban discourse to reference masculinities. He is wearing a harlequinesque
leotard, and as the sole character facing the viewer, he is speaking to the viewer,
telling us to playfully consider the ways in which these words define and influence
the performance of masculinity.

The floor of the gym is a dirty, sweaty yellow orange with bloodlike red stains
and shadows. The walls are streaked with dripping colors evoking mold, mildew,
and distress (the architecture of decay that maintains a constant and pervasive
presence in everyday Cuba). All of the characters have narrow knees and tiny
calves, slightly out of proportion with their upper bodies. Biceps, hairy chests,
and well-defined abs are greater markers of masculinity than calves, knees, or
cardiovascular fitness. As if it weren't already evident, the bold, all-uppercase

text screams TESTOSTERONE. This overcompensation of text and image—the animal heads; dirty, decaying setting; masked clowns; and bulges—turns masculinity into parody.

Paralleling Beatriz Preciado's (2013b) autofictional *Testo Junkie*, we are asked to consider the ways in which testosterone relates not only to masculinity and sex but also to broader forms of political and social control. Preciado (2013a) describes the "explosion of the desire to fuck, walk, go out everywhere in the city" after taking a fifty-milligram dose of Testogel—not as treatment to change into a man or as a "physical strategy of transsexualism" but rather as a way to take control of a nonbinary body, to achieve pleasure, and to escape political management of one's body. Testosterone is used to enhance the embodiment of masculinity and its associated elements: "I am linked by T to electricity, to genetic research projects, to mega-urbanization, to the destruction of forests and the biosphere, to pharmaceutical exploitation of living species, to Dolly the cloned sheep, to the advance of the Ebola virus, to HIV mutation, to antipersonnel mines and the broadband transmission of information."

While both Maura and Preciado use testosterone to embody, enhance, and examine hegemonic forms of masculinity, the masks and clowns in *TESTOS-TEROMANIA* highlight the performativity and even parody of this identity. The parallel bars next to the mirror, the Lycra-clad harlequin, the stripped onesie clown, the vastness of space, and the near absence of actual gym equipment . . . it could also be a dance studio. This is a performance—an artificial and erotic voyeuristic fantasy that hides fragile individuality via the stigmatized vernacular: individuality is erased by the stigmatization of certain categories of identity. Maura is asking us to think about hypermasculinity and sexuality and how these categories limit our ability to see and hear individual voices. The pantomimic harlequin and clown direct their movements while stealing their voices and individuality. They add a layer of melancholy into a narcissistic space of masculine debauchery.

When I first met Giorge Michel Milian Maura in 2016, he was attempting to draw me in from the street to see the small art gallery above the famous Ediciones Vigía publisher and bookshop—sellers of handmade books for whom he had created a series of drawings and book-sculptures (books that act as sculptures). It is located near the historic center of Matanzas, situated on the north coast, a mere 36 km from Varadero (one of Cuba's largest and densest collections of all-inclusive tourist resorts) and 82 km from Havana (and a mere 171 km from the southern extremity of the Global North: Key West, Florida). As we wandered the gallery, he told us about his other artworks—more personal and erotic but less marketable in this tourist-centric district. After we stopped for refreshments and met several friends, he invited me to his house to show me the rest of his collection.

Maura shares a two-bedroom interior house with his grandmother. It is part of the interior courtyard of an older, crumbling structure that is connected to the street by a long, narrow walkway ("the gallery"). Every surface is filled with art: paintings on the walls, under the beds, and stacked in the loft, and sculptures and papier-mâché costumes hanging from windows and doorways and even built into the walls themselves. His creativity is slowly exploding into the street as he expands into murals and sculptures, often using bricolage—found objects and antiques that he has creatively repurposed. The streets outside immediately take me to the story of Fred Raleigh, an eclectic folk artist in Harrisburg, Pennsylvania—the bricoleur who decorates his row house while deconstructing abandoned properties and fighting gentrification in Simon Bronner's (1992) "The House on Penn Street: Creativity and Conflict in Folk Art." Maura isn't fighting gentrification; more so, he is trying to kick-start neighborhood pride. Noting the seemingly insurmountable urban decay, the lack of opportunities for economic development, and a personal struggle with depression, Maura has embraced the creating-something-out-of-nothing attitude by creating beauty and community through bricolage. He calls it the "Open Sesame" project, as it encourages neighbors to work together and to take pride in their shared public spaces. Neighbors have joined in to collect and contribute various objects. He has created a community of bricoleurs.

Maura works in acrylic, multimedia, costume, pantomime, set design, and performance art. He has designed and performed shows for tourist resorts, as well as multigenre exhibitions for the state-run Asociación Cubana de Artesanos Artistas. He lists Salvador Dalí, Roberto Fabelo, and Rocío García as his greatest influences. Fabelo (b. 1950) is a contemporary Cuban painter and sculptor who mixes expressionism and surrealism. García (b. 1951) is a contemporary Cuban painter who is well known for exploring psychological issues through eroticism and violence. Her 1998 series *Hombres, Machos, Marineros* marked her as "a pioneer in showing erect penises in an exhibition in Cuba" (Prieto 2015) and contains themes of homoeroticism, contrasts and blending of self-affirmation and narcissism, alongside fantasy and danger. Maura extends on Dalí, Fabelo, and García as he explores what he calls "social eroticism"—that is, communication and exploration of social issues through the erotic. This is the visual art equivalent of Renaldo Arenas's (2001) final novel, *The Color of Summer*, and Jaime Cortez's (2004) graphic novel *Sexile*—both of which tell tales of coming of age as gay in Cuba, facing persecution, facing the HIV/AIDS epidemic, and struggling to find peace while living in exile in the United States. Maura hasn't left Cuba. Gay life has gotten better here. As he explains through some of his other works, however, he has thought about it.

Clowns are pervasive throughout Maura's work, and he explained to me that he uses clowns for circus play and for specific roles. One of the clowns, the harlequin figure in *TESTOSTEROMANIA*, is measuring a man's bicep. The other is holding a man's feet while he does sit-ups. Clowns assist the main characters, and Maura describes them as the only ones permitted to attend court and joke with reality. Clowns help code and reveal the truth, while civilians must fully hide their true thoughts to avoid persecution; art imitates life in the communist state. As assistants, these two clowns help reframe the gymnasium into a dance studio and turn us, the viewers, into the audience—the voyeurs. The clowns control the narrative, whereas the bodybuilders are passive, stigmatized images of manliness. They are trapped. Not only are they voiceless, but worse, they are part animal. Do they have the consciousness to critically engage with this discourse? Or, do they surrender their voices and hide individuality as a form of self-defense?

While presenting the history of the harlequin clown motif, Benjamin Radford (2016) notes that "Harlequin, for much of his existence, was silent. Like most clowns he performed in pantomime. This silence is one aspect that makes a clown mysterious and unnerving, for his thoughts and motivations—whether benevolent or malicious—may be on his mind but are not on his tongue" (8). He also notes that historically, the clown figure is "generally devoid of allegiance; he has no masters and is a man in full and at his own command" (9). The clown provides a key role for both Copperi and Maura in moving us toward considering the intersections of disidentification and stigmatized vernacular—and the emergence of humble theory.

Maura created this painting for himself. When I first saw it in 2016, it was covered in dust and stacked out of reach in his loft. I asked about it. He proudly showed it to me, explained it, and then put it away: "It is not for sale." Two years later he asked if I was still interested. While his decision to sell was in part economic—the need for money—I like to think that it was also an indicator of assurance: Maura now trusted me to be its guardian. His resistance to letting go of it speaks to its importance: This is a painting about Maura's personal struggles with masculinity and desire. In much of the art world, particularly among folk art and outsider art circles, this may be read as a sign of "authenticity" (Fine 2003). It is an image of personal struggle, transformation, and acceptance. In "real life," Maura embodies a gender-fluid hypermasculinity while serving the role of contemporary harlequin, both in his attitude and in his occasional employment, in his ability to reveal and cross boundaries, hegemonic narratives, and the queerness of everyday life.

Similar to Arenas's use of fiction and parody to reveal the untellable tales of gay everyday life in 1960s–1970s Cuba, Maura uses clowns, carnivalesque, and the surreal as part of his personal struggle with masculinity, sexuality, and patriotism. In their analysis of Arenas's (2001) *The Color of Summer*, Christophe Panichelli and Stéphanie Panichelli-Batalla (2018) discuss how humor, sublimation, and creativity interact not only to complicate identity in everyday life but also to make such narratives palatable. Humor is a coping mechanism—a defense against anxiety and depression. Sublimation is a way to process emotional conflict, channeling it into socially acceptable behavior—creativity such as writing autofiction or painting surrealist personalized fantasies.

Maura's first public exhibition was titled *Hechos, Mitos y Leyendas* (*Facts, Myths, and Legends*, 1992), an exploration of Greek mythology and the male body. It was followed by *Tentación y Pecado* (*Temptation and Sin*, 1993). In the series *Identidad* (*Identity*, 2010), he began exploring themes of the Cuban flag and patriotism (from the perspective of marginalization and alternate ways "to be revolutionary"), painting on antique door panels both as symbol (portals with layered histories) and as practicality (bricolage by necessity—a scarcity of materials). Parts of this series speak to the longings, fears, and temptations to leave Cuba (for anywhere, with or without legal documentation). In *Fábulas de la Gran Carpa* (*Fables of the Great Tent*, 2011), he dove into harlequins, clowns, and the carnivalesque, as if attempting to escape the dolorous heavyheartedness of *Identity*. Some of these figures became characters in Varadero tourist shows, where he was then working in stage design. His series *Pink Power Machine* (original title in English; 2015) was an expression of his own sexuality while battling depression—playfully but firmly masculine, with effeminate flourishes. I'd like to call it genderqueer, but as per Quiroga's (2000) critique of North theory / South practice, I use this term cautiously. There is a fluidity of gender that is unmarked, playful, and depoliticized; it is a queering of gender that is Cuban, Latino, and distinct from Northern white-centric queer theory.

Maura's most recent series, *Rosas a los Cerdos* (*Roses to Pigs*, 2016), is the most sexually provocative of his collections, featuring muscular, naked, hairy men; leather; drag; sex toys; and the same Taurus heads and clowns featured in *TESTOSTEROMANIA*. Maura blends hypermasculinity, gender nonconformity, and sadomasochism to create scenes of playful debauchery—exposing a sexuality that goes well beyond Rocío García's pioneering display of erect penises.

*TESTOSTEROMANIA* both invites and mocks the male body as a vessel of power. Read in relation to his other paintings, we see how it is not only an exaggeration of stereotypically male characteristics; for gay men, it is a strategy of gender conformity and individual safety. As noted by Tristan Bridges (2016), "Gay identities among men are sometimes culturally situated as at odds with normative conceptualizations of masculinity. Thus, it is logical that some gay men will rely on hypermasculinity to acquire a status symbolically denied to gay men as a result of sexual inequality." Hypermasculinity and the "gay gym clone" are often linked with the desire not only to escape stereotypes and stigmas of homosexuality but also to defend from false narratives of gay men as weak and ill. It was no accident that the gym body became exaggerated during the HIV/AIDS crisis.

*TESTOSTEROMANIA* is an exploration of the stigmatized vernacular. As with disidentification, it examines the layering of conflicting identities. However, while Muñoz's (1999, 2000) disidentification is based in internal attachments and conflicts (how one accepts, processes, or denies imposed identities), the stigmatized vernacular emphasizes external application (how identities are attached to certain individuals regardless of their acceptance, processing, or denial). We cannot read the thoughts and emotions of these bodybuilders; instead, we are asked to lay identities onto them and contemplate the ways in which hypervisibility obscures individuality. The stigmatized vernacular helps hide their individual desires.

In their introduction to *The Stigmatized Vernacular: Where Reflexivity Meets Untellability*, Diane Goldstein and Amy Shuman (2016) bring work on stigma, "a form of hyper-visibility that obscures other experiences," alongside the "vernacular politics of narrative" (2). Much of this deals with the doubly stigmatized— "situations where not only are individuals stigmatized but so are the vernaculars associated with them" (2). For Goldstein, this is how the label *HIV/AIDS* has limited and continues to limit our ability to see and hear the stories of affected individuals, thus limiting or redirecting access to health care and the legal system. For Shuman, the stigmatized vernacular directs the questioning, interpretation, and ability of immigration officers to hear the voices and experiences of applicants for political asylum, many of whom are resisting the retelling (and thus reexperiencing) of physical and sexual violence, even though such narratives are often the key to achieving asylum. Returning to Yunieski, the stigmatized vernacular deals with his erasure from the Cuban public sphere. His individuality is irrelevant; his imposed identity as a pinguero stifles true visibility.

The stigmatized vernacular is a framework through which folklorists can address the weaknesses of queer theory—how to reconnect critical and queer theory to everyday life (i.e., how to reveal the role of politics of narrative and tradition). This is the core theme through all of Maura's opus. The stigmatized vernacular is a framework that helps us move beyond descriptive ethnography and toward vernacular theorization via engagement with various layers of coding. In the context of gay Cuban eroticism, it is a critique of Global North queer theory. Disidentification encourages us to question how "these" bodybuilders think about themselves. The stigmatized vernacular forces us to better analyze how we think about "them."

## EVERYDAY LIFE AND QUEER CRITICAL ETHNOGRAPHY

One of my longtime favorite definitions of *folklore* is Barbara Kirshenblatt-Gimblett's (1983) "the aesthetics of everyday life." As argued by

Berger and Del Negro (2004), however, while the concern for everyday life is strongly felt and the term is increasingly pervasive across folkloristics, it is frequently undertheorized. How is "everyday life" defined, and from whose perspective? As Erving Goffman (1959) and Richard Bauman (1984) taught us, the frameworks that indicate performance—that which shifts us from everyday (unmarked) into performance (marked)—are culturally and socially specific (aesthetics is an even more elusive definition). Copperi and Maura, however, assert a heightened awareness of the existence of performance within the everyday—thus supporting the folkloristic argument for the value of seemingly mundane, informal, repetitive, and traditionalized actions. My exploration of Cuban art in relation to ethnographic experience, read through the intersections of disidentification and the stigmatized vernacular, is an attempt to move beyond descriptive ethnography and to start to engage with these blurrings.

Muñoz (1999, 2000) highlights ethnic affect as inappropriate—that is, the lack of audibility, visibility, and thus power of nonwhite voices within hegemonic mainstream American discourse; even if we see or hear "them," we interpret through a "white" lens that filters our ways of seeing and hearing in favor of a hegemonic whiteness. Likewise, queer affect is filtered through institutionalized heteronormativity, as are other layers of identity. It is through Muñoz's work, as well as that of other queer theorists of color such as Ana-Maurine Lara (2017) and Thomas Glave (2005), that we increasingly see the limits of Global North queer theory—a view of identity that continues to center middle-class whiteness and to relegate nonwhite voices to the margins. To understand Yunieski, Maura, or Copperi, we must decenter and exoticize our experiences of Global North whiteness—attempt to see ourselves as surreal in relation to Latinx everyday life.

Yunieski's poverty (as arising from and contributing to his lack of traditional home, biological family structure, officially recognized employment, heteronormativity—in short, mainstreamness) renders him invisible even within the mundaneness of everyday life. However, he is the center, normal, unmarked category as experienced by millions of Cuban and Latinx individuals. Just as Muñoz (1999, 2000) argues that Latinx affect shouldn't be hidden but should serve as a critique of the "emotional impoverishment" of normative whiteness, I see Yunieski's affect (pinguero affect, queer affect, and even an affect of poverty most broadly) as a creative and necessary public performative critique of the conventions of mainstream society.

Artists, by contrast, specialize in identifying and highlighting the interrelations of disidentification, affect, and stigmatized vernacular—to spur communication with the mainstream through more formalized frameworks of performance, even while blurring those frameworks to reveal the performativities that surround us in the everyday. This is particularly apt for Maura, who stages public and spontaneous performance art and who engages his neighborhood through projects such as "Open Sesame." He is queering notions of identity through these instances, making his community less homo-, trans-, and xenophobic without directly referencing any such issues.

Yunieski's affect is over-the-top: hypermasculine, aggressively romantic, intensely playful, suspiciously honest and dishonest—too real for mainstream reality. From a Cuban perspective, he is so normal that he goes unnoticed. During my fieldwork, I often felt like I was in the midst of a telenovela—the intensity of the stories and experiences was beyond what I could initially conceive of as reality. The line between fact and fiction was often blurry; many of the factual experiences of Yunieski and his friends were so extraordinary in relation to my life experiences that they appeared surreal. Through the repetition, variation, and diversity of a collectivity of life histories, however, they demonstrated to me that life is surreal when we remove the filters of white affect and the stigmatized vernacular and recognize the power of disidentification. Copperi and Maura added to these voices, and the influence of surrealism on their life works is particularly apt. Their paintings are a critique of Global North white, heteronormative, middle-class affect. Art helps us escape these confines in a way that ethnography merely strives for, forcing us to consider a diversity of ways of seeing regardless of our own personal identities.

While I was writing this essay, Copperi sent me a copy of his latest painting (fig. 15.3)—untitled but with the text "De la serie 'Conflicto almado.'" It is an AK-47—the military assault rife that we might associate with the Cuban army (or with American mass shootings and, by association, white affect). Inside the barrel is a paintbrush. Two men are sitting on top, positioned as if they are sitting on the malecón—a seawall such as those found in Havana and Cienfuegos and a common site where pingueros seek out foreigners and foreigners seek out pingueros. Both men are shirtless, and one is partly exposing his ass. There is a bullet shell on the left with a rose sticking out of it. Blood is splattered down the right side, and on the very bottom there are four roses, fading in succession. Who is winning in this battle? Are their voices getting through?

When I asked Copperi for his interpretation and he responded by asking for mine, he was emphasizing his belief that it is the viewer that must take responsibility for the interpretation—and that this interpretation would be a demonstration of personal identity and understanding of context. Rather than impose more of my ideas on this narrative, I ask my readers to look closely at this image (fig. 15.3), share it, and discuss it. What might this image say about everyday life in the so-called Global South? Or perhaps we should reverse this question: In a world of mass shootings, white nationalism, and populist

Fig. 15.3 *Untitled*, dry pastels and crayon on Strathmore paper, 2018,
© Luis Alberto Pérez Copperi.

politics, what might this Latino artist teach us about the perils of everyday life
in the Global North?

During the final stages of editing for this publication, I received news that a friend
from this community had died under mysterious conditions. According to a news
release by *Cibercuba* (Costa 2020), Dairo Jovelar Ruiz (Havana 1987–Barcelona
2020) was found dead in a room on calle Villarroel in Barcelona on August 27, 2020.
The police described the circumstances as a natural nonviolent death; however;
friends and family claim that there were two bodies at the scene and evidence of
violence (blunt force trauma to the back). This raises concern for how stories of
black queer immigrant lives are reported and investigated in the Global North—an
example of how the experiences of sex workers are exiled from the public sphere.
I met Dairo in Havana before beginning this research. He spent time at the ranch
and helped me understand what questions to ask, where to look, and what to focus
on. I dedicate this article in his memory. Dairo Jovelar Ruiz was the embodiment
of Cuban queer hypermasculinity. He found success under the stage name Ridder
Rivera. His face is hidden beneath the masks in each of these paintings.

BIBLIOGRAPHY

Alexander, Jonathan, and Jacqueline Rhodes. 2012. "Queer Rhetoric and the Pleasures of the Archive." *Enculturation*, no. 13 (January 16, 2012). http://www.enculturation.net/queer-rhetoric-and-the-pleasures-of-the-archive.

Allen, Jafari S. 2007. "Means of Desire's Production: Male Sex Labor in Cuba." *Identities* 14 (102): 183–202.

———. 2011. *Venceremos!? The Erotics of Black Self-Making in Cuba*. Durham, NC: Duke University Press.

Arenas, Reinaldo. 2001. *The Color of Summer or the New Garden of Earthly Delights*. Middlesex: Penguin Books.

Bauman, Richard. 1984. *Verbal Art ad Performance*. Prospect Heights, IL: Waveland.

Berger, Harris M., and Giovanna P. Del Negro. 2004. *Identity and Everyday Life: Essays in the Study of Folklore, Music, and Popular Culture*. Middletown, CT: Wesleyan University Press.

Blume, Libby Balter, and Rosemary Weatherston. 2018. "Queering the Campus Gender Landscape through Visual Arts Praxis." In *Mapping Queer Space(s) of Praxis*, edited by Elizabeth McNeil, James E. Wermers, and Joshua O. Lunn., 71–103. Cham, Switzerland: Palgrave Macmillan. http://doi.org/10.1007/978-3-319-64623-7_5.

Bridges, Tristan. 2016. "Hypermasculinity." In *The SAGE Encyclopedia of LGBTQ Studies*, edited by Abbie E. Goldberg. Thousand Oaks, CA: SAGE. http://dx.doi.org/10.4135/9781483371283.n207.

Bronner, Simon J. 1992. "The House on Penn Street: Creativity and Conflict in Folk Art." In *Folk Art and Art Worlds*, edited by John Michael Vlach and Simon J. Bronner, 123–149. Logan: Utah State University Press.

Butler, Judith. 1993. *Bodies That Matter: On the Discursive Limits of "Sex."* New York: Routledge.

Costa, Tania. 2020. "Muere en Barcelona actor cubano de cine de adultos." *Cibercuba*, September 1, 2020. https://www.cibercuba.com/noticias/2020-09-01-u192519-e192519-s27061-muere-espana-actor-modelo-cubano?fbclid=IwAR1nafoC83CgEilN_ZHxSCfa1fh9sShgGwqRG6EmEg7vAzZ6bdVDWaaA-uc.

Copperi, Luis Alberto Pérez. n.d. "Copperi Gallery." Accessed September 1, 2020. http://www.copperi.gallery.

Cortez, Jamie. 2004. *Sexile*. Los Angeles: Institute for Gay Men's Health.

Fine, Gary Alan. 2003. "Crafting Authenticity: The Validation of Identity in Self-Taught Art." *Theory and Society* 32:153–180.

Glave, Thomas. 2005. *Words to Our Now: Imagination and Dissent*. Minneapolis: University of Minnesota Press.

Goffman, Erving. 1959. *The Presentation of Self in Everyday Life*. Garden City, NY: Doubleday Anchor Books.

Goldstein, Diane W., and Amy Shuman, eds. 2016. *The Stigmatized Vernacular: Where Reflexivity Meets Untellability*. Encounters: Explorations in Folklore and Ethnomusicology. Bloomington: Indiana University Press.

Hodge, G. Derrick. 2014. "'Dangerous' Youth: Tourism Space, Gender Performance, and the Policing of Havana Street Hustlers." *Journal of Latin American and Caribbean Anthropology* 19 (3): 441–472. http://doi.org/10.1111/jlca.12104.

Kirshenblatt-Gimblett, Barbara. 1983. "The Future of Folklore Studies in America: The Urban Frontier." *Folklore Forum* 16:175–234.

Lara, Ana-Maurine. 2017. "I Wanted to Be More of a Person: Conjuring [Afro] [Latinx] [Queer] Futures." *Bilingual Review* 33 (4): 1–14.

Muñoz, José Esteban. 1999. *Disidentifications: Queers of Color and the Performance of Politics*. Minneapolis: University of Minnesota Press.

———. 2000. "Feeling Brown: Ethnicity and Affect in Ricardo Bracho's 'The Sweetest Hangover (and Other STDs).'" *Theatre Journal* 52 (1): 67–79.

Noyes, Dorothy. 2016. *Humble Theory: Folklore's Grasp on Social Life*. Bloomington: Indiana University Press.

Panichelli, Christophe, and Stéphanie Panichelli-Batalla. 2018. "Humorous Sublimation of a Dying Cuban Writer in Reinaldo Arenas' *The Color of Summer*." *Humor* 31 (4): 623–643.

Preciado, Beatriz. 2013a. "Testo Junkie: Sex, Drugs and Biopolitics." *E-flux* 44 (April). https://www.e-flux.com/journal/44/60141/testo-junkie-sex-drugs-and-biopolitics/.

———. 2013b. *Testo Junkie: Sex, Drugs, and Biopolitics in the Pharmacopornographic Era*. Translated by Bruce Benderson. New York: Feminist Press at the City University of New York.

Prieto, Augusto F. 2015. "Rocío García, en torno a la erótica y al poder." *Aladar*, June 6, 2015. http://aladar.es/rocio-garcia-en-torno-a-la-erotica-y-al-poder/.

Quiroga, José. 2000. *Tropics of Desire: Interventions from Queer Latino America*. New York: New York University Press.

Radford, Benjamin. 2016. *Bad Clowns*. Albuquerque: University of New Mexico Press.

slithis [pseud.]. 2007. "We Don't Want Gays (But We Do!!)." YouTube, April 7, 2007. Video, 02:27. https://www.youtube.com/watch?v=_nisMqIKkOs.

Stout, Noelle. 2014. *Queer Intimacy and Erotic Economies in Post-Soviet Cuba*. Durham, NC: Duke University Press.

CORY W. THORNE is Associate Professor of Folklore at Memorial University of Newfoundland, with a cross-appointment in music/ethnomusicology. His primary interests are in queer and vernacular theory, underground economies, popular culture, music, critical regionalism, vernacular religion, vernacular architecture, material culture, and tangible/intangible cultural heritage. Since 2008, he has been conducting ethnographic research within Havana's queer community, focused on a suburban ranch that was once the site of underground gay parties.

# SIXTEEN

# Complexifying Identity through Disability

Critical Folkloristic Perspectives on Being a Parent and
Experiencing Illness and Disability through My Child

PHYLLIS M. MAY-MACHUNDA

Absent in folklore studies is theorizing about and analyzing the lives of families living with children with disabilities or chronic illnesses. In fact, documentation of the experiences of children with disabilities or chronic illnesses has been ig-nored, as if their human experiences are without significance. Instead, the exami-nation of children's traditions has emphasized the expressive cultures of typically developing children and rarely explores the experiences of children outside that construct. In truth, except for a few works (Krell 1980; Gwaltney 1980; Goldstein 2004; Shuman 2011; Blank and Kitta 2015; Prahlad 2017), folklore scholarship has barely included people with disabilities, chronic illnesses, or trauma within its purview in any way. Similarly, folklore studies has highlighted stories of families whose lives excellently exemplify idealistic "normal" experiences of society rather than those families, in all their intersectionalities, whose life stories deviate from those norms. Thus, the spectrum of stories from the perspectives of parents and families tackling disability or chronic illness is virtually absent from folklore scholarship. As an African American parent of a now young adult with multiple disabilities, I see little scholarship in the field that addresses the lives of families with disabilities or chronic illnesses, like mine—yet millions of families, in a variety of social positionalities in the United States, generate such experiences. Therefore, from folkloristic lenses, I explore some critical aspects of parenting a child with disabilities, drawing on autoethnography and the scholarship and personal narratives of others.

My family's story begins early one June morning with an emergency drive
to the hospital for preterm labor. After a hospital debate over whether
I was really in labor, I stayed at the hospital overnight while the labor
intensified and proved resistant to control. By the next morning, I had

birthed my first child by C-section, an extremely premature baby born
3.5 months early at 26.5 instead of 40.0 weeks of gestation, weighing one
pound, fourteen ounces.[1] She was so tiny that she almost completely
fit in my left hand. Although she arrived so early, she was born with no
problems except that she faced a rough and lengthy journey to survive
such an early birth. We still do not know the causes of her early arrival,
and we weren't even prepared for her to come yet, as she was due in the
fall. I had been at work until ten o'clock the night before I went into
the hospital. A few days before her arrival, my husband, Zachary, while
working on his dissertation, had moved to DC from Indiana University
Bloomington to be with me during the final months of my pregnancy.
After crashing into parenthood, we trudged on this journey hour by
hour and day by day, on an unfamiliar and often rocky path for months,
without the presence of anyone except the doctors and nurses to guide
us through.

Folklore studies as a discipline has historically chosen to explore and emphasize extraordinary performances of behavioral norms. Disability and the
sometimes intersecting experiences of chronic illness have been deemed outside
behavioral norms. As esteemed disability scholar Rosemarie Garland-Thomson
(2017) has long observed about disability, these are fundamental and pervasive
attributes of human lives. We, as folklorists, have yet to fully interrogate these
human experiences and the traditions generated and shaped by such experiences.

When parents of children with disabilities talk about disability in the United
States, the term conflates two components of the concept, separated by some disabilities studies scholars: *impairment*, which speaks to the physiological (physical,
mental, or sensory) limitations that a person may have that makes it harder to
do normal daily activities; and *disability*, which Colin Barnes and Geof Mercer
(2003, 2) define as "the loss or limitations of opportunities to take part in the
normal life of the community on an equal level with others due to physical and
social barriers." Parents in the United States tend to use the term *disability* to refer
to both dimensions of the concept.

Our daughter was immediately placed in the neonatal intensive care
unit (NICU) so she could continue to develop to sustainability. I was
not allowed to see or hold her for several days after my emergency
C-section; Zachary did get to see but not touch her sometime on the
first day. Although she did well at first, she was not strong enough to
sustain breathing and vital functions by herself on a continuous basis,
so she was put on oxygen and lots of monitors. For weeks, she was in an
incubator that had lights to prevent jaundice and tubes for oxygen, and

she was fed with eyedroppers and IVs. Against hope, within the first month, her life journey intersected with illness.

A related lay term, *illness* can be described as a health condition where some facet of the body is unable to function as it usually does in a way that disrupts everyday functioning (Charmaz 1991). Illness is a bodily experience that can be short lived, can generate disability, or can be a chronic condition that persists in its effects or becomes a disease over a lengthy time. Illness does not have to be caused by disease, nor does it necessarily result in a condition of impairment, although it may.

> Whenever life-saving technology is used, there are upsides and downsides. With oxygen, our daughter had several small brain bleeds or intraventricular hemorrhages. Those are graded on a scale of I to IV, with IV meaning severe brain injury. While our daughter's brain bleeds were initially not severe, at around one month old, she acquired sepsis, a blood infection, which produced a larger brain bleed. It still was not the worst possible, but we were told that she was on the verge of death numerous times and that she would require several tiny blood transfusions over several days. Over several weeks, she recovered and continued to gain weight, ounce by ounce, until she was four pounds and large enough to come home. This first part of the journey took three months of daily visits to the NICU with Zachary singing "Twinkle, Twinkle, Little Star" to her each day. We devotedly did what we could to support the doctors and nurses in getting her to grow and begin to thrive in the NICU with a body that was not fully ready to take on the world.

Arnold van Gennep's (1960) theory of rites of passage offers a useful three-part metaphor for the process that abruptly plunged us into the ambiguous status of parents in the world of disability. My preliminary separation story is a bit embarrassing to admit to. I had not grown in consciousness in this area until *after* encountering my daughter's circumstances.[2]

> Before the birth of our daughter, I did not personally know people with moderate or severe disabilities. When I was a child, over several holidays, my father, who in the last part of his career worked with children with disabilities, took my brother and me to the local university school for children with disabilities to play music for children in residence there. I had no relationship with these children and, in ignorance, had no desire to ever build relationships with children whose bodies betrayed them, because I felt uncomfortable around them.

Crises and receiving tentative and then more definite diagnoses for our daughter plunged us deeper into extended and repeated periods of liminality—"betwixt and between" periods (Turner 1967) characterized by floundering episodes of discontinuity and unpredictability—that lasted serially for several years. In these traumatic liminal periods, we arrived at new levels of consciousness, were abruptly propelled into new rules of existence, began to grasp numerous ways that our lives would be forced to change, and, in stages, started to acquire fundamental information about our daughter's health and treatments. We were journeying on a new and unexpected path.

> For us, the liminal periods were multiple and frequently unpredictable. The first began at her birth. Would she survive? Would she be normal or have disabilities? What would that mean for her and for us? Those questions took months and then years to be fully answered. After she had been home three weeks, she ran a 102-degree fever, and we rushed her to the ER at Children's National Hospital. There we learned that she had acquired strep B meningitis, and she was put in the intensive care unit. Never had I seen someone so little, so sick. Because we had bonded with her, this experience was more devastating than the first three months in the NICU. Over the next three weeks, she was at death's door multiple times in the ICU. Whereas the consequences of prematurity in the NICU had been thought to be a matter of developmental delay, the impact of strep B meningitis was more definitive, because she had a more serious intraventricular hemorrhage and was diagnosed with permanent brain injury, resulting in hydrocephalus, which would need surgical treatment. At eighteen months, she caught a viral form of meningitis, which added to the complexity of her situation. By this time, we began to grasp that we were permanently on an atypical and more complex child-rearing path with multiple episodes of crisis ahead. Over the next two decades, she had therapies two or three times per week and a couple of doctors' appointments weekly. To this day, she continues to see a primary-care physician and a multidisciplinary team of specialists at least every three to six months.

These liminal periods forged and transformed us into our new identities as parents of a child with disabilities, invested in the love, survival, and success of our daughter.

When our daughter's situation began stabilizing to the point where we could finally bring her home at four months old, we began entering our postliminal reincorporation into the world. Reentry into our disrupted everyday lives meant that we had to reconstruct all aspects of our lives incrementally. Friend and family relationships had to be redefined and our social and professional flexibilities renegotiated. Unlike in our preliminal lives, in this phase, our very existence has become permanently shaped by an always-tenuous stability based in the ever-present fragility and unpredictability of our daughter's condition. Any health or environmental disruption can instantaneously snap our family back into periods of liminality of indefinite duration.

> Crises and key diagnoses each brought their own liminal periods: sepsis—near death; strep B meningitis—near death; hydrocephalus—surgery for a shunt with prospects for future brain surgeries; developmental delays—progressing into long-term neurological and cognitive impairments that become partially mitigated by persistent therapies, medications, adaptations, and nurturing. Puberty arrived with new diagnoses and more complicating factors that took years and several attempts before we found treatment with the right combination of medications in the appropriate doses. Emergency gallbladder removal—near death again, with full recovery taking years. In the stress of the search for appropriate housing and support in adult foster care and transitioning to life away from parents, the variety, frequency, and intensity of seizures increased. Labeled pharmaco-resistant, they diminished her stamina and tolerances. It has taken more than a decade for her to return to previous levels of performance. The volatility and fragility of our daughter's situation has forced us to scrutinize activities for accessibility and take less for granted in terms of our time and planning. In reality, her journey has meant that as parents, we have had to *always* be on alert for crises and available to intervene at any time, even as she has become an adult.

When disability or chronic illness permeates the processes of parenting, the experience of nurturing, protecting, supporting, and guiding a child toward full maturity transmogrifies into a qualitatively different and more complex parenting experience than for parents of typically developing children (Kelly 2005). Reflecting on my husband's and my journey as parents of a child with disabilities, it appears that some parents may choose to transform their identities in order to build lives integrally entwined with that of their child with disabilities. These transformed identities often express themselves through parental or family relationships, which I label as *differentially extended disability identities*. Coping with diagnoses and experiences of disability generates new identities, not only for the child with disabilities but frequently for the parents (and sometimes other family members), whose lives are intimately integrated with a child with disabilities on a daily basis. Having committed to supporting their child for years or even a lifetime, these parents may choose to develop a strongly empathetic and inter-subjective relationship with the child, in which the parent's and child's identities overlap, especially if the child's ability to express themselves verbally has been impaired. Assuming this vested role in their child's life (and not all parents or family members are willing to make such a commitment), these parents meld aspects of their world with that of their child, and frequently the parents' own identities, and life paths too, become transformed through their investment in caretaking and advocacy from the positionality of their child. Ethnographer Susan Kelly (2005, 184) notes, "Parents' stories of impairment are not direct experiences of the impaired embodied self and yet they are intimately centered on impairment—materially, discursively, phenomenologically—through embodied acts of caregiving and as an agent of an impaired child to the world. They therefore provide an opportunity to examine spaces of social interaction that are both intimate and public in which impairment is produced and made meaningful." Because of their embodied and intersubjective experiences, parents of children with disabilities can embrace and be reinforced in identities infused with the impairment in discursive, symbolic, representative, and interactive ways (Kelly 2005, 190). This familial identity experience goes beyond that of a basic caregiver because it carries many of the contextual aspects of living as a disabled person in the world but without the impairing illness or condition of the child. Parents adopting the positionalities of their children engage with the ways that ableism is embedded in the systems and structures of our society.

Disability as a category is negatively charged as a deficit identity in many cultures, including in mainstream American society. This stigmatized identity places people with disabilities in a less-than status—less deserving of access to the resources, rights, and opportunities of society because their body deviates in significant ways from an able-bodied ideal. In fact, bodies viewed as deviant and abnormal have often been used to rationalize treating people with disabilities as incompetent and incapable of attaining personhood (Kirshenblatt-Gimblett 1989, 124).[3] Our society has organized impairment into categories, which group sets of similar characteristics designated as "pathological" and their correspond-ing symptoms together, culminating in diagnostic labels that predict a narrow range of outcomes. Diagnoses form a dominating medically based social frame-work that carries the weight for assembling medical data and social services, inventorying treatment options, and predicting social expectations and out-comes that parents of children with disabilities have to navigate. Diagnoses are not valenced neutrally. As a result, children with disabilities are often labeled by their diagnoses and limitations rather than their capabilities. In the socially constructed system of ableism, diagnoses are ranked hierarchically in value and social acceptability according to the location of the affected body part and the severity and permanence of the impairment. Each diagnosis carries cultural expectations for outcomes and prognoses about possibilities that shape life options, treatment choices, and perceptions of personhood for children with disabilities. Cognitive impairments, physical disfigurement, and profoundly disabling impairments seem to be ranked near the bottom of this hierarchy because of their limited capacity to move toward normalcy.

> When she was an infant, several doctors bluntly crushed us with the prediction that she would never walk or talk, which we could not accept. Fortunately, this prediction never became our story. Yet when she achieved key milestones (delayed as they were), other doctors celebrated with us. Frustrated that she could not effectively communicate, she began to learn sign language at 2, began to speak words at 2.5 years, and learned to walk at 3.5 years. She is neurologically atypical, meaning that her neurological processing system can frequently be overwhelmed by social, environmental, or internal stimuli. As she has matured, she has been able to communicate verbally (but not consistently engage in fully reciprocal conversations), run track in Special Olympics, live away from us in her own apartment with support staff, be employed in a supported work environment, love listening to music, and become a whiz at playing UNO!

Many parents (primarily mothers) embrace this identity journey with their child with disabilities through life and create autoethnographic narratives of their experiences of disability as tools for understanding, coping with, and sharing such liminal and postliminal experiences in a positive way. In discussing the processes of autoethnographic writing, communications theorist Carolyn Ellis (2004, 33) observes that she writes these pieces when she encounters "experiences that knock me for a loop and challenge the construction of meaning I have put together for myself." I believe her revelation captures a driving force behind the creation of these disability autoethnographies. Whether the child's impairment is acquired through birth-process anomalies, developmental trajectories, illnesses, accidents, or genetic conditions, parents have to grapple with a steep learning curve and rapidly reassess their own life paths and those of their families. Autoethnography and personal experience narratives lend themselves as excellent tools for exploring postliminal experiences of disability and their nonnormative life paths from the voices of those directly impacted. With few visible societal role models illuminating the paths for raising a child with disabilities, parents turn to these books for help in making sense out of their experiences and for the assembled lists of resources that they frequently provide.

These autoethnographic narratives address the family's entry into the world of disability or chronic illness, as well as offer ways to negotiate and advocate in the medical, educational, social service, and employment systems that parents must navigate daily with and for their children. In these narratives, parents frequently discuss medical innovations for a particular diagnosis and ways to monitor and take joy in the achievement of milestones and small steps of advancement, or to cope with stages of grief in the worsening of their child's condition. The narratives reveal parent-constructed frameworks that seek to share and make sense of knowledge around specific diagnoses in order to model and illuminate strategies for postliminal survival and resilience in uncertain circumstances, provide tools to alleviate unwarranted blame for their children's situations, connect parents with networks of support, and suggest avenues for advocacy for treatments and policy development on behalf of their children.

Most of these self-generated narratives came into prominence in the late twentieth century after the passage of disability rights education laws in 1975, and they provide a site for theorizing about how to neutralize a stigmatized identity and navigate many of the social barriers and medical challenges facing their children (and families) in order to build a full life. In an incisive review of a sampling of these works, Alison Piepmeier (2012) has noted that these narratives typically offer a personalized cultural road map, a story of how one family has managed their multipoint journey within the American cultural context for disabilities, with the hope that others in similar situations may see and present the full humanity of their children.

> My role as mother to our daughter has been as her advocate, interpreter, confidant, planner and scheduler, guardian, conservator, caretaker, and protector. Sometimes her disabilities make it hard for her to put her feelings into words, and in those instances, she communicates in embodied ways. To support our daughter's developmental disabilities, we have taken on the role of assisting her with communication and sometimes communicate for her. I, in particular, as her mother, am her mediator and translator who interprets her behavior and unique expressions so that others can understand what she is communicating. In order to do this, I have to be tuned in to her in ways that are beyond typical relationships; our identities have to meld so I can interpret her standpoint. Since she understands more than she can express, I check with her to see if I am expressing what she wants said. She trusts me to interpret for her. This tends to be a role that she does not select my husband, Zachary, to take. Although he is also her stalwart caretaker, protector, guardian, and advocate, she confides in me and expects me

to interpret her feelings. I am able to assume this particular role only with her intimate and deep trust in me.

Philosopher Eva Feder Kittay (2010, 406–407) sums up the importance of these intersubjective experiences with our children as she discusses her relationship with her daughter: "It is because I see Sesha close up, because I have a deep and intimate relationship with her, that I am able to see what is hidden from those are not privileged enough to see her when she opens up to another. . . . Without a strong affective bond with people with severe cognitive disabilities, we often fail to get a glimpse into the lives of these persons."

The autoethnographic and personal experience narratives of disability, expressed in books, blogs, articles, and support group sharings, would qualify as an additional strand of what folklorist Sandra Dolby (2005) identifies as self-help books, works of "popular nonfiction written with the aim of enlightening readers about some of the negative effects of our culture and worldview and suggesting new attitudes and practices that might lead them to more satisfying and more effective lives" (38). Like the books Dolby examined, these works use condensed personal narratives to highlight "accessible wisdom" (153) and "bought" knowledge. As a type of self-help book, they represent "individual effort[s] to grow in wisdom and lead a satisfying life" (viii) and "incorporate elements of American worldviews and function in ways similar to personal narratives" with "stories people tell based on their own real experiences but incorporating the frame of narrative borrowed from tradition" in a genre that mixes original with formulaic materials (2). These works also follow the "lack and lack liquidated structure"[4] that Dolby identified as fundamental to all self-help books (4). Structured to present a problem (specific disability diagnosis) with a solution (example of a viable alternate path), these narratives offer educational guides through examples with the goal of directing readers toward more effective and satisfying journeys with children with disabilities (37). Not only do these autoethnographies offer an interpretative critique and analysis of existing social structures that can harm people with disabilities, but they present lessons learned and information useful to parents for transforming those social systems in ways to help their children (11), as well as highlight traditional, alternative, and complementary paths to selecting the best possible options for their children's diagnoses.

More critically, these disability autoethnographic works are both cultural narratives and transformative counternarratives of resistance that are "not only expressions of lived experience but important sites of knowledge production to resist hegemonic representations that valorize individuals, groups and bodies of knowledge deemed 'normal' and marginalize the 'other'" (Ferri 2010, 140). Disenchanted with conventional ways of thinking about disability as a deficit, many

mothers have created these autoethnographies to lead parents in similar situations to recognize the potential of their children, grasp the medical and service
options for them, and provide successful examples for families navigating their
own individual journeys within the Western system of ableism in the United
States.[5] By revealing the embodied experiences of children and their families
through the radically different lenses of disability, these narratives assert visibility for the lives of children with disabilities who may not be able to speak
for themselves and visibility for their families (Piepmeier 2012). The writers of
these narratives assert personhood for their own children and persons like them
though framing stories from the positionalities of their children and their relationships with them. The narratives lay out alternative paths that defy and rebuff
denigrating ideologies about their children's incapacities and instead replace
them with the construction of counternarrative discourses that foreground the
children's full humanity and capabilities and offer alternative visions for parents
as they wrestle with emotions ranging from grief, sorrow, rejection, and anger to
joy, acceptance, acknowledgement, and affirmation on their journeys with their
children.

While many narratives express parents' feelings of shock, grief, and loss as
they process and orient themselves to their new circumstances, others offer witness to the investments that parents of children with disabilities or chronic illnesses make to construct survival and resilience strategies for their families.
In her singular book, *In Sickness and in Play*, anthropologist Cindy Dell Clark
(2003) shared a story from a parent who intimately guided her seriously ill child
through a challenging examination in order to get a more detailed diagnosis for
further treatment:

> Our five and a half year old daughter has an inoperable brain tumor. Our
> only hope to remove the tumor is radiation. On the first day of her radiation
> treatment, she screamed and cried when she found out she would have to be in
> the room all by herself. . . . We kept saying that it would only take a minute. . . .
> Finally she asked me, "What is a minute?" . . . I looked at my watch and
> started singing, "It's a beautiful day in this neighborhood, a beautiful day for a
> neighbor," and before I could finish the song I said, "Oops, the minute is up. I
> can't even finish Mr. Rogers' song." Then Michelle said, "Is that a minute? I can
> do that." And she did. She laid perfectly still for the entire treatment; but, there
> was a catch to it. I have to sing your song every time over the intercom. Letter to
> Fred Rogers. (139)

Stories similar to this one are embedded throughout autoethnographic disability
narratives and illustrate the intimate ways parents engage with their children to
cajole them through daunting lab work, painful procedures, and intimidating
treatments in order to attain improvement in their situations.

In her groundbreaking article "On the Verge: Phenomenology and Empathic Unsettlement," folklorist Amy Shuman (2011) remarks on the power of autoethnography to "sustain a conversation" between "the personal, the methodological, and the theoretical" (147). Autoethnographic disability narratives use personal experience to examine knowledge and theories about specific diagnoses in order to humanize the experience and to understand the manifestation of impairment for the child. Using their own and other's personal experiences, the narrators question and critique methodological practices and resources tied to those diagnoses, and they share their assessments and resources with others who face similar diagnoses through stories about which practices have benefitted and which might harm or hinder their children. This disability-alike approach has begun to establish traditions around specific disability diagnoses in a social world that renders invisible and denigrates people with disabilities and their families. Shuman questions whether disability groups are true communities, since children with diagnoses under the same label can generate very disparate experiences, and not all disabilities are valued equally (156).

The autoethnographic disability books illustrate that disparate manifestations of specific disabilities are not a hindrance to building disability-alike communities, or even a pan-disability community. In fact, these communities are built around different assumptions than those identified by Shuman (2011). While children do not have exactly the same manifestations of their disabilities, these narratives do not assume that there is a single story for the experience of a diagnosis. Instead, a narrative describes a specific embodied experience of that diagnosis, which affirms the humanity of the child with disabilities and makes space for comparative narratives to expand a spectrum of emotions and embodied child and familial experiences—good and bad—tied to the diagnoses. These narratives are stories of lives "lived against the grain of normalcy" (Rapp and Ginsburg 2001, 552), lives lived on alternate paths than those of bodies normalized by society as ideal. As with any aspect of life, there are at least as many variations making up parents' interpretations of these experiences as there are children diagnosed with various impairments. The invaluable knowledge shared in this genre tends to be polyvocal because it is rare for only a single autoethnographic work to be available for any particular diagnosis category. Having access to multiple personal experience stories about a particular diagnosis expands the chances that parents will find examples from which they can extrapolate knowledge to apply toward understanding their own child's specific circumstances.

> Our daughter's experience with multiple disabilities cannot fit easily into the category of a single diagnosis. Instead, these symptoms often work in synergy with each other, taking on different characteristics

than would normally be recognized and making them more difficult to diagnose. In fact, the state has labeled our daughter's disabilities as low incidence—meaning that there are so few children with her combination of impairments that she cannot be predictably categorized. Moreover, some of the recognized aspects of her impairments have not remained fixed over time. Rather, as she progressed through various developmental stages, different facets of her impairment became foregrounded, and others morphed or seemed to retreat. Variability has been *the* constant of our daughter's experience. She is often unable to maintain a constant level of performance. A simple cold or a shift in hormones or an illness can knock her off her equilibrium and make her become primarily nonverbal, so that she cannot execute fundamental skills that she was able to do at another time. We don't know whether this is an attribute of her particular combination of disabilities or of multiple disabilities in general. We know she is not singular in this attribute, but it seems that the medical and social service agencies have not been geared to tackle the level of complexity that she brings. We have been forced to find ways to address her situation within systems designed to serve single diagnoses.

These narratives also frequently seek to build coalitions of resistance across diagnoses in order for parents to unite as they face navigations of pervasive social, cultural, and environmental barriers generated by ableism. Responses to ableism have begun to foster collaborative consciousnesses for some parents of children with disabilities, in similar ways to how racism has forged coalitions across racial group boundaries. Parents of children with disabilities or chronic illnesses often confront more unpredictable circumstances, more intense parental and financial responsibilities, more uncertain and judgmental social support services, and more highly regulated oversight of our parenting performances than parents of typically developing children. With pervasive and invasive scrutiny, we operate at the mercy of administrative bureaucracies that control our access to resources and opportunities for managing aspects of our lives in every arena: health, medicine, housing, finances, education, laws, transportation, and more. For and with their children, parents collide with ableism through legal and service barriers, stigma, stereotypes, and marginalization from the mainstream. Parents of children with disabilities encounter many discourses socially constructed by cultural professionals (doctors, therapists, attorneys, and educators), nonprofits and service providers, and institutional practices emphasizing the limitations caused by impairments of the child (Goodley and Tregaskis 2006, 631). If disability is about functioning within a societal worldview in which impairment is stigmatized, seen as abnormal, and invalidated as a significant human experience, then many parents see their job as helping their children navigate a dismissive, hostile, and often denigrating world so as to mitigate its impact. Many mothers organize pan- or specific disability support groups as safe spaces where some-times beaten-down participants tell their stories of fighting ableism; share their feelings of grief, loss, and suffering while in liminality; learn to decipher hidden but specialized knowledge; and see examples of restructured and adapted post-liminal lives teeming with resilience that illustrate alternate ways of being in the world, despite the barriers.

Transforming trauma into resilience has been a significant purpose of both the support groups and autoethnographic disability books. Through the guiding networks of support groups, parents of children with disabilities can obtain some of the care that they need to develop new and supportive relationships, mentor-ships, and friendships. Within these groups, they can acknowledge and tackle the emotional tolls of caring for children with disabilities, and they can gain tools to equip themselves with critical knowledge, skills, and coping mechanisms to support and advocate for their children's rights and needs.

Another purpose of these narratives and support groups has been to rally parents into becoming civic advocates to create appropriate institutional services and governmental policies on behalf of their children and to counsel parents so that they can respond to the structural, institutional, and societal inequities of ableism. Some parents (mostly mothers) have chosen to engage in activism on behalf of their children and others with disabilities. This activism ranges from seeking and critiquing treatments and cures for specific diagnoses to devising ways of negotiating or petitioning for or against traditions, laws, policies, and practices of ableism in educational, medical, or social service institutions. Gail Landsman (1998), a parent of a daughter with disabilities and an anthropologist, cites an interview she did with a mother illustrating a typical type of advocacy that mothers have to engage in on behalf of their nonverbal children, in her pio-neering article on mothers of children with illnesses and disabilities:

> A mother told the story of her second child born in a small rural hospital. The child seemed to her to be weak, a poor nurser. The child's complexion seemed duskier than she would have expected and she had to shake the child awake to nurse. Calling the hospital nurses with her concerns, she was told she was not feeding the baby enough, that she should nurse more often. Angry, the woman demanded a referral to a cardiologist. . . . On being given an appointment for one month later, she called the cardiologist's office herself, demanded to see the doctor sooner, and an appointment for the following week was arranged. When she arrived at the cardiologist's office, the doctor ran some tests and

immediately called for an ambulance to take the child to [the hospital] for
emergency surgery; the baby was about to go into congestive heart failure. (82)

Although this woman's knowledge of her child was initially trivialized, her inter-
subjective and embodied motherhood knowledge was eventually validated by the
fact that she persisted to save her child's life. I have very similar personal experience stories (about seeking treatment for my daughter's necrotized gallbladder
or her seizures), and many other mothers have stories like this, too. These stories
reaffirm that parents in similar situations have knowledge based in the connected
knowing and deep emotional bonds with their children and that they must be able
to trust this knowledge to advocate assertively for their children to receive the
care they need and deserve. Many mothers of children with disabilities believe
that this interdependent embodied knowledge is a defining characteristic of their
experiences of motherhood (Franits 2011, 138; Landsman 1998, 83).

Critical folklore studies, through its emphasis on bringing respectful visibility
to underrecognized cultures, can contribute significant insights to understanding
parental and familial experiences of disability in several ways. Folklore studies
could examine traditions of care, an area to which parents of children with disabilities and caregivers of children would have much knowledge to contribute
through examinations of how care is culturally conceptualized, constructed,
and enacted. Parents often have to make difficult decisions between how to economically support their families and how to care for their children's health needs.
These choices, shaped by social positionalities, are not without social, economic,
and cultural costs in lost professional opportunities, pay, and status.

> When our Miracle Baby finally came home, Zachary and I had to sleep
> in shifts because she needed to be fed every two hours. I would stay
> up until the 2:00 a.m. feeding, and Zachary would take the 4:00 a.m.
> feeding so I could sleep until 6:00 a.m. When she moved to eating
> every four hours, I would go to bed after the midnight feeding, and
> he would take the 4:00 a.m. feeding, so I could get up at 6:00 a.m. for
> work. Because I had the health insurance and she was too fragile for
> daycare, Zachary was a (rare—at that time) father who stayed home
> to raise his infant daughter. It was not without professional and social
> costs for him.

If they have to or decide to work outside the home, parents of children with
disabilities must rely on the help of caregivers, often paid direct service providers
from social service agencies. These providers are disproportionately nonfamilial
working-class women, often women of color or new immigrants, who hopefully
possess the necessary skills to care for the special needs of the child. Many of

them are leaving their own children at home to work with our children. Further-more, parents and caregivers can have qualitatively different experiences taking care of the same person. The gendered nature of caregiving and the intimate and nested interdependency between children, parents, and direct service workers are integral and distinguishing facets of the experiences of parents with children with disabilities.

Additionally, as parents, we select and try traditional care techniques, then hone them for use with our children. Parents communicate this embodied and experiential knowledge to the staff who support our children as well as to medical professionals, and we document their accounts of successful and unsuccessful strategies in the autoethnographic narratives and support groups.

Folklorists also could investigate the worldviews that support the conceptions of disability as a burden, as sin or a curse, as contagious, as infantilizing, or as an inferior human experience, which generate the conceptual basis for many of the barriers that parents and families of children with disabilities continually face. Diane Goldstein and Amy Shuman (2012), drawing on Erving Goffman's (1963) work on stigma, and Shuman (2011), drawing on Lennard Davis's (1995, 2013) unpacking of the concept of normalcy, have begun to explore concepts of stigma and normalcy in disability with folkloristic lenses. Certainly, folkloristic inves-tigations of disability stereotyping, objectification, and marginalization would contribute to revealing the power of community resilience and societal traditions of family rejection, dissolution, and disidentification around disability.

Families of children with disabilities commonly encounter stereotypes such the family being labeled as saints for caring for such a "burden." This ste-reotype suggests that having a child with disabilities in the family negates the parents' responsibilities to invest in that child by stating that parents are going *way beyond* their parental obligations to care for such a child. Therefore, viewing children with disabilities as "damaged goods," unworthy of care, lessens and even dismisses parental and familial obligations to care for them as children. These stereotypes are so pervasive that some parents do distance themselves or run away from the parental obligations to care for their children if the child has disabilities—and there is even cultural sanction for such distancing.[6]

> When our daughter was in the NICU, another family had a child there.
> Day after day, for months, the father would come and scrub up to go
> into the NICU but could never get through the door to enter the NICU
> to hold his child. We referred to him as "Jetsetter."

Another related stereotype is captured in the saying that "God gives 'special children' to special parents." The assumption is that children with disabilities are not everyone's concern, and only parents that can "handle disabilities" should be to be rewarded with this situation. Some family members and friends reject the child *and* their parents because they stigmatize disability or define disability to be tainted, a burden, contagious, or dangerous to associate with; therefore, the stigma spreads, objectifying and discounting the entire family. As a result, it is not uncommon for familial, friend, and acquaintance relationships to become strained or broken because of the discomfort people feel about associating with parents raising children with disabilities. What are the cultural roots of such biased beliefs?

> One of my students, a parent of a child with disabilities, revealed to me a not uncommon situation: she had been disowned by her own parents because they rejected her son with disabilities. Several other student parents spoke of divorces from spouses, usually leaving the mother to raise the child, or having to navigate increased static in extended family relationships because of family fears, prejudices, anger, or disappointment about having to deal with children diagnosed with disabilities. Others mentioned the loss of friendships that ended because their friends' "typically developing" children were engaged in qualitatively different activities and interests from their own children with disabilities and their paths no longer crossed.

Thus, many families like mine emerge from liminality more vulnerable to fracture, isolation, disruption, and rejection. We journey on substantially different paths from our children's typically developing peers. As parents, many of us also have encountered friends who say, "Well, I can't imagine what you've gone through. Thank God I have . . . children and they're healthy" (Landsman 1998, 87), or "At least they aren't more damaged!" Most parents reject views that their lives are pitiful, tragic, or in denial. Instead, most parents of children with disabilities seek to build lives with the necessary accommodations to live their everyday lives with quality.

Through the body of autoethnographic disability narratives, we know very little about the full experiences of parents from communities of color or parents from ethnicities, religions, social classes, sexual orientations, or abilities outside the mainstream. Mostly raced white, these disability works rarely engage issues of race, class, or sexual orientation, and they only superficially address issues of gender and religion. These works do not encompass the full range of disability experiences for families of color, like mine. Instead, they emphasize retelling the more common experiences of families with disabilities, without regard to exploring the perspectives from intersectional positionalities. Few parents of color (or from these other groups) have created these autoethnographies, perhaps because these works have been primarily generated by those privileged by the time, educational status, and economic means to create them. What are the cultural perspectives about disability and illness that shape their experiences? What are the embodied experiences of their children? What barriers do they routinely face?

> When we first arrived at our current community, we encountered a dentist and a doctor who were afraid to touch our daughter, who was an infant at the time. Because my husband was born in Africa, they feared our daughter might carry AIDS, even though Zachary had been in the States before the AIDS outbreak in Africa and there was absolutely no medical evidence for coming to such a conclusion. We also encountered other medical professionals that did not try to interact directly with her and would only talk to us as her parents, as if she were not even there. How can a professional examine a child's teeth or body if he doesn't touch her, even with gloves, or respect her as a human being? Needless to say, we had to search for and find other health-care providers.

Some of these experiences are not part of the parenting experiences of white families of children with disabilities. What have been the experiences of parents of color with children with disabilities (who may have less education, economic means, or community visibility than my family)?

> We have had paid direct service providers that did not want to work at our home or who broke toys and equipment in our home because they didn't want to be working with people of color. A few have even scolded me about going out with my husband for an event (most often work related), saying, "I am staying with your child while *you* are going out!"

Our intersectional social positionalities significantly impact parental interactions with individuals in the institutions and systems addressing disability, and these positionalities shape our capacities to advocate for and fulfill the needs of our children as parents.

> Our daughter has multiple impairments. At an IEP meeting for our daughter at the elementary school, one of the therapists suggested that our daughter *should not* get all the services to which she was entitled because "white students were not getting as many services." Fortunately, other team members confronted her because the Individuals with Disabilities Education Act (IDEA) of 1975 mandated that our daughter's needs be addressed, and the therapist was promptly fired by the school district.
>
> As our daughter was growing up, we attended several parent workshops. These were structured self-help events usually centered on

the broad experiences of living with a child with any disability. I can't remember a single event where we weren't the only parents of color there. These events shared valuable materials and information about navigating the social systems servicing disabilities. We noticed that other parents of color frequently did not obtain the same information because they were not able to access the same parent networks due to needing to work or care for other children or to not feeling welcome at such workshops, which were held in white, upper-middle-class environments.

So, questions for future critical folkloristic analysis include the following: What does folklore look like when disability is moved from the outskirts of the field to the center of the intersectional experiences of humanity that we study? How do culture, ethnicity, race, and other social statuses shape parents' experiences of their children's disabilities? How do parents of color communally construct their own knowledge networks and resources and shape them to meet their cultural needs within their cultural communities? How do stereotypes and prejudices work to keep parents of color within specified social hierarchical constraints? What cultural knowledges, worldviews, and beliefs shape parents' interpretations of their children's health conditions and treatment options? In what ways do parents of color raise boys and girls with disabilities differently? How do parents of color navigate the social systems providing services to support their children? If parental experiences navigating health and disability services are anything like dealing with the educational experiences of children of color with disabilities, then their stories will reflect qualitatively different journeys than those of their white counterparts. To complicate these questions even more, what are the stories of *parents with disabilities* (in all their diversities) raising children with disabilities and the people (often grandparents) who support them? What are the stories of their challenges and embodied and accumulated knowledges?

Although disability is a fundamental and pervasive aspect of human experiences, the multifaceted voices and narratives of parents of children with disabilities and their communities have rarely been noticed or explored in folklore scholarship. Creating personal narratives, autoethnographies, and disability support communities have been strategies and tools for some of these families to forge transformed identities and to make their experiences visible. Folklore studies needs to be able to not only account for these experiences but also understand how parents, families, and persons with disabilities communicate and interpret their expressivities from their social positionalities. Folklorists could provide a valuable service to the field and to disability communities by bringing their humanizing perspectives to these stories and experiences in order to uplift these communities, illuminate the structures and traditions upholding ableism, and contribute to its dismantlement.

## NOTES

1. I have not disclosed my daughter's name to maintain her privacy as a vulnerable adult.

2. May-Machunda ([1998] 2017) was my first attempt to write about my growing analysis of ableism and the systemic privilege awarded to able-bodied people from the lens of being a mother.

3. Barbara Kirshenblatt-Gimblett (1989, 24) discusses the significance of the concept of personhood, conceptualized with a conscience and internal identity, as a prerequisite for holding citizenship rights.

4. See Alan Dundes (1965) for his discussion of the lack and lack liquidated structure.

5. Few of these autoethnographies include the experiences of parents who provide guardianship for their children over age twenty-one, because most of the major new situations that parents encounter occur before age twenty-one.

6. Landsman (1998, 79) also notes this.

## BIBLIOGRAPHY

*Secondary Sources*

Barnes, Colin, and Geof Mercer. 2003. *Disability.* Cambridge: Polity.

Blank, Trevor J., and Andrea Kitta, eds. 2015. *Diagnosing Folklore: Perspectives on Disability, Health, and Trauma.* Jackson: University of Mississippi Press.

Charmaz, Kathy. 1991. *Good Days, Bad Days: The Self in Chronic Illness and Time.* New Brunswick, NJ: Rutgers University Press.

Clark, Cindy Dell. 2003. *In Sickness and in Play: Children Coping with Chronic Illness.* New Brunswick, NJ: Rutgers University Press.

Davis, Lennard J. 1995. *Enforcing Normalcy: Disability, Deafness, and the Body.* New York: Verso.

———. 2013. "Introduction: Disability, Normality and Power." In *The Disability Studies Reader,* 4th ed., edited by Lennard J. Davis, 1–14. New York: Routledge.

Dolby, Sandra K. 2005. *Self-Help Books: Why Americans Keep Reading Them.* Urbana: University of Illinois Press.

Dundes, Alan. 1965. "Structural Typology in North American Indian Folktales." In *The Study of Folklore,* 206–215. Englewood Cliffs, NJ: Prentice-Hall.

Ellis, Carolyn. 2004. *The Ethnographic I: A Methodological Novel about Autoethnography.* Walnut Creek, CA: AltaMira.

Ferri, Beth. 2010. "A Dialogue We've Yet to Have: Race and Disability Studies." In *The Myth of the Normal Curve,* edited by Curt Dudley-Marling and Alex Gurn, 139–150. New York: Peter Lang.

Franits, Linnea E. 2011. "Mothers as Storytellers." In *Disability and Mothering: Liminal Spaces of Embodied Knowledge,* edited by Cynthia Lewiecki-Wilson and Jen Cellio, 129–139. Syracuse, NY: Syracuse University Press.

Garland-Thomson, Rosemarie. 2017. "Building a World with Disability in It." In *Culture—Theory—Disability: Encounters between Disability Studies and Cultural Studies*, edited by Anne Waldschmidt, Hanjo Berressem, and Moritz Ingwersen, 51–62. Bielefeld, Germany: Transcript.

Goffman, Erving. 1963. *Stigma: Notes on the Management of Spoiled Identity*. Englewood Cliffs, NJ: Spectrum.

Goldstein, Diane E. 2004. *Once upon a Virus: AIDS Legends and Vernacular Risk Perception*. Logan: Utah State University Press.

Goldstein, Diane E., and Amy Shuman. 2012. "The Stigmatized Vernacular: Where Reflexivity Meets Untellability." *Journal of Folklore Research* 49 (2): 113–126.

Goodley, Dan, and Claire Tregaskis. 2006. "Storying Disability and Impairment: Retrospective Accounts of Disabled Family Life." *Qualitative Health Research* 16 (5): 630–646.

Gwaltney, John Langston. 1980. *Drylongso: A Self Portrait of Black America*. New York: Random House.

Kelly, Susan E. 2005. "'A Different Light': Examining Impairment though Parent Narratives of Childhood Disability." *Journal of Contemporary Ethnography* 34 (2): 180–205.

Kirshenblatt-Gimblett, Barbara. 1989. "Authoring Lives." *Journal of Folklore Research* 26 (2): 123–149.

Kittay, Eva Feder. 2010. "The Personal Is Philosophical Is Political: A Philosopher and Mother of a Cognitively Disabled Person Sends Notes from the Battlefield." In *Cognitive Disability and Its Challenge to Moral Philosophy*, edited by Eva Feder Kittay and Licia Carlson, 393–413. Malden, MA: Wiley-Blackwell.

Krell, Roberta. 1980. "At a Children's Hospital: A Folklore Survey." *Western Folklore* 39 (3): 223–231.

Landsman, Gail H. 1998. "Reconstructing Motherhood in the Age of 'Perfect' Babies: Mothers of Infants and Toddlers with Disabilities." *Signs* 24 (1): 69–99.

May-Machunda, Phyllis. (1998) 2017. "Unpacking the Knapsack of Able-Bodied Privilege." In *Saluting 30 Voices That Helped Shape the SEED Project in the First 30 Years*, edited by Emily Style, 141–147. Wellesley, MA: Wellesley Center for Women.

Piepmeier, Alison. 2012. "Saints, Sages and Victims: Endorsement of and Resistance to Cultural Stereotypes in Memoirs by Parents of Children with Disabilities." *Disability Studies Quarterly* 32 (1). http://dx.doi.org/10.18061/dsq.v32i1.3031.

Prahlad, Anand. 2017. *The Secret Life of a Black Aspie: A Memoir*. Fairbanks: University of Alaska Press.

Rapp, Rayna, and Faye D. Ginsburg. 2001. "Enabling Disability: Rewriting Kinship, Reimagining Citizenship." *Public Culture* 13 (3): 533–556.

Shuman, Amy. 2011. "On the Verge: Phenomenology and Empathetic Unsettlement." *Journal of American Folklore* 194 (493): 147–174.

Turner, Victor W. 1967. *The Forest of Symbols: Aspects of Ndembu Ritual*. Ithaca, NY: Cornell University Press.

van Gennep, Arnold. 1960. *The Rites of Passage*. Chicago: University of Chicago Press.

*A Representative Sampling of Parent Disability Narratives*

Barnhill, Press, and Gena P. Barnhill. 2010. *Parents of Children with Disabilities: A Survival Guide for Fathers and Mothers.* Lynchburg, VA: Liberty University.

Conroy, Helen, and Lisa Joyce Goes, eds. 2015. *The Thinking Moms' Revolution: Autism beyond the Spectrum.* Rev. ed. New York: Skyhorse.

Ford, Jill Rose. 2000. *Motherhood Magnified: Inspiring Stories of Insight and Lessons Learned from Raising a Child with Special Needs.* Lincoln, NE: Writers Club.

Gill, Barbara. 1997. *Changed by a Child: Companion Notes for Parents of a Child with Disability.* New York: Doubleday.

Harmel, Kristen. 2011. "Forever Parents." *Ladies Home Journal,* November 11, 2011, 112–117.

Kingston, Anna Karin. 2007. *Mothering Special Needs: A Different Maternal Journey.* London: Jessica Kingsley.

Marsh, Jayne D. B., ed. 1994. *From the Heart: On Being the Mother of a Child with Special Needs.* Bethesda, MD: Woodbine House.

Meyer, Donald J., ed. 1995. *Uncommon Fathers: Reflections on Raising a Child with a Disability.* Bethesda, MD: Woodbine House.

Naseef, Robert A. 2001. *Special Children, Challenged Parents: The Struggles and Rewards of Raising a Child with a Disability.* Rev. ed. Baltimore: Paul H. Brookes.

Pacer Center. 2012. *I Wish I Knew Then What I Know Now . . . : Wisdom and Advice from Parents of Children with Disabilities.* Minneapolis, MN: Pacer Center.

Paradiz, Valerie. 2002. *Elijah's Cup: A Family's Journey into the Community and Culture of High Functioning Autism and Asperger's Syndrome.* New York: Free Press.

PHYLLIS M. MAY-MACHUNDA is Professor of American Multicultural Studies at Minnesota State University Moorhead and earned her MA and PhD in folklore/ethnomusicology from Indiana University Bloomington. Her research interests center on African American folklore and music traditions, emphasizing traditions of African American women and children; multicultural and social justice education; and folklore and disability studies. She has curated exhibitions, published numerous articles, and cofacilitated several community-based collaborative social justice education initiatives. Her forthcoming book, *Say, Uhn! Ain't It Funky, Now? African American Cheerleading as Embodied Play and Display,* examines performative, aesthetic, and communicative dimensions of the African American cheerleading tradition in Washington, DC.

# INDEX

Lightning Source UK Ltd.
Milton Keynes UK
UKHW010706130521
383296UK00017B/503